Data Mining Patterns:
New Methods and Applications

Pascal Poncelet
Ecole des Mines d'Ales, France

Maguelonne Teisseire
Université Montpellier, France

Florent Masseglia
Inria, France

Information Science
REFERENCE

Acquisitions Editor:	Kristin Klinger
Development Editor:	Kristin Roth
Senior Managing Editor:	Jennifer Neidig
Managing Editor:	Sara Reed
Copy Editor:	Erin Meyer
Typesetter:	Jeff Ash
Cover Design:	Lisa Tosheff
Printed at:	Yurchak Printing Inc.

Published in the United States of America by
Information Science Reference (an imprint of IGI Global)
701 E. Chocolate Avenue, Suite 200
Hershey PA 17033
Tel: 717-533-8845
Fax: 717-533-8661
E-mail: cust@igi-pub.com
Web site: http://www.igi-global.com/reference

and in the United Kingdom by
Information Science Reference (an imprint of IGI Global)
3 Henrietta Street
Covent Garden
London WC2E 8LU
Tel: 44 20 7240 0856
Fax: 44 20 7379 0609
Web site: http://www.eurospanonline.com

Library of Congress Cataloging-in-Publication Data

Data mining patterns : new methods and applications / Pascal Poncelet, Florent Masseglia & Maguelonne Teisseire, editors.

p. cm.

Summary: "This book provides an overall view of recent solutions for mining, and explores new patterns, offering theoretical frameworks and presenting challenges and possible solutions concerning pattern extractions, emphasizing research techniques and real-world applications. It portrays research applications in data models, methodologies for mining patterns, multi-relational and multidimensional pattern mining, fuzzy data mining, data streaming and incremental mining"--Provided by publisher.

Includes bibliographical references and index.

ISBN 978-1-59904-162-9 (hardcover) -- ISBN 978-1-59904-164-3 (ebook)

1. Data mining. I. Poncelet, Pascal. II. Masseglia, Florent. III. Teisseire, Maguelonne.

QA76.9.D343D3836 2007

005.74--dc22

2007022230

British Cataloguing in Publication Data
A Cataloguing in Publication record for this book is available from the British Library.

Table of Contents

Preface x

Acknowledgment xiv

Chapter I
Metric Methods in Data Mining / *Dan A. Simovici* 1

Chapter II
Bi-Directional Constraint Pushing in Frequent Pattern Mining / *Osmar R. Zaïane
and Mohammed El-Hajj* 32

Chapter III
Mining Hyperclique Patterns: A Summary of Results / *Hui Xiong, Pang-Ning Tan,
Vipin Kumar, and Wenjun Zhou* 57

Chapter IV
Pattern Discovery in Biosequences: From Simple to Complex Patterns /
Simona Ester Rombo and Luigi Palopoli 85

Chapter V
Finding Patterns in Class-Labeled Data Using Data Visualization / *Gregor Leban,
Minca Mramor, Blaž Zupan, Janez Demšar, and Ivan Bratko* 106

Chapter VI
Summarizing Data Cubes Using Blocks / *Yeow Choong, Anne Laurent, and
Dominique Laurent* 124

Chapter VII
Social Network Mining from the Web / *Yutaka Matsuo, Junichiro Mori, and
Mitsuru Ishizuka* 149

Chapter VIII

Discovering Spatio-Textual Association Rules in Document Images /
Donato Malerba, Margherita Berardi, and Michelangelo Ceci.. 176

Chapter IX

Mining XML Documents / *Laurent Candillier, Ludovic Denoyer, Patrick Gallinari*
Marie Christine Rousset, Alexandre Termier, and Anne-Marie Vercoustre 198

Chapter X

Topic and Cluster Evolution Over Noisy Document Streams / *Sascha Schulz,*
Myra Spiliopoulou, and Rene Schult 220

Chapter XI

Discovery of Latent Patterns with Hierarchical Bayesian Mixed-Membership
Models and the Issue of Model Choice / *Cyrille J. Joutard, Edoardo M. Airoldi,*
Stephen E. Fienberg, and Tanzy M. Love.. 240

Compilation of References 276

About the Contributors 297

Index... 305

Detailed Table of Contents

Preface x

Acknowledgment.. xiv

Chapter I

Metric Methods in Data Mining / *Dan A. Simovici* 1

This chapter presents data mining techniques that make use of metrics defined on the set of partitions of finite sets. Partitions are naturally associated with object attributes and major data mining problem such as classification, clustering and data preparation which benefit from an algebraic and geometric study of the metric space of partitions. The metrics we find most useful are derived from a generalization of the entropic metric. We discuss techniques that produce smaller classifiers, allow incremental clustering of categorical data and help users to better prepare training data for constructing classifiers. Finally, we discuss open problems and future research directions.

Chapter II

Bi-Directional Constraint Pushing in Frequent Pattern Mining / *Osmar R. Zaïane and Mohammed El-Hajj*... 32

Frequent itemset mining (FIM) is a key component of many algorithms that extract patterns from transactional databases. For example, FIM can be leveraged to produce association rules, clusters, classifiers or contrast sets. This capability provides a strategic resource for decision support, and is most commonly used for market basket analysis. One challenge for frequent itemset mining is the potentially huge number of extracted patterns, which can eclipse the original database in size. In addition to increasing the cost of mining, this makes it more difficult for users to find the valuable patterns. Introducing constraints to the mining process helps mitigate both issues. Decision makers can restrict discovered patterns according to specified rules. By applying these restrictions as early as possible, the cost of mining can be constrained. For example, users may be interested in purchases whose total priceexceeds $100, or whose items cost between $50 and $100. In cases of extremely large data sets, pushing constraints sequentially is not enough and parallelization becomes a must. However, specific design is needed to achieve sizes never reported before in the literature.

Chapter III

Mining Hyperclique Patterns: A Summary of Results / *Hui Xiong, Pang-Ning Tan,*
Vipin Kumar, and Wenjun Zhou 57

This chapter presents a framework for mining highly correlated association patterns named hyperclique patterns. In this framework, an objective measure called h-confidence is applied to discover hyperclique patterns. We prove that the items in a hyperclique pattern have a guaranteed level of global pairwise similarity to one another. Also, we show that the h-confidence measure satisfies a cross-support property, which can help efficiently eliminate spurious patterns involving items with substantially different support levels. In addition, an algorithm called hyperclique miner is proposed to exploit both cross-support and anti-monotone properties of the h-confidence measure for the efficient discovery of hyperclique patterns. Finally, we demonstrate that hyperclique patterns can be useful for a variety of applications such as item clustering and finding protein functional modules from protein complexes.

Chapter IV

Pattern Discovery in Biosequences: From Simple to Complex Patterns /
Simona Ester Rombo and Luigi Palopoli 85

In the last years, the information stored in biological datasets grew up exponentially, and new methods and tools have been proposed to interpret and retrieve useful information from such data. Most biological datasets contain biological sequences (e.g., DNA and protein sequences). Thus, it is more significant to have techniques available capable of mining patterns from such sequences to discover interesting information from them. For instance, singling out for common or similar subsequences in sets of biosequences is sensible as these are usually associated to similar biological functions expressed by the corresponding macromolecules. The aim of this chapter is to explain how pattern discovery can be applied to deal with such important biological problems, describing also a number of relevant techniques proposed in the literature. A simple formalization of the problem is given and specialized for each of the presented approaches. Such formalization should ease reading and understanding the illustrated material by providing a simple-to-follow roadmap scheme through the diverse methods for pattern extraction we are going to illustrate.

Chapter V

Finding Patterns in Class-Labeled Data Using Data Visualization / *Gregor Leban,*
Minca Mramor, Blaž Zupan, Janez Demšar, and Ivan Bratko 106

Data visualization plays a crucial role in data mining and knowledge discovery. Its use is however often difficult due to the large number of possible data projections. Manual search through such sets of projections can be prohibitively timely or even impossible, especially in the data analysis problems that comprise many data features. The chapter describes a method called VizRank, which can be used to automatically identify interesting data projections for multivariate visualizations of class-labeled data. VizRank assigns a score of interestingness to each considered projection based on the degree of separation of data instances with different class label. We demonstrate the usefulness of this approach on six cancer gene expression datasets, showing that the method can reveal interesting data patterns and can further be used for data classification and outlier detection.

Chapter VI

Summarizing Data Cubes Using Blocks / *Yeow Choong, Anne Laurent, and Dominique Laurent* 124

In the context of multidimensional data, OLAP tools are appropriate for the navigation in the data, aiming at discovering pertinent and abstract knowledge. However, due to the size of the dataset, a systematic and exhaustive exploration is not feasible. Therefore, the problem is to design automatic tools to ease the navigation in the data and their visualization. In this chapter, we present a novel approach allowing to build automatically blocks of similar values in a given data cube that are meant to summarize the content of the cube. Our method is based on a levelwise algorithm (a la Apriori) whose complexity is shown to be polynomial in the number of scans of the data cube. The experiments reported in the chapter show that our approach is scalable, in particular in the case where the measure values present in the data cube are discretized using crisp or fuzzy partitions.

Chapter VII

Social Network Mining from the Web / *Yutaka Matsuo, Junichiro Mori, and Mitsuru Ishizuka* 149

This chapter describes social network mining from the Web. Since the end of the 1990's, several attempts have been made to mine social network information from e-mail messages, message boards, Web linkage structure, and Web content. In this chapter, we specifically examine the social network extraction from the Web using a search engine. The Web is a huge source of information about relations among persons. Therefore, we can build a social network by merging the information distributed on the Web. The growth of information on the Web, in addition to the development of a search engine, opens new possibilities to process the vast amounts of relevant information and mine important structures and knowledge.

Chapter VIII

Discovering Spatio-Textual Association Rules in Document Images / *Donato Malerba, Margherita Berardi, and Michelangelo Ceci* 176

This chapter introduces a data mining method for the discovery of association rules from images of scanned paper documents. It argues that a document image is a multi-modal unit of analysis whose semantics is deduced from a combination of both the textual content and the layout structure and the logical structure. Therefore, it proposes a method where both the spatial information derived from a complex document image analysis process (layout analysis), and the information extracted from the logical structure of the document (document image classification and understanding) and the textual information extracted by means of an OCR, are simultaneously considered to generate interesting patterns. The proposed method is based on an inductive logic programming approach, which is argued to be the most appropriate to analyze data available in more than one modality. It contributes to show a possible evolution of the unimodal knowledge discovery scheme, according to which different types of data describing the unitsof analysis are dealt with through the application of some preprocessing technique that transform them into a single double entry tabular data.

Chapter IX

Mining XML Documents / *Laurent Candillier, Ludovic Denoyer, Patrick Gallinari*
Marie Christine Rousset, Alexandre Termier, and Anne-Marie Vercoustre 198

XML documents are becoming ubiquitous because of their rich and flexible format that can be used for a variety of applications. Giving the increasing size of XML collections as information sources, mining techniques that traditionally exist for text collections or databases need to be adapted and new methods to be invented to exploit the particular structure of XML documents. Basically XML documents can be seen as trees, which are well known to be complex structures. This chapter describes various ways of using and simplifying this tree structure to model documents and support efficient mining algorithms. We focus on three mining tasks: classification and clustering which are standard for text collections; discovering of frequent tree structure, which is especially important for heterogeneous collection. This chapter presents some recent approaches and algorithms to support these tasks together with experimental evaluation on a variety of large XML collections.

Chapter X

Topic and Cluster Evolution Over Noisy Document Streams / *Sascha Schulz,*
Myra Spiliopoulou, and Rene Schult 220

We study the issue of discovering and tracing thematic topics in a stream of documents. This issue, often studied under the label "topic evolution" is of interest in many applications where thematic trends should be identified and monitored, including environmental modeling for marketing and strategic management applications, information filtering over streams of news and enrichment of classification schemes with emerging new classes. We concentrate on the latter area and depict an example application from the automotive industry—the discovery of emerging topics in repair & maintenance reports. We first discuss relevant literature on (a) the discovery and monitoring of topics over document streams and (b) the monitoring of evolving clusters over arbitrary data streams. Then, we propose our own method for topic evolution over a stream of small noisy documents: We combine hierarchical clustering, performed at different time periods, with cluster comparison over adjacent time periods, taking into account that the feature space itself may change from one period to the next. We elaborate on the behaviour of this method and show how human experts can be assisted in identifying class candidates among the topics thus identified.

Chapter IX

Discovery of Latent Patterns with Hierarchical Bayesian Mixed-Membership
Models and the Issue of Model Choice / *Cyrille J. Joutard, Edoardo M. Airoldi,*
Stephen E. Fienberg, and Tanzy M. Love 240

Statistical models involving a latent structure often support clustering, classification, and other datamining tasks. Parameterizations, specifications, and constraints of alternative models can be very different, however, and may lead to contrasting conclusions. Thus model choice becomes a fundamental issue in applications, both methodological and substantive. Here, we work from a general formulation of hierarchical Bayesian models of mixed-membership that subsumes many popular models successfully applied to problems in the computing, social and biological sciences. We present both parametric and nonparametric specifications for discovering latent patterns. Context for the discussion is provided by novel analyses of the following two data sets: (1) 5 years of scientific publications from the Proceedings of the National Academy of Sciences; (2) an extract on the functional disability of Americans age 65+ from the National Long Term Care Survey. For both, we elucidate strategies for model choice and our analyses bring new insights compared with earlier published analyses.

Compilation of References 276

About the Contributors 297

Index 305

Preface

Since its definition a decade ago, the problem of mining patterns is becoming a very active research area, and efficient techniques have been widely applied to problems either in industry, government or science. From the initial definition and motivated by real applications, the problem of mining patterns not only addresses the finding of itemsets but also more and more complex patterns. For instance, new approaches need to be defined for mining graphs or trees in applications dealing with complex data such as XML documents, correlated alarms or biological networks. As the number of digital data are always growing, the problem of the efficiency of mining such patterns becomes more and more attractive.

One of the first areas dealing with a large collection of digital data is probably text mining. It aims at analyzing large collections of unstructured documents with the purpose of extracting interesting, relevant and nontrivial knowledge. However, patterns became more and more complex, and led to open problems. For instance, in the biological networks context, we have to deal with common patterns of cellular interactions, organization of functional modules, relationships and interaction between sequences, and patterns of genes regulation. In the same way, multidimensional pattern mining has also been defined, and a lot of open questions remain regarding the size of the search space or to effectiveness consideration. If we consider social network in the Internet, we would like to better understand and measure relationships and flows between people, groups and organizations. Many real-world applications data are no longer appropriately handled by traditional static databases since data arrive sequentially in rapid, continuous streams. Since data-streams are contiguous, high speed and unbounded, it is impossible to mine patterns by using traditional algorithms requiring multiple scans and new approaches have to be proposed.

In order to efficiently aid decision making, and for effectiveness consideration, constraints become more and more essential in many applications. Indeed, an unconstrained mining can produce such a large number of patterns that it may be intractable in some domains. Furthermore, the growing consensus that the end user is no more interested by a set patterns verifying selection criteria led to demand for novel strategies for extracting useful, even approximate knowledge.

The goal of this book is to provide an overall view of the existing solutions for mining new kinds of patterns. It aims at providing theoretical frameworks and presenting challenges and possible solutions concerning pattern extraction with an emphasis on both research techniques and real-world applications. It is composed of 11 chapters.

Often data mining problems require metric techniques defined on the set of partitions of finite sets (e.g., classification, clustering, data preparation). The chapter "Metric Methods in Data Mining" proposed by D. A. Simovici addresses this topic. Initially proposed by R. López de Màntaras, these techniques formulate a novel splitting criterion that yields better results than the classical entropy gain splitting techniques. In this chapter, Simovici investigates a family of metrics on the set of partitions of finite sets that is linked to the notion of generalized entropy. The efficiency of this approach is proved through experiments conducted for different data mining tasks: classification, clustering, feature extraction and discretization. For each approach the most suitable metrics are proposed.

Mining patterns from a dataset always rely on a crucial point: the interest criterion of the patterns. Literature mostly proposes the minimum support as a criterion; however, interestingness may occur in constraints applied to the patterns or the strength of the correlation between the items of a pattern, for instance. The next two chapters deal with these criteria.

In "Bidirectional Constraint Pushing in Frequent Pattern Mining" by O.R. Zaïane and M. El-Hajj, proposes consideration of the problem of mining constrained patterns. Their challenge is to obtain a sheer number of rules, rather than the very large set of rules usually resulting from a mining process. First, in a survey of constraints in data mining (which covers both definitions and methods) they show how the previous methods can generally be divided into two sets. Methods from the first set consider the monotone constraint during the mining, whereas methods from the second one consider the antimonotone constraint. The main idea, in this chapter, is to consider both constraints (monotone and antimonotone) early in the mining process. The proposed algorithm (BifoldLeap) is based on this principle and allows an efficient and effective extraction of constrained patterns. Finally, parallelization of BifolLeap is also proposed in this chapter. The authors thus provide the reader with a very instructive chapter on constraints in data mining, from the definitions of the problem to the proposal, implementation and evaluation of an efficient solution.

Another criterion for measuring the interestingness of a pattern may be the correlation between the items it contains. Highly correlated patterns are named "Hyperclique Patterns" in the chapter of H. Xiong, P. N. Tan, V. Kumar and W. Zhou entitled "Mining Hyperclique Patterns: A Summary of Results". The chapter provides the following observation: when the minimum support in a pattern mining process is too low, then the number of extracted itemsets is very high. A thorough analysis of the patterns will often show patterns that are poorly correlated (i.e., involving items having very different supports). Those patterns may then be considered as spurious patterns. In this chapter, the authors propose the definition of hyperclique patterns. Those patterns contain items that have similar threshold. They also give the definition of the h-confidence. Then, h-confidence is analyzed for properties that will be interesting in a data mining process: antimonotone, cross-support and a measure of association. All those properties will help in defining their algorithm: hyperclique miner. After having evaluated their proposal, the authors finally give an application of hyperclique patterns for identifying protein functional modules.

This book is devoted to provide new and useful material for pattern mining. Both methods afore-mentioned are presented in the first chapters in which they focus on their efficiency. In that way, this book reaches part of the goal. However, we also wanted to show strong links between the methods and their applications. Biology is one of the most promising domains. In fact, it has been widely addressed by researchers in data mining those past few years and still has many open problems to offer (and to be defined). The next two chapters deal with bioinformatics and pattern mining.

Biological data (and associated data mining methods) are at the core of the chapter entitled "Pattern Discovery in Biosequences: From Simple to Complex Patterns" by S. Rombo and L. Palopoli. More precisely, the authors focus on biological sequences (e.g., DNA or protein sequences) and pattern extraction from those sequences. They propose a survey on existing techniques for this purpose through a synthetic formalization of the problem. This effort will ease reading and understanding the presented material. Their chapter first gives an overview on biological datasets involving sequences such as DNA or protein sequences. The basic notions on biological data are actually given in the introduction of this chapter. Then, an emphasis on the importance of *patterns* in such data is provided. Most necessary notions for tackling the problem of mining patterns from biological sequential data are given: definitions of the problems, existing solutions (based on tries, suffix trees), successful applications as well as future trends in that domain.

An interesting usage of patterns relies in their visualization. In this chapter, G. Leban, M. Mramor, B. Zupan, J. Demsar and I. Bratko propose to focus on "Finding Patterns in Class-labeled Data Using

Data Visualization." The first contribution of their chapter is to provide a new visualization method for extracting knowledge from data. WizRank, the proposed method, can search for interesting multidimensional visualizations of class-labeled data. In this work, the interestingness is based on how well instances of different classes are separated. A large part of this chapter will be devoted to experiments conducted on gene expression datasets, obtained by the use of DNA microarray technology. Their experiments show simple visualizations that clearly visually differentiate among cancer types for cancer gene expression data sets.

Multidimensional databases are data repositories that are becoming more and more important and strategic in most of the main companies. However, mining these particular databases is a challenging issue that has not yet received relevant answers. This is due to the fact that multidimensional databases generally contain huge volumes of data stored according to particular structures called star schemas that are not taken into account in most popular data mining techniques. Thus, when facing these databases, users are not provided with useful tools to help them discovering relevant parts. Consequently, users still have to navigate manually in the data, that is—using the OLAP operators—users have to write sophisticated queries. One important task for discovering relevant parts of a multidimensional database is to identify homogeneous parts that can summarize the whole database. In the chapter "Summarizing Data Cubes Using Blocks," Y. W. Choong, A. Laurent and D. Laurent propose original and scalable methods to mine the main homogeneous patterns of a multidimensional database. These patterns, called blocks, are defined according to the corresponding star schema and thus, provide relevant summaries of a given multidimensional database. Moreover, fuzziness is introduced in order to mine for more accurate knowledge that fits users' expectations.

The first social networking website began in 1995 (i.e., classmates). Due to the development of the Internet, the number of social networks grew exponentially. In order to better understand and measuring relationships and flows between people, groups and organizations, new data mining techniques, called social network mining, appear. Usually social network considers that nodes are the individual actors within the networks, and ties are the relationships between the actors. Of course, there can be many kinds of ties between the nodes and mining techniques try to extract knowledge from these ties and nodes. In the chapter "Social Network Mining from the Web," Y. Matsuo, J. Mori and M. Ishizuka address this problem and show that Web search engine are very useful in order to extract social network. They first address basic algorithms initially defined to extract social network. Even if the social network can be extracted, one of the challenging problems is how to analyze this network. This presentation illustrates that even if the search engine is very helpful, a lot of problems remain, and they also discuss the literature advances. They focus on the centrality of each actor of the network and illustrate various applications using a social network.

Text-mining approaches first surfaced in the mid-1980s, but thanks to technological advances it has been received a great deal of attention during the past decade. It consists in analyzing large collections of unstructured documents for the purpose of extracting interesting, relevant and nontrivial knowledge. Typical text mining tasks include text categorization (i.e., in order to classify document collection into a given set of classes), text clustering, concept links extraction, document summarization and trends detection.

The following three chapters address the problem of extracting knowledge from large collections of documents. In the chapter "Discovering Spatio-Textual Association Rules in Document Images", M. Berardi, M. Ceci and D. Malerba consider that, very often, electronic documents are not always available and then extraction of useful knowledge should be performed on document images acquired by scanning the original paper documents (document image mining). While text mining focuses on patterns involving words, sentences and concepts, the purpose of document image mining is to extract high-level spatial objects and relationships. In this chapter they introduce a new approach, called WISDOM++, for processing documents and transform documents into XML format. Then they investigate the discovery of spatio-textual association rules that takes into account both the layout and the textual dimension on XML documents. In order to deal with the inherent spatial nature of the layout structure, they formulate the problem as multi-level relational association rule mining and extend a spatial rule miner SPADA (spatial pattern discovery algorithm) in order to cope with spatio-textual association rules. They show that discovered patterns could also be used both for classification tasks and to support layout correction tasks.

L. Candillier, L. Dunoyer, P. Gallinari, M.-C. Rousset, A. Termier and A. M. Vercoustre, in "Mining XML Documents," also consider an XML representation, but they mainly focus on the structure of the documents rather than the content. They consider that XML documents are usually modeled as ordered trees, which are regarded as complex structures. They address three mining tasks: frequent pattern extraction, classification and clustering. In order to efficiently perform these tasks they propose various tree-based representations. Extracting patterns in a large database is very challenging since we have to consider the two following problems: a fast execution and we would like to avoid a memory-consuming algorithm. When considering tree patterns the problem is much more challenging due to the size of the research space. In this chapter they propose an overview of the best algorithms. Various approaches to XML document classification and clustering are also proposed. As the efficiency of the algorithms depends on the representation, they propose different XML representations based on structure, or both structure and content. They show how decision-trees, probabilistic models, k-means and Bayesian networks can be used to extract knowledge from XML documents.

In the chapter "Topic and Cluster Evolution Over Noisy Document Streams," S. Schulz, M. Spiliopoulou and R. Schult also consider text mining but in a different context: a stream of documents. They mainly focus on the evolution of different topics when documents are available over streams. As previously stated, one of the important purpose in text mining is the identification of trends in texts. Discover emerging topics is one of the problems of trend detection. In this chapter, they discuss the literature advances on evolving topics and on evolving clusters and propose a generic framework for cluster change evolution. However discussed approaches do not consider non-noisy documents. The authors propose a new approach that puts emphasis on small and noisy documents and extend their generic framework. While cluster evolutions assume a static trajectory, they use a set-theoretic notion of overlap between old and new clusters. Furthermore the framework extension consider both a document model describing a text with a vector of words and a vector of n-gram, and a visualization tool used to show emerging topics.

In a certain way, C. J. Joutard, E. M. Airoldi, S. E. Fienberg and T. M. Love also address the analysis of documents in the chapter "Discovery of Latent Patterns with Hierarchical Bayesian Mixed-Membership Models and the Issue of Model Choice." But in this chapter, the collection of papers published in the Proceedings of the National Academy of Sciences is used in order to illustrate the issue of model choice (e.g., the choice of the number of groups or clusters). They show that even if statistical models involving a latent structure support data mining tasks, alternative models may lead to contrasting conclusions. In this chapter they deal with hierarchical Bayesian mixed-membership models (HBMMM), that is, a general formulation of mixed-membership models, which are a class of models very well adapted for unsupervised data mining methods and investigate the issue of model choice in that context. They discuss various existing strategies and propose new model specifications as well as different strategies of model choice in order to extract good models. In order to illustrate, they consider both analysis of documents and disability survey data.

Acknowledgment

The editors would like to acknowledge the help of all involved in the collation and review process of the book, without whose support the project could not have been satisfactorily completed.

Special thanks go to all the staff at IGI Global, whose contributions throughout the whole process from inception of the initial idea to final publication have been invaluable.

We received a considerable amount of chapter submissions for this book, and the first idea for reviewing the proposals was to have the authors review their papers with each other. However, in order to improve the scientific quality of this book, we finally decided to gather a high level reviewing committee. Our referees have done an invaluable work in providing constructive and comprehensive reviews. The reviewing committee of this book is the following: Larisa Archer, Gabriel Fung, Mohamed Gaber, Fosca Giannotti, S.K. Gupta, Ruoming Jin, Eamonn Keogh, Marzena Kryszkiewicz, Mark Last, Paul Leng, Georges Loizou, Shinichi Morishita, Mirco Nanni, David Pearson, Raffaele Perego, Liva Ralaivola, Christophe Rigotti, Claudio Sartori, Gerik Scheuermann, Aik-Choon Tan, Franco Turini, Ada Wai-Chee Fu, Haixun Wang, Jeffrey Xu Yu, Jun Zhang, Benyu Zhang, Wei Zhao, Ying Zhao, Xingquan Zhu.

Warm thanks go to all those referees for their work. We know that reviewing chapters for our book was a considerable undertaking and we have appreciated their commitment.

In closing, we wish to thank all of the authors for their insights and excellent contributions to this book.

- Pascal Poncelet, Maguelonne Teisseire, and Florent Masseglia

About the Editors

Pascal Poncelet (Pascal.Poncelet@ema.fr) is a professor and the head of the data mining research group in the computer science department at the Ecole des Mines d'Alès in France. He is also co-head of the department. Professor Poncelet has previously worked as lecturer (1993-1994), as associate professor, respectively, in the Méditerranée University (1994-1999) and Montpellier University (1999-2001). His research interest can be summarized as advanced data analysis techniques for emerging applications. He is currently interested in various techniques of data mining with application in Web mining and text mining. He has published a large number of research papers in refereed journals, conference, and workshops, and been reviewer for some leading academic journals. He is also co-head of the French CNRS Group "I3" on data mining.

Maguelonne Teisseire (teisseire@lirmm.fr) received a PhD in computing science from the Méditer-ranée University, France (1994). Her research interests focused on behavioral modeling and design. She is currently an assistant professor of computer science and engineering in Montpellier II University and Polytech'Montpellier, France. She is head of the Data Mining Group at the LIRMM Laboratory, Montpellier. Her interests focus on advanced data mining approaches when considering that data are time ordered. Particularly, she is interested in text mining and sequential patterns. Her research takes part on different projects supported by either National Government (RNTL) or regional projects. She has published numerous papers in refereed journals and conferences either on behavioral modeling or data mining.

Florent Masseglia is currently a researcher for INRIA (Sophia Antipolis, France). He did research work in the Data Mining Group at the LIRMM (Montpellier, France) (1998-2002) and received a PhD in computer science from Versailles University, France (2002). His research interests include data min-ing (particularly sequential patterns and applications such as Web usage mining) and databases. He is a member of the steering committees of the French working group on mining complex data and the Inter-national Workshop on Multimedia Data. He has co-edited several special issues about mining complex or multimedia data. He also has co-chaired workshops on mining complex data and co-chaired the 6th and 7th editions of the International Workshop on Multimedia Data Mining in conjunction with the KDD conference. He is the author of numerous publications about data mining in journals and conferences and he is a reviewer for international journals.

Chapter I
Metric Methods in Data Mining *

Dan A. Simovici
University of Massachusetts – Boston, USA

ABSTRACT

This chapter presents data mining techniques that make use of metrics defined on the set of partitions of finite sets. Partitions are naturally associated with object attributes and major data mining problem such as classification, clustering and data preparation which benefit from an algebraic and geometric study of the metric space of partitions. The metrics we find most useful are derived from a generalization of the entropic metric. We discuss techniques that produce smaller classifiers, allow incremental clustering of categorical data and help users to better prepare training data for constructing classifiers. Finally, we discuss open problems and future research directions.

INTRODUCTION

This chapter is dedicated to metric techniques applied to several major data mining problems: classification, feature selection, incremental clustering of categorical data and to other data mining tasks.

These techniques were introduced by R. López de Màntaras (1991) who used a metric between partitions of finite sets to formulate a novel splitting criterion for decision trees that, in many cases, yields better results than the classical entropy gain (or entropy gain ratio) splitting techniques.

Applications of metric methods are based on a simple idea: each attribute of a set of objects induces a partition of this set, where two objects belong to the same class of the partition if they have identical values for that attribute. Thus, any metric defined on the set of partitions of a finite set generates a metric on the set of attributes. Once a metric is defined, we can evaluate how far these attributes are, cluster the attributes, find centrally located attributes and so on. All these possibilities can be exploited for improving existing data mining algorithms and for formulating new ones.

Important contributions in this domain have been made by J. P. Barthélemy (1978), Barthélemy and Leclerc (1995) and B. Monjardet (1981) where a metric on the set of partitions of a finite set is introduced starting from the equivalences defined by partitions.

Our starting point is a generalization of Shannon's entropy that was introduced by Z. Daróczy (1970) and by J. H. Havrda and F. Charvat (1967). We developed a new system of axioms for this type of entropies in Simovici and Jaroszewicz (2002) that has an algebraic character (being formulated for partitions rather than for random distributions). Starting with a notion of generalized conditional entropy we introduced a family of metrics that depends on a single parameter. Depending on the specific data set that is analyzed some of these metrics can be used for identifying the "best" splitting attribute in the process of constructing decision trees (see Simovici & Jaroszewicz, 2003, in press). The general idea is to use as splitting attribute the attribute that best approximates the class attribute on the set of objects to be split. This is made possible by the metric defined on partitions.

The performance, robustness and usefulness of classification algorithms are improved when relatively few features are involved in the classification. Thus, selecting relevant features for the construction of classifiers has received a great deal of attention. A lucid taxonomy of algorithms for feature selection was discussed in Zongker and Jain (1996); a more recent reference is Guyon and Elisseeff (2003). Several approaches to feature selection have been explored, including wrapper techniques in Kohavi and John, (1997) support vector machines in Brown, Grundy, Lin, Cristiani, Sugnet, and Furey (2000), neural networks in Khan, Wei, Ringner, Saal, Ladanyi, and Westerman (2001), and prototype-based feature selection (see Hanczar, Courtine, Benis, Hannegar, Clement, & Zucker, 2003) that is close to our own approach. Following Butterworth, Piatetsky-Shapiro, and Simovici (2005), we shall introduce an algorithm for feature selection that clusters attributes using a special metric and, then uses a hierarchical clustering for feature selection.

Clustering is an unsupervised learning process that partitions data such that similar data items are grouped together in sets referred to as clusters. This activity is important for condensing and identifying patterns in data. Despite the substantial effort invested in researching clustering algorithms by the data mining community, there are still many difficulties to overcome in building clustering algorithms. Indeed, as pointed in Jain, Murthy and Flynn (1999) "there is no clustering technique that is universally applicable in uncovering the variety of structures present in multidimensional data sets." This situation has generated a variety of clustering techniques broadly divided into hierarchical and partitional; also, special clustering algorithms based on a variety of principles, ranging from neural networks and genetic algorithms, to tabu searches.

We present an incremental clustering algorithm that can be applied to nominal data, that is, to data whose attributes have no particular natural ordering. In general, objects processed by clustering algorithms are represented as points in an n-dimensional space R^n and standard distances, such as the Euclidean distance, are used to evaluate similarity between objects. For objects whose attributes are nominal (e.g., color, shape, diagnostic, etc.), no such natural representation of objects as possible, which leaves only the Hamming distance as a dissimilarity measure; a poor choice for discriminating among multivalued attributes of objects. Our approach is to view clustering as a partition of the set of objects and we focus our attention on incremental clustering, that is, on clusterings that build as new objects are added to the data set (see Simovici, Singla, & Kuperberg, 2004; Simovici & Singla, 2005). Incremental clustering has attracted a substantial amount of attention starting with algorithm of Hartigan (1975) implemented in Carpenter and

Box 1.

$$\{\{a\},\{b\},\{c\},\{d\}\} \quad \{\{a,b\},\{c\},\{d\}\} \quad \{\{a,c\},\{b\},\{d\}\} \quad \{\{a,d\},\{b\},\{c\}\}$$

$$\{\{a\},\{b,c\},\{d\}\} \quad \{\{a\},\{b,d\},\{c\}\} \quad \{\{a\},\{b\},\{c,d\}\} \quad \{\{a,b,c\},\{d\}\}$$

$$\{\{a,b\},\{c,d\}\} \quad \{\{a,b,d\},\{c\}\} \quad \{\{a,c\},\{b,d\}\} \quad \{\{a,c,d\},\{b\}\}$$

$$\{\{a,d\},\{b,c\}\} \quad \{\{a\},\{b,c,d\}\} \quad \{\{a,b,c,d\}\}$$

Grossberg (1990). A seminal paper (Fisher, 1987) contains an incremental clustering algorithm that involved restructurings of the clusters in addition to the incremental additions of objects. Incremental clustering related to dynamic aspects of databases were discussed in Can (1993) and Can, Fox, Snavely, and France (1995). It is also notable that incremental clustering has been used in a variety of areas (see Charikar, Chekuri, Feder, & Motwani, 1997; Ester, Kriegel, Sander, Wimmer, & Xu, 1998; Langford, Giraud-Carrier, & Magee, 2001; Lin, Vlachos, Keogh, & Gunopoulos, 2004). Successive clusterings are constructed when adding objects to the data set in such a manner that the clusterings remain equidistant from the partitions generated by the attributes.

Finally, we discuss an application to metric methods to one of the most important pre-processing tasks in data mining, namely data discretization (see Simovici & Butterworth, 2004; Butterworth, Simovici, Santos, & Ohno-Machado, 2004).

PARTITIONS, METRICS, ENTROPIES

Partitions play an important role in data mining. Given a nonempty set S, a *partition of S* is a nonempty collection $\pi = \{B_1, ..., B_n\}$ such that $i \neq j$ implies $B_i \cap B_j = \varnothing$, and:

$$\bigcup_{i=1}^{n} B_i = S.$$

We refer to the sets $B_1, ..., B_n$ as the *blocks* of π. The set of partitions of S is denoted by *PARTS(S)*.

The set of partitions of S is equipped with a partial order by defining $\pi \leq \sigma$ if every block B of π is included in a block C of σ. Equivalently, we have $\pi \leq \sigma$ if every block C of σ is a union of a collection of blocks of π. The smallest element of the partially ordered set $(PART(S) \leq)$ is the partition α_S whose blocks are the singletons $\{x\}$ for $x \in S$; the largest element is the one-block partition ω_S whose unique block is S.

Example 1
Let $S = \{a, b, c, d\}$ be a four-element set. The set *PARTS(S)* consists of the 15 partitions shown in Box 1.

Box 2.

$$\{\{a\},\{b\},\{c\},\{d\}\} \leq \{\{a\},\{b,c\},\{d\}\} \leq \{\{a,b,c\},\{d\}\} \leq \{\{a,b,c,d\}\}$$

Among many chains of partitions we mention that as shown in Box 2.

A partition σ *covers* another partition π (denoted by $\pi \prec \sigma$) if $\pi \le \sigma$ and there is no partition τ such that $\pi \le \tau \le \sigma$. The partially ordered set *PARTS(S)* is actually a lattice. In other words, for every two partitions $\pi, \sigma \in PARTS(S)$ both $\inf\{\pi, \sigma\}$ and $\sup\{\pi, \sigma\}$ exist. Specifically, $\inf\{\pi, \sigma\}$ is easy to describe. It consists of all nonempty intersections of blocks of π and σ:

$$\inf\{\pi, \sigma\} = \{B \cap C \mid B \in \pi, C \in \sigma, B \cap C \ne \varnothing\}.$$

We will denote this partition by $\pi \cap \sigma$. The supremum of two partitions $\sup\{\pi, \sigma\}$ is a bit more complicated. It requires that we introduce the graph of the pair π, σ as the bipartite graph $G(\pi, \sigma)$ having the blocks of π and σ as its vertices. An edge (B, C) exists if $B \cap C \ne \varnothing$. The blocks of the partition $\sup\{\pi, \sigma\}$ consist of the union of the blocks that belong to a connected component of the graph $G\{\pi, \sigma\}$. We will denote $\sup\{\pi, \sigma\}$ by $\pi \cup \sigma$.

Example 2

The graph of the partitions $\pi = \{\{a,b\}, \{c\}, \{d\}\}$ and $\sigma = \{\{a\}, \{b,d\}, \{c\}\}$ of the set $S = \{a, b, c, d\}$ is shown in Figure 1. The union of the two

connected components of this graph are $\{a,b,d\}$ and $\{c\}$, respectively, which means that $\pi \cup \sigma = \{\{a,b,d\}, \{c\}\}$.

We introduce two new operations on partitions. If S, T are two disjoint sets and $\pi \in PARTS(S)$, $\sigma \in PARTS(T)$, the *sum* of π and σ is the partition: $\pi + \sigma = \{B_1, ..., B_n, C_1, ..., C_p\}$ of $S \cup T$, where $\pi = \{B_1, ..., B_n\}$ and $\sigma = \{C_1, ..., C_p\}$.

Whenever the "+" operation is defined, then it is easily seen to be associative. In other words, if S, U, V are pairwise disjoint and nonempty sets, and $\pi \in PARTS(S), \sigma \in PARTS(U)$, and $\tau \in PARTS(V)$, then $(\pi + \sigma) + \tau = \pi + (\sigma + \tau)$. Observe that if S, U are disjoint, then $\alpha_S + \alpha_U = \alpha_{S \cup U}$. Also, $\omega_S + \omega_U$ is the partition $\{S, U\}$ of the set $S \cup U$.

For any two nonempty sets S, T and $\pi \in PARTS(S)$, $\sigma \in PARTS(T)$ we define the *product* of π and σ, as the partition $\pi \times \sigma \{B \times C \mid B \in \pi, C \in \sigma\}$ of the set product $B \times C$.

Example 3

Consider the set $S = \{a_1, a_2, a_3\}$, $T = \{a_4, a_5, a_6, a_7\}$ and the partitions $p = \{\{a_1, a_2\}, \{a_3\}\}$, $s = \{\{a_4\}\{a_5, a_6\}\{a_7\}\}$ of S and T, respectively. The sum of these partitions is: $\pi + \sigma = \{\{a_1, a_2\}, \{a_3\}, \{a_4\}, \{a_5, a_6\}, \{a_7\}\}$, while their product is:

Figure 1. Graph of two partitions

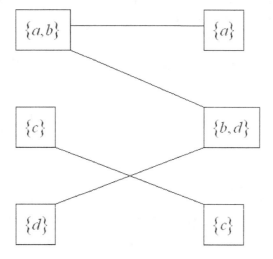

$\pi \times s = \{\{a_1,a_2\} \times \{a_4\}, \{a_1,a_2\} \times \{a_5,a_6\}, \{a_1,a_2\} \times \{a_7\}, \{a_3\} \times \{a_4\}, \{a_3\} \times \{a_5, a_6\}, \{a_3\} \times \{a_7\}\}.$

A *metric* on a set S is a mapping $d: S \times S \to R_{\geq 0}$ that satisfies the following conditions:

(M1) $d(x, y) = 0$ if and only if $x = y$
(M2) $d(x,y) = d(y,x)$
(M3) $d(x,y) + d(y,z) \geq d(x,z)$

for every $x,y,z \in S$. In equality (M3) is known as the *triangular axiom* of metrics. The pair (S,d) is referred to as a *metric space*.

The *betweeness relation* of the metric space (S,d) is a ternary relation on S defined by $[x,y,z]$ if $d(x,y) + d(y,z) = d(x,z)$. If $[x, y, z]$ we say that y *is between x and z.*

The Shannon entropy of a random variable X having the probability distribution $\boldsymbol{p} = (p_1,...,p_n)$ is given by:

$$H(p_1,...,p_n) = \sum_{i=1}^{n} -p_i \log_2 p_i.$$

For a partition $\pi \in PARTS(S)$ one can define a random variable X_π that takes the value i whenever a randomly chosen element of the set S belongs to the block B_i of π. Clearly, the distribution of X_π is $(p_1,...,p_n)$, where:

$$p_i = \frac{|B_i|}{|S|}.$$

Thus, the entropy $H(\pi)$ of π can be naturally defined as the entropy of the probability distribution of X and we have:

$$H(\pi) = -\sum_{i=1}^{n} \frac{|B_i|}{|S|} \log_2 \frac{|B_i|}{|S|}.$$

By the well-known properties of Shannon entropy the largest value of $H(\pi)$, $\log_2 |S|$, is obtained for $\pi = \alpha_S$, while the smallest, 0, is obtained for $\pi = \omega_S$.

It is possible to approach the entropy of partitions from a purely algebraic point of view that takes into account the lattice structure of $(PARTS(S) \leq)$ and the operations on partitions that we introduced earlier. To this end, we define the β-entropy, where β>0, as a function defined on the class of partitions of finite sets that satisfies the following conditions:

(P1) If $\pi_1,\pi_2 \in$ PARTS(S) are such that $\pi_1 \leq \pi_2$, then $H_\beta(\pi_2) \leq H_\beta(\pi_1)$.
(P2) If S,T are two finite sets such that $|S| \leq |T|$, then $H_\beta(\alpha_T) \leq H_\beta(\alpha_S)$.
(P3) For every disjoint sets S,T and partitions $p \in PARTS(S)$ and $\sigma \in PARTS(T)$ see Box 3.
(P4) If $\pi \in PARTS(S)$ and $\sigma \in PARTS(T)$, then $H_\beta(\pi \times \sigma) = \varphi(H_\beta(\pi), H_\beta(\sigma))$, where $\varphi: R_{\geq 0} \to R_{\geq 0}$ is a continuous function such that $\varphi(x,y) = \varphi(y,x)$, and $\varphi(x,0) = x$ for $x,y \in R_{\geq 0}$.

In Simovici and Jaroszewicz (2002) we have shown that if $\pi = \{B_1,...,B_n\}$ is a partition of S, then:

$$H_\beta(\pi) = \frac{1}{2^{1-\beta} - 1} \left(\sum_{i=1}^{n} \left(\frac{|B_i|}{|S|} \right)^\beta - 1 \right)$$

In the special case, when $b \to 1$ we have:

Box 3.

$$H_\beta(\pi + \sigma) = \left(\frac{|S|}{|S| + |T|} \right)^\beta H_\beta(\pi) + \left(\frac{|T|}{|S| + |T|} \right)^\beta H_\beta(\sigma) + H_\beta(\{S,T\})$$

$$\lim_{\beta \to 1} H_\beta (\pi) = -\sum_{i=1}^{n} \frac{|B_i|}{|S|} \log_2 \frac{|B_i|}{|S|}$$

This axiomatization also implies a specific form of the function φ. Namely, if $\beta \neq 1$ it follows that $\varphi(x,y) = x+y+(2^{1-\beta}-1)xy$. In the case of Shannon entropy, obtained using $\beta = 1$ we have $\varphi(x,y) = x+y$ for $x,y \in R_{\geq 0}$.

Note that if $|S| = 1$, then *PARTS(S)* consists of a unique partition $\alpha_S = \omega_S$ and $H_\beta(\omega_S) = 0$. Moreover, for an arbitrary finite set S we have $H_\beta(\pi) = 0$ if and only if $\pi = \omega_S$. Indeed, let U,V be two finite disjoint sets that have the same cardinality. Axiom **(P3)** implies Box 4.

Since $\omega_U + \omega_V = \{U,V\}$ it follows that $H_\beta(\omega_U) = H_\beta(\omega_V) = 0$.

Conversely, suppose that $H_\beta(\pi) = 0$. If $\pi \leq \omega_S$ there exists a block B of π such that $\varnothing \subset B \subset S$. Let θ be the partition $\theta = \{B, S-B\}$. It is clear that $\pi \leq \theta$, so we have $0 \leq H_\beta(\theta) \leq H_\beta(\pi)$ which implies $H_\beta(\theta) = 0$. This in turn yields:

$$\left(\frac{|B|}{|S|} \right)^\beta + \left(\frac{|S-B|}{|S|} \right)^\beta - 1 = 0$$

Since the function $f(x) = x^\beta + (1-x)^\beta - 1$ is concave for b > 1 and convex for b < 1 on the interval [0,1], the above equality is possible only if $B = S$ or if $B = \varnothing$, which is a contradiction. Thus, $\pi = \omega_S$.

These facts suggest that for a subset T of S the number $H_\beta(\pi_T)$ can be used as a measure of the purity of the set T with respect to the partition π. If T is π-pure, then $\pi_T = \omega_T$ and, therefore, $H_\beta(\pi_T) = 0$. Thus, the smaller $H_\beta(\pi_T)$, the more pure the set T is.

The largest value of $H_\beta(\pi)$ when p ∈ *PARTS(S)* is achieved when $\pi = \alpha_S$; in this case we have:

$$H_\beta(\alpha_S) = \frac{1}{2^{1-\beta}-1} \left(\frac{1}{|S|^{\beta-1}} - 1 \right)$$

GEOMETRY OF THE METRIC SPACE OF PARTITIONS OF FINITE SETS

Axiom **(P3)** can be extended as follows:

Theorem 1: Let $S_1, ..., S_n$ be n pairwise disjoint finite sets, $S = \prod S_i$ and let $p_1, ..., p_n$ be partitions of $S_1, ..., S_n$, respectively. We have:

$$H_\beta(\pi_1 + ... + \pi_n) = \sum_{i=1}^{n} \left(\frac{|S_i|}{|S|} \right)^\beta H_\beta(\pi_i) + H_\beta(\theta),$$

where θ is the partition $\{S_1, ..., S_n\}$ *of S.*

The β-entropy defines a naturally conditional entropy of partitions. We note that the definition introduced here is an improvement over our previous definition given in Simovici and Jaroszewicz (2002). Starting from conditional entropies we will be able to define a family of metrics on the set of partitions of a finite set and study the geometry of these finite metric spaces.

Let $\pi, \sigma \in$ *PARTS(S)*, where $\sigma = \{C_1, ..., C_n\}$. The β-*conditional entropy of the partitions* π,σ ∈ *PARTS(S)* is the function defined by:

$$H_\beta(\pi \mid \sigma) = \sum_{j=1}^{n} \left(\frac{|C_j|}{|S|} \right)^\beta H_\beta(\pi_{C_j}).$$

Observe that $H_\beta(\pi|\omega_S) = H_\beta(\pi)$ and that $H_\beta(\omega_S \pi) = H_\beta(\pi|\alpha_S) = 0$ for every partition. $\pi \in$ *PARTS(S)*

Box 4.

$$H_\beta(\omega_U + \omega_V) = \left(\frac{1}{2} \right)^\beta (H_\beta(\omega_U) + H_\beta(\omega_V)) + H_\beta(\{U,V\})$$

Also, we can write that which is seen in Box 5. In general, the conditional entropy can be written explicitly as seen in Box 6.

Theorem 2: Let π, σ be two partitions of a finite set S. We have $H_\beta (p \mid s) = 0$ if and only if $\sigma \leq \pi$.

The next statement is a generalization of a well-known property of Shannon's entropy.

Theorem 3: Let π, σ be two partitions of a finite set S. We have:

$$H_\beta (\pi \wedge \sigma) = H_\beta (\pi \mid \sigma) + H_\beta (\sigma) = H_\beta (\sigma \mid \pi) + H_\beta (\pi).$$

The β –conditional entropy is dually monotonic with respect to its first argument and is monotonic with respect to its second argument, as we show in the following statement:

Theorem 4: Let π, σ, σ' be two partitions of a finite set S. If $\sigma \leq \sigma'$, then $H_\beta (\sigma \mid \pi) \geq H_\beta (\sigma' \mid \pi)$ and $H_\beta (\pi \mid \sigma) \leq H_\beta (\beta \mid \sigma')$.

The last statement implies immediately that $H_\beta (\pi) \geq H_\beta (\pi \mid \sigma)$ for every π, σ *PARTS(S)*

The behavior of β -conditional entropies with respect to the sum of partitions is discussed in the next statement.

Theorem 5: Let S be a finite set, and let π, $\theta \in$ *PARTS(S)* where $\theta = \{D_1,...,D_h\}$. If $\sigma_i \in PARTS(D)$ for $1 \leq i \leq h$, then:

$$H_\beta (\pi \mid \sigma_1 + ... + \sigma_h) = \sum_{i=1}^{h} \left(\frac{\mid D_i \mid}{\mid S \mid} \right)^\beta H_\beta (\pi_{D_i} \mid \varsigma).$$

If $t = \{F_1,...,F_k\}$, $\sigma = \{C_1,...,C_n\}$ are two partitions of S and $\pi_i \in PARTS(F)$ for $1 \leq i \leq k$ then:

$$H_\beta (\pi_1 + ... + \pi_k \mid \sigma) = \sum_{i=1}^{k} \left(\frac{\mid F_i \mid}{\mid S \mid} \right)^\beta H_\beta (\pi_i \mid \sigma_{F_i}) + H_\beta (\tau \mid \sigma).$$

López de Màntaras, R. (1991) proved that Shannon's entropy generates a metric $d\colon S \times S \to R_{\geq 0}$ given by $d(\pi,\sigma) = H(\pi \mid \sigma) + H(\sigma \mid \pi)$, for $\pi,\sigma \in$ *PARTS(S)*. We extended his result to a class of

Box 5.

$$H_\beta (\alpha_S \mid \sigma) = \sum_{j=1}^{n} \left(\frac{\mid C_j \mid}{\mid S \mid} \right)^\beta H_\beta (\alpha_{\varsigma_j}) = \frac{1}{2^{1-\beta} - 1} \left(\frac{1}{\mid S \mid^{\beta-1}} - \sum_{j=1}^{n} \left(\frac{\mid C_j \mid}{\mid S \mid} \right)^\beta \right)$$

where $s = \{C_1,...,C_n\}$

Box 6.

$$H_\beta (\pi \mid \sigma) = \frac{1}{2^{1-\beta} - 1} \sum_{i=1}^{m} \sum_{j=1}^{n} \left(\left(\frac{\mid B_i \cap C_j \mid}{\mid S \mid} \right)^\beta - \left(\frac{\mid C_j \mid}{\mid S \mid} \right)^\beta \right),$$

where $\pi = \{B_1,...,B_m\}$.

metrics $\{d_\beta \mid \beta \in R_{\geq 0}\}$ that can be defined by β-entropies, thereby improving our earlier results.

The next statement plays a technical role in the proof of the triangular inequality for d_β.

Theorem 6: Let π, σ, τ be three partitions of the finite set S. We have:

$$H_\beta(\pi \mid \sigma \wedge \tau) + H_\beta(\sigma \mid \tau) = H_\beta(\pi \wedge \sigma \mid \tau).$$

Corollary 1: Let π, σ, τ be three partitions of the finite set S. Then, we have:

$$H_\beta(\pi \mid \sigma) + H_\beta(\sigma \mid \tau) \geq H_\beta(\pi \mid \tau).$$

> **Proof:** By theorem 6, the monotonicity of β-conditional entropy in its second argument and the dual monotonicity of the same in its first argument we can write that which is seen in Box 7, which is the desired inequality. QED.

We can show now a central result:

Theorem 7: The mapping $d_\beta : S \times S \rightarrow R_{\geq 0}$ defined by $d_\beta(\pi, \sigma) = H_\beta(\pi \mid \sigma) + H_\beta(\sigma \mid \pi)$ for π, $\sigma \in$ *PARTS(S)* is a metric on *PARTS(S)*.

> **Proof:** A double application of Corollary 1 yields $H_\beta(\pi \mid \sigma) + H_\beta(\sigma \, \tau) \geq H_\beta(\pi \mid \tau)$ and $H_\beta(\sigma \mid \pi) + H_\beta(\tau \mid \sigma) \geq H_\beta(\tau \mid \pi)$. Adding these inequality gives: $d_\beta(\pi, \sigma) + d_\beta(\sigma, \tau) \geq$

$d_\beta(\pi, \tau)$, which is the triangular inequality for d_β.

The symmetry of d_β is obvious and it is clear that $d_\beta(\pi, \pi) = 0$ for every $\beta \in$ *PARTS(S)*.

Suppose now that $d_\beta(\pi, \sigma) = 0$. Since the values of β-conditional entropies are non-negative this implies $H_\beta(\pi \mid \sigma) = H_\beta(\sigma \mid \pi) = 0$. By theorem 2, we have both $\sigma \leq \pi$ and $\pi \leq \sigma$, respectively, so $\pi = \sigma$. Thus, d_β is a metric on *PARTS(S)*. QED.

Note that $d_\beta(\pi, \omega_S) = H_\beta(\pi)$ and $d_\beta(\pi, \alpha_S) = H_\beta(\alpha_S \mid \pi)$.

The behavior of the distance d_β with respect to partition sum is discussed in the next statement.

Theorem 8: Let S be a finite set, $\pi, \theta \in$ *PARTS(S)*, where $\theta = \{D_1, ..., D_h\}$. If $\sigma_i \in$ *PARTS(D)* for $1 \leq i \leq h$ then:

$$d_\beta(\pi, \sigma_1 + ... + \sigma_h) = \sum_{i=1}^{h} \left(\frac{|D_i|}{|S|}\right)^\beta d_\beta(\pi_{D_i}, \sigma_i) + H_\beta(\theta \mid \pi).$$

The distance between two partitions can be expressed using distances relative to the total partition or to the identity partition. Indeed, note that for π, $\sigma \in$ *PARTS(S)* where $\pi = \{B_1, ..., B_m\}$ and $\sigma = \{C_1, ..., C_n\}$ we have:

$$d_\beta(\pi, \sigma) = \frac{1}{(2^{1-\beta} - 1)|S|^\beta}$$

$$\left(2 \sum_{i=1}^{m} \sum_{j=1}^{n} |B_i \cap C_j|^\beta - \sum_{i=1}^{m} |B_i|^\beta - \sum_{j=1}^{n} |C_j|^\beta\right)$$

Box 7.

$$H_\beta(\pi \mid \sigma) + H_\beta(\sigma \mid \tau) \geq H_\beta(\pi \mid \sigma \wedge \tau) + H_\beta(\sigma \mid \tau) = H_\beta(\pi \wedge \sigma \mid \tau) \geq H_\beta(\pi \mid \tau),$$

In the special case, when $\sigma = \omega_S$ we have:

$$d_\beta(\pi, \omega_S) = \frac{1}{(2^{1-\beta} - 1)|S|^\beta}\left(\sum_{i=1}^m |B_i|^\beta - |S|^\beta\right).$$

Similarly, we can write:

$$d_\beta(\alpha_S, \sigma) = \frac{1}{(2^{1-\beta} - 1)|S|^\beta}\left(|S| - \sum_{j=1}^n |C_j|^\beta\right).$$

These observations yield two metric equalities:

Theorem 9: Let $\pi, \sigma \in PARTS(S)$ be two partitions. We have:

$$d_\beta(\pi, \sigma) = 2d_\beta(\pi \wedge \sigma, \omega_S) - d_\beta(\pi, \omega_S) - d_\beta(\sigma, \omega_S)$$
$$= d_\beta(\alpha_S, \pi) + d_\beta(\alpha_S, \sigma) - 2d_\beta(\alpha_S, \pi \wedge \sigma).$$

It follows that for $\theta, \tau \in PARTS(S)$, if $q \leq t$ and we have either $d_\beta(\theta, \omega_S) = d_\beta(\tau, \omega_S)$ or $d_\beta(\theta, \alpha_S) = d_\beta(\tau, \alpha_S)$, then $\theta = \tau$. This allows us to formulate:

Theorem 10: Let $\pi, \sigma \in PARTS(S)$. The following statements are equivalent:

1. $\sigma \leq \pi$
2. We have $[\sigma, \pi, \omega_S]$ in the metric space $(PARTS(S), d_\beta)$
3. We have $[\alpha_S, \sigma, \pi]$ in the metric space $(PARTS(S), d_\beta)$

Metrics generated by β-conditional entropies are closely related to lower valuations of the upper semimodular lattices of partitions of finite sets. This connection was established Birkhoff (1973) and studied by Barthèlemy (1978), Barthèlemy and Leclerc (1995) and Monjardet (1981).

A *lower valuation* on a lattice $(L, \wedge, \vee)$ is a mapping $v: L \to R$ such that:

$$v(\pi \wedge \sigma) + v(\pi \vee \sigma) \geq v(\pi) + v(\sigma)$$

for every $\pi, \sigma \in L$. If the reverse inequality is satisfied, that is, if:

$$v(\pi \wedge \sigma) + v(\pi \vee \sigma) \leq v(\pi) + v(\sigma)$$

for every $\pi, \sigma \in L$ then v is referred to as an *upper valuation*.

If v is both a lower and upper valuation, that is, if:

$$v(\pi \wedge \sigma) + v(\pi \vee \sigma) = v(\pi) + v(\sigma)$$

for every $\pi, \sigma \in L$ then v is a valuation on L. It is known (see Birkhoff (1973) that if there exists a positive valuation v on L, then L must be a modular lattice. Since the lattice of partitions of a set is an upper-semimodular lattice that is not modular it is clear that positive valuations do not exist on partition lattices. However, lower and upper valuations do exist, as shown next.

Theorem 11: Let S be a finite set. Define the mappings $v_\beta: PARTS(S) \to R$ and $w_\beta: PARTS(S) \to R$ by $v_\beta(\pi) = d_\beta(\alpha_S, \pi)$ and $w_\beta(\pi) = d_\beta(\pi, \omega_S)$, respectively, for $\sigma \in PARTS(S)$. Then, v_β is a lower valuation and w_β is an upper valuation on the lattice $(PARTS(S), \wedge, \vee)$.

METRIC SPLITTING CRITERIA FOR DECISION TREES

The usefulness of studying the metric space of partitions of finite sets stems from the association between partitions defined on a collection of objects and sets of features of these objects. To formalize this idea, define an *object system* as a pair $T = (T, H)$, where T is a sequence of objects and H is a finite set of functions, $H = \{A_1, ..., A_n\}$, where $A_i: T \to D_i$ for $1 \leq i \leq n$. The functions A_i are referred to as *features* or *attributes* of the system. The set D_i is the domain of the attribute A_i; we assume that each set A_i contains at least to elements. The cardinality of the domain of attribute A will be denoted by m_A. If $X = (A_{i_1}, ..., A_{i_n})$ is a sequence of attributes and $t \in T$ the projection of t on is the sequence $t[X] = (A_{i_1}(t),...,A_{i_n}(t))$. The partition π^X defined by the sequence of attributes is obtained by grouping together in the same block all objects having the same projection on X. Observe that if X, Y are two sequences of attributes, then $\pi^{XY} = \pi^X \wedge \pi^Y$.

Thus, if U is a subsequence of V (denoted by $U \subseteq V$) we have $\pi^V \leq \pi^U$.

For example, if X is a set of attributes of a table T, any SQL phrase such as:

select count(*) **from** T **group by** X

computes the number of elements of each of the blocks of the partition π^X of the set of tuples of the table T.

To introduce formally the notion of decision tree we start from the notion of tree domain. A tree domain is a nonempty set of sequences D over the set of natural numbers N that satisfies the following conditions:

1. Every prefix of a sequence $\sigma \in D$ also belongs to D.
2. For every m ≥ 1, if $(p_1,...,p_{m-1}, p_m) \in D$, then $(p_1,...,p_{m-1}, q) \in D$ for every $q \leq p_m$.

The elements of D are called the *vertices* of D. If u,v are vertices of D and u is a prefix of v, then we refer to v as a *descendant* of u and to u as an *ancestor* of v. If $v = ui$ for some $i \in N$, then we call v an *immediate descendant* of u and u an *immediate ancestor* of v. The *root* of every tree domain is the null sequence λ. A *leaf* of D is a vertex of D with no immediate descendants.

Let S be a finite set and let D be a tree domain. Denote by $P(S)$ the set of subsets of S. An S-tree is a function $T: D \rightarrow P(S)$ such that $T(l) = S$, and if $u1,...,um$ are the immediate descendants of a vertex u, then the sets $T(u1),...,T(um)$ form a partition of the set $T(u)$.

A *decision tree* for an object system $T = (T,H)$ is an S-tree T, such that if the vertex v has the descendants $v1, ..., vm$, then there exists an attribute

A in H (called the *splitting attribute* in v) such that $\{T(vi) \mid 1 \leq i \leq m\}$ is the partition $\pi_A^{T(v)}$.

Thus, each descendant vi of a vertex v corresponds to a value a of the attribute A that was used as a splitting attribute in v. If $l = v_1,...,v_k = u$ is the path in T that was used to reach the vertex u, $A_1,...,A_{k-1}$ are the splitting attributes in $v_1,...,v_{k-1}$ and $a_1,...,a_{k-1}$ are the values that correspond to $v_2,...,v_k$, respectively, then we say that u is reached by the selection $A_{i_1} = a_1 \wedge ... \wedge A_{i_{k-1}} = a_{k-1}$.

It is desirable that the leaves of a decision tree contain C-pure or almost C-pure sets of objects. In other words, the objects assigned to a leaf of the tree should, with few exceptions, have the same value for the class attribute C. This amounts to asking that for each leaf w of T we must have $H_\beta(\pi_{S_w}^C)$ as close to 0 as possible. To take into account the size of the leaves note that the collection of sets of objects assigned to the leafs is a partition k of S and that we need to minimize:

$$\sum_w \left(\frac{|S_w|}{|S|} \right)^\beta H_\beta(\pi_{S_w}^C),$$

which is the conditional entropy $H_\beta(\pi^C \mid k)$. By theorem 2 we have $H_\beta(\pi^C \mid k) = 0$ if and only if $k \leq \pi^C$, which happens when the sets of objects assigned to the leafs are C-pure.

The construction of a decision tree $T_\beta(T)$ for an object system $T = (T,H)$ evolves in a top-down manner according to the following high-level description of a general algorithm (see Tan, 2005). The algorithm starts with an object system $T = (T,H)$, a value of β and with an impurity threshold ε and it consists of the following steps:

1. If $H_\beta(\pi_S^C) \leq \varepsilon$, then return T as a one-vertex tree; otherwise go to 2.
2. Assign the set S to a vertex v, choose an attribute A as a splitting attribute of S (using a splitting attribute criterion to be discussed in the sequel) and apply the algorithm to the object systems $T_1 = (T_1, H_1),...,T_p = (T_p,H_p)$, where for $1 \leq i \leq p$. Let $T_1,...,T_p$ the decision

trees returned for the systems $T_1,...,T_p$, respectively. Connect the roots of these trees to v.

Note that if ε is sufficiently small and if $H_\beta(\pi_S^C) \leq \varepsilon$, where $S = T(u)$ is the set of objects at a node u, then there is a block Q_k of the partition π_S^C that is dominant in the set S. We refer to Q_k as the *dominant class* of u.

Once a decision tree T is built it can be used to determine the class of a new object $t \notin S$ such that the attributes of the set H are applicable. If $A_{i_1}(t) = a_1,...,A_{i_{k-1}}(t) = a_{k-1}$, a leaf u was reached through the path $l = v_1,...,v_k = u$, and $a_1 a_2,...,a_{k-1}$ are the values that correspond to $v_2,...,v_k$, respectively, then t is classified in the class Q_k, where Q_k is the dominant class at leaf u.

The description of the algorithm shows that the construction of a decision tree depends essentially on the method for choosing the splitting attribute. We focus next on this issue.

Classical decision tree algorithms make use of the information gain criterion or the gain ratio to choose splitting attribute. These criteria are formulated using Shannon's entropy, as their designations indicate.

In our terms, the analogue of the information gain for a vertex w and an attribute A is: $H_\beta(\pi_{S_w}^C) - H_\beta(\pi_{S_w}^C | \pi_{S_w}^A)$. The selected attribute is the one that realizes the highest value of this quantity. When $\beta \to 1$ we obtain the information gain linked to Shannon entropy. When $\beta = 2$ one obtains the selection criteria for the Gini index using the CART algorithm described in Breiman, Friedman, Olshen and Stone (1998).

The monotonicity property of conditional entropy shows that if A,B are two attributes such that $\pi^A \leq \pi^B$ (which indicates that the domain of A has more values than the domain of B), then $H_\beta(\pi_{S_w}^C | \pi_{S_w}^A) \leq H_\beta(\pi_{S_w}^C | \pi_{S_w}^B)$, so the gain for A is larger than the gain for B. This highlights a well-known problem of choosing attributes based on information gain and related criteria: these criteria favor attributes with large domains, which in turn, generate bushy trees. To alleviate this problem information gain was replaced with the information gain ratio defined as $(H_\beta(\pi_{S_w}^C) - H_\beta(\pi_{S_w}^C | \pi_{S_w}^A))/H_\beta(\pi_{S_w}^A)$, which introduces the compensating divisor $H_\beta(\pi_{S_w}^A)$.

We propose replacing the information gain and the gain ratio criteria by choosing as splitting attribute for a node w an attribute that minimizes the distance $d_\beta(\pi_{S_w}^C, \pi_{S_w}^A) = H_\beta(\pi_{S_w}^C | \pi_{S_w}^A) + H_\beta(\pi_{S_w}^A | \pi_{S_w}^C)$. This idea has been developed by López de Màntaras (1991) for the metric d_1 induced by Shannon's entropy. Since one could obtain better classifiers for various data sets and user needs by using values of β that are different from one, our approach is an improvement of previous results.

Besides being geometrically intuitive, the minimal distance criterion has the advantage of limiting both conditional entropies $H_\beta(\pi_{S_w}^C | \pi_{S_w}^A)$ and $H_\beta(\pi_{S_w}^A | \pi_{S_w}^C)$. The first limitation insures that the choice of the splitting attribute will provide a high information gain; the second limitation insures that attributes with large domains are not favored over attributes with smaller domains.

Suppose that in the process of building a decision tree for an object system $T = (T,\mathit{II})$ we constructed a stump of the tree T that has m leaves and that the sets of objects that correspond to these leaves are $S_1,...,S_n$. This means that we created the partition $\kappa = \{S_1,...,S_n\} \in PARTS(S)$, so $\kappa = \omega_{S_1} + ... + \omega_{S_n}$. We choose to split the node v_i using as splitting attribute the attribute A that minimizes the distance $d_\beta(\pi_{S_i}^C, \pi_{S_i}^A)$. The new partition κ' that replaces κ is:

$$\kappa' = \omega_{S_1} + ... + \omega_{S_{i-1}} + \pi_{S_i}^A + \omega_{S_{i+1}} + ... + \omega_{S_n}.$$

Note that $\kappa \leq \kappa'$. Therefore, we have that which is seen in Box 8 because $[\pi^C \wedge \kappa, \kappa, \omega_S]$. This shows that as the construction of the tree advances the current partition k gets closer to the partition $\pi^C \wedge \kappa$. More significantly, as the stump of the tree grows, κ gets closer to the class partition π^C.

Indeed, by theorem 8 we can write:

$$d_\beta(\pi^C, \kappa) = d_\beta(\pi^C, \omega_{S_1} + \ldots + \omega_{S_n})$$

$$= \sum_{j=1}^{n} \left(\frac{|S_j|}{|S|} \right)^\beta d_\beta(\pi^C_{S_j}, \omega_{S_j}) + H_\beta(\theta \mid \pi^C),$$

where $\theta = \{S_1, \ldots, S_n\}$. Similarly, we can write that which is seen in Box 9.

These equalities imply that which is seen in Box 10.

We tested our approach on a number of data sets from the University of California Irvine (see Blake & Merz, 1978). The results shown in Table 1 are fairly typical. Decision trees were constructed using metrics d_β, where β varied between 0.25 and 2.50. Note that for $\beta = 1$ the metric algorithm coincides with the approach of Lopez de Màntaras (1991).

If the choices of the node and the splitting at-tribute are made such that $H_\beta(\pi^C_{S_i}) > d_\beta(\pi^C_{S_i}, \pi^A_{S_i})$, then the distance between π^C and the current partition k of the tree stump will decrease. Since the distance between $\pi^C \wedge$ k and k decreases in any case when the tree is expanded it follows that the "triangle" determined by π^C, $\pi^C \wedge$ k, and k will shrink during the construction of the decision tree.

In all cases, accurracy was assessed through 10-fold crossvalidation. We also built standard decision trees using the J48 technique of the well-known WEKA package (see Witten & Frank, 2005), which yielded the results shown in Table 2.

The experimental evidence shows that β can be adapted such that accuracy is comparable, or better than the standard algorithm. The size of the trees and the number of leaves show that the proposed approach to decision trees results consistently in smaller trees with fewer leaves.

Box 8.

$$d_\beta(\pi^C \wedge \kappa, \kappa) = d_\beta(\pi^C \wedge \kappa, \omega_S) - d_\beta(\kappa, \omega_S)$$

$$= H_\beta(\pi^C \wedge \kappa) - H_\beta(\kappa) \geq H_\beta(\pi^C \wedge \kappa') - H_\beta(\kappa'),$$

Box 9.

$$\kappa' = d_\beta(\pi^C, \omega_{S_1} + \ldots + \omega_{S_{i-1}} + \pi^A_{S_i} + \omega_{S_{i+1}} + \ldots + \omega_{S_n})$$

$$= \sum_{j=1, j \neq i}^{n} \left(\frac{|S_j|}{|S|} \right)^\beta d_\beta(\pi^C_{S_j}, \omega_{S_j}) + \left(\frac{|S_i|}{|S|} \right)^\beta d_\beta(\pi^C_{S_i}, \pi^C_{S_i}) + H_\beta(\theta \mid \pi^C).$$

Box 10.

$$d_\beta(\pi^C, \kappa) - d_\beta(\pi^C, \kappa') = \left(\frac{|S_i|}{|S|} \right)^\beta \left(d_\beta(\pi^C_{S_i}, \omega_{S_i}) - d_\beta(\pi^C_{S_i}, \pi^A_{S_i}) \right)$$

$$= \left(\frac{|S_i|}{|S|} \right)^\beta \left(H_\beta(\pi^C_{S_i}) - d_\beta(\pi^C_{S_i}, \pi^A_{S_i}) \right)$$

Table 1. Decision trees constructed by using the metric splitting criterion

Audiology			
β	Accuracy	Size	Leaves
2.50	34.81	50	28
2.25	35.99	31	17
2.00	37.76	33	18
1.75	36.28	29	16
1.50	41.89	40	22
1.25	42.18	38	21
1.00	42.48	81	45
0.75	41.30	48	27
0.50	43.36	62	35
0.25	44.25	56	32

Hepatitis			
β	Accuracy	Size	Leaves
2.50	81.94	15	8
2.25	81.94	9	5
2.00	81.94	9	5
1.75	83.23	9	5
1.50	84.52	9	5
1.25	84.52	11	6
1.00	85.16	11	6
0.75	85.81	9	5
0.50	83.23	5	3
0.25	82.58	5	3

Primary Tumor			
β	Accuracy	Size	Leaves
2.50	34.81	50	28
2.25	35.99	31	17
2.00	37.76	33	18
1.75	36.28	29	16
1.50	41.89	40	22
1.25	42.18	38	21
1.00	42.48	81	45
0.75	41.30	48	27
0.50	43.36	62	35
0.25	44.25	56	32

Vote			
β	Accuracy	Size	Leaves
2.50	94.94	7	4
2.25	94.94	7	4
2.00	94.94	7	4
1.75	94.94	7	4
1.50	95.17	7	4
1.25	95.17	7	4
1.00	95.17	7	4
0.75	94.94	7	4
0.50	95.17	9	5
0.25	95.17	9	5

Table 2. Decision trees built by using J48

Data Set	Accuracy	Size	Leaves
Audiology	77.88	54	32
Hepatitis	83.87	21	11
Primary Tumor	39.82	88	47
Vote	94.94	7	4

INCREMENTAL CLUSTERING OF CATEGORICAL DATA

Clustering is an unsupervised learning process that partitions data such that similar data items are grouped together in sets referred to as clusters. This activity is important for condensing and identifying patterns in data. Despite the substantial effort invested in researching clustering algorithms by the data mining community, there are still many difficulties to overcome in building clustering algorithms. Indeed, as pointed in Jain (1999) "there is no clustering technique that is universally applicable in uncovering the variety of structures present in multidimensional data sets."

We focus on an incremental clustering algorithm that can be applied to nominal data, that is, to data whose attributes have no particular natural ordering. In general clustering, objects to be clustered are represented as points in an *n*-dimensional space R^n and standard distances, such as the Euclidean distance is used to evaluate similarity between objects. For objects whose attributes are nominal (e.g., color, shape, diagnostic, etc.), no such natural representation of objects is possible, which leaves only the Hamming distance as a dissimilarity measure, a poor choice for discriminating among multivalued attributes of objects.

Incremental clustering has attracted a substantial amount of attention starting with Hartigan (1975). His algorithm was implemented in Carpenter and Grossberg (1990). A seminal paper, Fisher (1987), introduced COBWEB, an incremental

clustering algorithm that involved restructurings of the clusters in addition to the incremental additions of objects. Incremental clustering related to dynamic aspects of databases were discussed in Can (1993) and Can et al. (1995). It is also notable that incremental clustering has been used in a variety of applications: Charikar et al. (1997), Ester et al. (1998), Langford et al. (2001) and Lin et al. (2004)). Incremental clustering is interesting because the main memory usage is minimal since there is no need to keep in memory the mutual distances between objects and the algorithms are scalable with respect to the size of the set of objects and the number of attributes.

A clustering of an object system (*T, H*) is defined as a partition k of the set of objects *T* such that similar objects belong to the same blocks of the partition, and objects that belong to distinct blocks are dissimilar. We seek to find clusterings starting from their relationships with partitions induced by attributes. As we shall see, this is a natural approach for nominal data.

Our clustering algorithm was introduced in Simovici, Singla and Kuperberg (2004); a semisupervised extension was discussed in Simovici and Singla (2005). We used the metric space (*PARTS(S), d*), where *d* is a multiple of the d_2 metric given by that which is seen in Box 11.

This metric has been studied in Barthélemy (1978) and Barthélemy and Leclerc (1978) and in Monjardet (1981), and we will refer to it as the *Barthélemy-Monjardet distance*. A special property of this metric allows the formulation of an incremental clustering algorithm.

Box 11.

$$d(\pi,\sigma) = \sum_{i=1}^{m} |B_i|^2 + \sum_{j=1}^{n} |C_j|^2 - 2\sum_{i=1}^{m}\sum_{j=1}^{n} |B_i \cap C_j|^2 = \frac{|S|^2}{2} d_2(\pi,\sigma),$$

where $\pi = \{B_1,...,B_m\}$ and $\sigma = \{C_1,...,C_n\}$.

The main idea of the algorithm is to seek a clustering $k = \{C_1,...,C_n\} \in PARTS(T)$, where T is the set of objects such that the total distance from k to the partitions of the attributes:

$$D(\kappa) = \sum_{i=1}^{n} d(\kappa, \pi^{A_i})$$

is minimal. The definition of d allows us to write:

$$d(\kappa, \pi^A) = \sum_{i=1}^{n} |C_i|^2 + \sum_{j=1}^{m_A} |B_{a_j}^A|^2 - 2 \sum_{i=1}^{n} \sum_{j=1}^{m_A} |C_i \cap B_{a_j}^A|^2.$$

Suppose now that t is a new object, $t \notin T$, and let $Z = T \cup \{t\}$. The following cases may occur:

1. The object t is added to an existing cluster C_k.
2. A new cluster, C_{n+1} is created that consists only of t.

Also, the partition π^A is modified by adding t to the block $B_{t[A]}^A$, which corresponds to the value $t[A]$ of the A-component of t. In the first case let:

$$\kappa_k = \{C_1,...,C_{k-1}, C_k \cup \{t\}, C_{k+1},...,C_n\},$$
$$\pi^{A'} = \{B_{a_1}^A,..., B_{t[A]}^A \cup \{t\},..., B_{m_A}^A\}$$

be the partitions of Z. Now, we have what is shown in Box 12.

The minimal increase of $d(\kappa_k, \pi^{A'})$ is given by

$$\min_k \sum_A 2|C_k \oplus B_{t[A]}^A|.$$

In the second case we deal with the partitions:

$$\kappa_k = \{C_1,...,C_n, \{t\}\},$$
$$\pi^{A'} = \{B_{a_1}^A,..., B_{t[A]}^A \cup \{t\},..., B_{m_A}^A\}$$

and we have $d(\kappa', \pi^{A'}) - d(\kappa, \pi^A) = 2|B_{t[A]}^A|$. Consequently, we have:

$$D(\kappa') - D(\kappa) = 2 \sum_A |C_k \oplus B_{t[A]}^A|$$

in the first case and in the second case. Thus, if:

$$D(\kappa') - D(\kappa) = 2 \sum_A |B_{t[A]}^A|$$

we add t to a cluster C_k for which:

$$\min_k \sum_A |C_k \oplus B_{t[A]}^A|$$

is minimal; otherwise, we create a new one-object cluster.

Incremental clustering algorithms are affected, in general, by the order in which objects are processed by the clustering algorithm. Moreover, as pointed out in Cornuéjols (1993), each such algorithm proceeds typically in a hill-climbing fashion that yields local minima rather than global ones. For some incremental clustering algorithms certain object orderings may result in rather poor clusterings. To diminish the ordering effect problem we expand the initial algorithm by adopting the "not-yet" technique introduced by Roure and Talavera (1998). The basic idea is that a new cluster is created only when the inequality:

Box 12.

$$d(\kappa_k, \pi^{A'}) - d(\kappa, \pi^A) = (|C_k|+1)^2 - |C_k|^2 + (|B_{t[A]}^A|+1)^2 - |B_{t[A]}^A|^2 - 2(|C_k \cap B_{t[A]}^A|+1)$$
$$= 2|C_k \oplus B_{t[A]}^A|.$$

$$r(t) = \frac{\sum_A |B^A_{t[A]}|}{\min_k \sum_A |C_k \oplus B^A_{t[A]}|} < \xi,$$

is satisfied, that is, only when the effect of adding the object t on the total distance is significant enough. Here ξ is a parameter provided by the user, such that $\xi \leq 1$.

Now we formulate a metric incremental clustering algorithm (referred to as AMICA, an acronym of the previous five words) that is using the properties of distance d. The variable nc denotes the current number of clusters.

If $\xi < r(t) \leq 1$ we place the object t in a buffer known as the NOT-YET buffer. If $r(t) \leq \xi$ a new cluster that consists of the object t is created. Otherwise, that is, if $r(t) > 1$, the object t is placed in an existing cluster C_k that minimizes:

$$\min_k \sum_A |C_k \oplus B^A_{t[A]}|;$$

this limits the number of new singleton clusters that would be otherwise created. After all objects of the set T have been examined, the objects contained by the NOT-YET buffer are processed with $\xi = 1$. This prevents new insertions in the buffer and results in either placing these objects in existing clusters or in creating new clusters. The pseudo-code of the algorithm is given next:

Input: Data set T and threshold ξ
Output: Clustering $\{C_1, ..., C_{nc}\}$
Method: $nc = 0$; $l = 1$

while $(T \neq \varnothing)$ **do**
    select an object t;
    $T = T - \{t\}$;
    if $\sum_A |B^A_{t[A]}| \leq \xi \min_{1 \leq k \leq nc} \sum_A |C_k \oplus B^A_{t[A]}|$

    then
        $nc + +$;
        create a new single-object cluster $C_{nc} = \{t\}$;
    else

$$r(t) = \frac{\sum_A |B^A_{t[A]}|}{\min_k \sum_A |C_k \oplus B^A_{t[A]}|};$$

        if $(r(t) \geq 1)$

    then
        $k = \arg\min_k \sum_A |C_k \oplus B^A_{t[A]}|$;

        add t to cluster C_k;
    else /* this means that $\xi < r(t) \leq 1$ */
        place t in NOT-YET buffer;
    end if;
endwhile;
process objects in the NOT-YET buffer as above with $\xi = 1$.

We applied AMICA to synthetic data sets produced by an algorithm that generates clusters of objects having real-numbered components grouped around a specified number of centroids. The resulting tuples were discretized using a specified number of discretization intervals, which allowed us to treat the data as nominal. The experiments were applied to several data sets with an increasing number of tuples and increased dimensionality and using several permutations of the set of objects. All experiments used $\xi = 0.95$.

The stability of the obtained clusterings is quite remarkable. For example, in an experiment applied to a set that consists of 10,000 objects (grouped by the synthetic data algorithm around 6 centroids) a first pass of the algorithm produced 11 clusters; however, most objects (9895) are concentrated in the top 6 clusters, which approximate very well the "natural" clusters produced by the synthetic algorithm.

Table 3 compares the clusters produced by the first run of the algorithm with the cluster produced from a data set obtained by applying a random permutation.

Note that the clusters are stable; they remain almost invariant with the exception of their numbering. Similar results were obtained for other random permutations and collections of objects.

As expected with incremental clustering algorithms, the time requirements scale up very well with the number of tuples. On an IBM T20 system equipped with a 700 MHz Pentium III and with a

Table 3. Comparison between clusters produced by successive runs

Initial Run		Random Permutation		
Cluster	Size	Cluster	Size	Distribution (Original Cluster)
1	1548	1	1692	1692 (2)
2	1693	2	1552	1548 (1),3 (3), 1 (2)
3	1655	3	1672	1672 (5)
4	1711	4	1711	1711 (4)
5	1672	5	1652	1652 (3)
6	1616	6	1616	1616(6)
7	1	7	85	85 (8)
8	85	8	10	10 (9)
9	10	9	8	8 (10)
10	8	10	1	1 (11)
11	1	11	1	1 (7)

Table 4. Time for three random permutations

Number of Objects	Time for 3 permutations (ms)	Average time (ms)
2000	131, 140, 154	141.7
5000	410, 381, 432	407.7
10000	782,761, 831	794.7
20000	1103, 1148, 1061	1104

256 MB RAM, we obtained the results shown in Table 4 for three randomly chosen permutations of each set of objects.

Another series of experiments involved the application of the algorithm to databases that contain nominal data. We applied AMICA to the mushroom data set from the standard UCI data mining collection (see Blake & Merz, 1998). The data set contains 8124 mushroom records and is typically used as test set for classification algorithms. In classification experiments the task is to construct a classifier that is able to predict the poisonous/edible character of the mushrooms based on the values of the attributes of the mushrooms. We discarded the class attri-

bute (poisonous/edible) and applied AMICA to the remaining data set. Then, we identified the edible/poisonous character of mushrooms that are grouped together in the same cluster. This yields the clusters $C_1,...,C_9$.

Note that in almost all resulting clusters there is a dominant character, and for five out of the total of nine clusters there is complete homogeneity.

A study of the stability of the clusters similar to the one performed for synthetic data shows the same stability relative to input orderings. The clusters remain essentially stable under input data permutations (with the exception of the order in which they are created).

Table 5. Purity of clusters for the mushrooms data set

Class number	Poisonous/Edible	Total	Dominant Group (%)
1	825/2752	3557	76.9%
2	8/1050	1058	99.2%
3	1304/0	1304	100%
4	0/163	163	100%
5	1735/28	1763	98.4%
6	0/7	7	100%
7	1/192	192	100%
8	36/16	52	69%
9	8/0	8	100%

Thus, AMICA provides good quality, stable clusterings for nominal data, an area of clustering that is less explored than the standard clustering algorithms that act on ordinal data. Clusterings produced by the algorithm show a rather low sensitivity to input orderings.

CLUSTERING FEATURES AND FEATURE SELECTION

The performance, robustness and usefulness of classification algorithms are improved when relatively few features are involved in the classification. The main idea of this section, which was developed in Butterworth et al. (2005), is to introduce an algorithm for feature selection that clusters attributes using a special metric, and then use a hierarchical clustering for feature selection.

Hierarchical algorithms generate clusters that are placed in a cluster tree, which is commonly known as a *dendrogram*. Clusterings are obtained by extracting those clusters that are situated at a given height in this tree.

We show that good classifiers can be built by using a small number of attributes located at the centers of the clusters identified in the dendrogram. This type of data compression can be achieved with little or no penalty in terms of the accuracy of the classifier produced. The clustering of attributes helps the user to understand the structure of data, the relative importance of attributes. Alternative feature selection methods, mentioned earlier, are excellent in reducing the data without having a severe impact on the accuracy of classifiers; however, such methods cannot identify how attributes are related to each other.

Let m, $M \in N$ be two natural numbers such that $m \leq M$. Denote by $PARTS(S)_{m,M}$ the set of partitions of S such that for every block $B \in \pi$ we have $m \leq |B| \leq M$. The lower valuation v defined on $PARTS(S)$ is given by:

$$v(\theta) = \sum_{i=1}^{p} |D_i|^2,$$

where $\theta = \{D_1,...,D_p\}$.

Let $\pi = \{B_1,...,B_n\}$, $\sigma = \{C_1,...,C_p\}$ be two partitions of a set S. The *contingency matrix* of π, σ is the matrix $P_{\pi,\sigma}$ whose entries are given by $p_{ij} = |B_i \cap C_j|$ for $1 \leq i \leq n$ and $1 \leq j \leq p$. The Pearson $\chi^2_{\pi,\sigma}$ association index of this contingency matrix can be written in our framework as:

$$\chi^2_{\pi,\sigma} = \sum_i \sum_j \frac{(p_{ij} - |B_i||C_j|)^2}{|B_i||C_j|}.$$

It is well known that the asymptotic distribution of this index is a χ^2-distribution with $(n\text{-}1)(p\text{-}1)$ degrees of freedom. The next statement suggests that partitions that are correlated are close in the sense of the *Barthélemy-Monjardet distance*; therefore, if attributes are clustered using the corresponding distance between partitions we could replace clusters with their centroids and, thereby, drastically reduce the number of attributes involved in a classification without significant decreases in accuracy of the resulting classifiers.

Theorem 12: Let S be a finite set and let p,s $\in PARTS(S)_{m,M}$, where $\pi = \{B_1,...,B_n\}$ and $\sigma = \{C_1,...,C_p\}$. We have that which is seen in Box 13.

Thus, the Pearson coefficient decreases with the distance and, thus, the probability that the partitions π and σ and are independent increases with the distance.

We experimented with several data sets from the UCI dataset repository (Blake & Merz, 1998); here we discuss only the results obtained with the *votes* and *zoo* datasets, which have a relative small number of categorical features. In each case, starting from the matrix $(d(\pi^{A_i}, \pi^{A_j}))$ of *Barthélemy-Monjardet distances* between the partitions of the attributes $A_1,...,A_n$, we clustered the attributes using *AGNES*, an agglomerative hierarchical algorithm described in

Kaufman and Rousseeuw (1990) that is implemented as a component of the *cluster* package of system R (see Maindonald & Brown, 2003).

Clusterings were extracted from the tree produced by the algorithm by cutting the tree at various heights starting with the maximum height of the tree created above (corresponding to a single cluster) and working down to a height of 0 (which consists of single-attribute clusters). A "representative" attribute was created for each cluster as the attribute that has the minimum total distance to the other members of the cluster, again using the Barthélemy-Monjardet distance. The J48 and the Naïve Bayes algorithms of the WEKA package from Witten and Frank (2005) were used for constructing classifiers on data sets obtained by projecting the initial data sets on the sets of representative attributes.

The dataset *votes* records the votes of 435 U.S. Congressmen on 15 key questions, where each attribute can have the value "y", "n", or "?" (for abstention), and each Congressman is classified as a Democrat or Republican.

The attributes of this data set are listed in Table 6.

It is interesting to note that by applying the *AGNES* clustering algorithm with the Ward method of computing the intercluster distance the voting issues group naturally into clusters that involve larger issues, as shown in Figure 1.

For example, "El Salvador aid," "Aid to Nicaraguan contras," "Mx missile" and "Antisatellite test ban" are grouped quite early into a cluster that can be described as dealing with defense policies. Similarly, social budgetary legislation issues such as "Budget resolution," "Physician fee freeze" and "Education spending," are grouped together.

Two types of classifiers (J48 and Naïve Bayes) were generated using ten-fold cross validation by extracting centrally located attributes from cluster obtained by cutting the dendrogram at successive levels. The accuracy of these classifiers is shown in Figure 2.

Box 13.

$$\frac{v(\pi) + v(\sigma) - d(\pi, \sigma)}{2M^2} - 2np + |S|^2 \le \chi^2_{\pi,\sigma} \le \frac{v(\pi) + v(\sigma) - d(\pi, \sigma)}{2m^2} - 2np + |S|^2 .$$

Table 6.

1	Handicapped infants	9	Mx missile
2	Water project cost sharing	10	Immigration
3	Budget resolution	11	Syn fuels corporation cutback
4	Physician fee freeze	12	Education spending
5	El Salvador aid	13	Superfund right to sue
6	Religious groups in schools	14	Crime
7	Antisatellite test ban	15	Duty-free exports
8	Aid to Nicaraguan contras		

Figure 2. Dendrogram of votes data set using AGNES and the Ward method

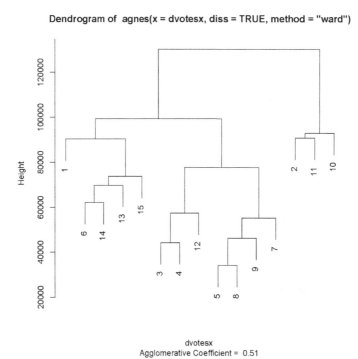

Dendrogram of agnes(x = dvotesx, diss = TRUE, method = "ward")

dvotesx
Agglomerative Coefficient = 0.51

This experiment shows that our method identifies the most influential attribute 5 (in this case "*El_Salvador_aid*"). So, in addition to reducing number of attributes, the proposed methodology allows us to assess the relative importance of attributes.

A similar study was undertaken for the *zoo* database, after eliminating the attribute *animal* which determines uniquely the type of the animal. Starting from a dendrogram build by using the Ward method shown in Figure 3 we constructed J48 and Naïve Bayes classifiers for several sets of attributes obtained as successive sections of the cluster tree.

The attributes of this data set are listed in Table 8.

The results are shown in Figure 3. Note that attributes that are biologically correlated (e.g., hair, milk and eggs, or aquatic, breathes and fins) belong to relatively early clusters.

The main interest of the proposed approach to attribute selection is the possibility of the supervision of the process allowing the user to opt between quasi-equivalent attributes (that is, attributes that are close relatively to the Barthélemy-Monjardet distance) in order to produce more meaningful classifiers.

We compared our approach with two existing attribute set selection techniques: the correlation-based feature (CSF) selection (developed in Hall (1999) and incorporated in the WEKA package) and the wrapper technique, using the "best first" and the greedy method as search methods, and the J48 classifier for the classifier incorporated by the wrapper. The comparative results for the zoo database show that using either the "best first" or the "greedy stepwise" search methods in the case of CSF the accuracy for the J48 classifier is 91.08%, and for the naïve Bayes classifier is 85.04%; the corresponding numbers for the wrapper method with J48 are 96.03% and 92.07%, respectively. These results suggest that this method is not as good for accuracy as the wrapper method or CSF. However, the tree of attributes helps to understand

Table 7. Accuracy of classifiers for the votes data set

Attribute Set (class attribute not listed)	J48%	ND%
1,2,3,4,5,6,7,8,9,10,11,12,13,14,15	96.78	90.34
1,2,3,4,5,6,7,9,10,11,12,13,14,15	96.78	91.03
1,2,3,4,5,6,7,10,11,12,13,14,15	96.55	91.26
1,2,4,5,6,7,10,11,12,13,14,15	95.17	92.18
1,2,4,5,6,10,11,12,13,14,15	95.17	92.64
1,2,4,5,6,10,11,13,14,15	95.40	92.18
1,2,6,8,10,11,13,14,15	86.20	85.28
1,2,8,10,11,13,14,15	86.20	85.74
1,2,8,10,11,14,15	84.13	85.74
1,2,8,10,11,14	83.69	85.74
2,8,10,11,14	83.67	84.36
2,5,10,11	88.73	88.50
2,5,10	84.82	84.82
2,5	84.82	84.82
5	84.82	84.82

Table 8.

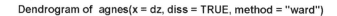

1	hair	10	breathes
2	feathers	11	venomous
3	eggs	12	fins
4	milk	13	legs
5	airborne	14	tail
6	aquatic	15	domestic
7	predator	16	cat size
8	toothed	17	type
9	backbone		

Figure 3. Dendrogram of zoo dataset using AGNES and the Ward method

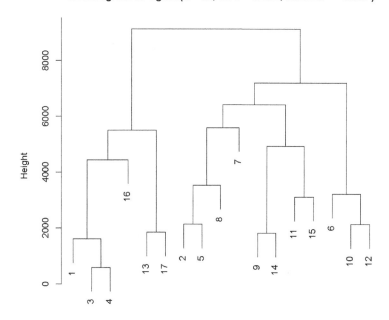

Table 9. Accuracy of classifiers for the zoo data set

Attribute Set (class attribute not listed)	J48%	NB%
1,2,3,4,5,6,7,8,9,10,11,12,13,14,15,16	92.07	93.06
1,2,4,5,6,7,8,9,10,11,12,13,14,15,16	92.07	92.07
2,4,5,6,7,8,9,10,11,12,13,14,15,16	87.12	88.11
2,4,5,6,7,8,9,10,11,12,13,15,16	87.12	88.11
2,4,6,7,8,9,10,11,12,13,15,16	88.11	87.12
2,4,6,7,8,9,10,11,13,15,16	91.08	91.08
2,4,6,7,8,9,10,11,13,16	89.10	90.09
2,4,7,8,9,10,11,13,16	86.13	90.09
2,4,7,9,10,11,13,16	84.15	90.09
2,4,7,9,10,11,13	87.12	89.10
4,5,7,9,10,11	88.11	88.11
4,5,7,9,10	88.11	90.09
4,5,9,10	89.10	91.09
4,5,10	73.26	73.26
4,10	73.26	73.26
4	60.39	60.39

the relationships between attributes and their relative importance.

Attribute clustering helps to build classifiers in a semisupervised manner allowing analysts a certain degree of choice in the selection of the features that may be considered by classifiers, and illuminating relationships between attributes and their relative importance for classification.

A METRIC APPROACH TO DISCRETIZATION

Frequently, data sets have attributes with numerical domains which makes them unsuitable for certain data mining algorithms that deal mainly with nominal attributes, such as decision trees and naïve Bayes classifiers. To use such algorithms we need to replace numerical attributes with nominal attributes that represent intervals of numerical domains with discrete values. This process, known to as *discretization*, has received a great deal of attention in the data mining literature and includes a variety of ideas ranging from fixed *k*-interval discretization (Dougherty, Kohavi, & Sahami, 1995), fuzzy discretization (see Kononenko, 1992; 1993), Shannon-entropy discretization due to Fayyad and Irani presented in Fayyad (1991) and Fayyad and Irani (1993), proportional κ-interval discretization (see Yang & Webb, 2001; 2003), or techniques that are capable of dealing with highly dependent attributes (cf. Robnik & Kononenko, 1995).

The discretization process can be described generically as follows. Let *B* be a numerical attribute of a set of objects. The set of values of the components of these objects that correspond to the attribute *B* is the *active domain* of *B* and is denoted by *adom(B)*. To discretize *B* we select a sequence of numbers $t_1 < t_2 < ... < t_l$ in *adom(B)*. Next, the attribute *B* is replaced by the nominal attribute *B'* that has $l+1$ distinct values in its active domain $\{k_0, k_1, ...k_l\}$. Each B-component b of an object t is replaced by the discretized B'-component k defined by $k = k_0$ if $b \le t_1$, $t = k$ if $t_i < b \le t_{i+1}$ for $1 \le i \le l-1$, and $k = k_l$ if $t_l < b$. The numbers t_1, $t_2, ...t_l$ define the discretization process and they will be referred to as *class separators*.

There are two types of discretization (see Witten & Frank, 2005): *unsupervised discretization*, where the discretization takes place without any knowledge of the classes to which objects belong, and *supervised discretization* which takes into account the classes of the objects. Our approach involves supervised discretization. Within our framework, to discretize an attribute B amounts to constructing a partition of the active domain *adom(B)* taking into account the partition π^A determined by the nominal class attribute A.

Partitions of active attribute domains induce partitions on the set of objects. Namely, the partition of the set of objects T that corresponds to a partition θ of *adom(B)*, where B is a numerical attribute, is denoted by θ_*. A block of θ_* consists of all objects whose B-components belong to the same block of θ. For the special case when $\theta = \alpha_{adom(B)}$ observe that $\theta_* = \pi^B$.

Let $P = (t_1, ..., t_l)$ a sequence of class separators of the active domain of an attribute B, where $t_1 < t_2 < ... < t_l$. This set of cut points creates a partition $\theta_B^P = \{Q_0, ..., Q_l\}$ of *adom(B)* where $Q_i = \{b \in adom(B) \mid t_i \le b < t_{i+1}\}$ for $0 \le i \le l$, where $t_0 = -\infty$ and $t_{l+1} = \infty$.

It is immediate that for two sets of cut points P, P' we have $\theta_B^{P \cup P'} = \theta_B^P \wedge \theta_B^{P'}$. If the sequence P consists of a single cut point t we shall denote θ_B^P simply by θ_B^t. The discretization process consists of replacing each value that falls in the block Q_i of θ_B^P by i for $0 \le i \le l$.

Suppose that the list of objects *sorted on the values of a numerical attribute B* is $t_1, ..., t_n$ and let $t_1[B], ..., t_n[B]$ be the sequence of B-components of those objects, where $t_1[B] < ... < t_n[B]$. For a nominal attribute A define the partition $\pi_{B,A}$ of *adom(B)* as follows. A block of $\pi_{B,A}$ consists of a maximal subsequence $t_i[B], ..., t_l[B]$ of the previous sequence

such that every object $t_i, ..., t_l$ of this subsequence belongs to the same block K of the partition π^A. If $x \in adom(B)$, we shall denote the block of $\pi_{B,A}$ that contains x by $\langle x \rangle$. The *boundary points* of the partition $\pi_{B,A}$ are the least and the largest elements of each of the blocks of the partition $\pi_{B,A}$. The least and the largest elements of $\langle x \rangle$ are denoted by $x^{\downarrow}$ and $x^{\uparrow}$, respectively. It is clear that $\pi_{B,A} \le \pi^A$ for any attribute B.

Example 4

Let $t_1, ..., t_9$ be a collection of nine objects such that the sequence $t_1[B], ..., t_9[B]$ is sorted in increasing order of the value of the B-components as seen in Table 10.

The partition π^A has two blocks corresponding to the values "Y" and "N" and is given by

$$\pi^A = \{\{t_1, t_3, t_4, t_7, t_8, t_9\}, \{t_2, t_5, t_6\}\}.$$

The partition $\pi_{B,A}$ is:

$$\pi_{B,A} = \{\{t_1\}, \{t_2\}, \{t_3, t_4\}, \{t_5, t_6\}, \{t_7, t_8, t_9\}\}.$$

The blocks of this partition correspond to the longest subsequences of the sequence $t_1, ..., t_9$ that consists of objects that belong to the same π^A-class.

Fayyad (1991) showed that to obtain the least value of the Shannon's conditional entropy $H(\pi^A \mid \theta_{B*}^P)$ the cut points of P must be chosen among the boundary points of the partition $\pi_{B,A}$. This is a powerful result that drastically limits the number of possible cut points and improves the tractability of the discretization.

We present two new basic ideas: a generalization of Fayyad-Irani discretization techniques that relies on a metric on partitions defined by generalized entropy, and a new geometric criterion for halting the discretization process. With an appropriate choice of the parameters of the discretization process the resulting decision trees are smaller, have fewer leaves, and display

Table 10.

	...	B	...	A
t_1	...	95.2	...	Y
t_2	...	110.1	...	N
t_3	...	120.0	...	Y
t_4	...	125.5	...	Y
t_5	...	130.1	...	N
t_6	...	140.0	...	N
t_7	...	140.5	...	Y
t_8	...	168.2	...	Y
t_9	...	190.5	...	Y

higher levels of accuracy as verified by stratified cross-validation; similarly, naïve Bayes classifiers applied to data discretized by our algorithm yield smaller error rates.

Our main results show that the same choice of cut points must be made for a broader class of impurity measures, namely the impurity measures related to generalized conditional entropy. Moreover, when the purity of the partition π^A is replaced as a discretization criterion by the minimality of the entropic distance between the partitions π^A and θ_{B*}^P the same method for selecting cut points can be applied. This is a generalization of the approach proposed in Cerquides and López de Màntaras (1997).

We are concerned with supervised discretization, that is, with discretization of attributes that takes into account the classes where the objects belong. Suppose that the class of objects is determined by the nominal attribute A and we need to discretize a numerical attribute B. The discretization of B aims to construct a set P of cut points of *adom(B)* such that the blocks of π^A are as pure as possible relative to the partition θ_{B*}^P, that is, the conditional entropy $H(\pi^A | \theta_{B*}^P)$ is minimal.

The following theorem extends a result of Fayyad (1991):

Theorem 13: Let T be a collection of objects, where the class of an object is determined by the attribute A and let $\beta \in (1,2]$. If P is a set of cut points such that the conditional entropy $H(\pi^A | \theta_{B*}^P)$ is minimal among the set of cut points with the same number of elements, then P consists of boundary points of the partition $\pi_{B,A}$ of *adom(B)*.

The next theorem is a companion to Fayyad's (1991) result and makes use of the same hypothesis as theorem 13.

Theorem 14: Let β be a number, $\beta \in (1,2]$. If P is a set of cut points of *adom(B)* such that the distance $d_\beta (\pi^A | \theta_{B*}^P)$ is minimal among the set of cut points with the same number of elements, then P consists of boundary points of the partition $\pi_{B,A}$ of *adom(B)*.

This result plays a key role. To discretize *adom(B)* we seek a set of cut points P such that:

$$d_\beta (\pi^A, \theta_{B*}^P) = H_\beta (\pi^A | \theta_{B*}^P) + H_\beta (\theta_{B*}^P | \pi^A)$$

is minimal. In other words, we shall seek a set of cut points such that the partition θ_{B*}^B induced on the set of objects T is as close as possible to the target partition π^A.

Initially, before adding cut points, we have $P = \varnothing$, $\theta_{B*}^B = \omega_S = \{S\}$, and therefore $H_\beta (\pi^A | \omega_S) = H_\beta (\pi^A)$. Observe that when the set P grows the entropy $H_\beta (\pi^A | \theta_{B*}^P)$ decreases. Note that the use of conditional entropy $H_\beta (\pi^A | \theta_{B*}^P)$ tends to favor large cut point sets for which the partition θ_{B*}^B is small in the partial ordered set $(PARTS(P), \leq)$. In the extreme case, every point would be a cut point, a situation that is clearly unacceptable. Fayyad-Irani (Fayyad & Irani, 1993) technique halts the discretization process using the principle of minimum description. We adopt another technique that has the advantage of being geometrically intuitive and produces very good experimental results.

Using the distance $d_\beta (\pi^A | \theta_{B*}^P)$ the decrease of $H_\beta (\pi^A | \theta_{B*}^P)$ when the set of cut points grows is balanced by the increase in $H_\beta (\theta_{B*}^P | \pi^A)$. Note that initially we have $H_\beta (\omega_T | \pi^A) = 0$. The discretization process can thus be halted when the distance $d_\beta (\pi^A | \theta_{B*}^P)$ stops decreasing. Thus, we retain as a set of cut points for discretization the set P that determines the closest partition to the class partition π^A. As a result, we obtain good discretizations (as evaluated through the results of various classifiers that use the discretize data) with relatively small cut point sets.

The greedy algorithm shown below is used for discretizing an attribute B. It makes successive passes over the table and, at each pass it adds a new cut point chosen among the boundary points of $\pi_{B,A}$.

Input: An object system (T, H), a class attribute A and a real-valued attribute B
Output: A discretized attribute B
Method: Sort (T, H) on attribute B;
    compute the set BP of boundary points of partition $\pi_{B,A}$;
    $P = \varnothing$, $d = \infty$;

```
while BP ≠ ∅ do
    let p = arg min_{p∈BP} d_β (π^A, θ_{B*}^{P∪{p}});
    if d ≥ d_β (π^A, θ_{B*}^{P∪{p}}) then
        begin
            P = P ∪ {t};
            BP = BP − {t};
            d = d_β (π^A, θ_{B*}^P);
        end
                            else
        exit while loop;
end while;
for θ_{B*}^P = {Q_0,...,Q_l} replace every value in Q_i by i for 0 ≤ i ≤ l.
```

The while loop runs for as long as candidate boundary points exist, and it is possible to find a new cut point p such that the distance $d_\beta (\pi^A | \theta_{B*}^P)$ is less than the previous distance $d_\beta (\pi^A | \theta_{B*}^P)$. An experiment performed on a synthetic database shows that a substantial amount of time (about 78% of the total time) is spent on decreasing the distance by the last 1%. Therefore, in practice we run a search for a new cut point only if: $|d - d_\beta (\pi^A, \theta_{B*}^P)| > 0.01d$.

To form an idea on the evolution of the distance between $\pi^A = \{P_1,...,P_n\}$ and the partition of objects determined by the cut points θ_{B*}^P let $p \in BP$ be a new cut point added to the set P. It is clear that the partition θ_{B*}^P covers the partition $\theta_{B*}^{P∪\{p\}}$ because $\theta_{B*}^{P∪\{p\}}$ is obtained by splitting a block of θ_{B*}^P. Without loss of generality we assume that the blocks Q_{m-1} and Q_m of $\theta_{B*}^{P∪\{p\}}$ result from the split of the block $Q_{m-1} \cup Q_m$ of θ_{B*}^P. Since $\beta > 1$ we have $d_\beta (\pi^A, \theta_{B*}^{P∪\{p\}}) < d_\beta (\pi^A, \theta_{B*}^P)$ if and only if:

$$| \sum_{i=1}^{n} |P_i| \ + \sum_{j=1}^{m} |Q_j|^\beta \ -2 \sum_{i=1}^{n} \sum_{j=1}^{m} |P_i \cap Q_j|^\beta \ < \sum_{i=1}^{n} |P_i|^\beta \ +$$

$$\sum_{j=1}^{m-2} |Q_j|^\beta \ + |Q_{m-1} \cup Q_m|^\beta \ -2 \sum_{i=1}^{n} \sum_{j=1}^{m-2} |P_i \cap Q_j|^\beta \ \beta$$

which is equivalent to:

$$|Q_{m-1}|^\beta \ + |Q_m|^\beta \ -2 \sum_{i=1}^{n} |P_i \cap Q_{m-1}|^\beta \ -2 \sum_{i=1}^{n} |P_i \cap Q_m|^\beta$$

$$\lhd |Q_{m-1} \cup Q_m|^\beta \ -2 \sum_{i=1}^{n} (|P_i \cap Q_{m-1}| + |P_i \cap Q_m|)^\beta.$$

Suppose that $Q_{m-1} \cup Q_m$ is intersected by only by P_1 and P_2 and that $\beta = 2$ Then, the previous inequality that describes the condition under which a decrease of $d_\beta (\pi^A | \theta_{B*}^P)$ can be obtained becomes:

$$(|P_1 \cap Q_{m-1}| - |P_2 \cap Q_{m-1}|)(|P_1 \cap Q_m| - |P_2 \cap Q_m|) < 0$$

and so, the distance may be decreased by splitting a block $Q_{m-1} \cup Q_m$ into Q_{m-1} and Q_m only when the distribution of the fragments of the blocks P_1 and P_2 in the prospective blocks Q_{m-1} and Q_m satisfies the previous condition. If the block $Q_{m-1} \cup Q_m$ of the partition θ_{B*}^P contains a unique boundary point, then choosing that boundary point as a cut point will decrease the distance.

We tested our discretization algorithm on several machine learning data sets from UCI data sets that have numerical attributes. After discretizations performed with several values of β (typically with $\beta \in \{1.5, 1.8, 1.9, 2\}$) we built the decision trees on the discretized data sets using the WEKA J48 variant of C4.5. The size, number of leaves and accuracy of the trees are described in Table 11, where trees built using the Fayyad-Irani discretization method of J48 are designated as "standard."

It is clear that the discretization technique has a significant impact of the size and accuracy of the decision trees. The experimental results shown

in Table 8 suggest that an appropriate choice of β can reduce significantly the size and number of leaves of the decision trees, roughly maintaining the accuracy (measured by stratified five-fold cross validation) or even increasing the accuracy.

Our supervised discretization algorithm that discretizes each attribute B based on the relationship between the partition π^B and π^A (where A is the attribute that specifies the class of the objects). Thus, the discretization process of an attribute is carried out independently of similar processes performed on other attributes. As a result, our algorithm is particularly efficient for naïve Bayes classifiers, which rely on the essential assumption of attribute independence. The error rates of naïve Bayes Classifiers obtained for different discretization methods are shown in Table 12.

The use of the metric space of partitions of the data set in discretization is helpful in preparing the data for classifiers. With an appropriate choice of the parameter β that defines the metric used in discretization, standard classifiers such as C4.5 or J48 generate smaller decision trees with comparable or better levels of accuracy when applied to data discretized with our technique.

CONCLUSION AND FUTURE RESEARCH

The goal of this chapter is to stress the significance of using metric methods in typical data mining tasks. We introduced a family of metrics on the set of partitions of finite sets that is linked to the notion of generalized entropy and we demonstrated its use in classification, clustering, feature extraction and discretization.

In the realm of classification these metrics are used for a new splitting criterion for building decision trees. In addition to being more intuitive than the classic approach, this criterion results in

Table 11. Comparative experimental results for decision trees

Database	Experimental Results			
	Discretization method	Size	Number of Leaves	Accuracy (strat. cross-validation)
Heart-c	*Standard*	*51*	*30*	*79.20*
	β = 1.5	20	14	77.36
	β = 1.8	28	18	77.36
	β = 1.9	35	22	76.01
	β = 2	54	32	76.01
Glass	*Standard*	*57*	*30*	*57.28*
	β = 1.5	32	24	71.02
	β = 1.8	56	50	77.10
	β = 1.9	64	58	67.57
	β = 2	92	82	66.35
Ionosphere	*Standard*	*35*	*18*	*90.88*
	β = 1.5	15	8	95.44
	β = 1.8	19	12	88.31
	β = 1.9	15	10	90.02
	β = 2	15	10	90.02
Iris	*Standard*	*9*	*5*	*95.33*
	β = 1.5	7	5	96
	β = 1.8	7	5	96
	β = 1.9	7	5	96
	β = 2	7	5	96
Diabetes	*Standard*	*43*	*22*	*74.08*
	β = 1.8	5	3	75.78
	β = 1.9	7	4	75.39
	β = 2	14	10	76.30

Table 12. Error rate for naive Bayes classifiers

Discretization method	Diabetes	Glass	Ionosphere	Iris
β = 1.5	34.9	25.2	4.8	2.7
β = 1.8	24.2	22.4	8.3	4
β = 1.9	24.9	23.4	8.5	4
β = 2	25.4	24.3	9.1	4.7
Weighted proportional	25.5	38.4	10.3	6.9
Proportional	26.3	33.6	10.4	7.5

decision trees that have smaller sizes and fewer leaves than the trees built with standard methods, and have comparable or better accuracy. The value of β that results in the smallest trees seems to depend on the relative distribution of the class attribute and the values of the feature attributes of the objects.

Since clusterings of objects can be regarded as partitions, metrics developed for partitions present an interest for the study of the dynamics of clusters, as clusters are formed during incremental algorithms, or as data sets evolve.

As stated in Guyon and Elisseeff (2003), in early studies of relevance published in the late 1990's (Blum & Langley, 1997; Kohavi & John, 1997), few applications explored data with more than 40 attributes. With the increased interest of data miners in bio-computing in general, and in microarray data in particular, classification problems that involve thousands of features and relatively few examples came to the fore. Applications of metric feature selection techniques should be useful to the analysis of this type of data.

An important open issue is determining characteristics of data sets that will inform the choice of an optimal value for the β parameter. Also, investigating metric discretization for data with missing values seems to present particular challenges that we intend to consider in our future work.

REFERENCES

Barthélemy, J. P. (1978). Remarques sur les propriétés metriques des ensembles ordonnés, *Math. sci. hum.*, 61, 39-60.

Barthélemy, J. P., & Leclerc, B. (1995). The median procedure for partitions. In *Partitioning data sets*, (pp. 3-34), Providence, RI: American Mathematical Society.

Blake, C. L., & Merz, C. J. (1998). *UCI Repository of machine learning databases*. Retrieved February 27, 2007, from University of California Irvine Department of Information and Computer Science Web site: http://www.ics.uci.edu/~mlearn/ML-Repository.html

Blum A., & Langley, P. (1997). Selection of relevant features and examples in machine learning. *Artificial Intelligence*, 245-271.

Breiman, L., Friedman, J. H., Olshen, R. A., & Stone, C. J. (1998). *Classification and regression trees*. Chapman and Hall, Boca Raton.

Brown, M. P. S., Grundy, W. N., Lin, D., Cristiani, N., Sugnet, C. W., Furey, T. S, Ares, M., & Haussler, D. (2000). Knowledge-based analysis of microarray gene expression data by using support vector machines. *PNAS, 97,* 262-267.

Butterworth, R., Piatetsky-Shapiro, G., & Simovici, D. A. (2005). On feature extraction through clustering. In *Proceedings of ICDM*, Houston, Texas.

Butterworth, R., Simovici, D. A., Santos, G. S., & Ohno-Machado, L. (2004). A greedy algorithm for supervised discretization. *Journal of Biomedical Informatics*, 285-292.

Can, F. (1993). Incremental clustering for dynamic information processing. *ACM Transactions for Information Systems, 11,* 143-164.

Can, F., Fox, E. A., Snavely, C. D. & France, R. K. (1995). Incremental clustering for very large document databases: Initial {MARIAN} experience. *Inf. Sci., 84,* 101-114.

Carpenter, G., & Grossberg, S. (1990). Art3: Hierachical search using chemical transmitters in self-organizing pattern recognition architectures. *Neural Networks, 3,* 129-152.

Cerquides, J., & López de Mántaras, R. (1997). Proposal and empirical comparison of a parallelizable distance-based discretization method. In *Proceedings of the 3rd International Confer-*

ence on Knowledge Discovery and Data Mining (KDD '97).

Charikar, M., Chekuri, C., Feder, T., & Motwani, R (1997). Incremental clustering and dynamic information retrieval. In *STOC*, (pp. 626-635).

Cornujols, A. (1993). Getting order independence in incremental learning. In *Proceeding of the European Conference on Machine Learning*, pages (pp. 192-212).

Daróczy, Z. (1970). Generalized information functions. *Information and Control, 16*, 36-51.

Dougherty, J., Kohavi, R., & Sahami, M. (1995). Supervised and unsupervised discretization of continuous features. In *Proceedings of the 12th International Conference on Machine Learning*, (pp. 194-202).

Ester, M., Kriegel, H. P., Sander, J., Wimmer, M., & Xu, X. (1998). Incremental clustering for mining in a data warehousing environment. In *VLDB*, (pp. 323-333).

Fayyad, U. M. (1991). *On the induction of decision trees for multiple concept learning.* Unpublished doctoral thesis, University of Michigan.

Fayyad, U. M., & Irani, K. (1993). Multi-interval discretization of continuous-valued attributes for classification learning. In *Proceedings of the 12th International Joint Conference of Artificial intelligence*, (pp. 1022-1027).

Fisher, D. (1987). Knowledge acquisition via incremental conceptual clustering. *Machine Learning, 2*, 139-172.

Guyon, E., & Elisseeff, A. (2003). An introduction to variable and feature selection. *Journal of Machine Learning Research*, 1157-1182.

Hall, M.A. (1999). Correlation-based feature selection for machine learning. Unpublished doctoral thesis, University of Waikato, New Zeland.

Hartigan, J. A. (1975). *Clustering algorithms.* New York: John Wiley.

Hanczar, B., Courtine, M., Benis, A., Hannegar, C., Clement, K., & Zucker, J. D. (2003). Improving classification of microarray data using prototype-based feature selection. *SIGKDD Explorations*, 23-28.

Havrda, J. H., & Charvat, F. (1967). Quantification methods of classification processes: Concepts of structural α-entropy. *Kybernetica, 3*, 30-35.

Jain, A. K., Murty, M. N., & Flynn, P. J. (1999). Data clustering: A review. *ACM Computing Surveys, 31*, 264-323.

Kaufman, L., & Rousseeuw, P. J. (1990). *Finding groups in data—An introduction to cluster analysis.* New York: Wiley Interscience.

Kohavi, R., & John, G. (1997). Wrappers for feature selection. *Artificial Intelligence*, 273-324.

Khan, J., Wei, J. S., Ringner, M., Saal, L. H., Ladanyi, M., Westerman, F., Berthold, F., Schwab, M., Antonescu, C. R., Peterson, C., & Meltzer, P. S. (2001). Classification and diagnostic prediction of cancers using gene expression profiling and artificial neural networks. *Nature Medicine, 7*, 673-679.

Kononenko, I. (1992). Naïve bayes classifiers and continuous attributes. *Informatica, 16*, 1-8.

Kononenko, I. (1993). Inductive and Bayesian learning in medical diagnosis. *Applied Artificial Intelligence, 7*, 317-337.

Langford, T., Giraud-Carrier, C. G., & Magee, J. (2001). Detection of infectious outbreaks in hospitals through incremental clustering. In *Proceedings of the 8th Conference on AI in Medicine (AIME)*.

Lin, J., Vlachos, M., Keogh, E. J., & Gunopulos, D. (2004). Iterative incremental clustering of time series. In *EDBT*, (pp. 106-122).

López de Màntaras, R. (1991). A distance-based attribute selection measure for decision tree induction. *Machine Learning, 6*, 81-92.

Maindonald, J., & Brown, J. (2003). *Data analysis and graphics using R.* Cambridge: Cambridge University Press.

Monjardet, B. (1981). Metrics on partially ordered sets—A survey. *Discrete Mathematics, 35*, 173-184.

Robnik, M. & Kononenko, I. (1995). Discretization of continuous attributes using relieff. In *Proceedings of ERK-95.*

Roure, J., & Talavera, L. (1998). Robust incremental clustering with bad instance ordering: A new strategy. In *IBERAMIA*, 136-147.

Simovici, D. A., & Butterworth, R. (2004). A metric approach to supervised discretization. In *Proceedings of the Extraction et Gestion des Connaisances* (EGC 2004) (pp. 197-202). Toulouse, France.

Simovici, D. A., & Jaroszewicz, S. (2000). On information-theoretical aspects of relational databases. In C. Calude & G. Paun (Eds.), *Finite versus infinite*. London: Springer Verlag.

Simovici, D. A., & Jaroszewicz, S. (2002). An axiomatization of partition entropy. *IEEE Transactions on Information Theory, 48*, 2138-2142.

Simovici, D. A., & Jaroszewicz, S. (2003). Generalized conditional entropy and decision trees. In *Proceedings of the Extraction et gestion des connaissances* - EGC 2003 (pp. 363-380). Paris, Lavoisier.

Simovici, D. A., & Jaroszewicz, S. (in press). A new metric splitting criterion for decision trees. In *Proceedings of PAKDD 2006*, Singapore.

Simovici, D. A., & Singla, N. (2005). Semi-supervised incremental clustering of categorical data. In *Proceedings of EGC* (pp. 189-200).

Simovici, D. A., Singla, N., & Kuperberg, M. (2004). Metric incremental clustering of categorical data. In *Proceedings of ICDM* (pp. 523-527).

Witten, I., & Frank, E. (2005). *Data mining – Practical machine learning tools and techniques (2nd ed)*. Amsterdam: Morgan Kaufmann.

Yang, Y., & Webb, G. I. (2001). Proportional *k* -interval discretization for naive Bayes classifiers. In *Proceedings of the 12th European Conference on Machine Learning*, (pp. 564-575).

Yang, Y., & Webb, G. I. (2003). Weighted proportional *k* -interval discretization for naive Bayes classifiers. In *Proceedings of the PAKDD*.

Zongker, D., & Jain, A. (1996). Algorithms for feature selection: An evaluation. In *Proceedings of the International Conference on Pattern Recognition* (pp. 18-22).

NOTE

To Dr. George Simovici,
In memoriam

Chapter II
Bi–Directional Constraint Pushing in Frequent Pattern Mining

Osmar R. Zaïane
University of Alberta, Canada

Mohammed El-Hajj
University of Alberta, Canada

ABSTRACT

Frequent itemset mining (FIM) is a key component of many algorithms that extract patterns from transactional databases. For example, FIM can be leveraged to produce association rules, clusters, classifiers or contrast sets. This capability provides a strategic resource for decision support, and is most commonly used for market basket analysis. One challenge for frequent itemset mining is the potentially huge number of extracted patterns, which can eclipse the original database in size. In addition to increasing the cost of mining, this makes it more difficult for users to find the valuable patterns. Introducing constraints to the mining process helps mitigate both issues. Decision makers can restrict discovered patterns according to specified rules. By applying these restrictions as early as possible, the cost of mining can be constrained. For example, users may be interested in purchases whose total price exceeds $100, or whose items cost between $50 and $100. In cases of extremely large data sets, pushing constraints sequentially is not enough and parallelization becomes a must. However, specific design is needed to achieve sizes never reported before in the literature.

INTRODUCTION

Frequent pattern discovery has become a common topic of investigation in the data mining research area. Its main theme is to discover the sets of items that occur together more than a given threshold defined by the decision maker. A well-known application domain that counts on the frequent pattern discovery is the market basket analysis. In most cases when the support threshold is low and the number of frequent patterns "explodes", the discovery of these patterns becomes problematic, not only because of the huge number of discovered rules, but also because of performance reasons such as: high memory dependencies, huge search space, and massive I/O operations. To reduce the effects of these problems new methods need to be investigated such as fast traversal techniques to reduce the search space or using constraints that lessen the output size whilst directly discovering patterns that are of interest to the user either sequentially or in parallel.

Constraint-based frequent pattern mining is an ongoing area of research. Two important categories of constraints are *monotone* and *anti-monotone* (Lakshmanan, Ng, Han, & Pang, 1999). *Anti-monotone* constraints are constraints that when valid for a pattern, they are consequently valid for any subset subsumed by the pattern. Monotone constraints when valid for a pattern are inevitably valid for any superset subsuming that pattern. The straightforward way to deal with constraints is to use them as a postmining filter. However, it is more efficient to consider the constraints during the mining process. This is what is referred to as "pushing the constraints" (Pie & Han, 2000). Most existing algorithms leverage (or push) one of these types during mining and postpone the other to a postprocessing phase.

New algorithms, such as Dualminer, apply both types of constraints at the same time (Bucila, Gehrke, Kifer, & White, 2002). It considers these two types of constraints in a double process, one mirroring the other for each type of constraint,

hence its name. However, *monotone* and *anti-monotone* constraints do not necessarily apply in duality. Especially when considering the mining process as a set of distinct phases, such as the building of structures to compress the data and the mining of these structures, the application of these constraints differ by type. Moreover, some constraints have different properties and should be considered separately. For instance, minimum support and maximum support are intricately tied to the mining process itself while constraints on item characteristics, such as price, are not. Algorithms such as BifoldLeap (El-Hajj & Zaïane, 2005) and DPC-COFI (El-Hajj & Zaïane, 2003) push both types of constraints at the same time. The first one uses a leap approach for finding the set of patterns, while the second employs a top-down approach. Those algorithms showed good performance results mainly when mining extremely large datasets. More details about those two algorithms are explained in the related work section.

Problem Statement

The problem of mining association rules over market basket analysis was introduced in (Agrawal, Imielinski, & Swami, 1993; Agrawal & Srikant, 1994). The problem consists of finding associations between items or itemsets in transactional data. The data is typically retail sales in the form of customer transactions, but can be any data that can be modeled into transactions.

Formally, the problem is stated as follows: Let I = $\{i_1, i_2, ... i_m\}$ be a set of literals, called items. Each item is an object with some predefined attributes such as price, weight, and so forth, and m is considered the dimensionality of the problem. Let Đ be a set of transactions, where each transaction Ŧ is a set of items such that $Ŧ \subseteq I$. A transaction Ŧ is said to contain X, a set of items in I, if $X \subseteq T$. A constraint ζ is a predicate on itemset X that yields either *true* or *false*. An itemset X satisfies a constraint ζ if and only if $\zeta(X)$ is *true*. An itemset

X has a support s in the transaction set Ð if s% of the transactions in Ð contain X. Two particular constraints pertain to the *support* of an itemset, namely the *minimum support* constraint and the *maximum support* constraint. An itemset X is said to be *infrequent* if its support s is smaller than a given minimum support threshold σ; X is said to be too *frequent* if its *support* s is greater than a given maximum support Σ; and X is said to be *large* or *frequent* if its *support* s is greater or equal than σ and less or equal than Σ.

Chapter Organization

This chapter starts by defining the main two types of constraints in section 2. Related work is illustrated in section 3. Our leap frequent mining algorithm COFI-Leap is explained in Section 4. The constraint pushing is explained in section 5. Section 6 presents HFP-Leap and the parallel version of the constraint frequent mining algorithm. Performance evaluations are explained in sections 7 and 8.

CONSTRAINTS

It is known that algorithms for discovering association rules generate an overwhelming number of those rules. While many new efficient algorithms were recently proposed to allow the mining of extremely large datasets, the problem due to the sheer number of rules discovered still remains. The set of discovered rules is often so large that it becomes useless. Different measures of interestingness and filters have been proposed to reduce the discovered rules, but one of the most realistic ways to find only those interesting patterns is to express constraints on the rules we want to discover. However, filtering the rules post-mining adds a significant overhead and misses the opportunity to reduce the search space using the constraints. Ideally, dealing with the constraints should be done as early as possible during the mining process.

Categories of Constraints

A number of types of constraints have been identified in the literature from Lakshmanan et al. (1999). In this work, we discuss two important categories of constraints – *monotone* and *anti-monotone*.

- **Definition 1 (*Anti-monotone* constraints):** A constraint ζ is *anti-monotone* if and only if an itemset X violates ζ, so does any superset of X. That is, if ζ holds for an itemset S then it holds for any subset of S.

☐

Table 1. Commonly used monotone and anti-monotone constraints

MONOTONE	ANTI-MONOTONE
min(S) ≤ v	*min(S) ≥ v*
max(S) ≥ v	*max(S) ≤ v*
count(S) ≥ v	*count(S) ≤ v*
sum(S) ≥ v(∀a ∈ S, a ≥ 0)	*sum(S) ≤ v(∀a ∈ S, a ≥ 0)*
range(S) ≥ v	*range(S) ≤ v*
support(S) ≤ v	*support(S) ≥ v*

Many constraints fall within the *anti-monotone* category. The minimum support threshold is a typical *anti-monotone* constraint. As an example, *sum(S) ≤ v(∀a ∈ S, a ≥ 0)* is an *anti-monotone* constraint. Assume that items A, B, and C have prices $100, $150, and $200 respectively. Given the constraint ζ =(sum(S) ≤ $200), then since itemset AB, with a total price of $250, violates the ζ constraint, there is no need to test any of its supersets (e.g., *ABC*) as they also violate the ζ constraint.

- **Definition 2 (Monotone constraints):** A constraint ζ is *monotone* if and only if an itemset *X* holds for ζ, so does any superset of *X*. That is, if ζ is violated for an itemset *S* then it is violated for any subset of *S*.

□

An example of a *monotone* constraint is *sum(S) ≥ v(∀a ∈ S, a ≥ 0)*. Using the same items A, B, and C as before, and with constraint ζ =(sum(S) ≥ 500), then knowing that ABC violates the constraint ζ is sufficient to know that all subsets of *ABC* will violate ζ as well.

Table 1 presents commonly used constraints that are either *anti-monotone* or *monotone*. From the definition of both types of constraints we can conclude that *anti-monotone* constraints can be pushed when the mining-algorithm uses the bottom-up approach, as we can prune any candidate superset if its subset violates the constraint. Conversely, the *monotone* constraints can be pushed efficiently when we are using algorithms that follow the top-down approach as we can prune any subset of patterns from the answer set once we find that its superset violates the *monotone* constraint.

As an example, assume we have a frequent pattern ABCDE where the prices of items A, B, C, D and E are $10, $20, $30, $40, and $50 respectively. Figure 1 presents the lattice for all possible frequent patterns that can be generated

from ABCDE along with their respective prices. From this figure we can see that we may need to generate and count five patterns of size 1, ten patterns of size 2, ten patterns of size 3, five patterns of size 4, and one pattern of size 5 for a total of 31 patterns. If the user wants to find all frequent itemsets that have prices ranging from more than $50 to less than $90, there are two alternatives: either use a bottom-up approach, pushing *anti-monotone* constraints and postprocessing the *monotone* ones, or use a top-down approach, pushing the *monotone* constraints and postprocessing *anti-monotone* ones. Let us consider the *anti-monotone* constraint price of X is less than $90. We can find that at the second level DE violates the constraint and consequently ADE, BDE, CDE, ABDE, ACDE, BCDE, and ABCDE should not be generated and counted, which saves us from generating seven patterns. At level three we find that ACE, BCD and BCE also violate the constraint, which means we do not need to generate and count ABCD and ABCE. In total, pushing the *anti-monotone* constraint allowed nine patterns to be pruned.

The second *monotone* constraint can be applied as a postprocessing step to remove any frequent patterns that violate it (i.e., price less than or equal to $50). Figure 1 illustrates this pruning. The other alternative is to consider the *monotone* constraints first starting from the long patterns. Once we find for example that AB has a price less than $50, we can directly omit single items A and B. The same applies to AC, AD and BC. As before, the *anti-monotone* constraint can be applied in a postprocessing step to remove generated patterns that violate it.

Bi-Directional Pushing of Constraints

Pushing constraints early means considering constraints while mining for patterns rather than postponing the checking of constraints until after the mining process. Considering all constraints

Figure 1. Lattice for all possible itemsets from ABCDE with their respective prices.

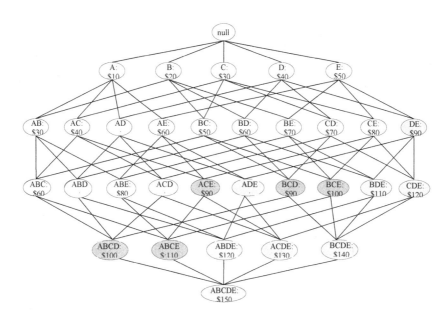

Figure 2. Pruning of the lattice: CDE and AB violate anti-monotone and monotone constraints respectively. All of their subsets and supersets are pruned respectively. BDE and AC satisfy the anti-monotone and monotone constraints respectively. There is no need to check their subsets and supersets respectively.

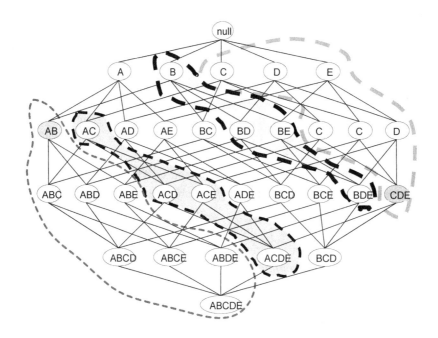

while mining is difficult given the intrinsic characteristics of existing algorithms for mining frequent itemsets, either going over the lattice of candidate itemsets top-down or bottom-up. Most algorithms attempt to push either type of constraints during the mining process hoping to reduce the search space in one direction: from subsets to supersets or from supersets to subsets. Dualminer (Bucila et al., 2002) pushes both types of constraints but at the expense of efficiency. Focusing solely on reducing the search space by pruning the lattice of itemsets is not necessarily a winning strategy. While pushing constraints early seems conceptually beneficial, in practice the testing of the constraints can add significant overhead. If the constraints are not selective enough, checking the constraint predicates for each candidate can be onerous. It is thus important that we also reduce the checking frequency. While the primary benefit of early constraint checking is the elimination of candidates that cannot pass the constraint, it can also be used to identify candidates which are guaranteed to pass the constraint and therefore do not need to be rechecked. In summary, the goal of pushing constraints early is to reduce the itemset search space, eliminating unnecessary processing and memory consumption, while at the same time limiting the amount of constraint checking performed. Figure 2 presents an example of how much we can gain by early pushing both types of constraints.

RELATED WORK

Mining frequent patterns with constraints has been studied in Lakshmanan et al. (1999) where the concept of *monotone, anti-monotone* and succinct were introduced to prune the search space. Pei and Han (2000) and Pei, Han, and Lakshmanan (2001) have also generalized these two classes of constraints and introduced a new convertible constraint class. In their work they proposed a new algorithm called FICM, which is

an FP-Growth based algorithm (Han, Pei, & Yin, 2000). This algorithm generates most frequent patterns before pruning them. Its main contribution is that it checks for *monotone* constraints early and once a frequent itemset is found to satisfy the *monotone* constraint, then all itemsets having this item as a prefix are sure to satisfy the constraint and consequently there is no need to apply further checks. Dualminer (Bucila et al., 2002) is the first algorithm to mine both types of constraints at the same time. Nonetheless, it suffers from many practical limitations and performance issues. First, it is built on the top of the MAFIA (Bucila et al., 2001) algorithm which produces the set of maximal patterns, and consequently all frequent patterns generated using this model do not have their support attached. Second, it assumes that the whole dataset can fit in main memory, which is not always the case. FP-Growth and our approach use a very condensed representation, namely FP-Tree, which uses significantly less memory (Han et al., 2000). Third, their top-down computation exploiting the *monotone* constraint often performs many useless tests for relatively large datasets, which raises doubts about the performance gained by pushing constraints in the Dualminer algorithm. In a recent study of parallelizing Dualminer (Ting, Bailey, & Ramamohanarao, 2004), the authors showed that by mining relatively small sparse datasets consisting of 10K transactions and 100K items, the sequential version of Dualminer took an excessive amount of time. Unfortunately, the original authors of Dualminer did not show any single experiment to depict the execution time of their algorithm but only the reduction in predicate executions (Bucila et al., 2002). A recent strategy dealing with *monotone* and *anti-monotone* constraints suggests reducing the transactional database input via pre-processing by successively eliminating transactions that violate the constraints and then applying any frequent itemset mining algorithm on the reduced transaction set (Bonchi et al., 2004). The main drawback of this approach is that it is highly I/O bound due to the iterative process needed in rewriting the reduced dataset to disk. This algorithm is also sensitive to the results of the initial *monotone* constraint checking which is applied to full transactions. In other words, if a whole transaction satisfies the *monotone* constraint, then no pruning is applied and consequently no gains are achieved even if parts of this transaction do not satisfy the same *monotone* constraint. To overcome some of the issues in Bonchi et al., (2004), the same approach has been tested against the FP-Growth approach in Bonchi et al., (2004) with new effective pruning heuristics. DPC-COFI (El-Hajj & Zaïane, 2003) pushes both types of constraints after building small COFI trees for each frequent pattern in the frequent 1-itemset. It uses a top-down approach for finding the frequent patterns that satisfy the constraints, where many pruning ideas are incorporated in this algorithm such as in some cases pruning the COFI trees themselves, if the algorithm detects early that all what will be generated from this COFI-tree violates one type of the constraints tested. BiFoldLeap (El-Hajj et al., 2005) also uses the concept of COFI tree. However, it extends this concept by applying a fast traversal approach called leap. In this approach it generates the maximal patterns first. During the pattern generation each type of constraints is checked early trying to prune any pattern that does not satisfy the constraints. In addition to its strong pruning strategies, this algorithm also uses a new idea of reducing the constraint checking by detecting in advance if a group of patterns satisfies one type of constraint, consequently this group will not be tested against this type of constraint.

LEAP ALGORITHMS: COFI-Leap, HFP-Leap

We start here by explaining our frequent pattern mining approach that is based on the leap idea. We have implemented this approach in two ways either by applying the COFI-Leap, or HFP-Leap

(Zaïane & El-Hajj, 2005) that is, the headerless Frequent Pattern Leap. The sequential constraint frequent mining algorithm, BifoldLeap, discussed in this chapter, is based on the COFI-Leap algorithm. The parallel BifoldLeap, discussed in the next section, is based on a parallel version of the HFP-Leap (El-Hajj & Zaïane, 2006). This is mainly due to the fact that we need to reduce the communication cost between processors. A detailed explanation for the COFI-Leap idea is outlined later in this section.

Most existing algorithms traverse the itemset lattice top-down or bottom-up, and search using a depth first or breadth first strategy. In contrast, we propose a leap traversal strategy that finds a su perset of pertinent itemsets by "leaping" between promising nodes in the itemset lattice. In addition to finding these relevant candidate itemsets, sufficient information is gathered to produce the frequent itemset patterns, along with their supports. Here, we use leap traversal in conjunction with the complementary COFI idea by El-Hajj and Zaïane (2003), where the locally frequent itemsets of each frequent item are explored separately. This creates additional opportunities for pruning. What is the COFI idea and what is this set of pertinent itemsets with their additional information? This set of pertinent itemsets is the set of maximals. We will first present the COFI tree structure, and then we will introduce our algorithm COFI-Leap that mines for frequent itemsets using COFI trees and jumping in the pattern lattice. In the next section, this same algorithm will be enhanced with constraint checking to produce algorithms BifoldLeap.

Important Patterns: Closed and Maximal

The set of all frequent itemsets is said to be redundant. Indeed, knowing a pattern X to be frequent, all its subsets are de-facto frequent. However, when knowing the frequency of this pattern X, nothing can be said about the exact

Algorithm 1. COFI-Leap: Leap-Traversal with COFI-tree

Input: Đ (transactional database; σ (Support threshold).

Output: Type patterns with their respective supports.

F1 ← Scan Đ to find the set of frequent 1-itemsets

FPT ← Scan Đ to build the FP-tree using *F1*

GlobalMaximals ←∅

FOR each item *I* in Header(*FPT*) in increasing support **DO**

    LF ← *FindlocalF requentW ithRespect(I)*

    IF Not ← (I ∪ *LF*) ⊆ *GlobalMaximals* **THEN**

        ICT ← Build COFT-Tree for I

        FPB ← *FindFrequentPathBases(ICT)*

        LocalMaximals ← *Frequent(FPB)*

        InFrequentFPB ← *notF requent(FPB)*

        FOR each pair (*A, B*) ∈ *InFrequentFPB* **DO**

            Pattern ← A ∩ B

            IF Pattern is frequent and not ∅ **THEN**

                Add *Pattern* in *LocalMaximals*

            ELSE

                Add Pattern in *InFrequentFPB* IF not ∅

            END IF

        END FOR

        FOR each pattern *P* in *LocalMaximals* **DO**

            IF *P* is not a subset of any *M* ∈ *GlobalMaximals* **THEN**

                Add *P* in *GlobalMaximals*

            END IF

        END FOR

    END IF

END FOR

Patterns ← *GeneratePatterns(FPB, GlobalMaximals)*

Output *Patterns*

---

respective frequencies of its subsets, except that they are frequent and their count is greater or equal than the support of X. This leads to the notion of Maximal patterns created by Bayardo (1998). A pattern is said to be maximal if there is no other frequent pattern that subsumes it.

In other words, maximals are a subset of frequent patterns from which we can straight-forwardly derive all frequent patterns without their exact support, but lower bounds. Another particular set of frequent patterns is called the set of frequent closed itemsets (Pasquier, Bastide,

Taouil & Lakhal 1999). A frequent itemset X is closed if and only if there is no X' such that X is a subset of X' and X' is contained in every transaction containing X. The difference with maximals is that with the closed itemsets and their support one can derive all frequent patterns with their exact support. The set of maximal frequent itemsets is found, in general, to be orders of magnitude smaller in size than the set closed itemsets, and the set of closed itemsets is found, in general, to be orders of magnitude smaller in size than the set of all frequent itemsets (Bucila et al., 2002).

The strategy of our algorithm COFI-Leap is to first find this small set of the maximal patterns and keep enough information in the process to then generate all frequent patterns with their exact counts.

COFI-Trees

The COFI-tree idea was introduced in El-Hajj and Zaïane (2003) as a means to reduce the memory requirement and speed up the mining strategy of FP-growth (Han et al., 2000). Rather than recursively building conditional trees from the FP-tree, the COFI strategy was to create COFI-trees for each frequent item and mine them separately. Conditional trees are FP-trees conditioned on the existence of a given frequent item. The FP-tree discussed in Han et al. (2000) is a compact prefix-tree representation of the subtransactions in the input data. Here, subtransactions are the original transactions with infrequent items removed. The FP-tree contains a header and internode links, which facilitate downward traversal (forward in the itemset pattern) as well as lateral traversal (next node representing a specific item).

Building COFI-trees based on the FP-tree. For each frequent item in the FP-tree, in order of increasing support, one COFI-tree is built (El-Hajj & Zaïane, 2003). This tree is based on subtransactions which contain the root item and are composed only of items locally frequent with

the root item that have not already been used as root items in earlier COFI-trees. The COFI-tree is similar to the FP-tree, but includes extra links for upward traversal (earlier in the itemset pattern), a new participation counter in each node, and a data structure to allow traversal of all leaves in the tree. This participation counter is used during the mining process to count up the participation of each node in the generation of a frequent pattern.

COFI-Leap

COFI-Leap is different than the algorithm presented in El-Hajj and Zaïane (2003) in the sense that it generates maximal patterns, where a pattern is said to be maximal if there is no other frequent pattern that subsumes it. COFI-Leap rather than traversing the pattern lattice top-down it leaps from one node to the other in search of the support border where maximals sit. Once maximals are found, with the extra information collected, all other patterns can be generated with their respective support.

Following is a brief summary of the COFI-Leap algorithm. First, a frequent pattern FP-tree (Han et al., 2000) is created, using two scans of the database. Second, for each frequent item, a COFI-tree is created including all co-occurant frequent items to the right (i.e., in order of decreasing support). Each COFI-tree is generated from the FP-tree without returning to the transactional database for scans. Unique subtransactions in the COFI-tree along with their count (called branch support) are obtained from the COFI-tree. These unique subtransactions are called frequent path bases (FPB). These can be obtained by traversing upward from each leaf node in the COFI-tree, updating the participation counter to avoid overcounting nodes. Clearly, there is at most one FPB for each subtransaction in the COFI-tree.

Frequent FPBs are declared candidate maximals. Infrequent FPBs are intersected iteratively, producing subsets that may be frequent. When an intersection of infrequent FPBs results in a frequent itemset, that itemset is declared as a candidate maximal and is not subject to further intersections. When an intersection is infrequent, it participates in further intersections looking for maximals. This is indeed how the leaps in the lattice are done. The result of the intersection of FPBs indicates the next node to explore. How is the support of a pattern calculated? Given the set of frequent path bases along with their branch supports, it is possible to count the support of any itemset. This is done by finding all FPBs that are supersets of the target itemset and summing their branch supports. For example, if there are two FPBs, ABC and ABCD, each with branch support 1, ABC has support 2, and ABCD has support 1.

Algorithm 1 shows the main steps of COFI-Leap. Notice that COFI-trees are not generated systematically for all frequent 1-itemsets. There is no need to look for maximals locally with respect to an item I, if I and its locally frequent items are already subset of known global maximals. Finally, in the function GeneratePatterns, the set of candidate maximal patterns is used along with the frequent path bases to produce the set of all frequent itemsets that satisfy the constraints along with their supports. Maximal itemsets can be found by filtering the candidate maximals to remove subsets. Supports for the candidate maximal patterns were computed as part of the intersection process (to discover that they were frequent), and therefore do not need to be recomputed. Once the maximal itemsets have been found, then all frequent itemsets can be found by iterating over all subsets of the maximals, suppressing duplicates resulting from overlap with other maximal patterns. Support counting for the frequent itemsets is done as for the FPBs, that is by summing the branch supports of all FPBs that are supersets of the pattern.

COFI-Leap WITH CONSTRAINTS, BifoldLeap

The algorithm COFI-Leap offers a number of opportunities to push the *monotone* and *anti-monotone* predicates, P() and Q() respectively. We start this process by defining two terms which are head (H) and tail (T) where H is a frequent path base or any subset generated from the intersection of frequent path bases, and T is the itemset generated from intersecting all remaining frequent path bases not used in the intersection of H. The intersection of H and T, $H \cap T$, is the smallest subset of H that may yet be considered. Thus Leap focuses on finding frequent H that can be declared as local maximals and candidate global maximals. BifoldLeap extends this idea to find local maximals that satisfy P(). We call these P-maximals.

Although we further constrain the P-maximals to itemsets that satisfy Q(), not all subsets of these P-maximals are guaranteed to satisfy Q(). To find the itemsets that satisfy both constraints, the subsets of each P-maximal are generated in order from long patterns to short. When a subset is found to fail Q(), further subsets do not need to be generated for that itemset, as they are guaranteed to fail Q() also.

There are three significant places where constraints can be pushed. These are:

a. While building the FP-tree
b. While building the COFI-trees
c. While intersecting the frequent path bases which is the main phase where both types of constraints are pushed at the same time (algorithm 2)

Constraint pushing opportunities during FP-tree construction. First, P() is applied to each 1-itemset. Items, which fail this test, are not included in FP-tree construction. Second, we use the idea from FP-Bonsai (Bonchi et al., 2004) where subtransactions which do not satisfy Q() are not used in the second phase of the FP-tree building process. The supports for the items within these transactions are decremented. This may result in some previously frequent items becoming infrequent. Such items will not be used to construct COFI-trees in the following phase.

Constraint pushing opportunities during COFI-tree construction. Let X be the set of all items that will be used to build the COFI-tree, that is the items which satisfy $P()$ individually but have not been used as the root of a previous COFI-tree. If X fails $Q()$, there is no need to build the COFI-tree, as no subset of X can satisfy $Q()$. Alternatively, if X satisfies $P()$, there is also no need to build the COFI-tree, as X is a candidate P-maximal.

Constraint pushing opportunities during intersection of Frequent-Path-Bases. There are two high-level strategies for pushing constraints during the intersection phase. First, $P()$ and $Q()$ can be used to eliminate an itemset or remove the need to evaluate its intersections with additional frequent path bases. Second, $P()$ and $Q()$ can be applied to the "head intersect tail" (H ∩ T), which is the smallest subset of the current itemset that can be produced by further intersections. These strategies are detailed in the following four theorems.

- **Theorem 1:** If an intersection of frequent path bases (H) fails $Q()$, it can be discarded,

and there is no need to evaluate further intersections with H.

  ° **Proof:** If an itemset fails $Q()$, all of its subsets are guaranteed to fail $Q()$ based on the definition of *monotone* constraints. Further intersecting H will produce subsets, all of which are guaranteed to violate $Q()$.

- **Theorem 2:** If an intersection of frequent path bases (H) passes $P()$, it is a candidate P-maximal, and there is no need to evaluate further intersections with H.

  ° **Proof:** Further intersecting H will produce subsets of H. By definition, no P-maximal is subsumed by another itemset that also satisfies $P()$. Therefore, none of these subsets of H are potential new P-maximals.

- **Theorem 3:** If a node's $H \cap T$ fails $P()$, the H node can be discarded, and there is no need to evaluate further intersections with H.

  ° **Proof:** If an itemset fails $P()$, then all of its supersets will also violate $P()$ from the definition of *anti-monotone* constraints. Since a node's $H \cap T$ represents the subset of H that results From intersecting H with all remaining frequent path bases, H and all combinations of intersections between H and remaining frequent path bases

Figure 3. Pushing P() and Q().

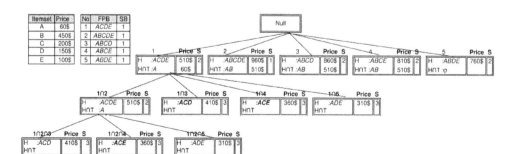

Algorithm 2. BifoldLeap: Pushing P() and Q()

Input: Ð (transactional database); σ; Σ; *P()*; *Q()*.
Output: Frequent patterns satisfying *P()*, *Q()*

PF1 ← Scan Ð to find the set of frequent P1-itemsets
FPT ← Scan D to build FP-tree using *PF1* and *Q()*
PGM(PGlobalMaximals) ←∅

FOR each item *I* in Header(*FPT*) **DO**
    LF ← *FindlocalFrequentWithRespect(I)*
    IF (*Not Q(I ∪ LF*)) **THEN**
        break
    END if
    IF *(P (I ∪ LF))* **THEN**
        Add *(I ∪ LF)* to *PGM* and break
    END if
    IF *Not (I ∪ LF) ⊆ PGM* **THEN**
        ICT ← Build COFI-Tree for *I*
        FPB ← *FindFrequentPathBases(ICT)*
        PLM(PLMaximals) ←{*P (FPB)* and frequent}
        InFrequentFPB ← *notFrequent(FPB)*
        FOR each pair (A, B) ∈ *InFrequentFPB* **DO**
            header ←A ∩ B
            Add *header* in *PLM* and Break IF (*P(header)* AND is frequent and not ∅)
            Delete *header* and break IF (Not *Q(header)*)
            tail ← Intersection(FPBs not in *header*)
            delete *header* and break IF (Not *P(header ∩ tail)*)
            Do not check for *Q()* in any subset of header IF (*Q(header ∩ tail)*)
        END FOR
        FOR each pattern *P* in *PLM* **DO**
            Add *P* in *PGM* IF ((*P* not subset of any M ∈ P GM)
        END FOR
    END IF
END FOR
PQ-Patterns ← *GPatternsQ(FPB, PGM)*
Output PQ-Patterns

---

are supersets of $H \cap T$ and therefore guaranteed to fail $P()$ also.

- **Theorem 4:** If a node's $H \cap T$ passes $Q()$, $Q()$ is guaranteed to pass for any itemset resulting from the intersection of a subset of the frequent path bases used to generate H plus the remaining frequent path bases yet to be intersected with H. $Q()$ does not need to be checked in these cases.
  - **Proof:** $Q()$ is guaranteed to pass for all of these itemsets because they are generated from a subset of the intersections used to produce the $H \cap T$ and are therefore supersets of the $H \cap T$.

The following example, shown in Figure 3, illustrates how BifoldLeap works. An A-COFI-tree is made from five items, A, B, C, D, and E, with prices $60, $450, $200, $150, and $100 respectively. In our example, this COFI-tree generates 5 frequent path bases, ACDE, ABCDE, ABCD, ABCE, and ABDE, each with branch support one. The *anti-monotone* predicate, $P()$, is Sum(prices) $\leq \$500$, and the *monotone* predicate, $Q()$, is Sum(prices) $\geq \$100$. Intersecting the first FPB with the second produces ACDE, which has a price of $510, and therefore violates $P()$ and passes $Q()$. Next, we examine the $H \cap T$, the intersection of this node with the remaining three FPBs, which yields A with price $60, passing $P()$ and failing $Q()$. None of these constraint checks provide an opportunity for pruning, so we continue intersecting this itemset with the remaining frequent path bases. The first intersection is with the third FPB, producing ACD with price $410, which satisfies both the *anti-monotone* and *monotone* constraints. The second intersection produces ACE, which also satisfies both constraints. The same thing occurs with the last intersection, which produces ADE. Going back to the second frequent path base, ABCDE, we find that the $H \cap T$, AB, violates the *anti-monotone* constraint with price $510. Therefore, we do not need to consider ABCDE or any further intersections with it. The remaining

nodes are eliminated in the same manner. In total, three candidate P-maximals were discovered. We can generate all of their subsets while testing only against $Q()$. Finally, the support for these generated subsets can be computed from the existing frequent path bases.

PARALLEL BifoldLeap: BUILDING THE STRUCTURES IN PARALLEL AND MINING THEM IN PARALLEL

The parallel BifoldLeap is based on a parallel version of the HFP-Leap (El-Hajj et al., 2005). The HFP-Leap employs the same idea of COFI-Leap, where both algorithms generate the FPBs before applying the leap approach to find the set frequent patterns. The main differences between them is that the COFI-Leap generates FPBs at the COFI-tree level, while the HFP-Leap generates the FPBs from a tree structure that is the same as the FP-tree except for the following differences. We call this tree Headerless-Frequent-Pattern-Tree or HFP-tree.

1. We do not maintain a header table, as a header table is used to facilitate the generation of the conditional trees in the FP-growth model (Han et al., 2000). It is not needed in our leap traversal approach.
2. We do not need to maintain the links between the same itemset across the different tree branches (horizontal links).
3. The links between nodes are bidirectional to allow top-down and bottom-up traversals of the tree.
4. All leaf nodes are linked together as the leaf nodes are the start of any pattern base and linking them helps the discovery of frequent pattern bases.
5. In addition to *support*, each node in the HFP-tree has a second variable called *participation*.

From the generated FPBs the leap approach is applied to produce the set of maximal patterns. In the work presented in this chapter we extend this parallelization idea by pushing constraints in parallel using a novel algorithm we call parallel BifoldLeap.

The parallel version of BifoldLeap favors using leap intersections on the HFP-Leap over the COFI-Leap approach. The reason for this is that during the parallelization of leap we mainly need to broadcast the results of each leap intersections at each node level, that is, broadcasting the locally generated maximals to produce the global maximals. In the case of COFI-Leap approach local maximals are generated per COFI tree that is, if we have n COFI-trees then n messages will be broadcast. However for HFP-Leap we apply one set of intersections per tree that is, per node. As a result of this, only one set of messages is needed to broadcast the set of local maximals among processors.

The parallel BifoldLeap starts by partitioning the data among the parallel nodes, where each node receives almost the same number of transactions. Each processor scans its partition to find the frequency of candidate items. The list of all supports is reduced to the master node to get the global list of frequent 1-itemsets. The second scan of each partition starts with the goal of building a local headerless frequent patterns tree. From each tree, the local set of frequent path bases is generated. Those sets are broadcast to all processors. Identical frequent path bases are merged and sorted lexicographically, the same as with the sequential process. At this stage the pattern bases are split among the processors. Each processor is allocated a carefully selected set of frequent pattern bases to build their respective intersection trees, with the goal of creating similar depth trees among the processors. This distribution is discussed further below. Pruning algorithms are applied at each processor to reduce the size of the intersection trees as it is done in the sequential version (Zaïane et al., 2005).

Maximal patterns that satisfy the $P()$ constraints are generated at each node. Each processor then sends its P-maximal patterns to one master node, which filters them to generate the set of global P-maximal patterns and then find all their subsets that satisfy $Q()$. Algorithm 3 presents the steps needed to generate the set of patterns satisfying both $P()$ and $Q()$ in parallel.

Load Sharing Among Processors

While the trees of intersections are not physically built, they are virtually traversed to complete the relevant intersections of pattern bases. Since each processor can handle independently some of these trees and the sizes of these trees of intersections are monotonically decreasing, it is important to cleverly distribute these among the processors to avoid significant load imbalance. A naïve and direct approach would be to divide the trees sequentially. Given p processors we would give the first $(1/p)^{th}$ trees to the first processor, the next fraction to the second processor, and so on. Unfortunately, this strategy eventually leads to imbalance among the processors since the last processor gets all the small trees and would undoubtedly terminate before the other nodes in the cluster. A more elegant and effective approach would be a round robin approach taking into account the sizes of the trees: when ordered by size, the first p trees are distributed one to each processor and so on for each set of p trees. This avoids having a processor dealing with only large trees while another processor is intersecting with only small ones. Although this strategy may still create imbalance among processors, it will be less acute than the naïve direct approach. The strategy that we propose, and call first-last, distributes two trees per processor at a time. The largest tree and the smallest tree are assigned to the first processor, then the second largest tree and penultimate small tree to the second processor, the third largest tree and third smallest tree to the third processor and so on in a loop. This

Algorithm 3. Parallel-BifoldLeap: Parallel-BifoldLeap with headerless FP-tree

---

Input: Đ (transactional database); $P()$; $Q()$; and σ (Support threshold).

Output: Patterns satisfying both $P()$ and $Q()$ with their respective supports.

- Đ is already distributed otherwise partition Đ between the available p processors;

- Each processor p scans its local partition $Đ_p$ to find the set of local candidate

1-itemsets L_pC1 with their respective local support;

- The supports of all $LiC1$ are transmitted to the master processor;

- Global Support is counted by master and $F1$ is generated;

- $F1$ is broadcasted to all nodes;

- Each processor p scans its local partition $Đ_p$ to build the local Headerless FP-tree L_pHFP based on $F1$;

- $L_pFPB \leftarrow FindFrequentPatternBases(L_pHFP)$;

-All L_pFPB are sent to the master node;

-Master node generates the global FPB from all L_pFPB;

-The global FPB are broadcast to all nodes;

-Each Processor p is assigned a set of local header nodes LHD from the global FPB; {this is the distribution of trees of intersections}

    FOR each i in LHD **DO**

        $LOCAL–P–Maximals \leftarrow Find-P-Maximals(FPB, σ, P(),Q())$;

    END FOR

- Send all $LOCAL– P –Maximals$ to the master node;

- The master node prunes all $LOCAL–P–Maximals$ that have supersets itemsets in $LOCAL–P –Maximals$ to produce $GLOBAL– P–Maximals$;

- The master node generates frequent patterns satisfying both $P()$ and $Q()$ from $GLOBAL–P–Maximals$.

---

approach seems to advocate a better load balance as is demonstrated by our experiments.

Parallel Leap Traversal Approach : An Example

The following example illustrates how the Bi-foldLeap approach is applied in parallel. Figure 4 (A) presents 7 transactions made of 8 distinct items which are: A, B, C, D, E, F, G, and H with prices $10, $20, $30, $40, $50, $60, and $70

respectively. Assuming we want to mine those transactions with a support threshold equals to at least 3 and generates patterns that their total prices are between $30 and $100 (i.e., $P()$: Sum of Prices < $100, and $Q()$Sum of Prices > $30, using two processors. Figures 4 (A) and Figure 4 (B) illustrate all the needed steps to accomplish this task. The database is partitioned between the two processors where the first three transactions are assigned to the first processor, $P1$, and the remaining ones are assigned to the second processor, $P2$

(Figure 4 (A)). In the first scan of the database, each processor finds the local support for each item: *P1* finds the support of A, B, C, D, E, F and G which are 3, 2, 2, 2, 2, 1 and 2 respectively, and P 2 the supports of A, B, C, D, E, F, and H which are 2, 3, 3, 3, 3, 3, 2. A reduced operation is executed to find that the global support of A, B, C, D, E, F, G, and H items is 5, 5, 5, 5, 5, 4, 2, and 2. The last two items are pruned as they do not meet the threshold criteria (support > 2), and the remaining ones are declared frequent items of size 1. The set of Global frequent 1-itemset is broadcast to all processors using the first round of messages.

The second scan of the database starts by building the local headerless tree for each processor. From each tree the local frequent path bases are generated. In *P1* the frequent-path-bases ABCDE, ABE, and ACDF with branch support equal to 1 are generated. *P2* generates ACDEF, BCDF, BEF, and ABCDE with branch supports equal to 1 for all of them (Figure 4 (B)). The second set of messages is executed to send the locally generated frequent path bases to *P1*. Here, identical ones are merged and the final global set of frequent path bases are broadcast to all processors with their branch support. (Figure 4 (C)).

Each processor is assigned a set of header nodes to build their intersection tree as in Figure 4.D. In our example, the first, third, and sixth frequent path bases are assigned to *P1* as header nodes for its intersection trees. *P2* is assigned to the second, fourth, and fifth frequent path bases. The first tree of intersection in *P1* produces 3 P-maximals (i.e., with total prices is less than $100) BCD: $90, ABE: $80, and ACD: $80 with support equal to 3, 3, and 4 respectively. The second assigned tree does not produce any P-maximals. *P1* produces 3 local P-maximals which are BCD: $90, ABE: $80, and ACD: $80. *P2* produced BE: $70, and AE: $60 with support equal to 4 and 4 respectively. All local P-maximals are sent to *P1* in which any local P-maximal that has any other superset of local P-maximals from other processors are removed.

The remaining patterns are declared as global P-maximals (Figure 4 (E)). Subsets of the Global P-maximals that satisfy *Q()* which is prices > 30 are kept and others are pruned. The final results set produces D: $40, E: $50, AC: $40, AD: $50, BC: $50, BD: $60, CD: $70, BE: $70, AE: $60, BCD: $90, ABE: $80, and ACD: $80

SEQUENTIAL PERFORMANCE EVALUATION

To evaluate our BifoldLeap algorithm, we conducted a set of experiments to test the effect of pushing *monotone* and *anti-monotone* constraints separately, and then both in combination for the same datasets. To quantify scalability, we experimented with datasets of varying size. We also measured the impact of pushing vs. postprocessing constraints on the number of evaluations of *P()* and *Q()*. Like in Bucila et al. (2002), we assigned prices to items using both uniform and zipf distributions. Our constraints consisted of conjunctions of tests for aggregate, minimum, and maximum price in relation to specific thresholds.

We received an FP-Bonsai code (base on FP-Growth) from its original authors Bonchi et al. (2004). Unfortunately, not all pruning and clever constraint considerations suggested in their FP-Bonsai paper were implemented in this code. Moreover, the implementation as received produced some false positives and false negatives. This is why we opted not to add it to our comparison study. Although, with simple and only *monotone* constraints, the received FP-Bonsai implementation was indeed fast. FP-Bonsai as described in the paper has merit, but because of lack of time we could not implement it ourselves (albeit adding implementation bias) or fix the received code.

We compared our algorithm with Dualminer (Bucila et al., 2002). Based on its authors' recommendations, we built the Dualminer framework on top of the MAFIA (Bucila et al., 2001) imple-

Figure 4. Example of parallel bifoldLeap: Finding the FPB, intersecting FPB

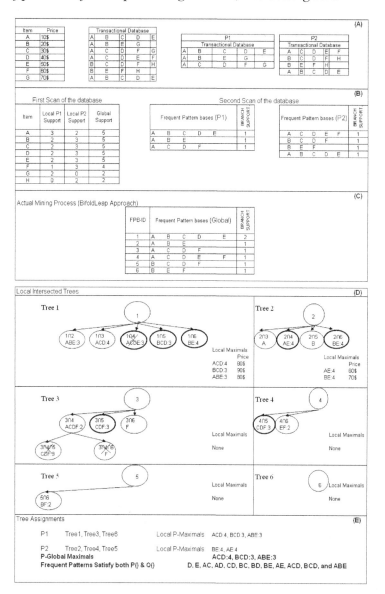

mentation provided by its original authors. Our experiments were conducted on a 3GHz Intel P4 with 2 GB of memory running Linux 2.4.25, Red Hat Linux release 9. The times reported also include the time to output all matching itemsets. We have tested these algorithms using both real datasets provided by FIMI (2003) and synthetic datasets generated using Q. synthetic data generation code (2000); we used "retail" as our primary real dataset reported here. A dataset with the same characteristics as the one reported in Bucila et al. (2002) was also generated. We also report some results with our DPC-COFI to illustrate the advantages of the Leap approach (BifoldLeap).

Figure 5. Pushing P(), Q(), and P() $\cap$ Q()

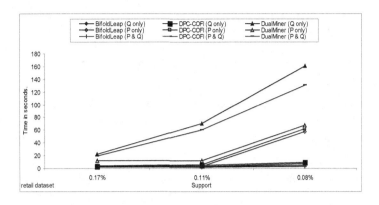

Figure 6. Pushing more selective P(), Q(), and P() $\cap$ Q()

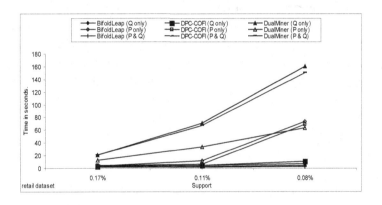

Figure 7. Pushing extremely selective P(), Q(), and P() $\square$ Q()

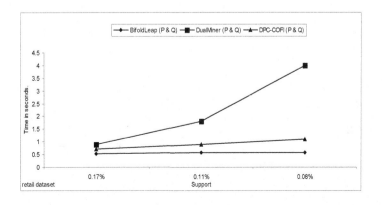

Impact of *P()* and *Q()* Selectivity on BifoldLeap and Dualminer

To differentiate between our DPC-COFI, Bifold-Leap algorithms and Dualminer, we experimented against the retail dataset. In the first experiment (Figure 5), we pushed *P()*, then *Q()*, and finally *P()* & *Q()*. We used the zipf distribution to assign prices to items. Both *P()* and *Q()* consisted of constraints on the sum of the prices. The constraint thresholds were chosen to not be very selective. Figure 6 presents the same experiment with more selective constraints.

Figure 7 presents pushing extremely selective constraints, using *anti-monotone* and *monotone* constraints on the sum of the prices, and on the minimum and maximum item price. In this experiment, we found that both DPC-COFI and BifoldLeap in most cases outperform Dualminer and in some cases by more than one order of magnitude, where DPC-COFI was always the runner up. The most interesting observation we found from this experiment was that if we push one type of constraint, for example, *P()*, that takes T 1 seconds and the other type of constraint, *Q()*, takes T 2 seconds where T 1 ≤ T 2, in Dualminer pushing both constraints together will take T 3 seconds, where T 3 is always between T 1 and T 2. In contrast, COFI approaches always take less time with the conjunction of the constraints than with either constraint in isolation. Monotone and

anti-monotone constraints can indeed be mutually assisting each other in the selectivity. DPC-COFI and BifoldLeap took better advantage of this reciprocal assistance in the pruning.

Scalability Tests

Scalability is an important issue for frequent itemset mining algorithms. Synthetic datasets were generated with 50K, 100K, 250K, and 500K transactions, with 5K or 10K distinct items. In this experiment, BifoldLeap demonstrated extremely good scalability vs. increasing dataset size. In contrast, Dualminer reached a point where it consumed almost three orders of magnitude more time than that needed by BifoldLeap. Figure 8 (A) depicts one of these results while mining datasets with only 5K unique items. As another experiment example, we tested both algorithms on datasets with up to 50 million transactions and 100K items. Dualminer finished the 1M dataset in 8534 seconds while BifoldLeap finished in 186s, 190s, 987s and 2034s for the 1M, 5M, 25M and 50M transactions datasets respectively.

Constraint Checking: Pushing Constraints vs. Postprocessing

One of the major challenging issues for constraint mining is reducing the number of evaluations of *P()* and *Q()*. In the following experiment,

Figure 8. (A) Scalability test; (B) Effect of changing the price distribution

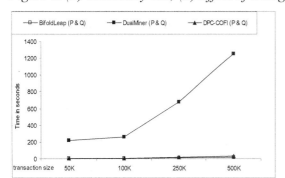
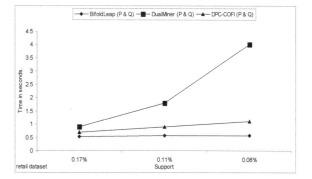

Figure 9. No. of P() and Q() evaluations, using constraint pushing vs. postprocessing

Uniform-distribution

dmT10K1KD15L	Absolute support = 25		Absolute support = 50		Absolute support = 75	
	Early Push	Post Prune	Early Push	Post Prune	Early Push	Post Prune
BifoldLeap (#P)	2266	3166	1483	1581	1212	1319
BifoldLeap (#Q)	4156	4650	299	351	166	189
DualMiner (#P)	25722	25649	18389	18028	14038	13720
DualMiner (#Q)	24946	298	17602	187	13221	160

# of generated patterns	255	158	134

(A)

Z-distribution

dmT10K1KD15L	Absolute support = 25		Absolute support = 50		Absolute support = 75	
	Early Push	Post Prune	Early Push	Post Prune	Early Push	Post Prune
BifoldLeap (#P)	1814	2184	1428	1778	1207	1436
BifoldLeap (#Q)	420	625	125	312	99	254
DualMiner (#P)	11971	11722	8019	7790	6148	5950
DualMiner (#Q)	11185	197	7178	119	5282	100

# of generated patterns	130	76	62

(B)

we generated a synthetic dataset with the same characteristics as the one reported in Bucila et al., (2002). Specifically, it was generated with 10,000 transactions, an average transaction length of 15, an average maximal pattern length of 10, 1000 unique items, and 10,000 patterns. We found that Dualminer was indeed good on this dataset as reported in Bucila et al. (2002). However, Bi-FoldLeap outperformed it with the same order of magnitude as the tests on timing. This shows that the predicate checking is indeed a significant overhead and BiFoldLeap outperforms Dualminer in time primarily because it does significantly less predicate checks.

The goal of these experiments was to test the number of evaluations and the effect of pushing constraints early vs. postprocessing them. We ran our experiments using this dataset with absolute support equal to 25, 50, and 75 using the two different distributions. We used a modified version of MAFIA with postprocessing as the postprocessing counterpart to Dualminer. Our implementation of Dualminer always tests minimum support and $P()$ together, while BifoldLeap's minimum support checks occur at different times and do not contribute to the count for $P()$. Figure 9 depicts the results of these experiments. Our first observation is that Dualminer performs a huge number of constraint evaluations as compared to BifoldLeap. Even in cases where we only generated 255 patterns, Dualminer needed more than 50,000 evaluations for both $P()$ and $Q()$, compared to almost 6,000 needed by BifoldLeap. Our second observation is that MAFIA with postprocessing requires fewer constraint evaluations than Dualminer.

Different Distributions

All of our experiments were conducted using uniform and/or zipf price distributions. In most of the experiments, we found that the effect of changing the distribution on Dualminer was greater than for BifoldLeap. This can be justified by the effectiveness of the pruning techniques used by BifoldLeap that also reduce the number of candidate checks which consequently affected its performance. Figure 8B depicts one of these results for the retail dataset.

PARALLEL PERFORMANCE EVALUATIONS

To evaluate our parallel BifoldLeap approach, we conducted a set of different experiments to test the effect of pushing *monotone Q()* and *anti-monotone P()* constraints separately, and then both in combination for the same datasets. These experiments were conducted using a cluster made of 20 boxes. Each box has Linux 2.4.18, dual processor 1.533 GHz AMD Athlon MP 1800+, and 1.5 GB of RAM. Nodes are connected by Fast Ethernet and Myrinet 2000 networks. In this set of experiments, we generated synthetic datasets using Q. synthetic data generation code (2000). All transactions are made of 100,000 distinct items with an average transaction length of 12 items per transaction. The size of the transactional databases used varies from 100 million transactions to 1 billion transactions.

With our best efforts and literature searches, we were unable to find a parallel frequent mining algorithm that could mine more than 10 million transactions, which is far less than our target size environment. Due to this large discrepancy in transaction capacity, we could not compare our algorithm against any other existing algorithms, as none of them could mine and reach our target data size.

We conducted a battery of tests to evaluate the processing load distribution strategy, the scalability vis-à-vis the size of the data to mine, and the speed-up gained from adding more parallel processing power. Some of the results are portrayed hereafter.

Effect of Load Distribution Strategy

We enumerated three possible strategies for tree of intersection distribution among the processors. As explained, the trees are in decreasing order of size and they can either be distributed arbitrarily using the naïve approach, or more evenly using a round robin approach, or finally with the first-last approach.

The naïve and simple strategy uses a direct and straightforward distribution. For example if we have six trees to assign to three processors, the first two trees are assigned to the first processor, the third and fourth trees are assigned to the second processor, and the last two trees are

Figure 10.

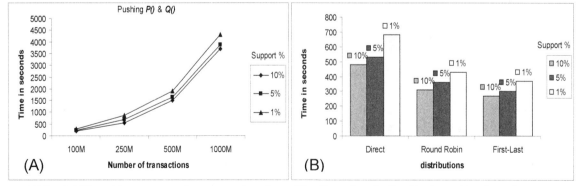

(A) Scalability with respect to the transaction size   (B) effect of node distributions, (number of processors + 32)

assigned to the last processor. Knowing that the last trees are smaller in size than the first trees, the third processor will inevitably finish before the first processor. In the round robin distribution, the first, second and third tree are allocated respectively to the first, second and third processor and then the remaining fourth, fifth and sixth trees are assigned respectively to processor one, two and three. With the last strategy of distribution, first-last, the trees are assigned in pairs: processor one works on the first and last tree, processor two receives the second and fifth tree, while the third processor obtains the third and fourth trees.

From our experiments in Figure 10 (B) we can see that the first-last distribution gave the best results. This can be justified by the fact that since trees are lexicographically ordered then in general trees on the left are larger than those on the right. By applying the first-last distributions we always try to assign largest and smallest tree to the same node. All our remaining experiments use the first-last distribution methods among intersected trees.

Scalability with Respect to Database Size

One of the main goals in this work is to mine extremely large datasets. In this set of experi-

ments we tested the effect of mining different databases made of different transactional databases varying from 100 million transactions up to 1 billion transactions while pushing both type of constraints $P()$ and $Q()$. To the best of our knowledge, experiments with such big sizes have never been reported in the literature. We mined those datasets using 32 processors, with 3 different support thresholds: 10%, 5% and 1%. We were able to mine 1 billion transactions in 3,700 seconds for a support of 0.1, up to 4300 seconds for a support of 0.01. Figure 10 (A) shows the results of this set of experiments. While the curve does not illustrate a perfect linearity in the scalability, the execution time for the colossal 1 billion transaction dataset was a very reasonable 1 hour and 40 minutes with a 0.01 support and 32 relatively inexpensive processors.

Scalability with Respect to Number of Processors

To test the speed-up of our algorithm with the increase of processors, we fixed the size of the database at 100 million transactions and examined the execution time on this dataset with one to 32 processors. The execution time is reduced sharply when two to four parallel processors are added, and continues to decrease significantly

Figure 11.

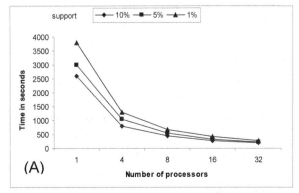

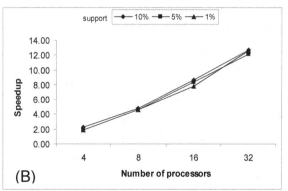

(A) Scalability with respect to the number of processors;

(B) Speedup with different support values (transaction size = 100M)

with additional processors (Figure 11 (A)). The speedup was significant: with 4 processors the speed doubled, with 8 processors it increased four-fold, and with 32 processors we achieved a thirteen-fold increase in speed. These results are depicted in Figure 11(B).

CONCLUSION

Since the introduction of association rules a decade ago and the launch of the research in efficient frequent itemset mining, the development of effective approaches for mining large transactional databases has been the focus of many research studies. Furthermore, it is widely recognized that mining for frequent items or association rules, regardless of its efficiency, usually yields an overwhelming, crushing number of patterns. This is one of the reasons it is argued that the integration of data mining and database management technologies is required Chaudhuri (1998). These large sets of discovered patterns could be queried. Expressing constraints using a query language could indeed help sift through the large pattern set to identify the useful ones.

We argue that pushing the consideration of these constraints at the mining process before discovering the patterns is an efficient and effective way to solve the problem. This does not exclude the integration of data mining and database systems, but suggests the need for data mining query languages intricately integrated with the data mining process.

In this chapter we address the issue of early consideration of *monotone* and *anti-monotone* constraints in the case of frequent itemset mining. We propose a leap traversal approach, BifoldLeap that traverses the search space by jumping from relevant node to relevant node and simultaneously checking for constraint violations. The approach we propose uses existing data structures, FP-tree and COFI-tree, but introduces new pruning techniques to reduce the search costs. We con-

ducted a battery of experiments to evaluate our constraint-based search and report a fraction of them herein for lack of space. The experiments show the advantages of pushing both *monotone* and *anti-monotone* constraints as early as possible in the mining process despite the overhead of constraint checking. We also compared our algorithm to Dualminer, a state-of-the-art algorithm in constraint-based frequent itemset mining, and showed how our algorithm outperforms it and can find all frequent itemsets, the closed and the maximal patterns that satisfy constraints along with their exact supports.

Parallelizing the search for frequent patterns plays an important role in opening the doors to the mining of extremely large datasets. Not all good sequential algorithms can be effectively parallelized and parallelization alone is not enough. An algorithm has to be well suited for parallelization, and in the case of frequent pattern mining, clever methods for searching are certainly an advantage. The algorithm we propose for parallel mining of frequent patterns while pushing constraints is based on a new technique for astutely jumping within the search space, and more importantly, is composed of autonomous task segments that can be performed separately and thus minimize communication between processors.

Our proposal is based on the finding of particular patterns, called pattern bases, from which selective jumps in the search space can be performed in parallel and independently from each other pattern base in the pursuit of frequent patterns that satisfy user's constraints. The success of this approach is attributed to the fact that pattern base intersection is independent and each intersection tree can be assigned to a given processor. The decrease in the size of intersection trees allows a fair strategy for distributing work among processors and in the course reducing most of the load balancing issues. While other published works claim results with millions of transactions, our approach allows the mining in reasonable time of databases in the order of billion transactions using relatively inexpensive clusters; 16 dual-processor boxes in our case. This is mainly credited to the low communication cost of our approach.

REFERENCES

Agrawal, R., Imielinski, T., & Swami, A. (1993). Mining association rules between sets of items in large databases. In *Proceedings of SIGMOD Int. Conf. Management of Data* (pp 207–216).

Agrawal, R., & Srikant, R. (1994). Fast algorithms for mining association rules. In *Proceedings of the Int. Conf. Very Large Data Bases* (pp 487–499).

Bayardo, R. J. (1998). *Efficiently mining long patterns from databases.* ACM SIGMOD.

Bonchi, F., Giannotti, Mazzanti, A., & Pedreschi, D. (2004). Examiner: Optimized level-wise frequent pattern mining with monotone constraints. In *Proceedings of the IEEE ICDM*, Melbourne, Florida.

Bonchi, F., & Goethals, B. (2004). FP-Bonsai: The art of growing and pruning small fp-trees. In *Proceedings of the Pacific-Asia Conference on Knowledge Discovery and Data Mining (PAKDD '04)* (pp.155–160).

Bonchi, F., & Lucchese, C. (2004). On closed constrained frequent pattern mining. In *Proceedings of the IEEE International Conference on Data Mining (ICDM'04).*

Bucila, C., Gehrke, J., Kifer, D., & White, W. (2002). Dualminer: A dual-pruning algorithm for itemsets with constraints. In *Proceedings of the Eight ACM SIGKDD International Conf. on Knowledge Discovery and Data Mining* (pp. 42–51), Edmonton, Alberta.

Burdick, D., Calimlim, M. J., & Gehrke, J. (2001). *Mafia: A maximal frequent itemset algorithm for transactional databases.* ICDE (pp 443–452).

Chaudhuri, S. (1998). Data mining and database systems: Where is the intersection? *Bulletin of the Technical Committee on Data Engineering,* p. 21.

El-Hajj, M., & Zaïane, O. R. (2003). Non recursive generation of frequent k-itemsets from frequent pattern tree representations. In *Proceedings of 5th International Conference on Data Warehousing and Knowledge Discovery (DaWak'2003).*

El-Hajj, M., & Zaïane, O. R. (2005). Mining with constraints by pruning and avoiding ineffectual processing. In *Proceedings of the 18th Australian Joint Conference on Artificial Intelligence*, Sydney, Australia.

El-Hajj, M., & Zaïane, O. R. (2006). Parallel leap: Large-scale maximal pattern mining in a distributed environment. In *Proceedings of the International Conference on Parallel and Distributed Systems (ICPADS'06)*, Minneapolis, Minnesota.

El-Hajj, M., Zaïane, O. R., & Nalos, P. (2005). Bifold constraint-based mining by simultaneous monotone and anti-monotone checking. In *Proceedings of the IEEE 2005 International Conference on Data Mining*, Houston, Texas.

Han, J., Pei, J., & Yin, Y. Mining frequent patterns without candidate generation. In *Proceedings of the ACM SIGMOD Intl. Conference on Management of Data* (pp 1–12).

FIMI (2003). Itemset mining implementations repository. Retrieved March 6, 2007, from http://fimi.cs.helsinki.fi/

Lakshmanan, L., Ng, R., Han, J., & Pang, A. (1999). Optimization of constrained frequent set queries with 2variable constraints. In *Proceedings of the ACM SIGMOD Conference on Management of Data* (pp 157–168).

Pasquier, N., Bastide, Y., Taouil, R., & Lakhal, L. Discovering frequent closed itemsets for association rules. In *Proceedings of the International Conference on Database Theory (ICDT),* (pp 398–416).

Pie, J., & Han, J. (2000). Can we push more constraints into frequent pattern mining? In *Proceedings of the ACM SIGKDD Conference* (pp 350–354).

Pie, J., Han, J., & Lakshmanan, L. Mining frequent itemsets with convertible constraints. In *Proceedings of the IEEE ICDE Conference* (pp 433–442).

Q. synthetic data generation code. (2000). Retrieved March 6, 2007, from http://www.almaden. ibm.com/software/quest/Resources/index.shtml

Ting, R. M., Bailey, J., & Ramamohanarao, K. (2004). Paradualminer: An efficient parallel implementation of the dualminer algorithm. In *Proceedings of the Eight Pacific-Asia Conference, PAKDD* (pp 96–105).

Zaïane, O. R., & El-Hajj, M. (2005). Pattern lattice traversal by selective jumps. In *Proceedings of the Int'l Conf. on Data Mining and Knowledge Discovery (ACM SIGKDD)* (pp 729–735).

Chapter III
Mining Hyperclique Patterns:
A Summary of Results

Hui Xiong
Rutgers University, USA

Pang-Ning Tan
Michigan State University, USA

Vipin Kumar
University of Minnesota, USA

Wenjun Zhou
Rutgers University, USA

ABSTRACT

This chapter presents a framework for mining highly correlated association patterns named hyperclique patterns. In this framework, an objective measure called h-confidence is applied to discover hyperclique patterns. We prove that the items in a hyperclique pattern have a guaranteed level of global pairwise similarity to one another. Also, we show that the h-confidence measure satisfies a cross-support property, which can help efficiently eliminate spurious patterns involving items with substantially different support levels. In addition, an algorithm called hyperclique miner is proposed to exploit both cross-support and anti-monotone properties of the h-confidence measure for the efficient discovery of hyperclique patterns. Finally, we demonstrate that hyperclique patterns can be useful for a variety of applications such as item clustering and finding protein functional modules from protein complexes.

INTRODUCTION

Many data sets have inherently skewed support distributions. For example, the frequency distribution of English words appearing in text documents is highly skewed—while a few of the words may appear many times, most of the words appear only a few times. Such a distribution has also been observed in other application domains, including retail data, Web click-streams, and telecommunication data.

This chapter examines the problem of mining association patterns (Agrawal, Imielinski & Swami, 1993) from data sets with skewed support distributions. Most of the algorithms developed so far rely on the support-based pruning strategy to prune the combinatorial search space. However, this strategy is not effective for data sets with skewed support distributions due to the following reasons.

- If the minimum support threshold is low, we may extract too many *spurious patterns involving items with substantially different support levels.* We call such patterns as weakly-related cross-support patterns. For example, {Caviar, Milk} is a possible weakly related cross-support pattern since the support for an expensive item such as caviar is expected to be much lower than the support for an inexpensive item such as milk. Such patterns are spurious because they tend to be poorly correlated. Using a low minimum support threshold also increases the computational and memory requirements of current state-of-the-art algorithms considerably.

- If the minimum support threshold is high, we may miss many *interesting patterns occurring at low levels of support* (Hastie, Tibshirani & Friedman, 2001). Examples of such patterns are associations among rare but expensive items such as caviar and vodka, gold necklaces and earrings, or TVs and DVD players.

As an illustration, consider the pumsb census data set,[1] which is often used as a benchmark data set for evaluating the computational performance of association rule mining algorithms. Figure 1 shows the skewed nature of the support distribution. Note that 81.5% of the items have support less than 0.01 while only 0.95% of them having support greater than 0.9.

Figure 1. The support distribution of pumsb

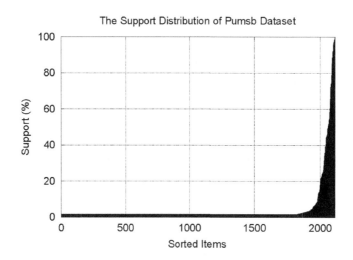

Table 1 shows a partitioning of these items into five disjoint groups based on their support levels. The first group, S_1, has the lowest support level (less than or equal to 0.01) but contains the most number of items (i.e., 1735 items). In order to detect patterns involving items from S_1, we need to set the minimum support threshold to be less than 0.01. However, such a low support threshold will degrade the performance of existing algorithms considerably. For example, our experiments showed that, when applied to the pumsb data set at support threshold less than 0.4,[2] state-of-the-art algorithms such as Apriori (Agrawal & Srikant, 1994) and Charm (Zaki & Hsiao, 2002) break down due to excessive memory requirements. Even if a machine with unlimited memory is provided, such algorithms can still produce a large number of weakly related cross-support patterns when the support threshold is low. Just to give an indication of the scale, out of the 18847 frequent pairs involving items from S_1 and S_5 at support level 0.0005, about 93% of them are cross-support patterns, that is, containing items from both S_1 and S_5. The pair wise correlations within these cross-support patterns are extremely poor because the presence of the item from S_5 does not necessarily imply the presence of the item from S_1. Indeed, the maximum correlation obtained from these cross-support patterns is only 0.029377. In contrast, item pairs from S_1 alone or S_5 alone have correlation as high as 1.0. The above discussion suggests that it will be advantageous to develop techniques that can automatically eliminate such patterns during the mining process.

Indeed, the motivation for this work is to strike a balance between the ability to detect patterns at very low support levels and the ability to remove spurious associations among items with substantially different support levels. A naive approach for doing this is to apply a very low minimum support threshold during the association mining step, followed by a post-processing step to eliminate spurious patterns. This approach may fail due to the following reasons: (1) the computation cost can be very high due to the large number of patterns that need to be generated; (2) current algorithms may break down at very low support thresholds due to excessive memory requirements. Although there have been recent attempts to efficiently extract interesting patterns without using support thresholds, they do not guarantee the completeness of the discovered patterns. These methods include sampling (Cohen, Datar, Fujiwara, Gionis, Indyk, & Motwani, 2000) and other approximation schemes (Yang, Fayyad, & Bradley, 2001).

A better approach will be to have a measure that can efficiently identify useful patterns even at low levels of support and can be used to automatically remove spurious patterns during the association mining process. Omiecinski (2003) recently introduced a measure called *all-confidence* as an alternative to the support measure. The all-confidence measure is computed by taking the minimum confidence of all association rules generated from a given item set. Omiecinski proved that all-confidence has the desirable anti-monotone property and incorporated this property directly into the mining process for efficient computation of all patterns with sufficiently high value of all-confidence. Note that we had independently proposed a measure called h-confidence (Xiong,

Table 1. Groups of items for pumsb *data set*

Group	S_1	S_2	S_3	S_4	S_5
Support	0-0.01	0.01-0.05	0.05-0.4	0.4-0.9	0.9-1.0
# Items	1735	206	101	51	20

Tan, & Kumar, 2003a) and had named the item sets discovered by the h-confidence measure as hyperclique patterns. As shown in the next section, h-confidence and all-confidence measures are equivalent. To maintain consistent notation and presentation, we will use the term h-confidence in the remainder of this chapter.

In this chapter, we extend our work (Xiong, Tan, & Kumar, 2003b) on hyperclique pattern discovery and makes the following contributions. First, we formally define the concept of the cross-support property, which helps efficiently eliminate spurious patterns involving items with substantially different support levels. We show that this property is not limited to h-confidence and can be generalized to some other association measures. Second, we prove that if a hyperclique pattern has an h-confidence value above the minimum h-confidence threshold, h_c, then every pair of objects within the hyperclique pattern must have a cosine similarity (uncentered Pearson's correlation coefficient[3]) greater than or equal to h_c. Also, we show that all derived size-2 hyperclique patterns guarantee to be positively correlated, as long as the minimum h-confidence threshold is above the maximum support of all items in the given data set. Moreover, we refine our algorithm (called hyperclique miner) that is used to discover hyperclique patterns. Our experimental results show that hyperclique miner can efficiently identify hyperclique patterns, even at low support levels. We also demonstrate that the utilization of the cross-support property provides significant additional pruning over that provided by the anti-monotone property of the h-confidence measure.

Finally, hyperclique patterns are valuable patterns in their own right because they correspond to item sets involving only tightly coupled items. Discovering such patterns can be potentially useful for a variety of applications such as item clustering and Bioinformatics. Indeed, we first demonstrate the application of hyperclique patterns in the area of item clustering, where such patterns can be used to provide high-quality hyperedges to seed the hypergraph-based clustering algorithms (Han, Karypis, & Kumar, 1998). In addition, we present an application of hyperclique patterns for identifying protein functional modules from protein complexes.

Related Work

Recently, there has been growing interest in developing techniques for mining association patterns without support constraints. For example, Wang, He, Cheung, and Chin, (2001) proposed the use of universal-existential upward closure property of confidence to extract association rules without specifying the support threshold. However, this approach does not explicitly eliminate cross-support patterns. Cohen et al. (2000) have proposed using the Jaccard similarity measure:

$$sim(x, y) = \frac{P(x \cap y)}{P(x \cup y)}$$

to capture interesting patterns without using a minimum support threshold. As we show later, the Jaccard measure has the cross-support property, which can be used to eliminate cross-support patterns. However, the discussion in Cohen et al. (2000) focused on how to employ a combination of random sampling and hashing techniques for efficiently finding highly correlated pairs of items.

Many alternative techniques have also been developed to push various types of constraints into the mining algorithm (Bayardo, Agrawal, & Gunopulous, 1999; Grahne, Lakshmanan & Wang, 2000; Liu, Hsu, & Ma, 1999). Although these approaches may greatly reduce the number of patterns generated and improve computational performance by introducing additional constraints, they do not offer any specific mechanism to eliminate weakly related patterns involving items with different support levels.

Besides all-confidence (Omiecinski, 2003), other measures of association have been proposed to extract interesting patterns in large data sets. For example, Brin, Motwani, and Silverstein (1997) introduced the *interest* measure and χ^2 test to discover patterns containing highly dependent items. However, these measures do not possess the desired anti-monotone property.

The concept of closed item sets (Pei, Han, & Mao, 2000; Zaki & Hsiao, 2002) and maximal item sets (Bayardo, 1998; Burdick, Calimlim, & Gehrke, 2001) have been developed to provide a compact presentation of frequent patterns and of the "boundary" patterns, respectively. Algorithms for computing closed item sets and maximal item sets are often much more efficient than those for computing frequent patterns, especially for dense data sets, and thus may be able to work with lower support thresholds. Hence, it may appear that one could discover closed or maximal item sets at low levels of support, and then perform a postprocessing step to eliminate cross-support patterns represented by these concepts. However, as shown by our experiments, for data sets with highly skewed support distributions, the number of spurious patterns represented by maximal or closed item sets is still very large. This makes the computation cost of postprocessing very high.

HYPERCLIQUE PATTERN

In this section, we present a formal definition of hyperclique patterns and show the equivalence between all-confidence (Omiecinski, 2003) and h-confidence. In addition, we introduce the anti-monotone property of the h-confidence measure. More properties will be discussed in the next section. These properties are useful for efficient computation and interpretation of hyperclique patterns.

Hyperclique Pattern Definition

A hypergraph $H = \{V, E\}$ consists of a set of vertices V and a set of hyperedges E. The concept of a hypergraph extends the conventional definition of a graph in the sense that each hyperedge can connect more than two vertices. It also provides an elegant representation for association patterns, where every pattern (item set) P can be modeled as a hypergraph with each item $i \in P$ represented as a vertex and a hyperedge connecting all the vertices of P. A hyperedge can also be weighted in terms of the magnitude of relationships among items in the corresponding item set. In the following, we define a metric called h-confidence as a measure of association for an item set.

- **Definition 1:** The **h-confidence** of an item set P = $\{i_1, i_2, ..., i_m\}$ is defined as follows:

$$hconf(P) = min\{conf\{i_1 \rightarrow i_2, ... , i_m\}, conf\{i_2 \rightarrow i_1, i_3, ... , i_m\}, ... , conf\{i_m \rightarrow i_1, ... , i_{m-1}\}\},$$

where conf follows from the conventional definition of association rule confidence (Agrawal et al., 1993).

- **Example 1:** Consider an item set $P = \{A, B, C\}$. Assume that $supp(\{A\}) = 0.1$, $supp(\{B\}) = 0.1$, $supp(\{C\}) = 0.06$, and $supp(\{A, B, C\}) = 0.06$, where $supp$ denotes the support (Agrawal et al., 1993) of an item set. Since

$$conf\{A \rightarrow B, C\} = supp(\{A, B, C\})/supp(\{A\})$$
$$= 0.6,$$
$$conf\{B \rightarrow A, C\} = supp(\{A, B, C\})/supp(\{B\})$$
$$= 0.6,$$
$$conf\{C \rightarrow A, B\} = supp(\{A, B, C\})/supp(\{C\})$$
$$= 1,$$

therefore, $hconf(P) = min\{0.6, 0.6, 1\} = 0.6$.

- **Definition 2:** Given a set of items $I = \{i_1, i_2, ..., i_n\}$ and a minimum h-confidence threshold h_c, an item set $P \subseteq I$ is a **hyperclique pattern** if and only if $hconf(P) \geq h_c$.

A hyperclique pattern P can be interpreted as follows: the presence of any item $i \in P$ in a transaction implies the presence of all other items $P - \{i\}$ in the same transaction with probability at least h_c. This suggests that h-confidence is useful for capturing patterns containing items, which are strongly related with each other, especially when the h-confidence threshold is sufficiently large.

Nevertheless, the hyperclique pattern-mining framework may miss some interesting patterns too. For example, an item set such as $\{A, B, C\}$ may have very low h-confidence, and yet it may be still interesting if one of its rules, say $AB \rightarrow C$, has very high confidence. Discovering such type of patterns is beyond the scope of this chapter.

The Equivalence Between All-Confidence Measure and H-Confidence Measure

The following is a formal definition of the all-confidence measure as given in Omiecinski (2003).

- **Definition 3:** The all-confidence measure (Omiecinski, 2003) for an item set $P = \{i_1, i_2, \ldots, i_m\}$ is defined as $allconf(P) = \min\{\{conf(A \rightarrow B \mid \forall A, B \in P, A \cup B = P, A \cap B = \phi\}\}$.

Conceptually, the all-confidence measure checks every association rule extracted from a given item set. This is slightly different from the h-confidence measure, which examines only rules of the form $\{i\} \rightarrow P - \{i\}$, where there is only one item on the left-hand side of the rule. Despite their syntactic difference, both measures are mathematically identical to each other, as shown in the lemma below.

- **Lemma 1.** *For an item set $P = \{i_1, i_2, \ldots, i_m\}$, $hconf(P) \equiv allconf(P)$.*
- **Proof:** The confidence for any association rule $A \rightarrow B$ extracted from an item set P is given by $conf\{A \rightarrow B\} = supp(A \cup B)/supp(A) = supp(P)/supp(A)$. From definition 3, we may write:

$$allconf(P) = \min(\{conf\{A \rightarrow B\}\}) = \frac{supp(P)}{\max(\{supp(A) \mid \forall A \subset P\})}$$

From the anti-monotone property of the support measure, $\max(\{supp(A) \mid A \subset P\}) = \max_{1 \leq k \leq m}\{supp(\{i_k\})\}$. Hence:

$$allconf(P) = \frac{supp(\{i_1, i_2, \ldots, i_m\})}{\max_{1 \leq k \leq m}(\{supp(\{i_k\})\})} \qquad (1)$$

Box 1.

$$
\begin{aligned}
hconf &(P) \\
&= \min\{conf\{i_1 \rightarrow i_2, \ldots, i_m\}, conf\{i_2 \rightarrow i_1, i_3, \ldots, i_m\}, \ldots, conf\{i_m \rightarrow i_1, \ldots, i_{m-1}\}, \} \\
&= \min\left\{\frac{supp(\{i_1, i_2, \ldots, i_m\})}{supp(\{i_1\})}, \frac{supp(\{i_1, i_2, \ldots, i_m\})}{supp(\{i_2\})}, \ldots, \frac{supp(\{i_1, i_2, \ldots, i_m\})}{supp(\{i_m\})}\right\} \\
&= supp(\{i_1, i_2, \ldots, i_m\})\min\left\{\frac{1}{supp(\{i_1\})}, \frac{1}{supp(\{i_2\})}, \ldots, \frac{1}{supp(\{i_m\})}\right\} \\
&= \frac{supp(\{i_1, i_2, \ldots, i_m\})}{\max_{1 \leq k \leq m}\{supp(\{i_k\})\}}.
\end{aligned}
$$

Also, we simplify h-confidence for an item set *P*, as shown in Box 1.

The expression in Box 1 is identical to equation (1), so Lemma 1 holds.

Anti-Monotone Property of H-Confidence

Omiecinski has previously shown that the all-confidence measure has the anti-monotone property (Omiecinski, 2003). In other words, if the all-confidence of an item set *P* is greater than a user-specified threshold, so is every subset of *P*. Since h-confidence is mathematically identical to all-confidence, it is also monotonically non-increasing as the size of the hyperclique pattern increases. Such a property allows us to push the h-confidence constraint directly into the mining algorithm. Specifically, when searching for hyperclique patterns, the algorithm eliminates every candidate pattern of size m having at least one subset of size $m - 1$ that is not a hyperclique pattern.

Besides being anti-monotone, the h-confidence measure also possesses other desirable properties. A detailed examination of these properties is presented in the following sections.

THE CROSS-SUPPORT PROPERTY

In this section, we describe the cross-support property of h-confidence and explain how this property can be used to efficiently eliminate cross-support patterns. Also, we show that the cross-support property is not limited to h-confidence and can be generalized to some other association measures. Finally, a sufficient condition is provided for verifying whether a measure satisfies the cross-support property or not.

Illustration of the Cross-Support Property

First, a formal definition of cross-support patterns is given as follows.

- **Definition 4:** (Cross-support patterns). Given a threshold *t*, a pattern *P* is a cross-support pattern with respect to *t* if *P* contains two items *x* and *y* such that $supp(\{x\})/supp(\{y\}) < t$, where $0 < t < 1$.

Let us consider the diagram shown in Figure 2, which illustrates cross-support patterns in a hypothetical data set. In the figure, the horizontal axis shows items sorted by support in nondecreasing order and the vertical axis shows the corresponding support for items. For example, in the figure, the pattern $\{x, y, j\}$ is a cross-support pattern with respect to the threshold $t = 0.6$, since this pattern contains two items *x* and *y* such that $supp(\{x\})/supp(\{y\}) = 0.3/0.6 = 0.5 < t = 0.6$.

Once we have the understanding of cross-support patterns, we present the cross-support property of h-confidence in the following lemma.

- **Lemma 2.** *(Cross-support property of the h-confidence measure). Any cross-support pattern P with respect to a threshold t is guaranteed to have hconf(P) < t.*
- **Proof:** Since *P* is a cross-support pattern with respect to the threshold *t*, by definition 4, we know P contains at least two items x and y such that $supp(\{x\})/supp(\{y\}) < t$, where $0 < t < 1$. Without loss of generality, let $P = \{..., x, ..., y, ...\}$. By equation (1), we have what is show in Box 2.

Note that the anti-monotone property of support is applied to the numerator part of the h-confidence expression in the proof.

- **Corollary 1.** *Given an item y, all patterns that contain y and at least one item with*

Box 2.

$$hconf(P) = \frac{supp(P)}{\max\{\ldots, supp(\{x\}), \ldots, supp(\{y\}), \ldots\}}$$

$$\leq \frac{supp(\{x\})}{\max\{\ldots, supp(\{x\}), \ldots, supp(\{y\}), \ldots\}} \leq \frac{supp(\{x\})}{supp(\{y\})} < t$$

support less than t·supp({y}) (for 0 < t < 1) are cross-support patterns with respect to t and are guaranteed to have h-confidence less than t. All such patterns can be automatically eliminated without computing their h-confidence if we are only interested in patterns with h-confidence greater than t.

- **Proof:** This corollary follows from definition 4 and Lemma 2.

For a given h-confidence threshold, the above Corollary provides a systematic way to find and eliminate candidate item sets that are guaranteed not to be hyperclique patterns. In the following, we present an example to illustrate the cross-support pruning.

- **Example 2:** Figure 2 shows the support distributions of five items and their support values. By Corollary 1, given a minimum h-confidence threshold $h_c = 0.6$, all patterns contain item y and at least one item with support less than $supp(\{y\}) \cdot h_c = 0.6 \times 0.6 = 0.36$ are cross-support patterns and are guaranteed to have h-confidence less than 0.6. Hence, all patterns containing item *y* and at least one of *l, m, x* do not need to be considered if we are only interested in patterns with h-confidence greater than 0.6.

Figure 2. An example to illustrate the cross-support pruning

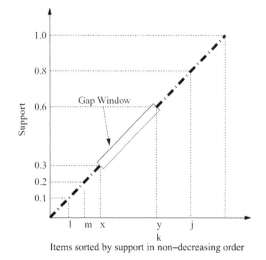

Item	Support
j	0.8
k	0.6
y	0.6
x	0.3
m	0.2
l	0.1

Generalization of the Cross-Support Property

In this subsection, we generalize the cross-support property to other association measures. First, we give a generalized definition of the cross-support property.

- **Definition 5:** (Generalized cross-support property). Given a measure f, for any cross-support pattern P with respect to a threshold t, if there exists a monotone increasing function g such that $f(P) < g(t)$, then the measure f has the cross-support property.

Given the h-confidence measure, for any cross-support pattern P with respect to a threshold t, if we let the function $g(l) = l$, then we have $hconf(P) < g(t) = t$ by Lemma 2. Hence, the h-confidence measure has the cross-support property. Also, if a measure f has the cross-support property, the following theorem provides a way to automatically eliminate cross-support patterns.

- **Theorem 1:** *Given an item y, a measure f with the cross-support property, and a threshold θ, any pattern P that contains y and at least one item x with support less than $g^{-1}(\theta) \cdot supp(\{y\})$ is a cross-support pattern*

with respect to the threshold $g^{-1}(\theta)$ and is guaranteed to have $f(P) < \theta$, where g is the function to make the measure f satisfy the generalized cross-support property.

- **Proof:** Since $supp(\{x\}) < g^{-1}(\theta) \cdot supp(\{y\})$, we have:

$$\frac{supp(\{x\})}{supp(\{y\})} < g^{-1}(\theta)$$

By definition 4, the pattern P is a cross-support pattern with respect to the threshold $g^{-1}(\theta)$. Also, because the measure f has the cross-support property, by definition 5, there exists a monotone increasing function g such that $f(P) < g(g^{-1}(\theta)) = \theta$. Hence, for the given threshold θ, all such patterns can be automatically eliminated if we are only interested in patterns with the measure f greater than θ.

Table 2 shows two measures that have the *cross-support* property. The corresponding monotone increasing functions for these measures are also shown in this table. However, some measures, such as support and odds ratio (Tan, Kumar, & Srivastava, 2002), do not possess such a property.

Table 2. Examples of measures of association that have the cross-support property (assuming that $supp(\{x\}) < supp(\{y\})$)

Measure	Computation formula	Upper bound	Function
Cosine	$\dfrac{supp(\{x, y\})}{\sqrt{supp(\{x\})supp(\{y\})}}$	$\sqrt{\dfrac{supp(\{x\})}{supp(\{y\})}}$	$g(l) = \sqrt{l}$
Jaccard	$\dfrac{supp(\{x, y\})}{supp(\{x\}) + supp(\{y\}) - supp(\{x, y\})}$	$\dfrac{supp(\{x\})}{supp(\{y\})}$	$g(l) = l$

THE H-CONFIDENCE AS A MEASURE OF ASSOCIATION

In this section, we first show that the strength or magnitude of a relationship described by h-confidence is consistent with the strength or magnitude of a relationship described by two traditional association measures: the Jaccard measure (Rijsbergen, 1979) and the correlation coefficient (Reynolds, 1977).

Given a pair of items $P = \{i_1, i_2\}$, the affinity between both items using these measures is defined as seen in Box 3.

Also, we demonstrate that h-confidence is a measure of association that can be used to capture the strength or magnitude of a relationship among several objects.

Relationship Between H-confidence and Jaccard

In the following, for a size-2 hyperclique pattern P, we provide a lemma that gives a lower bound for $jaccard(P)$.

- **Lemma 4.** If an item set $P = \{i_1, i_2\}$ is a size-2 hyperclique pattern, then $jaccard(P) \geq h_c/2$.

- **Proof:** By Eq. (1):

$$hconf(P) = \frac{supp(\{i_1, i_2\})}{\max\{supp(\{i_1\}), supp(\{i_2\})\}}$$

Without loss of generality, let $supp(\{i_1\}) \geq supp(\{i_2\})$. Given that P is a hyperclique pattern,

$$hconf(P) = \frac{supp(\{i_1, i_2\})}{supp(\{i_1\})} \geq h_c$$

Furthermore, since $supp(\{i_1\}) \geq supp(\{i_2\})$, (we have what is shown in Box 4).

Lemma 4 suggests that if the h-confidence threshold h_c is sufficiently high, then all size-2 hyperclique patterns contain items that are strongly related with each other in terms of the Jaccard measure, since the Jaccard values of these hyperclique patterns are bounded from below by $h_c/2$.

Relationship Between H-Confidence and Correlation

In this subsection, we illustrate the relationship between h-confidence and Pearson's correlation. More specifically, we show that if at least one item in a size-2 hyperclique pattern has a support value

Box 3.

$$jaccard(P) = \frac{supp(\{i_1, i_2\})}{supp(\{i_1\}) + supp(\{i_2\}) - supp(\{i_1, i_2\})},$$

$$correlation, \phi(P) = \frac{supp(\{i_1, i_2\}) - supp(\{i_1\})supp(\{i_2\})}{\sqrt{supp(\{i_1\})supp(\{i_2\})(1 - supp(\{i_1\}))(1 - supp(\{i_2\}))}}.$$

Box 4.

$$jaccard(P) = \frac{supp(\{i_1, i_2\})}{supp(\{i_1\}) + supp(\{i_2\}) - supp(\{i_1, i_2\})} \geq \frac{supp(\{i_1, i_2\})}{2supp(\{i_1\})} \geq h_c/2$$

less than the minimum h-confidence threshold, h_c, then two items within this hyperclique pattern must be positively correlated.

- **Lemma 5.** *Let S be a set of items and h_c be the minimum h-confidence threshold, we can form two item groups: S_1 and S_2 such that $S_1 = \{x|supp(\{x\}) < h_c$ and $x \in S\}$ and $S_2 = \{y|supp(\{y\}) \geq h_c$ and $y \in S\}$. Then, any size-2 hyperclique pattern $P = \{A, B\}$ has a positive correlation coefficient in each of the following cases: Case 1: $A \in S_1$ and $B \in S_2$. Case 2: $A \in S_1$ and $B \in S_1$.*

- **Proof:** For a size-2 hyperclique pattern $P = \{A, B\}$, without loss of generality, we assume that $supp(\{A\}) \leq supp(\{B\})$. Since $hconf(P) \geq h_c$, we know:

$$\frac{supp(\{A, B\})}{\max\{supp(\{A\}), supp(\{B\})\}} =$$
$$\frac{supp(\{A, B\})}{supp(\{B\})} \geq h_c$$

In other words, $supp(\{A, B\}) \geq h_c \cdot supp(\{B\})$.

From the definition of Pearson's correlation coefficient, we have what is shown in Box 5.

Also:

$$\sqrt{supp(\{A\})(1 - supp(\{A\}))} \leq (supp(\{A\}) + 1 - supp(\{A\}))/2 = 1/2$$

So

$$\phi(\{A, B\}) \geq 4(supp(\{A, B\}) - supp(\{A\})supp(\{B\}))$$
$$\geq 4supp(\{B\})(h_c - supp(\{A\}))$$

- **Case 1:** If $A \in S_1$ and $B \in S_2$

Since $A \in S_1$ and $B \in S_2$, we know $supp(\{A\}) < h_c$ due to the way that we construct S_1 and S2. As a result, $4supp(\{B\})(h_c - supp(\{A\})) > 0$. Hence, $\phi > 0$.

- **Case 2:** if $A \in S_1$ and $B \in S_1$

Since $A \in S_1$, we know $supp(\{A\}) < h_c$ due to the way that we construct S_1 and S_2. As a result, $4supp(\{B\})(h_c - supp(\{A\})) > 0$. Hence, $\phi > 0$.

- **Example 3.** Figure 3 illustrates the relationship between h-confidence and correlation. Assume that the minimum h-confidence threshold is 0.45. In the figure, there are four pairs including {a, b}, {c, d}, {c, e}, {d, e} with h-confidence greater than 0.45. Among these four pairs, {c, d}, {c, e}, {d, e} contain at least one item with the support value less than the h-confidence threshold, 0.45. By Lemma 5, all these three pairs have positive correlation. Furthermore, if we increase the minimum h-confidence threshold to be greater than 0.6 that is the maximum support of all items in the given data set, all size-2 hyperclique patterns are guaranteed to have positive correlation.

In practice, many real-world data sets, such as the point-of-sale data collected at department stores, contain very few items with considerably high support. For instance, the `retail` data set used in our own experiment contains items with

Box 5.

$$\phi(\{A, B\}) = \frac{supp(\{A, B\}) - supp(\{A\})supp(\{B\})}{\sqrt{supp(\{A\})supp(\{B\})(1 - supp(\{A\}))(1 - supp(\{B\}))}}$$

Figure 3. Illustration of the relationship between h-confidence and correlation

TID	Items
1	a
2	b
3	b, c, d
4	a
5	a, b
6	a, b
7	a, b, c, d, e
8	a
9	b
10	c, e

Item	Support
a	0.6
b	0.6
c	0.3
d	0.2
e	0.2

Pairwise Correlation	a	b	c	d	e
a		−0.25	−0.356	−0.102	−0.102
b			0.089	0.408	−0.102
c				0.764	0.764
d					0.375

Pairwise h−confidence	a	b	c	d	e
a		0.5	0.167	0.167	0.167
b			0.333	0.333	0.167
c				0.667	0.667
d					0.5

a maximum support equals to 0.024. Following the discussion presented above, if we set the minimum h-confidence threshold above 0.024, all size-2 hyperclique patterns guarantee to be positively correlated. To make this discussion more interesting, recall the well-known coffee-tea example given in (Brin et al., 1997). This example illustrates the drawback of using confidence as a measure of association. Even though the confidence for the rule *tea → coffee* may be high, both items are in fact negatively correlated with each other. Hence, the confidence measure can be misleading. Instead, with h-confidence, we may ensure that all derived size-2 patterns are positively correlated, as long as the minimum h-confidence threshold is above the maximum support of all items.

H-Confidence for Measuring the Relationship among Several Objects

In this subsection, we demonstrate that the h-confidence measure can be used to describe the strength or magnitude of a relationship among several objects.

Given a pair of items $P = \{i_1, i_2\}$, the cosine similarity between both items is defined as follows:

$$cosine(P) = \frac{supp(\{i_1, i_2\})}{\sqrt{supp(\{i_1\})supp(\{i_2\})}}$$

Note that the cosine similarity is also known as uncentered Pearson's correlation coefficient (when computing Pearson's correlation coefficient, the data mean is not subtracted). For a size-2 hyperclique pattern P, we first derive a lower bound for the cosine similarity of the pattern P, $cosine(P)$, in terms of the minimum h-confidence threshold h_c.

- **Lemma 6.** *If an item set $P = \{i_1, i_2\}$ is a size-2 hyperclique pattern, then cosine(P) $\geq h_c$.*

- **Proof:** By Eq. (1):

$$hconf(P) = \frac{supp(\{i_1, i_2\})}{\max\{supp(\{i_1\}), supp(\{i_2\})\}}$$

Without loss of generality, let $supp(\{i_1\}) \geq supp(\{i_2\})$. Given that P is a hyperclique pattern:

$$hconf(P) = \frac{supp(\{i_1, i_2\})}{supp(\{i_1\})} \geq h_c$$

Since $supp(\{i_1\}) \geq supp(\{i_2\})$:

$$cosine(P) = \frac{supp(\{i_1, i_2\})}{\sqrt{supp(\{i_1\})supp(\{i_2\})}} \geq$$

$$\frac{supp(\{i_1, i_2\})}{supp(\{i_1\})} \geq h_c$$

Lemma 6 suggests that if the h-confidence threshold h_c is sufficiently high, then all size-2 hyperclique patterns contain items that are strongly related with each other in terms of the cosine measure, since the cosine values of these hyperclique patterns are bounded from below by h_c.

For the case that hyperclique patterns have more than two objects, the following theorem guarantees that if a hyperclique pattern has an h-confidence value above the minimum h-confidence threshold, h_c, then every pair of objects within the hyperclique pattern must have a cosine similarity great than or equal to h_c.

- **Theorem 2:** *Given a hyperclique pattern P = {i_1, i_2, . . . , i_k} (k > 2) at the h-confidence-threshold h_c for any size-2 item set Q = {i_l, i_m} (1≤ l ≤ k, 1≤ m ≤ k, and l ≠ m) such that Q ⊂ P, we have cosine(Q) ≥ h_c.*
- **Proof:** By the anti-monotone property of the h-confidence measure and the given condition that Q ⊂ P, we know Q is a also hyperclique pattern. Then, by Lemma 6, we know cosine(Q) ≥ h_c.
- **Clique View:** Indeed, a hyperclique pattern can be viewed as a clique, if we construct a graph in the following way. Treat each object in a hyperclique pattern as a vertex and put an edge between two vertices if the cosine similarity between two objects is above the h-confidence threshold, h_c. According to Theorem 2, there will be an edge between

any two objects within a hyperclique pattern. As a result, a hyperclique pattern is a clique.

Viewed as cliques, hyperclique patterns have applications in many different domains.

For instance, Xiong, Steinbach, Tan, and Kumar (2004) show that the hyperclique pattern is the best candidate for pattern preserving clustering—a new paradigm for pattern based clustering. Also, Xiong, He, Ding, Zhang, Kumar and Holbrook (2005) describe the use of hyperclique pattern discovery for identifying functional modules in protein complexes.

HYPERCLIQUE MINER ALGORITHM

The hyperclique miner (see algorithm one) is an algorithm that can generate all hyperclique patterns with support and h-confidence above user-specified minimum support and h-confidence thresholds.

Explanation of the Detailed Steps of the Algorithm

Step 1 scans the database and gets the support for every item. Items with support above *min_supp* form size-1 candidate set C_1. The h-confidence values for size-1 item sets are 1. All items in the set C_1 are sorted by the support values and relabeled in alphabetic order.

Step 2 to *Step 4* loops through 2 to K–1 to generate qualified hyperclique patterns of size 2 or more. It stops whenever an empty candidate set of some size is generated.

Step 3 uses generalized *apriori_gen* to generate candidate hyperclique patterns of size k from hyperclique patterns of size k – 1. The generalized *apriori_gen* function is an adaptation of the *apriori_gen* function of the *Apriori* algorithm (Agrawal & Srikant, 1994). Let C_{k-1} indicate the set of all hyperclique patterns of size k–1. The

Algorithm 1.

Hyperclique Miner
Input:

(1) A set F of K Boolean feature types $F = \{f_1, f_2, \ldots, f_K\}$

(2) A set T of N transactions $T = \{t_1, t_2, \ldots, t_N\}$, each $t_i \in T$ is a record with K attributes $\{i_1, i_2, \ldots, i_K\}$ taking values in $\{0, 1\}$, where the i_p $(1 \leq p \leq K)$ is the Boolean value for the feature type f_p.

(3) A user specified minimum h-confidence threshold (h_c)

(4) A user specified minimum support threshold (min_supp)

Output:

hyperclique patterns with h-confidence > h_c and support > min_supp

Method:

(1) Get size-1 prevalent items

(2) **For** the size of item sets in $(2, 3, \ldots, K{-}1)$ **do**

(3) Generate candidate hyperclique patterns using the *generalized apriori_gen* algorithm

(4) Generate hyperclique patterns

(5) **End**;

---

function works as follows. First, in the join step, we join C_{k-1} with C_{k-1} and get candidate set C_k. Next in the prune step, we delete all candidate hyperclique patterns $c \in C_k$ based on two major pruning techniques:

a. **Pruning based on anti-monotone property of h-confidence and support:** If any one of the $k{-}1$ subsets of c does not belong to C_{k-1}, then c is pruned. (Recall that this prune step is also done in *apriori_gen* by Agrawal and Srikant because of the anti-monotone property of support. Omiecinski (2003) also applied the anti-monotone property of all-confidence in his algorithm.)

b. **Pruning of cross-support patterns by using the cross-support property of h-confidence:** By corollary 1, for the given h-confidence threshold h_c and an item y, all patterns that contain y and at least one

item with support less than $h_c \cdot supp(\{y\})$ are cross-support patterns and are guaranteed to have h-confidence less than t. Hence, all such patterns can be automatically eliminated.

Note that example 4 illustrates the major pruning techniques applied in this step.

Step 4 computes exact support and h-confidence for all candidate patterns in C_k and prunes this candidate set using the user specified support threshold min supp and the h-confidence threshold h_c. All remaining patterns are returned as hyperclique patterns of size k.

- **Example 4:** Figure 4 illustrates the process of pruning the candidate generation step (Step 3) of the hyperclique miner algorithm. In this example, we assume the minimum support threshold to be zero and the minimum h-confidence threshold to be 0.6. Consider the state after all size-1 hyperclique patterns

Figure 4. A running example with a support threshold = 0 and an h-confidence threshold = 0.6. Note that crossed nodes are pruned by the anti-monotone property and circled nodes are pruned by the cross-support property.

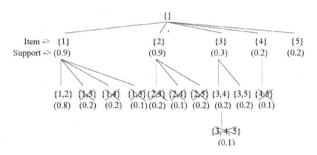

TID	Items
1	1, 2
2	1, 2
3	1, 3, 4
4	1, 2
5	1, 2
6	1, 2
7	1, 2, 3, 4, 5
8	1, 2
9	1, 2
10	2, 3, 5

Item	Support
1	0.9
2	0.9
3	0.3
4	0.2
5	0.2

have been generated. Note that all these singleton items have support greater than 0. Also, by equation (1), h-confidence of all size-1 item sets is 1.0, which is greater than the user-specified h-confidence threshold of 0.6. Hence, all these singleton item sets are hyperclique patterns.

There are two major pruning techniques that we can enforce in step 3 while generating size-2 candidate item sets from size-1 item sets.

a. **Pruning based on the anti-monotone property:** No pruning is possible using this property since all size-1 item sets are hyperclique patterns.

b. **Pruning based on cross-support patterns by using the cross-support property:** Given an h-confidence threshold 0.6, for the item 2, we can find an item 3 with $supp(\{3\}) = 0.3 < supp(\{2\}) \cdot 0.6 = 0.36$ in the sorted

item list $\{1, 2, 3, 4, 5\}$. If we split this item list into two item sets $L=\{1, 2\}$ and $U=\{3, 4, 5\}$, any pattern involving items from both L and U is a cross-support pattern with respect to the threshold 0.6. By Lemma 2, the h-confidence values for these cross-support patterns are less than 0.6. Since the h-confidence threshold is equal to 0.6, all cross-support patterns are pruned. In contrast, without applying cross-support pruning, we have to generate six cross-support patterns including $\{1, 3\}$, $\{1, 4\}$, $\{1, 5\}$, $\{2, 3\}$, $\{2, 4\}$, and $\{2, 5\}$ as candidate patterns and prune them later by computing the exact h-confidence values.

For the remaining size-2 candidate item sets, the h-confidence of the item set $\{4, 5\}$ is $supp(\{4, 5\})/\max\{supp(\{4\}), supp(\{5\})\} = 0.1/0.2 = 0.5.$, which is less than the h-confidence threshold,

0.6. Hence, the item set {4, 5} is not a hyperclique pattern and is pruned.

Next, we consider pruning in step 3 while generating size-3 candidate item sets from size-2 hyperclique patterns.

c. **Pruning based on the anti-monotone property:** From the above, we know that the item set {4, 5} is not a hyperclique pattern. Then, we can prune the candidate pattern {3, 4, 5} by the anti-monotone property of the h-confidence measure, since this pattern has one subset {4, 5}, which is not a hyperclique pattern.

HYPERCLIQUE-BASED ITEM CLUSTERING APPROACH

In this section, we describe how to use hyperclique patterns for clustering items in high dimensional space. For high dimensional data, traditional clustering schemes such as *Autoclass* (Cheeseman & Stutz, 1996) and K-means (Jain & Dubes, 1998) tend to produce poor results when directly applied to large, high-dimensional data sets (Agrawal, Gehrke, Gunopulos & Raghavan, 1998). One promising approach is to cluster the data using a hypergraph partitioning algorithm (Han et al., 1998). More specifically, a hypergraph is constructed with individual items as vertices and frequent itemsets as hyperedges connecting between these vertices. For example, if {A, B, C} is a frequent itemset, then a hyperedge connecting the vertices for A, B, and C will be added. The weight of the hyperedge is given by the average confidence of all association rules generated from the corresponding itemset. The resulting hypergraph is then partitioned using a hypergraph-partitioning algorithm such as HMETIS[4] to obtain clusters.

Although the hypergraph-based clustering algorithm has produced promising results (Han et al., 1998), we believe that it can be further

improved if the hypergraph contains a good representative set of high-quality hyperedges. We believe frequent itemsets may not provide such a good representation because they include cross-support patterns, which may have low affinity but relatively high average confidence. In addition, many low support items cannot be covered by frequent itemsets unless the minimum support threshold is sufficiently low. However, if the threshold is indeed low enough, a large number of frequent itemsets will be extracted, thus resulting in a very dense hypergraph. It will be difficult for a hypergraph partitioning algorithm to partition such a dense hypergraph, which often leads to poor clustering results.

In this chapter, we use hyperclique patterns as an alternative to frequent itemsets. In the hypergraph model, each hyperclique pattern is represented by a hyperedge whose weight is equal to the h-confidence of the pattern. For example, if {A, B, C} is a hyperclique pattern with h-confidence equals to 0.8, then the hypergraph contains a hyperedge that connects the vertices A, B, and C. The weight for this hyperedge is 0.8.

There are several advantages of using the hyperclique-based clustering algorithm. First, since hyperclique patterns are strong affinity patterns, they can provide a good representative set of hyperedges to seed a hypergraph-based clustering algorithm. Second, hyperclique patterns can be extracted for very low support items without making the hypergraph becomes too dense. Finally, hyperclique-based clustering algorithm is also more tolerant to noise compared to traditional clustering algorithms such as k-means because it can explicitly remove the weakly related items.

EXPERIMENTAL RESULTS

In this section, we present extensive experiments to show the performance of hyperclique miner, the quality of hyperclique patterns, and the applications of hyperclique patterns. Specifically, we demonstrate: (1) the effectiveness of h-confidence pruning, (2) the scalability of hyperclique miner, (3) the overall quality of hyperclique patterns, (4) hyperclique-based item clustering, and (5) the application of hyperclique patterns for identifying protein functional modules.

The Experimental Setup

Experimental Data Sets

Our experiments were performed on both real and synthetic data sets. By using the IBM Quest synthetic data generator (Agrawal & Srikant, 1994), synthetic data sets were generated which gives us the flexibility of controlling the size and dimensionality of the database. A summary of the parameter settings used to create the synthetic data sets is presented in Table 3, where $|T|$ is the average size of a transaction, N is the number of

items, and $|L|$ is the maximum number of potential frequent item sets. Each data set contains 1,00,000 transactions, with an average frequent pattern length equal to 4.

The real data sets are obtained from several application domains. Some characteristics of these data sets[5] are shown in Table 4. In the table, the pumsb and pumsb* data sets correspond to binary versions of a census data set. The difference between them is that pumsb* does not contain items with support greater than 80%. The LA1 data set is part of the TREC-5 collection[6] and contains news articles from the Los Angeles Times. In addition, retail is a market-basket data set obtained from a large mail-order company. The S&P 500 index data set consists of the daily price movement of various stocks that belong to the S&P 500 index from January 1994 to October 1996. Finally, the TAP-MS data set (Gavin, et al., 2002) is a protein complex data

Table 3. Parameter settings for synthetic data sets

Data set name	$|T|$	$|L|$	N	Size (MBytes)
T5.L100.N1000	5	100	1000	0.94
T5.L500.N5000	5	500	5000	2.48
T10.L1000.N10000	10	1000	10000	4.96
T20.L2000.N20000	20	2000	20000	10.73
T30.L3000.N30000	30	3000	30000	16.43
T40.L4000.N40000	40	4000	40000	22.13

Table 4. Real data set characteristics

Data set	# Item	# Record	Source
Pumsb	2113	49046	IBM Almaden
Pumsb*	2089	49046	IBM Almaden
LA1	29704	3204	TREC-5
Retail	14462	57671	Retail Store
S&P 500	932	716	Stock Market
TAP-MS	1440	232	Gavin's Protein Complexes

set, which summarizes large-scale experimental studies of multi-protein complexes for the yeast *Saccharomyces Cerevisiae*.

Experimental Platform

Our experiments were performed on a Sun Ultra 10 workstation with a 440 MHz CPU and 128 Mbytes of memory running the SunOS 5.7 operating system. We implemented hyperclique miner by modifying the publicly available Apriori implementation by Borgelt (http://fuzzy.cs.uni-magdeburg.de/~borgelt). When the h-confidence threshold is set to zero, the computational performance of hyperclique miner is approximately the same as the Borgelt's implementation of Apriori (Agrawal & Srikant, 1994).

The Pruning Effect of Hyperclique Miner

The purpose of this experiment is to demonstrate the effectiveness of the h-confidence pruning on hyperclique pattern generation. Note that hyperclique patterns can also be derived by first computing frequent patterns at very low levels of support, and using a post-processing step to

eliminate weakly-related cross-support patterns. Hence, we use the conventional frequent pattern mining algorithms as the baseline to show the relative performance of hyperclique miner.

First, we show how the performance of the algorithm changes as the h-confidence threshold is increased. Figure 5(a) shows the number of patterns generated from the LA1 data set at different h-confidence thresholds. As can be seen, at any fixed support threshold, the number of generated patterns increases quite dramatically with the decrease of the h-confidence threshold. For example, when the support threshold is 0.01 and the h-confidence threshold is zero, the number of patterns generated is greater than 10^7. In contrast, there are only several hundred hyperclique patterns when the h-confidence threshold is increased to 40%. Recall that, when the h-confidence threshold is equal to zero, the hyperclique miner essentially becomes the Apriori algorithm, as it finds all frequent patterns above certain support thresholds. As shown in Figure 5(a), Apriori is not able to find frequent patterns at support level less than 0.01 due to excessive memory requirements. This is caused by the rapid increase of the number of patterns generated as the support threshold is decreased. On the other

Figure 5.

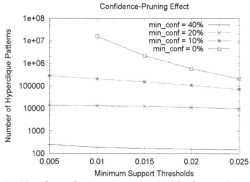

(a) Number of patterns generated by hyperclique miner on LA1 data set

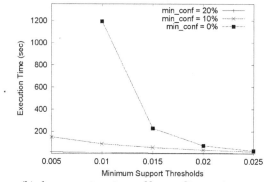

(b) the execution time of hyperclique miner on LA1 data set

hand, for an h-confidence threshold greater than or equal to 10%, the number of patterns generated increases much less rapidly with the decrease in the support threshold.

Figure 5(b) shows the execution time of hyperclique miner on the LA1 data set. As can be seen, the execution time reduces significantly with the increase of the h-confidence threshold. Indeed, our algorithm identifies hyperclique patterns in just a few seconds at 20% h-confidence threshold and 0.005 support threshold. In contrast, the traditional Apriori, which corresponds to the case that h-confidence is equal to zero in Figure 5(b), breaks down at 0.005 support threshold due to excessive memory and computational requirement.

The above results suggest a trade-off between execution time and the number of hyperclique patterns generated at different h-confidence thresholds. In practice, analysts may start with a high h-confidence threshold first at support threshold close to zero, to rapidly extract the strongly affiliated patterns, and then gradually reduce the h-confidence threshold to obtain more patterns that are less tightly-coupled.

Next, we evaluate the performance of hyperclique miner on dense data sets such as pumsb and pumsb*. Recently, Zaki and Hsiao proposed

the CHARM algorithm (Zaki & Hsiao, 2002) to efficiently discover frequent closed item sets. As shown in their paper, for the pumsb and pumsb* data sets, CHARM can achieve relatively better performance than other state-of-the-art pattern mining algorithms such as CLOSET (Pei et al., 2000) and MAFIA (Burdick et al., 2001) when the support threshold is low. Hence, for the pumsb and pumsb* data sets, we chose CHARM as the base line for the case when the h-confidence threshold is equal to zero.

Figure 6(a) shows the number of patterns generated by hyperclique miner and CHARM on the pumsb data set. As can be seen, when the support threshold is low, CHARM can generate a huge number of patterns, which is hard to analyze in real applications. In contrast, the number of patterns generated by hyperclique miner is several orders of magnitude smaller than the number of patterns found by CHARM. In addition, CHARM is unable to generate patterns when the support threshold is less than or equals to 0.4, as it runs out of memory. With a support threshold greater than 0.4, CHARM can only identify associations among a very small fraction of the items. However, hyperclique miner is able to identify many patterns containing items that are strongly related with

Figure 6. On the pumsb *data set*

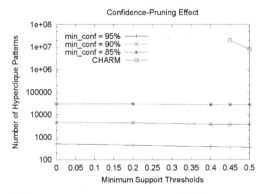

(a) Number of patterns generated by hyperclique miner and CHARM

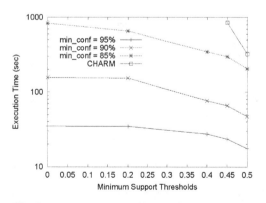

(b) The execution time of hyperclique miner and CHARM

each other even at very low levels of support. For instance, we obtained a long pattern containing 9 items with the support 0.23 and h-confidence 94.2%. Recall from Table 1 that nearly 96.6% of the items have support less than 0.4.

Figure 6(b) shows the execution time of hyperclique miner and CHARM on the pumsb data set. As shown in the figure, the execution time of hyperclique miner increases much less rapidly (especially at higher h-confidence thresholds) than that of CHARM. With h-confidence pruning, we can use hyperclique miner to discover hyperclique patterns even at support threshold equal to zero. Finally, when we continue to reduce the h-confidence threshold, the runtime of hyperclique miner goes up. However, it is possible to incorporate h-confidence pruning strategy into the CHARM implementation to further improve the performance of hyperclique miner on dense data sets.

Similar results are also obtained from the pumsb* data set, as shown in Figure 7(a) and (b). For the pumsb* data set, CHARM is able to find patterns for the support threshold as low as 0.04. This can be explained by the fact that the pumsb* data set do not include those items having support greater than 0.8, thus manually removing

a large number of weakly related cross-support patterns between the highly frequent items and the less frequent items. Hyperclique miner does not encounter this problem because it automatically removes the weakly related cross-support patterns using the cross-support property of the h-confidence measure. Note that, in the pumsb* data set, there are still more than 92% (1925 items) of the items that have support less than 0.04. CHARM is unable to find any patterns involving those items with support less than 0.04, since it runs out of memory when the support threshold is less than 0.04.

The Effect of Cross-Support Pruning

Figure 8(a) illustrates the effect of cross-support pruning on the LA1 data set. There are two curves in the figure. The lower one shows the execution time when both cross-support and anti-monotone pruning are applied. The higher one corresponds to the case that only anti-monotone pruning is applied. As can be seen, cross-support pruning leads to significant reduction in the execution time. Similarly, Figure 8(b) shows the effectiveness of cross-support pruning on the pumsb data set. Note that the pruning effect of the cross-support

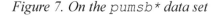

Figure 7. On the pumsb* *data set*

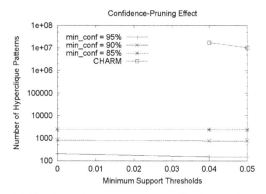

(a) Number of patterns generated by hyperclique miner and CHARM

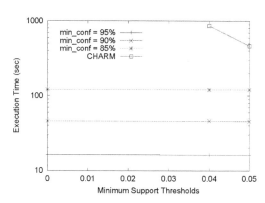

(b) The execution time of hyperclique miner and CHARM

property is more dramatic on the `pumsb` data set than on the `LA1` data set. This is because cross-support pruning tends to work better on dense data sets with skewed support distributions, such as `pumsb`.

Scalability of Hyperclique Miner

We tested the scalability of hyperclique miner with respect to the number of items on the synthetic data sets listed in Table 3. In this experiment, we set the support threshold to 0.01% and increase the number of items from 1,000 to 40,000. Figure 9(a) shows the scalability of hyperclique miner in terms of the number of patterns identified. As can be seen, without h-confidence pruning, the number of patterns increases dramatically and the algorithm breaks down for the data set with 40,000 items. With h-confidence pruning, the number of patterns generated is more manageable and does not grow fast. In addition, Figure 9(b) shows the execution time for our scale-up experiments. As can be seen, without h-confidence pruning, the execution time grows sharply as the number of items increases. However, this growth with respect to the number of items is much more moderate when the h-confidence threshold is increased.

Quality of Hyperclique Patterns

In this experiment, we examined the quality of patterns extracted by hyperclique miner.

Table 5 shows several interesting hyperclique patterns identified at low levels of support from the `LA1` data set. It can be immediately seen that the hyperclique patterns contain words that are closely related to each other. For example, the pattern {arafat, yasser, PLO, Palestine} includes words that are frequently found in news articles about Palestine. These patterns cannot be directly discovered using standard frequent pattern mining algorithms due to their low support values.

Table 6 shows some of the interesting hyperclique patterns extracted at low levels of support from the `retail` data set. For example, we identified a hyperclique pattern involving closely related items such as Nokia battery, Nokia adapter, and Nokia wireless phone. We also discovered several interesting patterns containing very low support items such as {earrings, gold ring, bracelet}. Customers rarely purchase these items, but they are interesting because they are expensive and belong to the same product category.

We also evaluated the affinity of hyperclique patterns by the correlation measure. Specifically,

Figure 8.

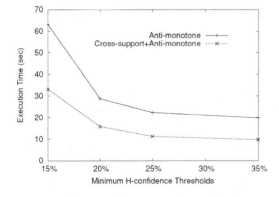

(a) *The effect of cross-support pruning on the LA1 data set*

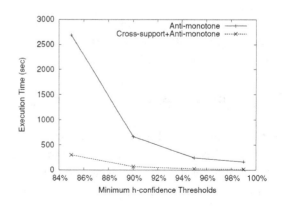

(b) *The effect of cross-support pruning on the `pumsb` data set*

Figure 9. With increasing number of items

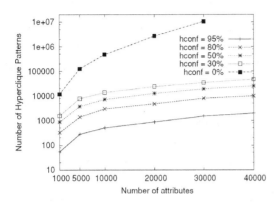

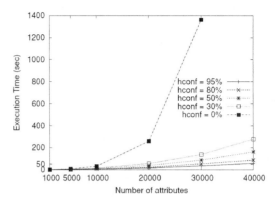

(a) *Number of patterns generated by hyperclique miner*

(b) *The execution time of hyperclique miner*

for each hyperclique pattern $X = \{x_1, x_2, ... x_k\}$, we calculate the correlation for each pair of items (x_i, x_j) within the pattern. The overall correlation of a hyperclique pattern is then defined as the average pair wise correlation of all the items. Note that this experiment was conducted on the `Retail` data set with the h-confidence threshold 0.8 and the support threshold 0.0005.

Figure 10 compares the average correlation for hyperclique patterns vs. non-hyperclique patterns. We sorted the average correlation and displayed them in increasing order. Notice that the hyperclique patterns have extremely high average pair wise correlation compared to the nonhyperclique patterns. This result empirically shows that hyperclique patterns contain items that are strongly related with each other, especially when the h-confidence threshold is relatively high.

Hyperclique-Based Item Clustering

In this section, we illustrate the application of hyperclique patterns as an alternative to frequent patterns in hypergraph-based clustering approach (Han et al., 1998). We use the S&P 500 index data set for our clustering experiments.

Table 7 shows the dramatic increase in the number of frequent patterns as the minimum support threshold is decreased. As can be seen, the number of frequent patterns increases up to 11,486,914 when we reduce the support threshold to 1%. If all these frequent item sets are used for hypergraph clustering, this will create an extremely dense hypergraph and makes the hypergraph-based clustering algorithm become computationally intractable. In Han et al. (1998), the authors have used a higher minimum support threshold, that is, 3%, for their experiments and obtained 19,602 frequent item sets covering 440 items. A hypergraph consisting of 440 vertices and 19,602 hyperedges was then constructed and 40 partitions were generated. Out of 40 partitions[6], 16 of them are clean clusters as they contain stocks primarily from the same or closely related industry groups.

With hyperclique patterns, we can construct hypergraphs at any support threshold, and thus covering more items. For instance, with a minimum h-confidence threshold 20% and a support threshold 0%, we obtain 11,207 hyperclique patterns covering 861 items. A hypergraph consisting of 861 vertices and 11,207 hyperedges is then constructed and partitioned into smaller clusters. For comparison purposes, we partitioned the hypergraph into 80 partitions to ensure that the average size of clusters is almost the same as the average size of the 40 clusters obtained using frequent patterns. Note that for both approaches, we only use patterns containing two or more items as hyperedges.

Our experimental results suggest that the hyperclique pattern approach can systematically produce better clustering results than the frequent pattern approach. First, many items with low levels of support are not included in the frequent pattern approach. Specifically, there are 421 items covered by hyperclique pattern based clusters that are not covered by frequent pattern based clusters. Second, the hypergraph clustering algorithm can produce a larger fraction of clean clusters using hyperclique patterns than frequent patterns—41 out of 80 partitions vs. 16 out of 40 partitions. Third, all the clean clusters identified by the frequent pattern approach were also present in the results by the hyperclique pattern approach.

Finally, for the same clean cluster identified by both approaches, there are more same category items included by the hyperclique-based approach.

Table 8 shows some of the clean hyperclique pattern based clusters that appear at low levels of support (around 1% support). Such clusters could not be identified by the frequent pattern approach. As the table shows, our hyperclique pattern approach was able to discover retail, chemical, health-product, power and communication clusters. A complete list of clusters is given in our Technical Report (Xiong et al., 2003a).

We have also applied the graph-partitioning scheme in CLUTO[7]. This algorithm takes the adjacency matrix of the similarity graph between the n objects to be clustered as input. The experiment results indicate that this approach can produce much worse clustering results than the hyperclique-based approach. For instance, out of the 80 clusters derived by CLUTO, less than 30 of them are clean clusters. This result is not surprising since the graph-partitioning scheme

Table 5. Hyperclique patterns from `LA1`

Hyperclique patterns	support	h-conf (%)
{najibullah, kabul, afghan}	0.002	54.5
{steak, dessert, salad, sauce}	0.001	40.0
{arafat, yasser, PLO, Palestine}	0.004	52.0
{shamir, yitzhak, jerusalem, gaza}	0.002	42.9
{amal, militia, hezbollah, syrian, beirut}	0.001	40.0

Table 6. Hyperclique patterns from `retail`

Hyperclique patterns	support	h-conf (%)
{earrings, gold ring, bracelet}	0.00019	45.8
{nokia battery, nokia adapter, nokia wireless phone}	0.00049	52.8
{coffee maker, can opener, toaster}	0.00014	61.5
{baby bumper pad, diaper stacker, baby crib sheet}	0.00028	72.7
{skirt tub, 3pc bath set, shower curtain}	0.0026	74.4
{jar cookie, canisters 3pc, box bread, soup tureen, goblets 8pc}	0.00012	77.8

considers only information about pairs of items but not higher order interactions.

In addition, we also applied the improved version of the k-means clustering algorithm in CLUTO. For this partition-based clustering algorithm, the similarity between objects can be computed using the cosine measure, the correlation coefficient, or the inverse Euclidean distance function. Our experiments show that measuring similarity using the Euclidean distance function tends to produce poor clustering results for high-dimensional data. Also, there is very little difference between the clustering results for cosine and correlation coefficient measures. When using cosine as the similarity measure, we were able to identify 36 clean clusters out of 80 clusters, which is worse than the hyperclique pattern approach.

Finally, we observed the following effects of the hyperclique-based clustering approach. If we set the minimum support threshold to 0% and h-confidence threshold to 20%, the discovered hyperclique patterns cover 861 items. Since there are 932 items in total, the hyperclique pattern mining algorithm must have eliminated 71 items. We examine the distribution of these 71 items in the CLUTO k-means clustering results. We observe

that 68 of the items are assigned to the wrong clusters by CLUTO. As a result, we believe that the items not covered by these hyperclique patterns are potentially noise items. We also observed that the quality of clusters for the hyperclique-based clustering approach tends to get better with the increase of h-confidence thresholds.

An Application of Hyperclique Patterns for Identifying Protein Functional Modules

In this subsection, we describe an application of hyperclique patterns for identifying protein functional modules—groups of proteins involved in common elementary biological function (Xiong et al., 2005).

Figure 11 shows the subgraphs of the Gene Ontology (www.geneontology.org) corresponding to a hyperclique pattern {Cus1, Msl1, Prp3, Prp9, Sme1, Smx2, Smx3, Yhc1} identified from the TAP-MS protein complex data. Figure 11 (a) is the molecular function annotation of the proteins in the pattern. Note that all eight proteins from this pattern are annotated to the term *RNA binding* with p-value 4.97e-10. The p-value is calculated as the probability that n or more proteins would be assigned to that term if proteins from the entire genome are randomly assigned to that pattern. The smaller the p-value, the more significant the annotation. Among the pattern, 4 proteins {Prp3, Sme1, Smx2, Smx3} are annotated to a more specific term *pre-mRNA splicing factor*

Figure 10. The average correlation of each pair of items for hyperclique and nonhyperclique patterns

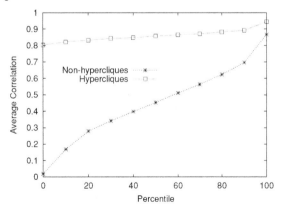

Table 7. Numbers of frequent patterns with the decrease of support thresholds on the S&P data set

Support	# Frequent patterns	# Items covered
3%	19602	440
2%	149215	734
1%	11486914	915

Figure 11. The gene ontology annotations of pattern {Cus1, Msl1, Prp3, Prp9, Sme1, Smx2, Smx3, Yhc1}. Proteins are listed in square box. Significant nodes are labeled with the number of proteins annotated directly or indirectly to that term and the p-value for the term.

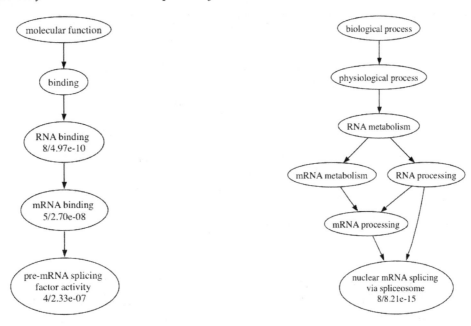

(a) shows function annotation of the pattern   *(b) shows subgraph of process annotation*

activity with p-value 2.33e-07. The annotation of these proteins confirms that each pattern form a module performing specific function. Figure 11 (b) shows the biological process this pattern is involved. The proteins are annotated to the term *nuclear mRNA splicing via spliceosome* with p-value 8.21^{-15}, which is statistically significant.

CONCLUSION

In this chapter, we introduced the problem of mining hyperclique patterns in data sets with skewed support distribution. We also presented the concept of cross-support property and showed how this property can be used to avoid generating spurious patterns involving items from different support levels. Furthermore, an algorithm called hyperclique miner was developed. This algorithm

utilizes cross-support and anti-monotone properties of h-confidence for the efficient discovery of hyperclique patterns. Finally, we demonstrated applications of hyperclique patterns for identifying protein functional modules as well as hyperclique-based item clustering.

There are several directions for future work on this topic. First, the hyperclique miner algorithm presented in this chapter is based upon the Apriori algorithm. It will be useful to explore implementations based upon other algorithms for mining hyperclique patterns, such as TreeProjection (Agarwal, Aggarwals, & Prasad, 2000) and FP-growth (Han, Pei, & Yin, 2000). Second, it is valuable to investigate the *cross-support* property on some other measures of association. Third, the current hyperclique pattern-mining framework is designed for dealing with binary data. The extension of the hyperclique concept to

Table 8. Some clean clusters appearing at low levels of support (around 1% support)

No	Discovered Clusters	Industry Group
1	Baltimore Gas↓, CINergy Corp↓, Amer Electric Power↓, Duke Power↓, Consolidated Edi↓, Entergy Corp↓, Genl Public Until↓, Houston Indus↓, PECO Energy↓, Texas Utilities↓	Power
2	Becton Dickinso↓, Emerson Electric↓, Amer Home Product↓, Johnson & Johnson↓, Merck↓, Pfizer↓, Schering-Plough↓, Warner-Lambert↓	Health Product
3	Bank of New York↓, Bank of Boston↓, CoreStates Financial↓, CIGNA Corp↓, Comerica Inc↓, Aetna Life & Cas↓, Amer General↓, Fleet financial↓, Morgan (J.P.↓), KeyCorp↓, Mellon Bank Corp↓, NationsBank Corp↓, Natl City Corp↓, Wells Fargo, BankAmerica Corp↓	Financial
4	Bell Atlantic Co↑, BellSouth Corp↑, CPC Intl↑, GTE Corp↑, Ameritech Corp↑, NYNEX Corp↑, Pacific Telesis↑, SBC Communication, US West Communication↑	Common
5	duPont (EI) deNemo↑, Goodrich (B.F.)↑, Nalco Chemical↑, Rohm & Haas, Avon Products↑	Chemical
6	Federated Dept↑, Gap Inc↑, Nordstrom Inc↑, Pep Boys-Man↑, Sears, TJX, Walmart↑	Retail

continuous-valued domains will be a challenging task. Finally, it is a very interesting direction to explore more efficient algorithms based on approximate clique partitioning algorithms (Feder & Motwani, 1995).

REFERENCES

Agarwal, R., Aggarwal, C., & Prasad, V. (2000). A tree projection algorithm for generation of frequent itemsets. *Journal of Parallel and Distributed Computing, 61*(3), 350-371.

Agrawal, R., Gehrke, J., Gunopulos, D., & Raghavan, P. (1998). Automatic subspace clustering of high dimensional data for data mining applications. In *Proceedings of the 1998 ACM SIGMOD International Conference on Management of Data*, (pp. 94-105).

Agrawal, R., Imielinski, T., & Swami, A. (1993). Mining association rules between sets of items in large databases. In *Proceedings of the 1993 ACM SIGMOD International Conference on Management of Data*, (pp. 207-216).

Agrawal, R., & Srikant, R. (1994). Fast algorithms for mining association rules. In *Proceedings of the 20th International Conference on Very Large Data Bases (VLDB) Conference*, (pp. 487-499).

Bayardo, R., Agrawal, R.. & Gunopulous, D. (1999). Constraint-based rule mining in large, dense databases. In *Proceedings of the 15th International Conference on Data Engineering (ICDE)*, (pp. 188-197).

Bayardo, R. J. (1998). Efficiently mining long patterns from databases. In *Proceedings of the ACM SIGMOD International Conference on Management of Data*, (pp. 85-93).

Brin, S., Motwani, R., & Silverstein, C. (1997). Beyond market baskets: Generalizing association rules to correlations. In *Proceedings of the 1997 ACM SIGMOD International Conference on Management of Data*, (pp. 265–276).

Burdick, D., Calimlim, M., & Gehrke, J. (2001). MAFIA: A maximal frequent itemset algorithm for transactional databases. In *Proceedings of the 2001 International Conference on Data Engineering (ICDE)*, (pp. 443-452).

Cheeseman, P., & Stutz, J. (1996). Bayesian classification (autoclass): Theory and results. In *Proceedings of the ACM KDD International Conference on Knowledge Discovery and Data Mining*, (pp. 61-83).

Cohen, E., Datar, M., Fujiwara, S., Gionis, A., Indyk, P., Motwani, R., Ullman, J., & Yang, C. (2000). Finding interesting associations without support pruning. In *Proceedings of the 2000 International Conference on Data Engineering (ICDE)*, (pp. 489-499).

Feder, T., & Motwani, R. (1995). Clique partitions, graph compression and speeding-up algorithms [Special Issue]. *Journal of Computer and System Sciences, 51*, 261–272

Gavin, A. et al. (2002). Functional organization of the yeast proteome by systematic analysis of protein complexes. *Nature, 415*, 141-147.

Grahne, G., Lakshmanan, L. V. S., & Wang, X. (2000). Efficient mining of constrained correlated sets. In *Proceedings of the 2000 International Conference on Data Engineering (ICDE)*, (pp. 512-524).

Han, E., Karypis, G., & Kumar, V. (1998). Hypergraph based clustering in high-dimensional data sets: A summary of results. *Bulletin of the Technical Committee on Data Engineering, 21*(1), 15-22.

Han, J., Pei, J., & Yin, Y. (2000) Mining frequent patterns without candidate generation. In *Proceedings of the 2000 ACM SIGMOD International Conference on Management of Data*, (pp. 1-12)

Hastie, T., Tibshirani, R., & Friedman, J. (2001). *The elements of statistical learning: Data mining, inference, and prediction.* Springer.

Jain, A. K., & Dubes, R. C. (1998). *Algorithms for clustering data.* Prentice Hall.

Liu, B., Hsu, W., & Ma, Y. (1999). Mining association rules with multiple minimum supports.

In *Proceedings of the 1999 ACM SIGMOD International Conference on Management of Data*, 175-186.

Omiecinski, E. (2003). Alternative interest measures for mining associations. *IEEE Transactions on Knowledge and Data Engineering (TKDE),15*(1), 57-69.

Pei, J., Han, J.. & Mao, R. (2000). CLOSET: An efficient algorithm for mining frequent closed itemsets. In *Proceedings of the ACM SIGMOD Workshop on Research Issues in Data Mining and Knowledge Discovery*, (pp. 21-30).

Reynolds, H. T. (1977). The analysis of cross-classifications. *The Free Press.*

Rijsbergen, C. J. V. (1979). *Information retrieval (2nd ed.).* Butterworths, London.

Tan, P., Kumar, V., & Srivastava, J. (2002). Selecting the right interestingness measure for association patterns. In *Proceedings of the 8th ACM SIGKDD International Conference on Knowledge Discovery and Data Mining*, (pp. 32-41).

Wang, K., He, Y., Cheung, D., & Chin, Y. (2001). Mining confident rules without support requirement. In *Proceedings of the 2001 ACM Conference on Information and Knowledge Management (CIKM)*, (pp. 236-245).

Xiong, H., He, X., Ding, C., Zhang, Y., Kumar, V., & Holbrook, S. R. (2005). Identification of functional mdodules in protein complexes via hyperclique pattern discovery. In *Proceedings of the Pacific Symposium on Biocomputing (PSB)*, (pp. 209-220).

Xiong, H., Steinbach, M., Tan, P-N., & Kumar, V. (2004). HICAP: Hierarchical clustering with pattern preservation. In *Proceedings of 2004 SIAM International Conference on Data Mining (SDM).* (pp. 279-290).

Xiong, H., Tan, P., & Kumar, V. (2003a). Mining hyperclique patterns with confidence pruning

(Tech. Rep. No. 03-006). University of Minnesota, Twin Cities, Department of Computer Science.

Xiong, H., Tan, P., & Kumar, V. (2003b). Mining strong affinity association patterns in data sets with skewed support distribution. In *Proceedings of the 3rd IEEE International Conference on Data Mining (ICDM)*, (pp. 387-394).

Yang, C., Fayyad, U. M., & Bradley, P. S. (2001). Efficient discovery of error-tolerant frequent itemsets in high dimensions. In *Proceedings of the 1999 ACM SIGKDD International Conference on Knowledge Discovery and Data Mining*, (pp. 194-203).

Zaki, M., & Hsiao, C.-J. (2002). CHARM: An efficient algorithm for closed itemset mining. In *Proceedings of the 2nd SIAM International Conference on Data Mining*.

ENDNOTES

[1] It is available at http://www.almaden.ibm.com/ software/quest/resources.

[2] This is observed on Sun Ultra 10 work station with a 440 MHz CPU and 128 Mbytes of memory.

[3] When computing Pearson's correlation coefficient, the data mean is not subtracted.

[4] http://www.cs.umn.edu/~karypis/metis/hmetis/index.html

[5] Note that the numbers of items shown in Table 4 for pumsb and pumsb* are somewhat different from the numbers reported in Zaki and Hsiao (2002), because we only consider item IDs for which the count is at least one. For example, although the minimum item ID in pumsb is 0 and the maximum item ID is 7116, there are only 2113 distinct item IDs that appear in the data set.

[6] The data set is available at http://trec.nist.gov.

[7] In Han et al. (1998), they also applied a fitness measure to eliminate partitions with bad quality and get 20 good clusters. Out of 20 good clusters, 16 clusters are clean.

[8] http://www.cs.umn.edu/~karypis/cluto/index.html.

Chapter IV
Pattern Discovery in Biosequences:
From Simple to Complex

Simona Ester Rombo
Università della Calabria, Italy

Luigi Palopoli
Università della Calabria, Italy

ABSTRACT

In the last years, the information stored in biological datasets grew up exponentially, and new methods and tools have been proposed to interpret and retrieve useful information from such data. Most biological datasets contain biological sequences (e.g., DNA and protein sequences). Thus, it is more significant to have techniques available capable of mining patterns from such sequences to discover interesting information from them. For instance, singling out for common or similar subsequences in sets of biosequences is sensible as these are usually associated to similar biological functions expressed by the corresponding macromolecules. The aim of this chapter is to explain how pattern discovery can be applied to deal with such important biological problems, describing also a number of relevant techniques proposed in the literature. A simple formalization of the problem is given and specialized for each of the presented approaches. Such formalization should ease reading and understanding the illustrated material by providing a simple-to-follow roadmap scheme through the diverse methods for pattern extraction we are going to illustrate.

INTRODUCTION

Biology has been one of the most important driving forces in science in the last century. Genome sequencing and the other important developments in molecular biology have been important conquests, but innumerable challenges still exist in this field, and it is reasonable to suppose that a very long quest lies ahead. On this subject, during an interview given in 1993, Donald Knuth stated, "Biology is so digital, and incredibly complicated, but incredibly useful. … I can't be as confident about computer science as I can about biology. Biology easily has 500 years of exciting problems to work on." In an evolving field such as this, continuously having new data to store and to analyze seems natural. Actually, the amount of available data is growing exponentially, and providing biologists with efficient tools to interpret data is imperative. Computer science can help in providing most appropriate answers, and the development of new, interdisciplinary, sciences, such as bioinformatics, is an immediate consequence of that. The intrinsic difficulty in understanding biological processes is connected to the necessity of both analyzing enormous data sets and facing different sorts of specific problems. Therefore, techniques to extract and manage biological information have been developed and implemented in the last few years, for example, developing useful software interfaces allowing for the management of large amounts of data through easy human-machine interactions. Several application programs accessible through Internet are available (e.g., Altschul, Gish, Miller, Myers, & Lipman, 1990; Altschul, Madden, Schaffer, Zhang, Anang, & Miller, 1997), and the widespread use of the Web represents a peculiar aspect of bioinformatics. Biological data-sets, such as GenBank (Benson, Mizrachi, Lipman, Ostell, & Wheeler, 2005), PDB (Berman, Bourne, & Westbrook, 2004), and Prosite (Hulo, Sigrist, Le Saux, Langendijk-Genevaux, Bordoli, & Gattiker, 2004), featuring an impressive number of entries and containing data representing from portions to entire genomes or protein sequences corresponding to different organisms, are continuously queried online. In this scenario, the availability of very large amounts of data does not imply necessarily an enlargement of the attained knowledge, since such data need to be interpreted in order to extract useful information. Thus, the discovery of information implicitly encoded in biological datasets nowadays is assuming a prominent role.

Most biological datasets contain DNA and protein sequences. DNA is a polymer, that is, a macromolecule made of small molecules joined together and called nucleotides. There are four nucleotides and the four bases can distinguish them: adenine (A), cytosine (C), guanine (G), and thymine (T). DNA is a central constituent of each living being, encoding the information required by an organism to function, and makes each organism transfer genetic information to its descendants. DNA can be viewed as a template to produce additional (duplicate) DNA for the purposes of transmitting genetic material to descendants, but also to produce another kind of important macromolecule, that is, proteins. Proteins are macromolecules made of units, called amino acids. The gene sequence inscribed in DNA is composed of triplets of nucleotides called codons, each coding for a single amino acid. There are twenty amino acids, and the sequence of the amino acids of a specific protein is determined by the sequence of the bases in the gene that encodes that protein. To briefly illustrate protein expression, let us recall that two main processes constitute the *Central Dogma* of biology:

- *Transcription = DNA → RNA*
- *Translation = RNA → protein*

During transcription, DNA serves as the template for the synthesis of RNA, thus the information encoded in DNA is transcribed into an RNA sequence. Translation consists of mapping the information encoded in the nucleotides of RNA into a defined sequence of amino acids of the synthesized protein. Taken together, the two processes make up:

* *DNA → RNA → protein.*

It is not difficult to understand that both DNA and proteins can be represented and stored by sequences of symbols corresponding, respectively, to bases or amino acids. These biological sequences are usually named *biosequences*. While the analysis of biological sequences represents a fundamental step in those studies concerning the identification of genetic diseases and the deciphering of biological mechanisms, extracting useful information from databases containing biosequences is a formidable task; the number of stored sequences is growing exponentially, and most of these sequences require interpretation before becoming useful for further studies. In particular, the discovery of regular expressions, that are, common subsequences, among sets of biosequences can often be related to important biological properties, for instance, the presence of similar biological functions in different macromolecules or the appearance of the same disease in different patients. In other words, regularities in sets of biosequences can model the presence of *interesting* common properties in the biological components associated with them.

The problem of pattern discovery might be formalized under several and more general keys (Pal, Mitra, & Pal, 2004), but we consider its application in the context of biological sequences. According to (Brazma, Jonassen, Eidhammer, & Gilbert, 1998a), a possible way to analyze biosequences is grouping them in families of biologically (i.e., evolutionary, structurally, or functionally) related ones. For each family, the matter is searching groups of common features that can be purely expressed in terms of the sequences. Such "syntactic" features are named *patterns*. For example, we can consider a subsequence common to several biosequences or repeated several times

in the same sequence to be a pattern. Common patterns in sets of biologically related sequences can be associated, for example, with the presence of conserved regions, usually corresponding to some important biological function of the macromolecules represented by such sequences. In this case, mining interesting patterns can be useful to predict properties of biological components. In other applications, finding frequent patterns repeated in sets of sequences can help in classifying such sequences. As an example, proteins can be grouped into families where those belonging to the same family have common biological functions. Since proteins with similar functions have also similar structures (Lesk, 2004), it is possible to group in families also the corresponding amino acid sequences. Thus, each family of sequences can be described by regular expressions, corresponding to substrings repeated in all the sequences of the family and representing interesting patterns for that family. If a pattern previously found in a family of sequences is discovered in a new sequence, then that sequence will (most probably) belong to that family. More in general, it might be interesting to mine *complex* structured patterns. If we refer to *interesting* patterns as substrings frequently occurring in a set of strings, it can happen that, for example, a pair of substrings occurs in most sequences, appearing in each of those sequences always separated by the same number of symbols. In that case, the pair of substrings *altogether* are to be considered as a *unique* pattern, whose structure is characterized, intuitively, as two *boxes* linked by a *gap*. These are the kinds of patterns that we call *structured* and are interesting since, again, they are often associated with biological functions expressed in a living being. An example is the prokaryotic transcription regulation regions: the most frequently observed prokaryotic promoter regions are in general composed of two parts positioned approximately *10* and *35* bases upstream from the transcription start. The biological reason for these particular positions is that the two parts are recognized by the same protein. Relevant mining tasks for structured patterns can involve patterns with very complex structures, for instance consisting of several boxes having different lengths, and separated by a varying number of symbols. These kinds of patterns can be particularly meaningful in those studies involving eukaryotic organisms, whose biological components and related processes are much more complex than the prokaryotes ones. Also, allowing a limited number of "errors" (insertions, deletions or symbol substitutions) in repeated patterns is biologically relevant, since (relatively limited) sequence modifications are produced through the evolution of species and individuals. Proteins are still a good example: many protein functional domains are associated with the same function even if they are different in some of the amino acids of the corresponding sequences.

Informally, we can say that pattern discovery consists in developing methods and tools to find *interesting patterns* that are unknown a priori in a sequence or in a given set of sequences. The concept of *interestingness* deserves some attention, since a pattern can be considered *interesting* according to different criteria, such as if it is frequent, unexpected, or contextually under- or over- represented. *Interesting* patterns are also called *motifs*. In several problems, a pattern is considered *interesting* if it appears at least q times, where q represents a quorum value associated with the problem. Moreover, in some biological problems, *interesting* patterns present complex structures, and many constraints are to be considered in the discovery process. The aim here is to consider the problem of discovering *interesting* patterns in biosequences, presenting an overview of the main methods presented in the literature and their applications, both consolidated or just developed in the past few years. In the following, we present a general formalization of the problem of pattern discovery, and then particularize it during exposition to some specific examined cases, in such a way that the reader will be able

to easily categorize the guiding thread of the different described approaches, thus providing an easy-to-use reading key of differences and similarities characterizing them.

The first step in our narration is giving the means to fully understand what is pattern discovery and how it can be applied to problems involving sets of sequences. To achieve that, we first introduce and explain some basic notions derived from string matching; then we shall present our formalization of the problem of pattern discovery applied to biosequences. Keeping in mind this formalization, the next step will be to go through a collection of selected works developed and consolidated in the last few years. Finally, we shall point out the emerging directions in the field.

The chapter is organized as follows: section 2 is devoted to providing some guidelines on surveys and collections of works already presented in the literature on the topic of interest, and to introducing some preliminary definitions useful to the illustration; section 3 is the central part of the chapter, in which we provide a simple yet general formalization of the problem of pattern discovery in biosequences and describe a number of approaches presented in the literature; in section 4 we underline some emergent approaches and discuss about some interesting future trends; finally, in section 5 we draw our conclusions.

BACKGROUND

The variety of biological data, their often high-dimensional nature, the enormous amount of information to manage necessitated approaching several problems in this field by applying data mining and knowledge discovery consolidated methods, suitably adapted to solve biological problems. The application of traditional data mining approaches to bioinformatics is not straightforward: differently from in other application fields, such as business and finance, biological data are characterized by both the absence of explicit features and the presence of numerous exceptions. Thus, inferring knowledge by applying classical data mining methods is highly nontrivial, and accurate studies are necessary to attain significant results. In (Liu & Wong, 2003), a number of data mining tools for analyzing biological sequence data are discussed. In particular, a general methodology is described based on: *(a)* the generation of candidate features from the sequences, where different types of features based on k-grams are presented; *(b)* the selection of relevant features from the candidates, where signal-to-noise, t-statistics, entropy measures and correlation-based feature selection methods are discussed; *(c)* the integration of the selected features to build a system to recognize specific properties in sequence data, using machine learning methods. The emphasis of the paper is on the application of this methodology to recognize translation initiation sites (TIS), even if a significant list of other data mining approaches for biomedical applications are reported. In particular, different classification techniques successful in the biomedical context are revised, including decision tree based approaches, Bayesian classifiers, artificial neural networks and support vector machines.

Data mining approaches have been proposed to classify biological data. To cite a recent example, in Elloumi and Maddouri (2005) a method based on voting strategies and called *Disclass* is presented to do classification of nucleic sequences. The approach has been applied to the analysis of *toll-like receptors* (TLR) macromolecules, to the discrimination between *exon* and *intron* regions in DNA macromolecules and to the identification of *junction regions* in DNA macromolecules. Besides classification, the discovery of knowledge by pattern extraction has been also successfully applied in the biological context, and this chapter focuses just on this subject. In general, given a database including a number of records, patterns can be simply defined considering common features characterizing related records. As already pointed out, in biological databases the records are often biosequences, and this chapter focuses on mining patterns in biosequences. Anyway, before starting with the main part of our narration, it is mandatory to point out that also other kinds of patterns may be usefully considered in bioinformatics contexts. As an example, one of the current trends is the study of biological networks, useful to represent interactions among molecules, such as protein-interaction, protein-DNA interaction, and metabolic reactions, or functional relationships derived from genomic data (e.g., microarray data). Biological networks may be modelled by using graphs and computational methods can be used to mine *graph patterns* that are similar subgraphs common to different graphs. Graph patterns are useful, for example, to discover common biological modules in biological multiple networks, or to search for similarities among networks modelling different kinds of interactions among molecules. In Hu, Yan, Huang, Han, and Zhou (2005) an algorithm for efficiently mining graph patterns is presented and applied to biological networks derived from microarray datasets, discovering numerous functionally homogenous clusters and making functional predictions for 169 uncharacterized yeast genes. Other interesting and recent references about this subject are found in Koyuturk, Kim, Subramaniam, Szpankowski, and Grama (2006) and Berg and Lassig (2004), describing approaches to discover graph patterns in biological networks. In particular, in Koyuturk et al. (2006), an algorithm for detecting frequently occurring patterns and modules in biological networks is proposed, using a graph simplification technique based on ortholog contraction, useful to make the problem computationally tractable and scalable to many networks. The authors apply their method to extract frequently occurring patterns in metabolic pathways and protein interaction networks from commonly used biological databases. In Berg and Lassig (2004) *topological motifs*, that is, graph patterns occurring repeatedly at different positions in the network, are considered. The authors establish a statistical model for the occurrence of such motifs, from which they derive a scoring function for their statistical significance. Based on this scoring function, they develop an algorithm for searching for topological motifs; the procedure is called *graph alignment*, because of its analogies to sequence alignment techniques. The algorithm is applied to the gene regulation network of Escherichia coli.

At this point, we have provided some reviews of possible data mining and mining patterns applications in the biological contexts, and we are ready to focus on the main subject of this chapter, that is, mining patterns in biosequences. A survey on approaches and algorithms used for the automatic discovery of patterns in biosequences is presented in Brazma et al. (1998a). In that work, a formulation of the problem of automatically discovering patterns from a set of sequences is given, where patterns with the expressive power in the class of regular languages are considered among those frequently used in molecular bioinformatics. That paper focuses on *families*, which are, groups of biologically related sequences, and two different but related problems of learning family descriptions thereof are described. The first problem considered is how to find a *classifier function* for a family of biosequences; this is a function that takes a sequence as an argument, and returns *true* over the members of the family, and *false* over nonmembers. The second problem is how to extract a description of *conserved* features in (i.e., characterizing) the family, expressed by a *conservation function*. Several solution spaces are discussed, illustrating different ways of defining such functions w.r.t. different biological problems, and the issue of ranking the solution space of discovered patterns is also discussed. Then, an in-depth review of algorithms used to find classification or conservation functions for sets of biosequences is given. The perspective put forward in Brazma et al. (1998a) highlights how the problem of pattern discovery in biosequences can be related to problems studied in the field of

machine learning, which is certainly interesting. However, here we deal with a different matter, focusing on the more structural properties characterizing sequences and their repetitions. Also, we point out approaches developed in the last few years to discover new classes of patterns having complex structures, whose identification is important in several biological problems, such as the individuation of regulatory regions of prokaryotes organisms and similar issues. In Rigoutsos, Floratos, Parida, Gao, and Platt (2000), a detailed discussion of several applications of pattern discovery in computational biology is reported. The authors present the problem of pattern discovery in terms of determining *interesting* combinations of events, which are contained in a database *D*. They observe that one of the possible ways to recast the notion of what is *interesting* in terms of the number of times some combination of events appears. Thus, given an interestingness threshold *k*, a combination of events is to be considered *interesting* if and only if it appears at least *k* times in the processed input database. The authors present a number of algorithmic approaches related to this problem, and several explored applications of pattern discovery in the context of biological problems. For more on this, the reader is referred also to Vilo (2002) and Wang, Shapiro, and Shasha (1999). In the remaining part of this section, we shall focus on introducing some preliminary notions useful in the foregoing.

String, Suffix, and Don't Care

As already stated, one of the most common ways to model biological components such as DNA and proteins is by sequences of symbols, where the set of symbols exploited for the representation changes according to both the specific components and the specific problems to analyze. Some basic concepts are recalled next.

Given a finite set of characters denoted by Σ and called *alphabet*, a *string s* of size (a.k.a., *length*) n over Σ is an ordered list of characters

$s=a_1a_2 \ldots a_n$ such that $a_i \in \Sigma$, for each i, $1 \leq i \leq n$. The length n of s is denoted by $|s|$. In the following, the terms "string" and "sequence" are used interchangeably. By a little abuse of notation, the cardinality of Σ is denoted by $|\Sigma|$. A *substring* of s, starting from position i and ending at position j, is a list of consecutive characters $a_i a_{i+1} \ldots a_j$ of s and is denoted by $s_{[i \ldots j]}$, where $1 \leq i \leq j \leq n$. The *suffix* s_k of a string s is the substring $s_{[k \ldots n]}$ of s.

Example 1: Consider the alphabet $\Sigma = \{a, b\}$. The size of Σ is $|\Sigma| = 2$. Then $s = abbbababba$ is a string of length $|s| = 10$ over Σ. The substring $s_{[2 \ldots 5]}$ of s is *bbba*. The suffix s_7 of s is *abba*.

Given two strings s' and s'' of size n' and n'', respectively, with $n'' \leq n'$, we say that s'' *occurs* in s' if $s'_{[i \ldots j]} = s''$ for some indexes i and j, $1 \leq i < j \leq n'$ such that $n'' = j - i + 1$. We also say that s' *matches* s''. Each substring of s' with this property represents an exact occurrence or, simply, an *occurrence* of s'' in s'.

Example 2: Consider the strings $s' = AKKTATAK$ and $s'' = KTAT$ on the alphabet $\Sigma = \{A, K, T\}$. Observe that, for $i = 3$ and $j = 6$, $s'_{[i \ldots j]} = s''$. Thus, $s'_{[3 \ldots 6]}$ represents an occurrence of s'' in s'.

In addition to the characters from Σ, called *solid characters*, we introduce a new special character denoted by '·' and called a *don't care* symbol. The don't care is a symbol not occurring in Σ and matching all the symbols in Σ. As an example, consider the strings $s' = bcabc$ and $s'' = baabc$. Then, both of them match the string $s = b \cdot abc$.

Distance Between Strings and Approximate Occurrences

It is often useful to define some notion of *distance* between two strings. The most common notions found in the literature are those of the Hamming and the Levenshtein distances, which are recalled next.

Let s' and s'' be two strings over the same alphabet Σ. The *Hamming distance* between s' and s'' is the minimum number of symbol substitutions to be applied on s' to obtain s''. The *Levenshtein distance* between s' and s'' is the minimum number of edit operations (i.e., symbol substitutions, insertions, and deletions) to be applied on s' to obtain s''. For instance, '*ACGTAG*' and '*ABGATG*' have Hamming distance equal to 3, whereas the Levenshtein distance between '*MISSPELL*' and '*MISTELL*' is equal to 2.

Given a maximum (e.g., Hamming or Levenshtein) allowed distance e (also called *error*), each substring of s' at a distance $d \leq e$ from the string s'' represents an *approximate occurrence* of s'' in s' w.r.t. e (also called an *e-occurrence* in the following).

Example 3: Consider the strings $s' = aaabcaaaad$ and $s'' = aadbaa$, and suppose that the maximum number of allowed errors is $e = 2$. Thus, with reference to the Hamming distance, the substring $s'_{[2 \ldots 7]} = aabcaa$ is an approximate occurrence of s'' in s'.

Data Structures: Tries and Suffix Trees

We report next a brief description of some data structures commonly adopted to store and manipulate strings. More detailed information can be found in Apostolico (1985), Apostolico (2000), and Gusfield (1997).

The first data structure we consider is the *trie*. A trie, introduced in Fredkin (1960), is an ordered tree structure. Each edge of the tree has a label representing a symbol. Any two edges out of the same node have distinct labels. Each node is associated with a string. Concatenating all the symbols in the path from the root to a node n, the string corresponding to n is obtained (the empty string for the root). All the descendants of the same node n are associated with strings having a common prefix, represented by the string corresponding to n. Figure 1 shows an example

Figure 1. An example of trie storing the strings: to, tea, te, ten, hi, he, her

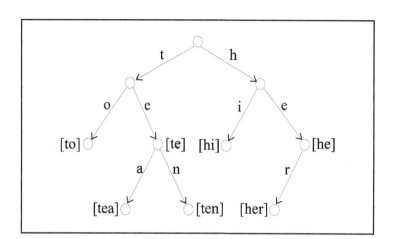

of a trie, where strings associated with nodes are shown in square brackets.

A trie can be also considered in a compressed form, obtained by merging single child nodes with their parents. This kind of trie is known in the literature as *PATRICIA trie* (Morrison, 1968), from the acronym of *Practical Algorithm To Retrieve Information Coded In Alphanumeric*. The term *compact trie* is often used to indicate a trie in the compressed form.

Given a string s of n characters on the alphabet Σ, a *suffix tree T* associated to s can be defined as a trie containing all the n suffixes of s. In a suffix tree, for each leaf i of T, the concatenation of the edge labels on the path from the root to that leaf will spell out the suffix s_i of s. Moreover, for any two suffixes s_i and s_j of s, their longest common prefix share the same subpath in T. Also for suffix trees compact forms can be defined, which can be built in $O(n)$ both in time and space (Apostolico, Iliopoulos, Landau, Schieber, & Vishkin, 1988; Apostolico & Crochemore, 2000; McCreight, 1976; Ukkonen, 1995), assuming as constant the time needed to traverse a node. Figure 2 shows a suffix tree.

In some applications, it can be useful to store in a suffix tree all the suffixes of *a set* of strings: the resulting tree is called *generalized* suffix tree.

FORMALIZATION AND APPROACHES

As already stated, the aim of this chapter is to provide the basic notions for understanding the different facets that the problem of mining patterns in biosequences can assume, providing also an overview of the main classes of approaches proposed in the last years and related references. As already stated, many biological problems involve the task of finding common substrings in sets of biosequences, representing common features that usually correspond to *interesting* patterns (motifs). According to the particular problem under examination, the criteria to establish whether a pattern is *interesting* change, and motifs may have from simple to more complex structure. Furthermore, also the choice of searching for exact or approximate repetitions depends on the analyzed biological problem. Thus, specifying constraints on both the selection criterion and the structure

Figure 2. An example of suffix tree for the string bbbabba

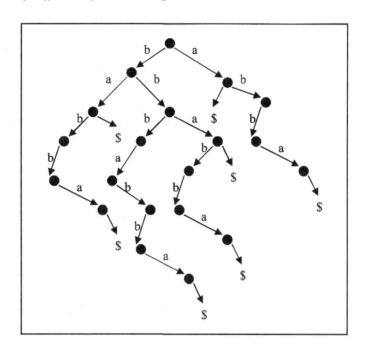

of the patterns, the problem can be particularized to different application contexts.

In the following we illustrate a simple formalization of the problem of pattern discovery in biosequences, with the aim of facilitating the reading, relieving it of different notations, and then analyzing a selection of approaches and applications developed in this field. We would like to stress here that this analysis is not exhaustive but, rather, aims at pushing the reader towards further reading.

A Formalization of the Problem

Before formalizing the problem of pattern discovery in biosequences, we need to introduce some definitions concerning structural properties of sets of strings. Indeed, we shall be interested in defining the problem of mining patterns that may have a significantly complex structure and possibly allowing errors or string repetitions. A possible way to go is to define the concept of *ex-*

traction constraints of a set of strings on a given sequence, in order to model the way in which the different portions of the pattern succeed to each other while occurring in an input sequence.

Definition 1 (Extraction Constraints): Given a string z on the alphabet Σ, the *extraction constraints* E_c can be defined as a seven-tuple of integers $<n, l_{min}, l_{max}, d_{min}, d_{max}, e_{min}, e_{max}>$, where $1 \leq n, l_{min}, l_{max} \leq |z|$ and $e_{min}, e_{max} \geq 0$. In particular, n represents a minimum number of substrings (boxes) over the extended alphabet $\Sigma \cup \{\}$ to be extracted from z; l_{min} and l_{max} denote the minimum and maximum allowed length for boxes, respectively; occurrences of boxes in z may be approximated w.r.t. an error e such that $e_{min} \leq e \leq e_{max}$; finally, the distance separating a generic pair of consecutive boxes must be less than d_{max} and greater than d_{min}.

Definition 2 (Satisfaction): Given a string z over the alphabet Σ, an ordered set of strings P over the alphabet $\Sigma \cup \{\}$, and the extraction constraints $E_c = <n, l_{min}, l_{max}, d_{min}, d_{max}, e_{min}, e_{max}>$, P satisfies E_c on z iff:

1. The cardinality $|P|$ of P is s.t. then $|P| \geq n$
2. For each string p_i in P, with $1 \leq i \leq |P|$, $l_{min} \leq |p_i| \leq l_{max}$
3. For $1 \leq i < |P|-1$, let d_i be the number of symbols in z separating p_i and p_{i+1}, then $d_{min} \leq d_i \leq d_{max}$
4. If e_i is the number of errors in the considered approximate occurrence of p_i in z (according to the given distance measure), then $e_{min} \leq e_i \leq e_{max}$

Example 4: Consider the string $z=abbaaababababbbaba$ on the alphabet $\Sigma=\{a, b\}$, the set of strings $P=<ab\cdot a, b\cdot\cdot a, b\cdot b>$ and the extraction constraints $E_c=<2, 3, 4, 1, 2, 1, 2>$. It is not difficult to see that P satisfies E_c on z, by virtue of the substrings $z_{[1...4]}$, $z_{[7...10]}$ and $z_{[13...15]}$ of z.

Definition 3 (Pattern and Box): Given a string z over the alphabet Σ and the extraction constraints $E_c = <n, l_{min}, l_{max}, d_{min}, d_{max}, e_{min}, e_{max}>$, all the ordered sets P of strings over the alphabet $\Sigma \cup \{\}$ satisfying E_c on z are *patterns* of z. For each such a P, its position is individuated by the leftmost symbol of the leftmost string of P in z. All the strings included in a pattern P are *boxes* of P, thus a pattern is an ordered set of *boxes* satisfying some extraction constraints on an input string. The pattern P will be denoted by $P=<b_1,...,b_k>$ where k is the number of its boxes.

Example 4 (cont'd.) The strings in P are the boxes of the pattern $P=<ab\cdot a, b\cdot\cdot a, b\cdot b>$ of z.

Also for patterns it is possible to define the concept of approximate occurrence, meaning that at least one of its boxes occurs in the string in input, not exactly, but with some errors. In the same way, a pattern satisfies some given extraction constraints on a string if the set of its boxes does.

The given formalization includes a large set of possible specializations. For instance, considering the extraction constraints in which the number of boxes is equal to one and, fixed the minimum and maximum lengths, all the other parameters are zero, the correspondent patterns to discover are strings with exact occurrences in a given input string. In some cases it can also be useful not to specify all the parameters of the extraction constraints, so as to enlarge the class of patterns considered. In this case, we refer to *extended* extraction constraints, where at least one of the parameters is not specified and denoted by '-'. As an example, $E_c = <n, l_{min}, l_{max}, d_{min}, -, e_{min}, e_{max}>$ denote extraction constraints in which the upper bound for the maximum distance between two adjacent boxes is not specified. Obviously, at least one of the parameters has to be in any case specified.

In many contexts the aim is to mine patterns from a set of biosequences, where the structure of the patterns to analyze can change according to the different analyzed cases, from the simplest to the most complicated ones. The problem is therefore to find all the patterns occurring in the given biosequences that can be considered *interesting* according to some predefined criteria. We point out that the simplest criteria to define the concept of *interesting* corresponds to searching for patterns occurring more than a given number of times in the strings in input.

For convention, if a pattern occurs more than once on one of the input strings, only the leftmost occurrence is considered. Indeed, usually, the reason to search for repeated patterns in sets of biosequences is that such patterns can represent biological features that are common to a relevant number of sequences; therefore, further repetitions in the same string are not significant. Thus, the number of occurrences of a pattern in a set of strings is taken to be the number of strings in which such a pattern occurs at least once.

Definition 4 (List of Occurrences): Given a set S of m strings, a pattern P and some extraction constraints E_c, we associate to P a list $L_{S,P,Ec}$ of couples of integer values, each indicating a string of S and the position in such string where the pattern occurs; this list is the *list of occurrences* of the pattern.

Example 5: Consider the set of string $S=\{abbaab,$ $aabba, abbbbb, ababbbab, babaab\}$, the pattern $P=<ab\cdot a>$ and the extraction constraints $E_c=<1, 2,$ $4, 0, 0, 0, 1>$. Observe that P satisfies E_c, having, for example, an occurrence in the first string of S. Then the list is $L_{S,P,Ec}=\{(1,1), (2,2), (4,5), (5,2)\}$.

The only patterns to be considered in the search are the ones occurring in at least one of the strings in input.

Definition 5 (Satisfaction of Some Extraction Constraints by a Pattern P on a Set of Strings): Given a set S of m strings, a pattern P and some extraction constraints E_c, P satisfies E_c on S iff there is at least one string in S where P satisfies E_c.

Now that the reader should have gained a clear vision of several basic concepts, we can continue our discussion by presenting a formalization of the problem of pattern discovery, which aims at including most of its possible instantiations within the biological contexts.

The Problem of Pattern Discovery

Given a set S of m strings, each representing a biosequence and denoted by s_i, with $1\leq i \leq m$, some extraction constraints E_c and a real value q, the problem of pattern discovery consists of extracting all the triplets $<p, L, f_q>$, where p is a pattern, L its list of occurrences and f_q a parameter associated with a value of interest for p, such that:

1. p satisfies E_c on S
2. $f_q \geq q$

Example 6: Consider the following instance of the problem of pattern discovery:

$S=\{babbaab, aabbaa, aabbbbaa, abaaab\text{-}$
$bab, babaab\}$
$E_c = <1, 3, 3, 0, 0, 0, 0>$
$q=4$

Suppose that f_q represents the frequence of occurrences of patterns. The only two patterns that can be considered *interesting* are $p_1=<abb>$, occurring 4 times and having a list of occurrences $L_1=\{(1,2),$ $(2,2), (3,2), (4,5)\}$, and $p_2=<baa>$, occurring 5 times and having a list of occurrences $L_2=\{(1,4),$ $(2,4), (3,6), (4,2), (5,3)\}$. The output is $\{<p_1, L_1,$ $4>, <p_2, L_2, 5>\}$.

The given formalization of the problem of pattern discovery can be useful in analyzing the approaches developed in the last few years towards solving various versions of the problem of mining patterns in biosequences. The next section is devoted to focusing on different ways in which pattern discovery can be applied to solve biological problems.

An Overview of the Proposed Approaches and Applications

We are in the central part of our discussion. In the following, a collection of methods and techniques exploiting pattern discovery to solve biological problems is presented. For all presented approaches, a possible specialization of the general problem of pattern discovery to the specific analyzed case is reported, in order to better focus on the different facets that mining patterns can assume in biological contexts. Notice that the expression of a specific pattern discovery task within our formal framework will not be, in general, unique. For simplicity, in what follows, only one of these specializations is reported. Furthermore, in some few cases, for example, Jonassen, Collins, and Higgins (1995), where the considered pattern classes are rather specific, our formalization turns out to be somehow weaker than needed in order for those approaches to be exactly captured. Indeed, as specified below, to rigorously encode those cases by our formalization scheme, our extraction constraints should be generalized by considering arrays of parameters values in the place of simple values thereof. However, our objective with the proposed formalization is to provide an easy-to-follow roadmap scheme through the diverse approaches to pattern extraction that have been proposed recently, rather than a completely general scheme precisely accounting for all of them. In this respect, a more complex extraction constraint scheme is arguably less suitable to serve our declared purpose than the one we have chosen to adopt.

RNA and proteins are encoded as sequences that can be also used to predict structures and functions of the corresponding macromolecules. In particular, the prediction of biological properties of proteins from their amino acid sequences can be made easier by grouping proteins in families, where the members of a family have similar structures. Indeed, if the structures of some members of a family are known, then the structures of the other members, for which only the sequences are known, can be in some cases obtained in an easier way. Protein family databases (Bateman, Coin, Durbin, Finn, Hollich, & Griffiths-Jones, 2004; Hulo et al., 2004) are available online, and an interesting task is finding common features in a family of functionally related proteins, since this implies that such features are important for the biological functions of that family. In some cases, this problem can be dealt with by aligning the sequences and looking for any conserved (i.e., common) blocks amongst aligned sequences; however, the sequences are not always easy to align since the conserved regions may be very short or repeated within the proteins. In this context, pattern discovery can be a successful solution to individuate common sequence patterns or motifs in groups of protein sequences that possibly reflect the presence of common ancestry or the conservative evolutionary pressure to maintain functionally important parts of the protein.

In Jonassen et al. (1995) a program, called Pratt, is presented that, given a set of unaligned protein sequences, which are sequences that have not been processed by any alignment algorithm to find the subsequences that better match, finds what the authors call *patterns* by matching a minimum number of these sequences. Note that this notion of a pattern is slightly different from the one presented here, as will be apparent below.

The user specifies the minimum number of sequences to be matched and the class of pattern to be searched for. Specifically, patterns that can be discovered by Pratt can be written in the form:

$$p = A_1\text{-}x(i_1, j_1)\text{-}A_2\text{-}x(i_2, j_2)\text{-}....A_{p-1}\text{-}x(i_{p-1}, j_{p-1})\text{-}A_p$$

where $A_1, ..., A_p$ are nonempty sets of amino acids, also called *components* of the pattern, and $i_1 \leq j_1$, $i_2 \leq j_2, ..., i_{p-1} \leq j_{p-1}$ are integers. Each A_k can either specify one amino acid, for example, C, or one out of a set of amino acids, for example *[ILVF]*; a pattern component A_k is an *identity component* if it specifies exactly one amino acid (for instance C or L), or an *ambiguous component* if it specifies more than one (for instance *[ILVF]* or *[FWY]*). The syntactic $x(i_k, j_k)$ specifies a wildcard region in the pattern made of from i_k to j_k arbitrary amino acids. A wildcard region $x(i_k, j_k)$ is *flexible* if j_k is bigger than i_k (for example $x(2,3)$). If j_k is equal to i_k, for example, $x(2,2)$ which can be written as $x(2)$, then the wildcard region is *fixed*. Biologically, considering variable spaces among regions is important. The purpose of Jonassen (1995) is to compile, from a set of protein sequences in input, a list of the most significant patterns (according to a nonstatistical significance measure) found to be matching at least for the user-defined minimum number of sequences. As already mentioned, our formalization does not allow to precisely capture such an extraction semantics. However, such patterns can be approximately encoded within our framework as follows. Given a set of strings S, the extraction constraints $E_c = <p, 1, 1, min (i_k),$ $max(j_k), 0, [A_k]_{max} - 1>$, for $1 \leq k \leq p$, and a value f_q, Pratt returns in output those patterns satisfying E_c and such that f_q is greater than a fixed threshold (we remind the reader that f_q is, in general, a function value according to which it is possible to discern whether a pattern is *interesting* for the specific analyzed problem). In particular, the number of components in a pattern is p, that is, the number of identity or ambiguous components; their length is fixed to be equal to 1; the distances between boxes express, in this case, the flexibility of the wildcard regions, thus they are bounded, respectively, by the minimum of the i_ks and the maximum of the j_ks; the number of errors might be zero, if all components are identity ones, or it is bounded by the maximum number of amino acids that can be specified in the ambiguous component (denoted by $[A_k]_{max}$) minus one (if the component A_k is ambiguous, then it specifies at least two different amino acids, thus the matching error is at least one); finally, f_q is a function of both the number of matched sequences and the pattern itself. Note that, formalizing the problem in this way, the class of patterns satisfying the extraction constrains might be larger than the one extracted by Jonassen et al. (1995). The basic algorithm in Pratt uses the block data structure when exploring the space of a restricted class of patterns. This is a variation of the algorithm in Neuwald and Green (1994), developed in order to allow for more general ambiguous positions and for variable length wildcard regions. The authors show that Pratt is able to retrieve known motifs for PROSITE families and has been also successfully applied to several known protein families.

Let us now to turn our attention to so-called *tandem repeats*. DNA can be subject to different mutational events. Tandem repeats occur when a sequence of two or more nucleotides is converted in two or more copies, each following contiguously the preceding one. As an example, the sequence *TCGGCGGCGGA* presents three copies of the triplet *CGG*: such a sequence, ob-

tained by duplication of *CGG* in three copies, is a tandem repeat. Moreover, since during the copying process further mutations can occur, also approximate copies of nucleotide sequences have to be considered. In other words, a tandem repeat is a string that involves consecutive (either exact or approximate) occurrences of a substring. Therefore, a tandem repeat is a pattern satisfying the extraction constraints $E_c = <2, 3, 3, 0, 0, 0,$ $e_{max}>$ on a DNA sequence. Researches on human genome proved that tandem repeats can be useful in human genetic analysis, for example they can be applied directly to problems of human identification, including parenthood testing (Jeffreys, Wilson, & Thein, 1985a; Jeffreys, Wilson, & Thein, 1985b). Furthermore, tandem repeats can be associated with human diseases caused by triplet repeat expansion (Benson, 1997; Kolpakov, Bana & Kucherov, 2003), such as Huntington Chorea or Myotonic Dystrophy. In Benson (1999) an algorithm is proposed to find tandem repeats in DNA sequences without the necessity to specify either the pattern or pattern size. The algorithm is based on the detection of k-tuple matches, and uses a probabilistic model of tandem repeats and a collection of statistical criteria based on that model. The program presented in Benson (1999) has both a detection and an analysis components. The detection component uses a set of statistically based criteria to find candidate tandem repeats, the analysis component attempts to produce an alignment for each candidate and, if successful, gathers a number of statistics about the alignment and the nucleotide sequence. The program was tested on human genes obtained from GenBank. In Hauth and Joseph (2002) an algorithm to identify two important complex pattern structures, that are, *variable length tandem repeats (VLTRs)* and *multi-period tandem repeats (MPTRs)*, is presented, and three application examples are given. A VLTR is a simple nested tandem repeat in which the copy number for some pattern is variable rather than constant, an MPTR is formed by the nested concatenation of two or more similar patterns. The repeats considered in Hauth and Joseph (2002) contain substitutions, insertions and deletions, and the three reported examples are a bovine sequence containing a highly conserved VLTR, a human sequence containing an MPTR region and an analysis of yeast chromosome I, in which there are similar regions. The main tasks of the algorithm of Hauth and Joseph (2002) refer to both locating and characterizing regions, similarly to Benson (1999), in that they analyze k-length substrings in a DNA sequence by finding recurring distances between identical substrings. The difference is that Hauth and Joseph (2002) does not use any statistical models to locate interesting periods, but rather a filter coupled with techniques to data mine sequence differences. The work presented in Gusfield and Stoye (2004) focuses on the problem of extracting a *vocabulary* of tandem repeats of a string, where a vocabulary is defined as a list reporting the start location and the length of different tandem repeat types. The definition of tandem repeats given in Gusfield and Stoye (2004) is a bit more general than the previous one reported here, since they consider a tandem repeat to be a string $\alpha\alpha$, where α is a non-empty string. Thus, two tandem repeats $\alpha\alpha$ and $\alpha'\alpha'$ are of different type iff $\alpha \neq \alpha'$. The authors propose a linear-time and space algorithm to find the vocabulary of an input string, based on a three-phase approach. In particular, during Phase I a subset of the occurrences of tandem repeats is found, then Phase II finds the end locations in the suffix tree of the input string for some of the tandem repeat types. Finally, Phase III traverses parts of the suffix tree from the endpoints found in phase II, to obtain the complete vocabulary of tandem repeats. In other words, the suffix tree of the input string is *decorated* with the endpoint of each tandem repeat in its vocabulary, compactly representing all the different tandem repeat types and the locations where they occur in the input string.

Other important applications of pattern discovery are in gene regulation. In fact, the regulation mechanisms of gene expression are not yet fully understood, and the identification of upstream regulatory sequences is not a simple task. In particular, the controls acting on gene expression (i.e., the ability of a gene to produce a biologically active protein) are much more complex in eukaryotes (complex organisms, such as, mammals) than in prokaryotes organisms (unicellular organisms), due to the presence of nuclear membranes preventing the two phases of transcription and translation to occur simultaneously as in prokaryotes. Proteins that activate or repress transcription by binding to short, specific DNA sequences is often regulated by gene expression. Such cis-acting sites are usually located close to the promoter (RNA polymerase binding site) for the regulated gene. Regulatory regions are thus regions associated with a gene to which proteins bind, regulating that gene expression. Promoter regions in DNA sequences are not always expressed exactly by the same sequence, thus their identification can be difficult. Although promoter regions vary, it is usually possible to find a DNA sequence (called the *consensus* sequence) encoding common subsequences thereof. For example, the consensus in the bacterium Escherichia coli, based on the study of *263* promoters, is *TTGACA* followed by *17* uncorrelated base pairs, followed by *TATAAT*, with the latter, called *TATA* box, located about *10* bases upstream of the transcription start site. None of the *263* promoter regions *exactly* match the above consensus sequence. Eukaryotic is more complicated than prokaryotic transcription regulation, since promoter sequences contain one or two boxes recognized by the same protein, but there may be more regulatory sites, appearing sometimes repeated, which are recognized by distinct proteins that interact with one another. In this context, an interesting problem is the discovery of motifs in the upstream regions shared by a given group of genes having common biological function or regulation. In Brazma (1998b) a sequence pattern discovery algorithm is described that searches exhaustively for a priori unknown regular expression patterns that are over-represented in a given set of sequences. The algorithm was applied to discovery patterns both in the complete set of sequences taken upstream of the putative yeast genes and in the regions upstream of the genes with similar expression profiles. The algorithm is able to discover various subclasses of regular expression type patterns of unlimited length common to as few as ten sequences from thousands. In particular, it was able to predict regulatory elements from gene upstream regions in the yeast Saccharomyces cerevisiae. Errors are allowed in the search, represented by wildcard positions. According to our notation, the problem dealt with in Brazma et al. (1998b) consists in discovering those patterns satisfying the extraction constraints $E_c = <2, 1, -, 0, d_{max}, 0, e_{max}>$, and such that the concept of *interest* is related, in this case, to the number of input sequences where the pattern P occurs and also to the specific positions where the errors appear. Those are, in some cases, fixed in the box included in the pattern and restricted to subsets of the alphabet in input (they call such sets of possible symbol substitutions *character groups*, referring to wildcards of fixed lengths). The paper by Jensen and Knudsen (2000) also deserves mentioning. It proposes two word-analysis algorithms for the automatic discovery of regulatory sequence elements, applied to the Saccharomyces cerevisiae genome and publicly available DNA array data sets. The approach relies on the functional annotation of genes. The aim is the identification of patterns that are over-represented in a set of sequences (positive set) compared to a reference set (negative set). In this case, the authors consider four numbers to decide whether a pattern is significantly overrepresented. The first represents the number of sequences in the positive set that contains the pattern; the second is the number of sequences in the negative set that contains the pattern; the last two denote the number of sequences in each of the two sets that do not contain the pattern. Distributions on such numbers are used to compute the significance

potential of being overrepresented for a pattern of fixed length, and then analyze all correlations found to have a significance potential of at least four. Some possible extraction constraints for the problem dealt with in Jensen (2000) are $E_c = <1, 4, k, 0, 0, 0, 0>$, observing that, in that algorithm, there is no specified minimal pattern length. In the paper, the authors also claim that, even if also patterns of length *1* are analyzed, patterns shorter than *4* nucleotides are not to be considered significant. In the same paper, two further techniques are presented. The first one consists in a systematic analysis of functional annotation, whereas the second aims at computing the significance of a given pattern using Kolmogorov-Smirnov statistics on DNA array data. The main experimental result presented in Jensen (2000) is the discovery of a highly conserved 9-mer occurring in the upstream regions of genes coding for proteasomal subunits, that is, the consensus sequence GGTGGCAAA, and several other putative and known regulatory elements. In particular, for the Cbf1p-Met2p-Met28p complex and MCB, patterns similar to AAAATTTT have been picked up by all three methods presented in Jensen (2000), and the pattern GTGACTCA as consensus sequence for Cbf1p-Met2p-Met28p and Met31p/Met32p has been found to have significant correlation to methionine biosynthesis.

In the context of regulatory processes for promoter regions, other approaches have been proposed, sometimes considering quite complex pattern structures. It can be observed that, the more an organism is complicated in terms of regulatory processes, the more the corresponding patterns to be searched for are characterized by the presence of complex structures. In Marsan and Sagot (2000) the authors address the problem of extracting consensus motifs for DNA binding sites, introducing two exact algorithms to extract conserved patterns from a set of DNA sequences. The patterns they search for have complex structures and are named *structured motifs*. Structured motifs may be described as an ordered collection of $p{\geq}1$ boxes, p substitution rates (one for each box) and $p-1$ intervals of distance (one for each pair of successive boxes in the collection). A suffix tree generalized on a set of N sequences is used for finding such motifs, building first single *models* of fixed length. For each node occurrence of this first box, considered in turn, a jump is made in the tree down to the descendants situated at lower levels. The second algorithm differs from the first one since it passes through the nodes at the lower levels, grabbing some information the nodes contain and jumping back up to the higher level again. Both algorithms time complexity scales linearly with N^2n, where n is the average length of the sequences and N their number. An application to the identification of promoter and regulatory consensus sequences in bacterial genomes is also shown. In particular, interesting considerations concerning the achieved results for E. coli set of non-coding sequences between divergent genes might be drawn. In fact, it has been experimentally observed in Marsan and Sagot (2000) that extracting a promoter consensus sequence for the organism E. coli seems much harder than for other organisms, although E. coli is believed to have less promoter sequence families. This may suggest that, for example, the promoter family called σ^{70} is more degenerate in E. coli than in the other organisms, and that it may contain more elements. Improvements to the techniques presented in Marsan and Sagot (2000) are illustrated in Carvalho, Freitas, Oliveira, and Sagot (2005) where a new data structure, called *box-link*, is used to store the information about conserved regions that occur in a well-ordered and regularly spaced manner in the dataset sequences. In Eskin (2002) an algorithm to discover composite motifs, named MITRA (MIsmatch TRee Algorithm), is proposed. The algorithm has two steps: in the first step, the problem of finding a larger simple motif (called *monad* in the paper) by preprocessing input data is considered; the preprocessing concatenates the various parts of the pattern into a set of virtual monads. In the second step, an exhaustive monad discovery algorithm is applied on the set of virtual monads. The authors define a "monad pattern discovery problem", representing patterns as *l-mers*, that are, continuous strings of length l, and defining the concept of *(l,d)-neighborhood* of an *l-mer P* to represent all possible *l-mers* with up to d mismatches as compared to *P*. They search for all *l-mers* that occur with up to d mismatches at least a fixed number of times in an input string. This problem can be easily related to the one described in this chapter, involving sets of sequences, simply using, in the place of the input string, the set of its suffixes. MITRA was evaluated on biological samples, applying it to upstream regions of orthologous genes with known motifs. Also Terracina (2005) addresses the problem of extracting frequent structured patterns, considering both exact and approximate repetitions within a set of sequences in input. In particular, the proposed approach allows the discovery of structured motifs composed of r highly conserved regions, separated by constrained spacers. Moreover, approximate repetitions are considered for each conserved region, allowing a maximum number e of errors, where e is a user-specified parameter. The approach exploits compact tries as support index structures and represents structured patterns as cross-links between trie nodes. Moreover, the concept of *e-neighbor pattern* is introduced allowing the approach to be made independent of the alphabet exploited to express input strings. Tests were reported both on synthetic data and on biological data, exploiting, in the former ones, the noncoding regions from the whole genomes of *B. subtilis*, *H. Pylori* and *E. coli*. The work of Fassetti (2006) represents an extension of Terracina (2005), providing an algorithm for the identification of novel classes of structured motifs, where several kinds of "exceptions" (whose biological relevance recently emerged in the literature) may be tolerated in pattern repetitions, such as skips between boxes, box swaps and box inverse. The papers by Carvalho et al. (2005), Eskin and Pevzner (2002), Fassetti, Greco, and Terracina (2006), Marsan and Sagot (2000), and Terracina (2005) all deal with a common version of the problem of pattern discovery, where the extraction constraints are of the type $E_c = <2, 1, l_{max}, d_{min}, d_{max}, e_{min}, e_{max}>$ and the *interest* for the patterns is related to the frequency of their occurrences.

In Palopoli, Rombo, and Terracina (2005) an approach is presented concerned with the definition and the implementation of a framework allowing for defining and resolving under-specified motif extraction problems where, for instance, the number and the length of boxes can be variable. The method is based on the observation that approaches presented in the literature are often tailored on specific classes of patterns and, as with most algorithms, even slight changes in the pattern class to be dealt with may cause significant problems in their effectiveness. In other words, algorithms are available that are efficient and effective when the class of patterns of interest is quite well defined, but when the class of interest is unknown the problem can shift away from motif extraction to the selection of the right approach to apply. The framework proposed in Palopoli et al. (2005) is general in that it covers a wide range of pattern classes, and the computed results can be exploited to guide the selection of specific, efficient, algorithms tailored on the resulting pattern classes. Moreover, it can be exploited as a "fast prototyping" approach to quickly verify the relevance of new pattern classes in specific biological domains. This framework is based on automatically generating logic programs starting from user-defined under-specified extraction problems for locating various kinds of motifs in a set of sequences. According to our formalization, the most general form of extraction constraints $E_c = <n, l_{min}, l_{max}, d_{min}, d_{max}, e_{min}, e_{max}>$ can be associated with this approach, since it includes a large number of pattern classes.

EMERGENT AND FUTURE TRENDS

This is the final part of our narration, and we can discuss some of the approaches recently emerging in this fascinating field. In the works presented in the third section, the concept of *interest* for patterns was usually related to the frequency of occurrences, that is, patterns were *interesting* if they were over-represented in a given set of sequences. In many biological contexts though, patterns occurring unexpectedly, often or rarely, often called *surprising words*, can be associated with important biological meanings, for example, they can be representative of elements having patterns repeated surprisingly differently from the rest of population due to some disease or genetic malformation. Distance measures based not only on the frequency of occurrences of a pattern, but also on its expectation, are assuming a fundamental role in these emergent studies. Thus, *interesting* patterns can be patterns such that the difference between observed and expected counts, usually normalized to some suitable moment, are beyond some preset threshold. The increasing volumes of available biological data makes exhaustive statistical tables become excessively large to guarantee practical accessibility and usefulness. In Apostolico, Bock, and Lonardi (2003) the authors study probabilistic models and scores for which the population of potentially surprising words in a sequence can be described by a table of size at worst linear in the length of that sequence, supporting linear time and space algorithms for their construction. The authors consider as candidate surprising words, only the members of an a priori (i.e., before any score is computed) identified set of representative strings, where the cardinality of that set is linear in the input sequence length. The construction is based on the constraint that the score is monotonic in each class of related strings described by such a score. In the direction of extracting over-represented motifs, the authors of Apostolico, Comin, and Parida (2005) introduce and study a characterization of *extensible motifs* in a sequence which tightly combines the structure of the pattern, as described by its syntactic specification, with the statistical measure of its occurrence count. They show that a prudent combination of saturation conditions (expressed in terms of minimum number of don't care compatible with a given list of occurrences) and monotonicity of probabilistic scores over regions of constant frequency afford significant parsimony in the generation and testing of candidate over-represented motifs. The approach is validated by tests on protein sequence families reported in the PROSITE database. In both the approaches illustrated in Apostolico et al. (2003) and Apostolico et al. (2005), the concept of interestingness is related to the concept of surprise. The main difference between them is that the former aims at showing how the number of over- and under-represented words in a sequence can be bound and computed in efficient time and space, if the scores under consideration grow monotonically, a condition that is met by many scores; the latter presents a novel way to embody both statistical and structural features of patterns in one measure of surprise.

If the emergent trends underline the importance of making the search for motifs occurring unexpectedly often or rarely in a given set of sequences in input efficient, further studies are driven towards the characterization of patterns representing outliers for a given population, looking at the structure of the pattern as the key to detect unexpected properties possessed by a single individual, being object of examination, belonging to a large reference collection of categorical data. Moreover, the complexity of biological processes, such as gene regulation and transcription, in eukaryotes organisms, leaves many challenges still open and requires the proposal of new and more efficient techniques to solve particular problems, such as the computation of distances on specific classes of patterns, or of operations on boxes more complex than swaps or skips.

CONCLUSION

The ever-increasing growth of the amount of biological data that are available and stored in biological databases, significant especially after the completion of human genome sequencing, has stimulated the development of new and efficient techniques to extract useful knowledge from biological data. Indeed, the availability of enormous volumes of data does not provide "per se" any increase in available information. Rather, suitable methods are needed to interpret them.

A particular class of biological data is biosequences, denoting DNA or protein sequences, and characterized by the presence of regular expressions associated with the presence of similar biological functions in the different macromolecules. Such regularities can be represented by substrings, that are, patterns, common to a number of sequences, meaning that sequences sharing common patterns are associated with a common biological function in the corresponding biological components.

The main aim of this chapter is that of addressing the problem of mining patterns that can be considered *interesting*, according to some predefined criteria, from a set of biosequences. First, some basic notions and definitions have been provided concerning concepts both derived from string matching and from pattern discovery for sets of sequences. Then, since in many biological problems such as, for example, gene regulation, the structure of the repeated patterns in the sequences can be fixed for the generic case, and maybe also complex and vary with the different analyzed cases, an intuitive formalization of the problem has been given considering structural properties in which parameters related to the structure of the patterns to search for can be specified according to the specific problem. This formalization aimed at guiding the reader in the discussion put forward about a number of approaches to pattern discovery that have been presented in the literature in recent years. The approaches regarded fundamental areas of application of pattern discovery in biosequences, such as protein family characterization, tandem repeats and gene regulation. A further section has been devoted to pointing out emergent approaches, dealing with the extraction of patterns occurring unexpectedly often or rarely and to pointing out possible future developments.

As a final remark, it is worth pointing out that mining patterns is central as well w.r.t. many biological applications. It has been applied to solve different problems involving sets of sequences, as an alternative to other existing methods (e.g., sequence alignment) but, especially, as a powerful technique to discover important properties from large data bunches. Biology is an evolving science, and emerging biological data are, in some cases, sets of aggregate objects rather than just biosequences. Therefore, it is anticipated that a very interesting evolution of the problem of pattern discovery presented in this chapter consists in its extension to more structured cases, involving objects that cannot be encoded as simple sequences of symbols.

REFERENCES

Altschul, S. F., Gish, W., Miller, W., Myers, E. W., & Lipman, D. J. (1990). Basic local alignment search tool. *Journal of Molecular Biology, 215,* 403-410.

Altschul, S. F., Madden, T. L., Schaffer, A. A., Zhang, J., Anang, Z., Miller, W., & Lipman, D. J. (1997). Gapped blast and psi-blast: A new generation of protein database search programs. *Nucleic Acids Research, 25,* 3389-3402.

Apostolico, A. (1985). The myriad virtues of subword trees. In A. Apostolico & Z. Galil (Eds.), *Combinatorial algorithms on words* (*12*, pp. 85-96). Springer-Verlag Publishing.

Apostolico, A., Bock, M. L., & Lonardi, S. (2003). Monotony of surprise and large-scale quest for unusual words. *Journal of Computational Biology 10*(3/4), 283-311.

Apostolico, A., & Crochemore, M. (2000). String pattern matching for a deluge survival kit. In P. M. Pardalos, J. Abello, & M. G. C. Resende (Eds.), *Handbook of massive data sets.* Kluwer Academic Publishers.

Apostolico, A., Comin, M., & Parida, L. (2005). Conservative extraction of over-represented extensible motifs. *ISMB* (Supplement of Bioinformatics), 9-18.

Apostolico, A., Iliopoulos, C., Landau, G., Schieber, B., & Vishkin, U. (1988). Parallel construction of a suffix tree with applications. *Algorithmica, 3,* 347-365.

Bateman, A., Coin, L., Durbin, R., Finn, R. D., Hollich, V., Griffiths-Jones, S., Khanna, A., Marshall, M., Moxon, S., Sonnhammer, E. L. L., Studholme, D. J., Yeats, C., & Eddy, S. R. (2004). The pfam protein families database. *Nucleic Acids Research, 32,* 138-141.

Benson, D. A., Mizrachi, I. K., Lipman, D. J., Ostell, J., & Wheeler, D. L. (2005). Genbank. *Nucleic Acids Research, 33.*

Benson, G. (1997). Sequence alignment with tandem duplication. *Journal of Computational Biology, 4*(3), 351-67.

Benson, G. (1999). Tandem repeats finder: A program to analyze DNA sequences. *Nucleic Acids Research, 27*(2), 573–580.

Berg, J., & Lassig, M. (2004). Local graph alignment and motif search in biological networks. In *Proceedings of the National Academy of Sciences of the United States of America,* (pp. 14689-14694).

Berman, H. M., Bourne, P. E., & Westbrook, J. (2004). The pdb: A case study in management of community data. *Current Proteomics, 1*, 49-57.

Brazma, A., Jonassen, I., Eidhammer, I., & Gilbert, D. (1998). Approaches to the automatic discovery of patterns in biosequences. *Journal of Computational Biology, 5*(2), 277-304.

Brazma, A., Jonassen, I., Vilo, J., & Ukkonen, E. (1998). Predicting gene regulatory elements in silico on a genomic scale. *Genome Research, 8*(11), 1998.

Carvalho, A. M., Freitas, A. T., Oliveira, A. L., & Sagot, M. F. (2005). A highly scalable algorithm for the extraction of cis-regulatory regions. In *Proceedings of the 3rd Asia-Pacific Bioinformatics Conference* (pp. 273-282).

Elloumi, M., & Maddouri, M. (2005). New voting strategies designed for the classification of nucleic sequences. *Knowledge and Information Systems, 1*, 1-15.

Eskin, E., & Pevzner, P. A. (2002). Finding composite regulatory patterns in DNA sequences. *Bioinformatics, 18*(Suppl. 1), S354-63.

Fassetti, F., Greco, G., & Terracina, G. (2006). Efficient discovery of loosely structured motifs in biological data. In *Proceedings of the 21st Annual ACM Symposium on Applied Computing,* (pp. 151-155).

Fredkin, E. (1960). Trie memory. *Communications of the ACM, 3*(9), 490-499.

Gusfield, D. (Ed.). (1997). *Algorithms on strings, trees and sequences: Computer science and computational biology.* Cambrige University Press.

Gusfield, D., & Stoye, J. (2004). Linear time algorithms for finding and representing all the tandem repeats in a string. *Journal of Computer and System Sciences, 69*, 525-546.

Hauth, A. M., & Joseph, D. A. (2002). Beyond tandem repeats: Complex pattern structures and distant regions of similarity. *Bioinformatics, 18*(1), 31-37.

Hu, H., Yan, X., Huang, Y., Han, J., & Zhou, X., J. (2005). Mining coherent dense subgraphs across massive biological networks for functional discovery. *Bioinformatics, 18*(1), 31-37.

Hulo, N., Sigrist, C. J. A., Le Saux, V., Langendijk-Genevaux, P. S., Bordoli, L., Gattiker, A., De Castro, E., Bucher, P., & Bairoch, A. (2004). Recent improvements to the PROSITE database. *Nucleic Acids Research, 32*, 134-137.

Kolpakov, R. M., Bana, G. & Kucherov, G. (2003). Mreps: Efficient and flexible detection of tandem repeats in DNA. *Nucleic Acids Research, 31*(13), 3672-3678.

Koyuturk, M., Kim, Y., Subramaniam, S., Szpankowski, W. & Grama, A. (2006). *Journal of Computational Biology, 13*(7), 1299-1322.

Jeffreys, A. J., Wilson, V., & Thein, S. L. (1985). Hypervariable "minisatellite" regions in human DNA. *Nature, 314*(6006), 67-73.

Jeffreys, A. J., Wilson, V., & Thein, S. L. (1985). Individual-specific "fingerprints" of human DNA. *Nature, 316*(6023), 76-9.

Jensen, L. J., & Knudsen, S. (2000). Automatic discovery of regulatory patterns in promoter regions based on whole cell expression data and functional annotation. *Bioinformatics, 16*(4), 326-333.

Jonassen, I., Collins, J. F., & Higgins, D.G. (1995). Finding flexible patterns in unaligned protein sequences. *Protein Science, 4*, 1587-1595.

Lesk, A. (Ed.). (2004). *Introduction to protein science architecture, function, and genomics.* Oxford University Press.

Liu, H., & Wong, L. (2003). Data mining tools for biological sequences. *Journal of Bioinformatics and Computational Biology, 1*(1), 139-167.

Marsan, L., & Sagot, M. F. (2000). Algorithms for extracting structured motifs using a suffix tree with application to promoter and regulatory site consensus identification. *Journal of Computational Biology, 7,* 345-360.

McCreight, E. M. (1976). A space-economical suffix tree construction algorithm. *Journal of the ACM, 23*(2), 262-272.

Morrison, D. R. (1968). Patricia: Practical algorithm to retrieve information coded in alphanumeric. *Journal of the ACM, 15*(4), 514-534.

Neuwald, A. F., & Green, P. (1994). Detecting patterns in protein sequences. *Journal of Molecular. Biology, 239* (5), 698-712.

Pal, K. P., Mitra, P., & Pal, S. K. (2004). *Pattern recognition algorithms for data mining.* CRC Press.

Palopoli, L., Rombo, S., & Terracina, G. (2005). In M.-S. Hacid, N. V. Murray, Z. W. Ras, & S. Tsumoto (Ed.) *Flexible pattern discovery with (extended) disjunctive logic programming.* (pp. 504-513). Lecture Notes in Computer Science.

Rigoutsos, I., Floratos, A., Parida, L., Gao, Y., & Platt, D. (2000). The emergence of pattern discovery techniques in computational biology. *Journal of Metabolic Engineering, 2*(3), 159-177.

Terracina, G. (2005). A fast technique for deriving frequent structured patterns from biological data sets. *New Mathematics and Natural Computation, 1*(2), 305-327.

Ukkonen, E. (1995). On-line construction of suffix trees. *Algorithmica, 14*(3), 249-260.

Vilo, J. (2002). *Pattern discovery from biosequences.* Academic Dissertation, University of Helsinki, Finland. Retrieved March 15, 2007, from http://ethesis.helsinki.fi/julkaisut/mat/tieto/vk/vilo/

Wang, J., Shapiro, B., & Shasha, D. (Eds.). (1999). *Pattern discovery in biomolecular data: Tools, techniques and applications.* New York: Oxford University Press.

Chapter V
Finding Patterns in Class–Labeled Data Using Data Visualization

Gregor Leban
University of Ljubljana, Slovenia

Minca Mramor
University of Ljubljana, Slovenia

Blaž Zupan
University of Ljubljana, Slovenia

Janez Demšar
University of Ljubljana, Slovenia

Ivan Bratko
University of Ljubljana, Slovenia

ABSTRACT

Data visualization plays a crucial role in data mining and knowledge discovery. Its use is however often difficult due to the large number of possible data projections. Manual search through such sets of projections can be prohibitively timely or even impossible, especially in the data analysis problems that comprise many data features. The chapter describes a method called VizRank, which can be used to automatically identify interesting data projections for multivariate visualizations of class-labeled data. VizRank assigns a score of interestingness to each considered projection based on the degree of separation of data instances with different class label. We demonstrate the usefulness of this approach on six cancer gene expression datasets, showing that the method can reveal interesting data patterns and can further be used for data classification and outlier detection.

INTRODUCTION

Data visualization can be a powerful tool for extracting knowledge from data. When displaying the right set of features, data visualization can uncover interesting and potentially useful patterns present in the data. The quality of visualization, and with it the clarity and interestingness of displayed patterns, depends on the particular set of visualized features and on the selected visualization method. The goal of data mining related to visualization is thus to identify relevant features and find the projections that uncover the patterns hidden in the data.

The notion of interestingness in the data depends on the type of data-mining task. In case of unsupervised data mining, that is, considering unlabeled (classless) data, interesting projections are those that show unusual trends, clusters of points or identify outliers. In supervised data mining, where data is annotated with class information, interesting projections are those where data instances of the same class are grouped and well separated from instances of other classes. Such projections can explain the role of various features, help us visually induce rules for discriminating between classes, and can even be used to predict the class label of a new data instance. In this chapter, we focus on supervised data mining and describe an automated approach that can find interesting data visualizations.

Today many popular visualization techniques are available to data miners, including one- and two-dimensional visualization methods like histograms, pie charts, scatterplots, and multidimensional visualizations like radviz, polyviz, parallel coordinates and survey plots (Harris, 1999). Multidimensional methods depict relations between several features at once and are more expressive than low-dimensional visualizations, which are more widely used due to their simplicity and wide availability in popular data analysis tools. Multidimensional visualizations can also become harder to interpret with increasing number of visualized features. A more important reason that limits the use of multidimensional visualizations is, however, the abundance of possible projections that can be used. For a low-dimensional visualization a data miner only needs to select a feature or (at most) a pair of features that yield an interesting and informative plot. For a visualization of multiple features, a correspondingly larger subset of features needs to be selected, properly arranged and optimized. Selecting an appropriate set of features is, as we also show in this chapter, far from trivial and most often cannot be done manually.

We have recently developed a method called VizRank (Leban, Zupan, Vidmar, & Bratko, 2006) that can search for interesting multidimensional visualizations of class-labeled data. VizRank assigns the "interestingness" score to projections based on how well they separate instances of different classes. Among many possible projections, the user is then presented only with a small subset of best-scored visualizations that provide the most informative insight into the data. For example, Figure 1 shows four different scatterplot projections of the microarray data from leukemia tissue samples (Golub, Slonim, Tamayo, Huard, Gaasenbeek, & Mesirov, 1999). The data set it considers consists of 7,071 features (gene expression measurements) and 72 data instances (tissue samples). The scatterplots in Figure 1 show the worst, two medium, and the best-ranked projection by VizRank. While in the best ranked-projection (Figure 1(d)) the separation between two classes (ALL and AML) is very clear and the visualization clearly suggests a classification rule, there is no such separation in the worst ranked projection. It is obvious that the choice of features to be displayed in the visualization can largely impact the utility of the visualization.

Also notice that with 7,071 features there are 7,071*7,070/2= 24,995,985 possible two-feature projections. Manual search among this many scatterplots is clearly unfeasible. VizRank automates this search, and uses a heuristic to inspect only

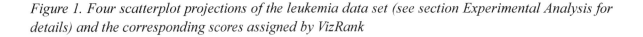

Figure 1. Four scatterplot projections of the leukemia data set (see section Experimental Analysis for details) and the corresponding scores assigned by VizRank

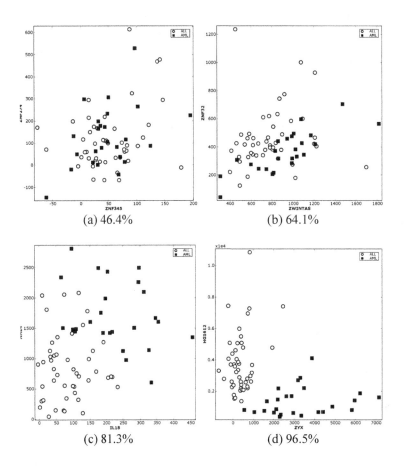

(a) 46.4%　　　　　　　　　　(b) 64.1%

(c) 81.3%　　　　　　　　　　(d) 96.5%

a small subset of candidate projection. In this chapter, we introduce the visualization techniques used together with VizRank, in detail describe VizRank's scoring algorithm and heuristic search technique, and demonstrate its utility on the analysis of various cancer microarray datasets, which recently gained substantial attention in data mining community and pose specific problems to data analysis due to inclusion of many features.

VISUALIZATION METHODS

A large number of techniques for visualizing multidimensional data are today available to data miners. Utilizing several taxonomies based on Keim and Kriegel (1996), we can classify all techniques into five different groups: geometric, pixel-oriented, icon-based, hierarchical, and graph based techniques.

VizRank can be applied to geometric visualization methods where data instances are visualized as points and the values of visualized features only influence the position of the point and not its size, shape or color (symbol's properties can, however, be used to represent class value). Examples of such methods that will be shown in this chapter are scatterplot, radviz, and polyviz. Since scatterplot is a well-known technique, we will only describe the latter two techniques.

Radviz (Hoffman, Grinstein, & Pinkney, 1999) is a nonlinear visualization method where the visualized features are represented as anchor points equally spaced around the perimeter of a unit circle. Data instances are shown as points inside the circle, with their positions determined by a metaphor from physics (see Brunsdon, Fotheringham, & Charlton, 1998) for a formal definition): each data point is held in place with springs that are at one end attached to the point and at the other to the feature anchors. The stiffness of each spring is proportional to the value of the corresponding feature and the point ends up at the equilibrium position. Prior to visualizing, the values of each feature are usually scaled to the interval between 0 and 1 to make all features equally influential. Figure 2(a) shows a radviz plot for the leukemia data set introduced in the chapter's first section, with lines representing springs for the selected data point. Radviz projection is defined by the selection of features that are visualized and by their specific order on the unit circle. The number of different projections can be very large: for a data set with n features, there are $n!/[2m(n-m)!]$ different radviz projections with m features. For illustration, for a thousand-feature data set there are more than 166 millions different three-feature projections. To obtain a six-featured visualization such as the one from Figure 2(a), one has to choose from 10^{22} different projections.

The polyviz visualization method (Hoffman et al., 1999) can be seen as an extension of the radviz method where each visualized feature is represented with an edge of a polygon and the ends of the edge represent the minimum and maximum values of that feature. When visualizing a data instance, first the appropriate position on each edge is determined based on the values of the data instance. These edge positions are then considered as anchors and the same principle as in radviz is applied, where each anchor attracts the data point with a force proportional to the feature value. A short line is usually drawn from the anchor position on the edge towards the final position of the point, which allows us to observe distribution of values along each edge (feature). An example of a polyviz plot of the cancer microarray data set (MLL data, see experimental analysis for description) that contains eight features and has an excellent class separation is shown in Figure 2(b).

Figure 2. A radviz projection of the leukemia data set (a) and polyviz projection of the MLL data set (b). Springs with corresponding feature values are drawn for one data instance (see section Experimental Analysis for description of the data sets)

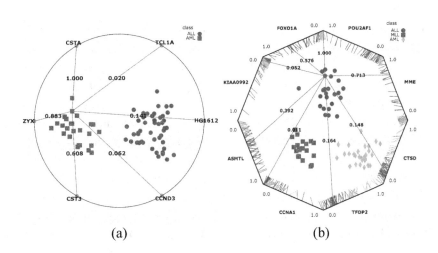

(a)   (b)

A useful multidimensional projection of supervised data that offers some insight into the observed data should clearly expose some class separation patterns. Such are both visualizations in Figure 2. Beyond class separation they also offer an interpretation, as the effect of the expression of genes presented as features in the visualization graph is clearly depicted. For instance, Figure 2(a) suggests that tissue samples of acute myeloid leukemia (AML) have higher expression at genes CSTA, ZYX and CST3 and lower expression at genes TCL1A, HG1612, and CCND3.

VizRank PROJECTION RANKING

VizRank (Leban et al., 2006), which is short for visualization ranking, is a method that considers a class-labeled data set and for a particular multidimensional visualization method obtains a list of most interesting projections with best class separation. Using VizRank, the data analyst does not have to manually search through all possible projections, but can focus on a small subset of top-ranked by VizRank that are likely to provide the best insight into the data and reveal most interesting classification patterns.

VizRank evaluates interestingness of each projection based on how well it separates data points with different class labels. For each subset of features and the related projection parameters (e.g., placement of the features in radviz), it computes the positions of data points. The quality of the projection is then judged based on performance of a machine learning method in developing a classification model using only the positional information of data points in a particular projection – the available features for learning are therefore only the x and y positions of points in the projection. With an appropriately chosen learning algorithm, the predictive accuracy assessed from such procedure corresponds to the degree of class separation in particular visualization. That is, a machine learning algorithm will perform more accurately

for projections where data instances of different class are well separated. Classification accuracy assessed in this way is then used as an indicator for the interestingness of the projection.

Projection Scoring and Selection of Machine Learning Method

Not all machine learning algorithms are suitable for evaluating projections. Some of them, such as Naive Bayes (Mitchell, 1997) consider each feature independently when classifying a data instance. This does not fit our purpose, as we want to evaluate planar projections and need to take into account possible relationships between x- and y-axis, that is, between two attributes that provide us with positional information. Machine learning methods may often have limitations regarding the type of decision boundaries they can infer from the data. Decision trees (Quinlan, 1986), for example, use straight vertical and horizontal decision boundaries that partition the projection into a set of rectangles, thus imposing a rather stringent constraint over the type of separation between instances of different class.

A machine learning method that we found most appropriate for our purpose is k-nearest neighbors (k-NN) (Cover & Hart, 1967). k-NN predicts the class of a data instance by observing class distribution of its k nearest data instances ("neighbors"). There is no constraint on the type of decision boundary, as this is implicitly inferred from the position of data instances and can in principle take any shape. We measure the distances by the Euclidean metric, which may well approximate the human's perception of distance between data instances in the two-dimensional plot. As for the number of neighbors, we follow the recommendation of Dasarathy (1991) who suggested to use $k = \sqrt{N}$, where N is the number of data instances.

To evaluate the performance of the k-NN classifier we can choose among many scoring functions. One of most often used measures in machine learning is classification accuracy, which is defined as the proportion of correctly classified instances. The classification accuracy is, however, too crisp of a measure that does not take into account the predicted probabilities of class labels. Among the measures that will treat the probabilities are Brier score, area under curve (AUC), and average probability of correct classification (Witten & Frank, 2005). While any of these could be used, we opted for the latter because of its intuitive simplicity. The measure is defined as:

$$\overline{P} = \frac{1}{N} \sum_{i=1}^{N} P(y_i | x_i)$$

where N is the number of data instances and $P(y_i|x_i)$ is the probability assigned to the correct (known) class value y_i for data instance x_i. The k-NN's accuracy is tested using the leave-one-out evaluation (Witten and Frank, 2005), in which each data instance is classified using a classifier trained on all instances except the tested one.

Search Heuristic

As we have illustrated in previous sections, the number of possible projections for a chosen multidimensional visualization method can rise exponentially with the number of features. Although in practice, VizRank can rank several thousands of projections in a minute of runtime, it cannot exhaustively search through all possible projections of datasets containing hundreds or possibly thousands of features. To be able to treat such cases, we have developed a heuristic approach. This starts with scoring each individual feature in the data set using some measure like ReliefF (Kononenko, 1994) or signal-to-noise ratio (S2N) (Golub et al., 1999). Assuming that the features which—considered on their own—bear some information on class discrimination are also more likely to be involved in interesting projections, VizRank searches for best projections by considering combinations of best-ranked features first.

Figure 3 shows the distribution of projection scores for 5,000 radviz projections from leukemia data set (see Introduction) as they were selected for evaluation with and without proposed search

Figure 3. Distribution of projection scores for 5,000 radviz projections of the leukemia data set as selected with and without the search heuristic

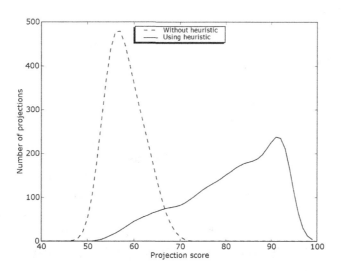

heuristic. Using heuristic search, we were able to find more informative visualizations. In particular, most informative projections, that is, projections with very high scores, were completely missed if heuristic search was not used. Use of the search heuristic is therefore both advisable and necessary in analyses of high-dimensional datasets where only a small fraction of possible projections can be evaluated due to runtime constraints.

Note on Complexity of the Algorithm

Scoring of the projection using leave-one-out and *k*-nearest neighbor algorithm has a complexity on the order of $O(N^2)$, where N is the number of instances in a data set. This complexity is high, especially for larger datasets, and can be reduced to $O(N*\log(N))$ using a more efficient implementation of nearest neighbor search (Krauthgamer & Lee, 2004). Notice that it is also unlikely that the data set considered by our approach will be extremely large, as these cannot be nicely visualized using point-based visualization. Typical datasets for which these visualizations are appropriate include from several hundreds to (at most) couple of thousand data items, where our implementation of VizRank typically evaluates about 1,000 to 10,000 projections per minute of runtime on a medium-scaled desktop PC.

Another major factor that contributes to the complexity of the procedure is the number of projections to evaluate. Consider radviz visualization, which can include arbitrary number of features in a single plot. The number of different projections grows exponentially with the number of features included in visualizations. Yet, in practice, visualizations with more than ten features are rarely considered since they are hard to interpret. Still, even with this limitation, it is impossible to evaluate all possible projections. The approach we propose is to consider only the projections that can be evaluated in some limited time. Due to the proposed heuristic search, and as we experimentally demonstrate on the studies with

microarray cancer data, the overall approach can find interesting projections with high predictive power in few minutes of runtime.

EXPERIMENTAL ANALYSIS

We tested VizRank on several microarray gene expression datasets. The analysis of such datasets has recently gained considerable attention in the data mining community. Typically, the datasets include up to few hundred data instances. Instances (tissue samples from different patients) are represented as a set of gene expression measurements; most often, datasets include measurements of several thousands genes. As tissue samples are labeled, with classes denoting malignant vs. nonmalignant tissue, or different cancer types, the task is to find if the cancer type can be diagnosed based on the set of gene expressions. Another important issue emerging from cancer microarray datasets is to consider what is the minimal number of genes for which we need to measure the expression in order to derive a reliable diagnosis.

In the following, we first describe six datasets used in our analysis and discuss the top-ranked projections. We then present a study in which we used top-ranked projections as simple and understandable prediction models and show that despite their simplicity we achieve high prediction accuracies. We also show how these projections can be used to find important features and identify possible outliers or misclassified instances.

Datasets

Gene expression datasets are obtained by the use of DNA microarray technology, which simultaneously measures expressions of thousands of genes in a biological sample. These datasets can be used to identify specific genes that are differently expressed across different tumor types. Several recent studies of different cancer types (Armstrong, Staunton, Silverman, Pieters, den

Table 1. Cancer-related gene expression datasets used in our study

Data set	Samples (Instances)	Genes (Features)	Diagnostic classes	Majority class
Leukemia	72	7,074	2	52.8%
DLBCL	77	7,070	2	75.3%
Prostate	102	12,533	2	51.0%
MLL	72	12,533	3	38.9%
SRBCT	83	2,308	4	34.9%
Lung cancer	203	12,600	5	68.5%

Boer, & Minden, 2002; Golub, et al., 1999; Nutt, Mani, Betensky, Tamayo, Cairncross, & Ladd, 2003; Shipp, Ross, Tamayo, Weng, Kutok, & Aguiar, 2002) have demonstrated the utility of gene expression profiles for cancer classification, and reported on the superior classification performance when compared to standard morphological criteria.

What makes microarray datasets unique and difficult to analyze is that they typically contain thousands of features (genes) and only a small number of data instances (patients). Analysts typically treat them with a combination of methods for feature filtering, subset selection and modeling. For instance, in the work reported by Khan, Wei, Ringner, Saal, Ladanyi, & Westermann (2001) on the SRBCT dataset, the authors first removed genes with low expression values throughout the data set, then trained 3,750 feed-forward neural networks on different subsets of genes as determined by principal component analysis, analyzed the resulting networks for most informative genes thus obtaining a subset of 96 genes expression of which clearly separated different cancer types when used in multidimensional scaling. Other approaches, often similar in their complexity, include k-nearest neighbors, weighted voting of informative genes (Golub et al., 1999) and support vector machines (Statnikov, Aliferis, Tsamardinos, Hardin, & Levy, 2005). In most

cases, the resulting prediction models are hard or even impossible to interpret and can not be communicated to the domain experts in a simple way that would allow reasoning about the roles genes play in separating different cancer types.

In our experimental study we considered six publicly available cancer gene expression datasets with 2 to 5 diagnostic categories, 40 to 203 data instances (patients) and 2,308 to 12,600 features (gene expressions). The basic information on these is summarized in Table 1. Three datasets, leukemia (Golub et al., 1999), diffuse large B-cell lymphoma (DLBCL) (Shipp et al., 2002) and prostate tumor (Singh, Febbo, Ross, Jackson, Manola, Ladd, 2002) include two diagnostic categories. The leukemia data consists of 72 tissue samples, including 47 with acute lymphoblastic leukemia (ALL) samples and 25 with acute myeloid leukemia (AML), each with 7,074 gene expression values. The DLBCL data set includes expressions of 7,070 genes for 77 patients, 59 with DLBCL and 19 with follicular lymphoma (FL). The prostate tumor data set includes 12,533 genes measured for 52 prostate tumor and 50 normal tissue samples.

The other three datasets analyzed in this work include more than two class labels. The mixed lineage leukemia (MLL) (Armstrong et al., 2002) data set includes 12,533 gene expression values for 72 samples obtained from the peripheral blood or bone marrow samples of affected individuals. The ALL samples with a chromosomal translocation involving the mixed lineage gene were diagnosed as MLL, so three different leukemia classes were obtained (AML, ALL, and MLL). The small round blue cell tumors (SRBCT) dataset (Khan et al., 2001) consists of four types of tumors in childhood, including Ewing's sarcoma (EWS), rhabdomyosarcoma (RB), neuroblastoma (NB) and Burkitt's lymphoma (BL). It includes 83 samples derived from both tumor biopsy and cell lines and 2,308 genes. The last dataset is the lung cancer dataset (Bhattacharjee, Richards, Staunton, Li, Monti, & Vasa, 2001) that contains 12,600 gene expression values for 203 lung tumor samples (139 adenocarcinomas (AD), 21 squamous cell lung carcinomas (SQ), 20 pulmonary carcinoids (COID), 6 small cell lung cancers (SMLC) and 17 normal lung samples (NL)).

Top-Ranked Projections

We applied VizRank to evaluate scatterplot, radviz, and polyviz projections. We limited radviz and polyviz projections to a maximum of eight features since projections with more features are harder to interpret. For each dataset and visualization method, VizRank evaluated 100,000 projections as selected by the search heuristic. With these constraints, the runtime for the largest

of the datasets in terms of number of instances was about half an hour.

Top projections for each dataset (Figures 1(c), 2, and 4) show that VizRank is able to find a projection with a relatively good to excellent class separation using only a fraction of available features. Scores for these projections in Table 2 show that radviz and polyviz projections consistently offer better class separation than scatterplots. This was expected since scatterplots present the data on only two features, while we searched for radviz and polyviz visualizations that included up to eight features. The advantage of using more features is especially evident in datasets with many class values (e.g., lung cancer) where two features alone are clearly insufficient for discrimination between all classes.

Important to our study was to answer the question if the features (genes) used in best projections bear also biological relevance, that is, were they expected to be associated with particular disease. Since most datasets try to discriminate between different tumor types, we assumed that most useful genes will mostly be markers of different tissue or cell origin and will not necessarily be related to cancer pathogenesis. However, we found that many of the genes appearing in the best projections are annotated as cancer or cancer-related genes according to the Atlas of Genetics and Cytogenetics in Oncology and Haematology (http://www.

Table 2. Scores of top projections found by VizRank using different visualization methods

Data set	$\overline{P}$ for best-ranked projection		
	Scatterplot	Radviz	Polyviz
Leukemia	96.54%	99.93%	99.91%
DLBCL	89.34%	99.90%	99.87%
Prostate	87.34%	96.58%	97.23%
MLL	90.12%	99.70%	99.75%
SRBCT	83.52%	99.94%	99.92%
Lung cancer	75.48%	93.49%	93.66%

Figure 4. Optimal radviz and polyviz projections for lung cancer, prostate tumor, SRBCT, and DLBCL data set.

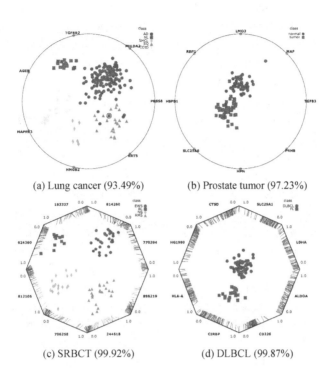

(a) Lung cancer (93.49%)   (b) Prostate tumor (97.23%)

(c) SRBCT (99.92%)   (d) DLBCL (99.87%)

infobiogen.fr/services/chromcancer/index.html). On the other hand, for the prostate dataset, where we try to differentiate between tumor and normal tissue samples, one would expect the "marker" genes to be cancer related. We support our hypothesis by ascertaining that six out of eight genes used in the best radviz projection (LMO3, RBP1, HSPD1, HPN, MAF, and TGFB3) (Figure 4(b)) are cancer related according to the cancer gene atlas.

For brevity, we here only present a biological interpretation of the genes used in the best visualizations of a single data set, and for this consider the MLL data. The best polyviz projection for this dataset is shown in Figure 2(b), and exhibits a clear separation of instances with different diagnostic class. In the visualization, class ALL instances lie closer to the anchor points of the MME and POU2AF1 gene. The anchor point of gene CCNA1 most strongly attracts the MLL class samples and, by some degree, also the AML samples. These

findings are consistent with the work of Armstrong et al. (2002), in which they report on genes MME and POU2AF1 to be specifically expressed in ALL and gene CCNA1 in MLL. There is also a well-founded biological explanation for the appearance of these genes in some of the other best projections separating different classes of the MLL dataset. For example, MME (membrane metalloendopeptidase), also known as common acute lymphocytic leukemia antigen (CALLA), is an important cell surface marker in the diagnosis of human acute lymphocytic leukemia (ALL) (http://www.ncbi.nlm.nih.gov/entrez/dispomim. cgi?id=120520). It is present on leukemic cells of pre-B phenotype, which represent 85% of cases of ALL, and is not expressed on the surface of AML or MLL cells. Similarly, gene POU2AF1 (Pou domain class 2 associating factor 1) is required for appropriate B-cell development (Schubart, Massa, Schubart, Corcoran, Rolink, & Matthias, 2001) and is therefore expressed in ALL samples but not in instances with AML or MLL class label. On the other hand, gene CCNA1 (cyclin A1) is a myeloid-specific gene, expressed in hematopoietic lineages other than lymphocytes (Liao, Wang, Wei, Li, Merghoub, & Pandolfi, 2001). Overexpression of CCNA1 results in abnormal myelopoiesis, which explains the higher expression in AML samples. According to Armstrong et al. (2002), lymphoblastic leukemias with MLL translocation (MLL class) constitute a distinct disease and are characterized by the expression of myeloid-specific genes such as CCNA1. Because this gene is myeloid-specific it is not expressed in ALL samples.

Instead of a single good projection, VizRank can often find a set of projections with high scores. We can then analyze what features are shared between these projections. For example, we may want to know whether a particular gene appears in only one good projection or in several top-ranked projections. In Figure 5(a) we show a plot that lists the first 20 genes present in the top-ranked

scatterplot projections of the MLL dataset. For each pair of genes (one from the *x* and one from the *y* axis), a black box indicates whether their scatterplot projection is ranked among the best 500. The figure shows that three genes—MME, DYRK3, and POU2AF1—stand out in the number of their appearances in the top-ranked projections. Interestingly, in the original study of this dataset (Armstrong et al., 2002) these three genes were listed as the 1st, 3rd, and 10th gene, respectively, among the top 15 genes most highly correlated with ALL class compared with the MLL and AML classes.

We have performed a similar experiment for the leukemia dataset. For each gene we counted how often it appears in the top 500 scatterplots. The histogram of 20 most frequent genes is shown in Figure 5(b). It is evident that gene ZYX (zyxin) particularly stands out as it was present in more than 260 out of 500 projections. ZYX is also one of the anchor genes in the best radviz projection of the leukemia dataset (Figure 2(a)). One can

Figure 5. (a) Genes on the x and y axis are the first 20 genes from the list of top-ranked scatterplot projections of the MLL data set. Black boxes indicate that the corresponding pair of genes on the x and y axis form a scatterplot that is ranked as one of the best 500 scatterplots. (b) Histogram of genes that appear most frequently in the list of 500 best ranked scatterplot projections of the leukemia data set.

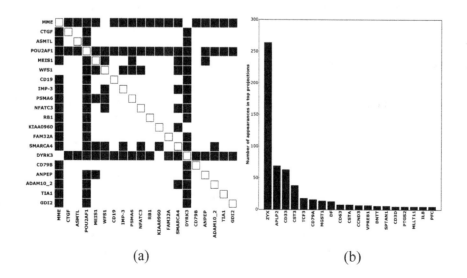

(a)   (b)

observe in the figure that instances from the AML class lie closer to this anchor; therefore, they have higher expression of this gene. Zyxin has been previously recognized as one of the most important genes in differentiating acute lymphoblastic and acute myeloid leukemia samples. In the original study of this dataset (Golub et al., 1999), zyxin was reported as one of the genes most highly correlated with ALL-AML class distinction. Wang and Gehan (2005) systematically investigated and compared feature selection algorithms on this dataset, and reported that zyxin was ranked as the most important gene in differentiating the two leukemias by most filter and wrapper feature selection methods. They also give a possible biological explanation for the involvement of zyxin in leukaemogenesis.

We found similar biological relevance of genes that participated in the best visualizations of other datasets. Besides finding projections with good class separations, VizRank therefore also pointed at specific important genes, which were already experimentally proven to be relevant in the diagnosis of different cancer types. Most of our visualizations included in this chapter point to nonlinear gene interactions, giving VizRank an advantage over univariate feature selection algorithms prevailingly used in the current related work in the area.

Visualization-Based Classification

Because of a huge number of possible projections and a relatively small number of data instances, one could argue that it is possible to find a projection with excellent class separation by chance. Even for a random dataset, if using enough features, VizRank could then find an excellent projection and would thus overfit the data.

To prove that this is not the case, we tested the predictive accuracy of the top-ranked projection using ten-fold cross-validation. The data was divided into ten subsets of approximately equal size and class distribution; in each of the ten iterations VizRank was given nine subsets and 20 minutes to find the best radviz projection with eight or less features. The resulting projection was then used to classify the data instances in the remaining data subset. To classify using the projection, we presented the positional information (x- and y-coordinates) together with the instance class to a machine learning algorithm, which built a model to classify the instances from the left-out data subset. For machine learning, we used the k-nearest neighbor classifier, with $k = \sqrt{N_t}$, where N_t is the number of instances in the training dataset, that is, in the nine subsets used for obtaining the best visualization.

Table 3. Classification accuracy of different classification methods on tested data sets

Data set	Classification accuracy				
	VizRank	SVM	k-NN	Naïve Bayes	Decision trees
Leukemia	93.06%	95.83%	88.89%	93.06%	77.78%
DLBCL	96.10%	98.70%	89.61%	81.82%	89.61%
Prostate	95.10%	93.14%	83.33%	60.78%	80.39%
MLL	93.06%	95.83%	84.72%	84.72%	87.50%
SRBCT	95.18%	100.0%	84.34%	92.77%	84.34%
Lung cancer	91.63%	91.63%	90.64%	73.17%	91.63%
Average rank	**1.91**	**1.33**	**3.91**	**4.16**	**3.66**

We compared this approach with four standard machine learning approaches, that infer the classification model from the entire training dataset: support vector machines with RBF kernel, k-NN using all genes (k=10), naive Bayesian classifier, and decision trees (C4.5 algorithm with default settings). The results are shown in Table 3. The best performance was achieved by support vector machines, which was somehow expected since they are believed to be the best classification method for microarray data (Statnikov et al., 2005). A more surprising result, however, is that simple projections found by VizRank proved to be very accurate predictors and were on average ranked just below support vector machines, but above or even well above other machine learning approaches.

Based on the above we can therefore conclude that the top-ranked projections are not the result of overfitting but actually show true regularities in the data. The results also demonstrate that we do not always have to resort to support vector machines in order to achieve a good classification performance. Instead, methods such as those presented in this chapter that in addition to a good performance offer also means of interpretation, may provide a good alternative.

Detecting Outliers

For all the examined datasets, the best radviz and polyviz projections (Figures 1(c), 2, and 4) clearly separate instances from different classes, with the exception of only a few outliers. Identification and analysis of these outliers can reveal interesting characteristics of the data, where outliers may be special cases of a specific disease or may perhaps even be misdiagnosed instances.

Figure 4(a) shows the best radviz projection for the lung cancer dataset, which contains 5 diag-

Figure 6. A visualization of class predictions for the selected data instance using best 100 radviz projections of the lung cancer data set. Although the data instance, which is selected in Figure 4.a, is in the data set classified as the AD instance it is often placed inside a group of SQ instances.

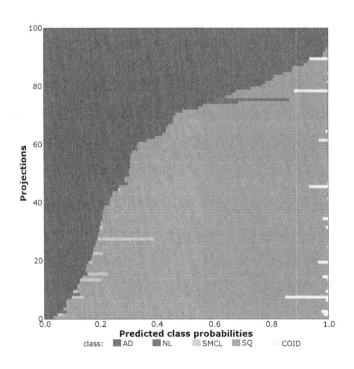

nostic classes and 203 examples. The diagnostic classes in the visualization are well separated, except for the adenocarcinomas (class AD) and squamous cell carcinomas (class SQ), where there is a region of overlap. To assess if these instances overlap also in other best-ranked projections we analyzed the class prediction of the adenocarcinomas in the overlapping region in the 100 best radviz projections. As a particular example, we analyzed the data instance marked with a circle in Figure 4(a); Figure 6 shows how this data instance was classified using the 100 best radviz projections. Each horizontal line in the figure represents the predicted class probabilities for each class value in one projection (horizontal lines are sorted by the decreasing probability of AD class). Although the observed data instance is classified as adenocarcinoma (AD) in some top-ranked projections, we can see that it is also classified as squamous cell carcinoma (SQ) in roughly half of the considered projections. Interestingly, after analyzing the supplemental information concerning the adenocarcinoma tissue samples, we noticed that some of the adenocarcinomas have been histologically diagnosed as adenocarcinomas with squamous features (Bhattacharjee et al., 2001). The instance marked in Figure 4(a) is therefore actually a mixture of AD and SQ classes, as can also be seen from the class prediction visualization shown in Figure 6.

Using VizRank with Parallel Coordinates

Parallel coordinates (Inselberg, 1981) are a visualization method where we were also able to (indirectly) apply VizRank. In parallel coordinates the features are visualized as parallel and equally spaced axes. Each data instance is then visualized as a broken line that extends from the first to the last axis, intersecting each axis at the position that corresponds to the value of the instance. If we have class labeled data we can color the lines according to class values. An example of a par-

allel coordinates plot for the leukemia dataset is shown in Figure 7.

The ability to perceive an interesting pattern in the parallel coordinates plot mainly depends on two factors. First is the selection of appropriate, informative features—visualizing an uninformative set of features cannot reveal any relevant patterns. The second factor is the order in which the axes are placed. If the data lines between neighboring axes flow in various unrelated directions, the plot is cluttered and does not show any pattern. Axes should therefore be placed in such a way that lines with the same class are as similar as possible and thus allow us to easily detect patterns common to instances of the same class.

Our experiments show that a good approach for selecting features and determining their optimal order is to find good radviz projections using VizRank and then place the features from radviz to a parallel coordinates plot in the same order. To understand why this works, let us assume that we found a radviz projection where instances with the same class label are grouped and nicely separated from other classes. The fact that data instances with the same class lie close together implies they have similar values at the neighboring visualized features, so their lines in parallel coordinates plot will be similar. On the other hand, because of the good separation of different classes in the radviz projection, we will also be able to notice a qualitative difference between the forms of lines with different class values.

Figure 7 shows a parallel coordinates plot of the features from the radviz projection in Figure 2(a). In the figure it is clearly visible that the ALL data instances have high values for the first three features and low for the last three features, while the opposite holds for the instances with AML class value. Because a parallel coordinates plot offers a different view of the data than radviz and polyviz projections, it makes sense to use it in combination with the aforementioned methods.

Figure 7. Parallel coordinates plot of the leukemia data set

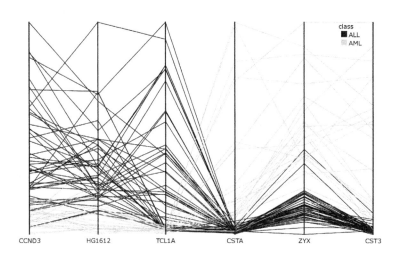

Related Work

There are several approaches that were developed (or can be adapted) for finding interesting data visualizations. Most of them search for the vectors in the original feature space that contain some interesting information. The two most important vectors are then visualized in a scatterplot, one vector on the x and the other on the y axis. Such projections are called linear projections since each axis is a linear combination of original features. Following is an overview of such methods.

In the area of unsupervised learning, one of the oldest techniques is principal component analysis (PCA). PCA is a dimension reduction technique that uses variance as a measure of interestingness and finds orthogonal vectors (principal components) in the feature space that account for the most variance in the data. Visualizing the two most important vectors can identify some elongated shapes or outliers. A more recent and general technique was developed by Friedman and Tukey (1974), and is known as projection pursuit. Diaconis and Friedman (1984) proved that a randomly selected projection of a high-dimensional dataset would show approximately Gaussian distribution of data points. Since we are interested in nonran-

dom patterns, such as clusters or long tails, they propose to measure interestingness as departure from normality. Several such measures, known as projection pursuit indices, were developed and can be used in a gradient-based approach to search for interesting projections.

Probably the most popular method for finding projections for labeled data is Fisher's linear discriminant analysis (LDA) (Duda, Hart & Stork, 2000), which finds a linear combination of features that best discriminate between instances of two classes. When we have more than two classes, we can compute discriminants for each pair of classes and visualize pairs of discriminants in scatterplots. LDA's drawbacks (sensitivity to outliers, assumption of equal covariance matrix for instances in each class, etc.) gave rise to several modifications of the method. One of the most recent ones is normalized LDA (Koren & Carmel, 2004), which normalizes the distances between instances and makes the method far more robust with respect to outliers. Another method that searches for projections with a good class separation is FreeViz (Demsar, Leban & Zupan, 2005), which could be considered as a projection pursuit for supervised learning. FreeViz plots the instances in a two dimensional projection where the instance's position in each dimension is computed as a linear combination of feature values. The optimization procedure is based on a physical metaphor in which the data instances of the same class attract, and instances of different classes repel each other. The procedure then searches for a configuration with minimal potential energy, which at the same time results in the optimal (as defined by the algorithm) class separation.

CONCLUSION

We presented a method called VizRank that can evaluate different projections of class labeled data and rank them according to their interestingness defined by the degree of class separation in the projection. Analysts can then focus only on the small subset of highest ranked projections that contain potentially interesting information regarding the importance of the features, their mutual interactions and their relation with the classes. We have evaluated the proposed approach on a set of cancer microarray datasets, all featuring about a hundred data instances but a large number of features, which, with the biggest datasets, went into several thousands.

Perhaps the most striking experimental result reported in this work is that we found simple visualizations that clearly visually differentiate among cancer types for all cancer gene expression datasets investigated. This finding complements a recent related work in the area that demonstrates that gene expression cancer data can provide ground for reliable classification models (Statnikov et al., 2005). However, our "visual" classification models are much simpler and comprise much smaller number of features, and besides provide means for a simple interpretation, as was demonstrated throughout the chapter.

The approach presented here is of course not limited to cancer gene expression analysis and can be applied to search for good visualizations on any class-labeled dataset that includes continuous

or nominal features. VizRank is freely available within Orange open-source data mining suite (Demsar et al., 2004; Demsar et al., 2004), and can be found on the Web at www.ailab.si/orange.

REFERENCES

Armstrong, S. A., Staunton, J. E., Silverman, L. B., Pieters, R., den Boer, M. L., Minden, M. D., Sallan, S. E., Lander, E. S., Golub, T. R., & Korsmeyer, S. J. (2002). MLL translocations specify a distinct gene expression profile that distinguishes a unique leukemia. *Nature Genetics, 30,* 41-47.

Bhattacharjee, A., Richards, W. G., Staunton, J., Li, C., Monti, S., Vasa, P., Ladd, C., Beheshti, J., Bueno, R., Gillette, M., Loda, M., Weber, G., Mark, E. J., Lander, E. S., Wong, W., Johnson, B. E., Golub, T. R., Sugarbaker, D. J., & Meyerson, M. (2001). Classification of human lung carcinomas by mRNA expression profiling reveals distinct adenocarcinoma subclasses. *PNAS, 98,* 13790-13795.

Brunsdon, C., Fotheringham, A. S., & Charlton, M. (1998). An investigation of methods for visualising highly multivariate datasets. In D. Unwin, & P. Fisher (Eds.), *Case studies of visualization in the social sciences* (pp. 55-80).

Cover, T. M., & Hart, P. E. (1967). Nearest neighbor pattern classification. *IEEE Transactions on Information Theory, 1,* 21-27.

Dasarathy, B. W. (1991) *Nearest neighbor (NN) norms: NN pattern classification techniques.* Los Alamitos, CA: IEEE Computer Society Press.

Demsar, J., Leban, G., & Zupan, B. (2005). FreeViz - An intelligent visualization approach for class-labeled multidimensional data sets. *IDAMAP-05 Workshop Notes.* Aberdeen, UK.

Demsar, J., Zupan, B., & Leban, G. (2004). Orange: From experimental machine learning to interactive data mining. White Paper, Faculty of

Computer and Information Science, University of Ljubljana.

Demsar, J., Zupan, B., Leban, G., & Curk, T. (2004). Orange: From experimental machine learning to interactive data mining. In *Proceedings of the European Conference of Machine Learning*. Pisa, Italy.

Diaconis, P., & Friedman, D. (1984). Asymptotics of graphical projection pursuit. *Annals of Statistics, 1*, 793-815.

Duda, R. O., Hart, P. E., & Stork, D. G. (2000). *Pattern classification*. Wiley-Interscience.

Friedman, J. H., & Tukey, J. W. (1974). A projection pursuit algorithm for exploratory data analysis, *IEEE Transactions on Computers, C-23*, 881-889.

Golub, T. R., Slonim, D. K., Tamayo, P., Huard, C., Gaasenbeek, M., Mesirov, J. P., Coller, H., Loh, M. L., Downing, J. R., Caligiuri, M. A., Bloomfield, C. D., & Lander, E. S. (1999). Molecular classification of cancer: Class discovery and class prediction by gene expression monitoring, *Science, 286*, 531-537.

Harris, R. L. (1999). *Information graphics: A comprehensive illustrated reference*. New York: Oxford Press.

Hoffman, P., Grinstein, G., & Pinkney, D. (1999). Dimensional anchors: A graphic primitive for multidimensional multivariate information visualizations. In *Proceedings of the 1999 Workshop on new paradigms in information visualization and manipulation*.

Inselberg, A. (1981). *N-dimensional graphics, part I-lines and hyperplanes* (Tech. Rep. No. G320-2711). IBM Los Angeles Scientific Center.

Keim, D. A., & Kriegel, H. (1996). Visualization techniques for mining large databases: A comparison, *Transactions on Knowledge and Data Engineering, 8*, 923-938.

Khan, J., Wei, J. S., Ringner, M., Saal, L. H., Ladanyi, M., Westermann, F., Berthold, F., Schwab, M., Antonescu, C. R., Peterson, C., & Meltzer, P. S. (2001). Classification and diagnostic prediction of cancers using gene expression profiling and artificial neural networks. *Nature Medicine, 7*, 673-679.

Kononenko, I. (1994). Estimating attributes: Analysis and extensions of RELIEF. In *Proceedings of the European Conference on Machine Learning (ECML)*.

Koren, Y., & Carmel, L. (2004). Robust linear dimensionality reduction. *IEEE Transactions on Visualization and Computer Graphics, 10*, 459-470.

Krauthgamer, R., & Lee, J. (2004). Navigating nets: Simple algorithms for proximity search. In *Proceedings of the 15th Annual Symposium on Discrete Algorithms*.

Leban, G., Zupan, B., Vidmar, G., & Bratko, I. (2006). VizRank: Data visualization guided by machine learning. *Data Mining and Knowledge Discovery, 13*, 119-136.

Liao, C., Wang, X. Y., Wei, H. Q., Li, S. Q., Merghoub, T., Pandolfi, P. P., & Wolgemuth, D. J. (2001). Altered myelopoiesis and the development of acute myeloid leukemia in transgenic mice overexpressing cyclin A1. *PNAS, 98*, 6853-6858.

Mitchell, T. M. (1997). *Machine learning*. New York: McGraw-Hill.

Nutt, C. L., Mani, D. R., Betensky, R. A., Tamayo, P., Cairncross, J. G., Ladd, C., Pohl, U., Hartmann, C., McLaughlin, M. E., Batchelor, T. T., Black, P. M., von Deimling, A., Pomeroy, S. L., Golub, T. R., & Louis, D. N. (2003). Gene expression-based classification of malignant gliomas correlates better with survival than histological classification. *Cancer Research, 63*, 1602-1607.

Quinlan, J. R. (1986). Induction of decision trees. *Machine Learning, 1*, 81-106.

Schubart, K., Massa, S., Schubart, D., Corcoran, L. M., Rolink, A. G., & Matthias, P. (2001). B cell development and immunoglobulin gene transcription in the absence of Oct-2 and OBF-1. *Nature Immunol, 2*, 69-74.

Shipp, M. A., Ross, K. N., Tamayo, P., Weng, A. P., Kutok, J. L., Aguiar, R. C., Gaasenbeek, M., Angelo, M., Reich, M., Pinkus, G. S., Ray, T. S., Koval, M. A., Last, K. W., Norton, A., Lister, T. A., Mesirov, J., Neuberg, D. S., Lander, E. S., Aster, J. C., & Golub, T. R. (2002). Diffuse large B-cell lymphoma outcome prediction by gene-expression profiling and supervised machine learning. *Nature Medicine, 8*, 68-74.

Singh, D., Febbo, P. G., Ross, K., Jackson, D. G., Manola, J., Ladd, C., Tamayo, P., Renshaw, A. A., D'Amico, A. V., Richie, J. P., Lander, E. S., Loda, M., Kantoff, P. W., Golub, T. R., & Sellers, W. R. (2002). Gene expression correlates of clinical prostate cancer behavior. *Cancer Cell, 1*, 203-209.

Statnikov, A., Aliferis, C. F., Tsamardinos, I., Hardin, D., & Levy, S. (2005). A comprehensive evaluation of multicategory classification methods for microarray gene expression cancer diagnosis. *Bioinformatics, 21*, 631-643.

Wang, A., & Gehan, E. A. (2005). Gene selection for microarray data analysis using principal component analysis, *Stat Med, 24*, 2069-2087.

Witten, I. H., & Frank, E. (2005). *Data mining: Practical machine learning tools and techniques with Java implementations* (2nd ed.). San Francisco: Morgan Kaufmann.

Chapter VI
Summarizing Data Cubes Using Blocks

Yeow Wei Choong
HELP University, Malaysia

Anne Laurent
Université Montpellier II, France

Dominique Laurent
Université de Cergy - Pontoise, France

ABSTRACT

In the context of multidimensional data, OLAP tools are appropriate for the navigation in the data, aiming at discovering pertinent and abstract knowledge. However, due to the size of the dataset, a systematic and exhaustive exploration is not feasible. Therefore, the problem is to design automatic tools to ease the navigation in the data and their visualization. In this chapter, we present a novel approach allowing to build automatically blocks of similar values in a given data cube that are meant to summarize the content of the cube. Our method is based on a levelwise algorithm (a la Apriori) whose complexity is shown to be polynomial in the number of scans of the data cube. The experiments reported in the chapter show that our approach is scalable, in particular in the case where the measure values present in the data cube are discretized using crisp or fuzzy partitions.

INTRODUCTION

As stated by Bill Inmon in 1990, "A data warehouse is a subject-oriented, integrated, time-variant and non-volatile collection of data in support of management's decision making process" (Inmon, 1992). As data warehouses are devoted to intensive decision-oriented querying, classical relational database management systems are known to be not suitable in this framework. To cope with this problem, the multidimensional model of databases has been proposed by E. F. Codd more than 10 years ago in Codd, Codd, and Salley (1993).

In the context of multidimensional databases, data are considered as belonging to multidimensional tables, the so-called data cubes or simply cubes, defined over several dimensions and in which measure values are associated to one value in each dimension. On-line analytical processing (OLAP) has become a major research issue, aiming at providing users with tools for querying data cubes.

Querying a cube is known to be a tedious process because, as data are often voluminous, an exhaustive exploration is not possible. Therefore, it is often the case that users wish to have a rough idea of the content of a cube in order to identify relevant data. In other words, summarizing the content of a data cube is one of the major needs of users. The OLAP operators called roll-up and drill-down are commonly used to this end. These operators allow to explore the data cube according to different levels of granularity defined on dimensions: while rolling-up according to one or several dimensions displays the data at a lower level of details, drilling-down has the reverse effect of displaying the data at a higher level of details. However, it should be noticed that these operators work based on predefined hierarchies on dimensions, and thus, do not allow to summarize a data cube based on its actual content, that is, the measure values.

In this chapter, we propose an approach to automatically summarize a data cube by comput-ing sub-cubes, which we call blocks, that mainly contain the same measure value. It is important to note that in this work, we do not consider the option of computing blocks containing exclusively the same measure value, which is very restrictive and thus, would prevent from obtaining relevant summaries. The way we characterize that a block b of a cube C mainly contains the measure value m can be outlined as follows: Assuming two user-given thresholds σ and γ, called the *support* and the *confidence* thresholds, respectively, b *mainly* contains m if the ratio of the number of occurrences of m in b over the cardinality of C is greater than σ, and if the ratio of the number of occurrences of m in b over the cardinality of b is greater than γ. These two ratios are called support and confidence of b for m, and as we shall see later, the support and the confidence thresholds are respectively related to the minimum size and to the purity of the block.

Moreover, as measure values are numerical, it can be relevant to consider close values as equal. We take such an option into account in the computations of support and confidence by considering two kinds of partitioning of the set of measure values present in the data cube, namely crisp and fuzzy partitioning.

As in either case the computation of blocks as roughly described above is NP-hard, we propose a levelwise algorithm *a la* Apriori and the ex-periments reported in this chapter show that our method is scalable even for data cubes with large cardinalities and large numbers of dimensions. However, it is important to note that the price to pay for scalability is the noncompleteness of our method, that is, a cube C may contain blocks with supports and confidences greater than the corresponding thresholds that are not output. We shall discuss this important point in details later in the chapter.

The set of all blocks computed by our approach is considered as a summary of the cube. In our previous work, we have argued that blocks can be associated with rules (see Choong, Laurent.

& Laurent, 2004), and that they can serve as a basis for an efficient visualization of the cube (see Choong, Laurent. & Laurent, 2007). It should be noticed that, since the computed blocks (obtained after partitioning or not) mainly contain a given measure value, it might be the case that two or more blocks overlap. This important feature of our approach is taken into account in Choong et al. (2004) by considering fuzzy rules, and in Choong et al. (2006) by defining a policy to display the most relevant block among all those that overlap. In this chapter, we do not address the issues of computing rules or of visualizing the blocks. Instead, we focus on the computation of the blocks in the following respects:

1. Based on the fact that the method presented in Choong et al. (2004) is not complete, we enhance our approach and we show some partial completeness results in this new framework.

2. As in practice, the measure values contained in a cube are numerical, we study the impact of discretizing these values, using crisp or fuzzy partitions.

3. We report experiments conducted on randomly generated datasets that show that our approach is still scalable for large data cubes with a high number of dimensions.

The following example illustrates our approach.

Example 1: Let us consider the cube C displayed in Figure 1. This cube is defined over two dimensions, namely CITY and PRODUCT, and contains measure values standing for the quantity of a given product sold in a given city. For instance, it can be seen that the quantity of product P1 sold in city C1 is six units.

Considering a support threshold $\sigma = 1/15$ and a confidence threshold $\gamma = 2/3$, our approach generates the blocks as represented in Figure 1. These blocks are defined as follows in our formalism:

1. $b1 = [C1;C1] \times [P1; P2]$ for value 6, because the support and the confidence for 6 are respectively 1/12 and 1,

2. $b2 = [C1;C3] \times [P3;P4]$ for value 8, because the support and the confidence for 8 are respectively 1/6 and 2/3,

3. $b3 = [C3;C4] \times [P1;P3]$ for value 5, because the support and the confidence for 5 are respectively 1/6 and 2/3,

4. $b4 = [C4;C6] \times [P3;P4]$ for value 2, because the support and the confidence for 2 are respectively 5/24 and 5/6.

First, we note that, for the measure value 6, the block defined by $b = [C1;C2] \times [P1;P2]$ has a support and a confidence equal to 1/8 and 3/4, respectively. Therefore, this illustrates the noncompleteness of our approach since $1/8 > \sigma$ and $3/4 > \gamma$.

Now, assume that instead of integer values, the cube of Figure 1 contains numbers that represent the quantity of sales in thousands of units for each city and each product. In this case, it is likely that, for instance, in place of 6 for city C1 and products P1 and P2, the cube contains values such as 5.996 and 6.002. In this case, computing blocks based on the exact measure value would not give the block b1, although the corresponding measure values are close to each other. To cope with this problem, we consider that the set of measure values can be partitioned so as to yield relevant blocks.

For instance, in our example, this partitioning could be defined by considering for every integer X that measure values in $[(X-1).500;X.500[$ are equal to X. Moreover, we generalize partitionings to fuzzy partitionings, so as to consider that $[(X-1).500;X.500]$ and $[(X-2).500;(X+1).500]$ are respectively the support and the kernel of the bin corresponding to the fuzzy notion about X thousands.

We mention that building blocks from a data cube facilitates its visualization, and the more the relevance of the blocks, the better the representation quality. The issue of data cube representation

Figure 1. A data cube and the associated blocks

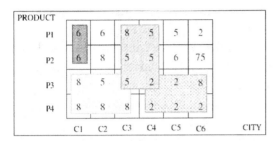

has been addressed in Choong, Laurent, and Marcel (2003), where the authors show that a data cube has several representations among which some are more relevant than others, according to user-specified criteria. In Choong et al. (2003), the criterion is that the measure is ordered in an increasing manner over all dimensions, and representations optimizing this criterion are studied. In the present chapter, we consider as relevant the representations where same measure values are grouped to form blocks as large as possible. However, in this chapter, contrary to Choong et al. (2003), our goal is not to compute relevant representations according to this criterion; in what follows, the representation of the data cube is assumed to be fixed, and the blocks are computed in this particular representation. In this setting, it is relevant to use the blocks computed by our approach in order to assess the quality of the representation of the cube. More precisely, this quality can be related to the following criteria:

- The proportion of elements in the cube that are included in the blocks (the higher the proportion, the less elements not covered by the rules)
- The number of blocks built (the more blocks there are, the more heterogeneous data are)

- The number of blocks in comparison with the number of measure values (if several blocks are built for the same measure value m, then the different occurrences of m are displayed in noncontiguous areas of the cube)
- The number of overlappings between blocks and their sizes (the higher the number of overlapping blocks, the more mixed the data)

The chapter is organized as follows: section 2 introduces the basic definitions concerning multidimensional databases and blocks, including interval based and fuzzy interval based-blocks. Section 3 presents the algorithms to build blocks from multidimensional databases and the corresponding complexity issues, as well as a thorough discussion about the completeness of our approach. Section 4 presents a method based on cell neighborhood to improve the completeness of our approach. Section 5 reports on the experiments performed on synthetic data and on a real dataset. Section 6 presents the related work from the literature, and in section 7, we conclude the chapter and we outline further research directions.

MULTIDIMENSIONAL DATABASES AND BLOCKS

Basic Definitions

Although no consensual definition has emerged for now concerning data representation and manipulation, a multidimensional database is generally defined as being a set of data cubes (hereafter cubes). A cube can be seen as a set of cells and a cell represents the association of a measure value with one member in each dimension. Moreover, hierarchies may be defined over dimensions, for instance to describe sales in function of states and not of cities. Since hierarchies are not considered in the present chapter, we do not include these in our definition.

Definition 1. Cube: A k-dimensional cube, or simply a cube, C is a tuple $\langle dom_1,..., dom_k, dom_m, m_C \rangle$ where:

- $dom_1,..., dom_k$ are k finite sets of symbols for the members associated with dimensions $1,..., k$ respectively,
- let dom_{mes} be a finite totally ordered set of measures. Let $\perp$ be a constant (to represent null values). Then $dom_m = dom_{mes} \cup \{\perp\}$
- m_C is a mapping: $dom_1 \times ... \times dom_k \rightarrow dom_m$.

A cell c of a k-dimensional cube C is a (k + 1)-tuple $\langle v_1,..., v_k, m \rangle$ such that for every $i = 1,..., k$, v_i is in dom_i and where $m = m_C(v_1,..., v_k)$. m is called the *content* of c and c is called an m-cell. Moreover, for every $i = 1,..., k$, dom_i is called the *domain* of dimension d_i and an element v_i in dom_i is called a *member value*.

We recall from Choong et al. (2003) that a given cube can be represented in several ways, based on the ordering of the member values in each set dom_i. For example, Figures 1 and 2 display two different representations of the cube C considered in Example 1. Although we do not consider the issue of computing particular representations, the notion of representation, as defined below, plays an important role in the present approach.

Definition 2. Representation: A representation of a k-dimensional cube C is a set R = $\{rep_1,..., rep_k\}$ where for every $i = 1,...,k$, rep_i is a one-to-one mapping from dom_i to $\{1,..., |dom_i|\}$.

In this chapter, we consider a fixed k-dimensional cube C and a fixed representation of C, that we denote by R = $\{rep_1,..., rep_k\}$.

Now, given a fixed representation of C, R = $\{rep_1,..., rep_k\}$, for every dimension d_i, v_1 and v_2 in dom_i are said to be *contiguous* if $rep_i(v_1)$ and $rep_i(v_2)$ are consecutive integers, *i.e.* if $|rep_i(v_1)-rep_i(v_2)| = 1$. Moreover, if $rep_i(v_1) \leq rep_i(v_2)$, the interval $[v_1;v_2]$ is the set of all contiguous values between v_1 and v_2, *i.e.*, $[v_1;v_2] = \{v \in dom_i \mid rep_i(v_1) \leq rep_i(v) \leq rep_i(v_2)\}$.

Blocks

In our approach, we define a block of C as follows:

Definition 3. Block: A block b is a set of cells defined over a k-dimensional cube C by $b = \delta_1 \times ... \times \delta_k$ where δ_i are intervals of contiguous values from dom_i, for $i = 1,..., k$.

Note that in the previous definition a block is specified by exactly one interval per dimension. In the case where an interval would not be specified on a dimension d_i, the corresponding interval is set to $[rep_i^{-1}(1), rep_i^{-1}(|dom_i|)]$, which is denoted by ALL_i.

Figure 2. Another representation of the cube of Figure 1

PRODUCT						
P4	8	8	8	2	2	2
P2	5	6	8	5	6	75
P1	8	6	6	5	5	2
P3	5	8	5	2	2	8
	C3	C1	C2	C4	C5	C6 CITY

For example, if we consider the cube of Figure 1, the interval [C1;C3] is associated with the block [C1;C3] × ALL$_{PRODUCT}$ where ALL$_{PRODUCT}$ is the interval [P4;P1].

Definition 4. Block Overlapping: Two blocks b and b' are said to *overlap* if they share at least one cell, *i.e.*, if b ∩ b' ≠ ∅.

It is easy to see that two blocks b = δ$_1$ ×... × δ$_k$ and b' = δ'$_1$ ×... × δ'$_k$ overlap if and only if for every dimension d$_i$, δ$_i$ ∩ δ'$_i$ ≠ ∅. As stated in the following definition, in our formalism, a slice is defined as a particular block.

Definition 5. Slice: Let v$_i$ be a member value in dom$_i$. The slice of C associated with v$_i$, denoted by T(v$_i$), is the block δ$_1$ × ... × δ$_k$ such that δ$_i$ = {v$_i$}, and for all j ≠i, j = ALL$_j$.

Given two member values v$_1$ and v$_2$ in the same domain dom$_i$, the slices T(v$_1$) and T(v$_2$), are said to be contiguous if v$_1$ and v$_2$ are contiguous, that is, if |rep$_i$(v$_1$) – rep$_i$(v$_2$)| = 1.

Referring to Figure 1, the slices T(P3) and T(P4) are contiguous since P3 and P4 are contiguous in the considered representation. It is important to note that the notion of contiguous cells (or slices) depends on the representation of the cube that is being considered. Indeed, two member values (or slices) can be contiguous in a given representation of C but not contiguous in another representation of C. For instance, considering the cube C of Example 1, the member values C2 and C3 are contiguous in the representation of C displayed in Figure 1, but are not contiguous in the representation of C displayed in Figure 2.

We now define the following specificity relation between blocks of a given cube C.

Definition 6. Specificity relation: Let b = δ$_1$ × ... × δ$_k$ and b' = δ'$_1$ × ... × δ'$_k$ be two blocks. b' is said to be *more specific* than b, denoted by b ∠ b', if for every i = 1,..., k, δ$_i$ ≠ δ'$_i$ ⟹ δ$_i$ = ALL$_i$.

For instance, in the cube of Figure 1, for b = [C1;C3] × ALL$_{PRODUCT}$ and b' = [C1;C3] × [P3;P4],

we have b ∠ b' since the intervals defining b and b' satisfy the above definition. It can be seen that the relation ∠ as defined above is a partial ordering over the set of all blocks of the cube C. Given a set of blocks B, the maximal (respectively minimal) elements of B are said to be most specific (respectively most general) in B. Most specific blocks and most general blocks are called MS-blocks and MG-blocks, respectively.

Moreover, it can be easily shown that if b and b' are two blocks such that b ∠ b', then b' ⊆ b.

Support and Confidence of a Block

The support and the confidence of a given block b are defined according to the content of the cells in b. In order to comply with our discussion in the introductory section (see example 1), we consider three different criteria in this respect: (1) single measure values, (2) partition based measure values, and (3) fuzzy partition based measure values.

In order to define the support and the confidence of a block for a given measure value, we introduce the following notation: let b be a block and m a measure value, Count(b, m) denotes the number of m-cells in b, and |b| denotes the total number of cells in b. In particular, |C| denotes the total number of cells in the whole cube C.

Definition 7. Support: The support of a block b from C for a measure value m is defined as:

$$sup(b,m) = \frac{count(b,m)}{|C|}$$

Considering a user-given minimum support threshold σ and a measure value m, a block b such that sup(b, m) > σ is called σ-frequent for m.

Definition 8. Confidence: The confidence of a block b for a measure value m is defined as:

$$conf(b,m) = \frac{count(b,m)}{|b|}$$

As argued in the introductory section, considering separately all measure values present in the cube can lead to consider nonrelevant blocks, which will be very small. For instance, in a cube containing billions of cells and where the measure values range from 1 to 1,000 with very few repetitions, almost 1,000 values have to be considered separately. Alternatively, in this case, 5 and 5.2 are likely to be considered as similar measure values and thus, should be processed as such.

In order to take this important point into account, we propose two ways to build blocks, based on intervals of measure values, on the one hand, and on fuzzy intervals, on the other hand. In these cases, the support and the confidence of a block are defined as follows.

Definition 9. Interval support and confidence:
The interval support of a block b in C for a measure value interval [m1;m2] is defined as:

$$i\_sup(b,[m1,m2]) = \frac{iCount(b,[m1,m2])}{|C|}$$

where iCount(b, [m1;m2]) is the number of m-cells in b such that m $\in$ [m1;m2]. Similarly, the interval confidence of b for [m1;m2] is defined as:

$$i\_conf(b,[m1,m2]) = \frac{iCount(b,[m1,m2])}{|b|}$$

When considering fuzzy intervals instead of intervals, counting cells in a block b with respect to a fuzzy interval φ can be computed according to the following methods (Dubois, Hülermeier & Prade, 2003):

1. The Σ-count sums up the membership degrees of all cells of b.

2. The threshold-count counts those cells of b whose membership degree is greater than a user-defined threshold.

3. The threshold-Σ-count sums up those cell membership degrees that are greater than a user-defined threshold.

In what follows, given a fuzzy interval φ and a cell c with content m, we denote by $\mu(c, \varphi)$ the membership value of m in φ. Moreover, given a block b, $\sum_{c \in b}^{f} \mu(c, \varphi)$ denotes the count of cells in b whose content is in φ, according to one of the three counting methods mentioned above. In this case, the support and confidence of a block b are defined as follows.

Definition 10: Fuzzy Support and Confidence

The fuzzy support of a block b in C for a fuzzy interval φ is defined as:

$$f\_sup(b,\varphi) = \frac{fCount(b,\varphi)}{|C|}$$

where:

$$fCount(b,\varphi) = \sum_{c \in b}^{f} \mu(c,\varphi)$$

Similarly, the fuzzy confidence of b for φ is defined as:

$$f\_conf(b,\varphi) = \frac{fCount(b,\varphi)}{|b|}$$

Properties

We first show that the support is anti-monotonic with respect to $\angle$, in either of the three cases defined above.

Proposition 1: For all blocks b and b' such that b $\angle$ b', we have:

1. For every measure value m, sup(b', m) $\leq$ sup(b, m).
2. For every interval [m1;m2], i_sup(b', [m1;m2]) $\leq$ i_sup(b, [m1;m2]).
3. For every fuzzy interval φ, f_sup(b', φ) $\leq$ f_sup(b, φ).

- **Proof:** If b and b' are two blocks such that b $\angle$ b' then we have that b' $\subseteq$ b. Moreover, in this case, we have Count(b, μ) $\leq$ Count(b', μ), iCount(b, [m1;m2]) $\leq$ iCount(b', [m1;m2]) and for every fuzzy counting method given above, fCount(b, φ) $\leq$ fCount(b', φ). Therefore, the proposition follows from the definitions of the support, which completes the proof.

In our levelwise algorithm for computing blocks given in the next section, proposition 1 is used in the following way in the case of single measure values (the other two cases being similar): given a block b, a measure value m and a support threshold σ, b is not σ-frequent for m if there exists a block b' such that b' $\angle$ b and b' is not σ-frequent for m.

The following proposition shows that the support (respectively confidence) of blocks based on intervals and fuzzy intervals are greater than the support (respectively confidence) blocks based on single values.

Proposition 2: For every block b and every measure value m, let m1 and m2 be measure values such that m $\in$ [m1;m2], and let φ be a fuzzy interval such that kernel(φ) = [m1;m2]. Then, for any of the three fuzzy counting methods Σ^f, we have:

Count(b, m) $\leq$ iCount(b, [m1;m2]) $\leq$ fCount(b, φ)

As a consequence:

- sup(b, m) $\leq$ i_sup(b, [m1;m2]) $\leq$ f_sup(b, φ) and
- conf(b, m) $\leq$ i_conf(b, [m1;m2]) $\leq$ f_conf(b, φ).

- **Proof:** For any cell c in b, if $m_C(c) = m$ then c contributes to 1 in Count(b, m), iCount(b, [m1;m2]) and fCount(b, φ). Similarly, if $m_C(c) \neq m$ but $m_C(c) \in [m_1;m_2]$ then c contributes to 1 in iCount(b, [m1;m2]) and fCount(b, φ). Finally, if $m_C(c) \notin [m_1;m_2]$ then it might be that c contributes to less than 1 only in fCount(b, φ). Therefore, the proof is complete.

ALGORITHMS

In this chapter, our goal is to discover blocks whose support and confidence are greater than user specified thresholds. To this end, our method is based on a levelwise Apriori-like algorithm (Agrawal, Imielinski, & Swami, 1993), for scalability reasons. In this section, we first present the algorithms for the discovery of blocks in the case of single values, and then we show how the cases of (fuzzy) interval based measure values can be processed.

Roughly speaking, in the case of single measure values, our method works as follows: for every single measure value m in C do the following:

1. For every i = 1,..., k, compute all maximal intervals I of values in dom_i such that, for every v in I, the slice T(v) is σ-frequent for m.
2. Combine the intervals in a levelwise manner as follows: at level l ($2 \leq l \leq k$), compute all σ-frequent blocks b = I_1 x...x I_k such that exactly l intervals defining b are different than ALL. Assuming that all blocks σ-frequent for m have been computed at the previous levels, this step can be achieved in much the

same way as frequent itemsets are computed in the algorithm Apriori.

3. Considering the set of all blocks computed in the previous step, sort out those that are not MS-blocks and those having a confidence for m less than γ.

It should be clear from definition 7 that a block can be frequent only if it contains at least σ.|C| cells. Similarly, it follows from definition 8 that, for a given confidence threshold γ, a block b is output only if it contains at least γ.|b| cells containing the measure value m. Therefore, when fixing the support and the confidence thresholds, the user actually determines thresholds concerning the size and the purity of the blocks the user wishes to obtain.

Block Generation for Single Measure Values

In the following algorithms, MS- or MG-blocks are computed according to the user's specification. Algorithm 1 performs step 1, while algorithm 2 performs steps 2 and 3.

Referring to the cube of example 1, the supports for measure value 8 of all slices of the cube is displayed in Figure 3, while Figure 1 depicts all blocks output by algorithm 2. These blocks are defined as follows:

b1 = [P1; P2] x [C1;C1] for value 6, b2 = [P3; P4] x [C1;C3] for value 8
b3 = [P1; P3] x [C3;C4] for value 5, b4 = [P3; P4] x [C4;C6] for value 2

Note that there are two overlappings: one between b2 and b3, and one between b3 and b4.

Processing Interval-Based Blocks

In this section, we consider the computation of blocks when intervals and fuzzy intervals are considered, instead of single measure values. In

this case, the following modifications must be made in the two algorithms given previously:

1. The supports and confidences must be computed accordingly. That is, in the case of interval based measure values, sup and conf must be replaced by i_sup and i_conf, respectively, and in the case of fuzzy interval based measure values, sup and conf must be replaced by f_sup and f_conf, respectively.

2. In algorithm 2, the most outer loop must range over the set of intervals (fuzzy or not according to the considered case), instead of over the set of all single measure values.

On the other hand, when considering intervals or fuzzy intervals, a preprocessing task must be applied on the data in order to discretize the measure values into (fuzzy) intervals. This discretization process can be automatically performed, provided that the user defines the number of intervals she wants to consider.

Denoting by N this number of intervals, and assuming that m_b (respectively m_t) is the bottom value (respectively the top value) of the measure values, $[m_b;m_t]$ can be divided into N intervals either in an equi-width manner (i.e., the widths of all intervals are equal), or in an equi-depth manner (i.e., all intervals cover the same number of cells). These intervals are denoted by $[bot_i;top_i]$ for i =1,...,N, and we note that for every i = 2,...,N, $bot_i = top_{i-1}$.

Then, in the case of fuzzy intervals, we consider N trapezoidal membership functions $μ_1$,..., $μ_N$ such that:

- $[bot_1;top_1]$ and $[bot_1;top_2]$ are respectively the kernel and the support of $μ_1$,
- $[bot_N;top_N]$ and $[bot_{N-1};top_N]$ are respectively the kernel and the support of $μ_N$,
- $[bot_{i-1};top_{i+1}]$ and $[bot_i;top_i]$ are respectively the support and kernel of $μ_i$, for i = 2,..., N-1.

Algorithm 1.

Algorithm 1: Computation of $\mathcal{L}_1(m)$

Data: A k-dimensional data cube C, a measure value m, a support
   threshold σ

Result: The set of intervals $\mathcal{L}_1(m)$, the set of corresponding blocks $\mathcal{B}_1(m)$

$\mathcal{L}_1(m) \leftarrow \emptyset$

foreach *dimension* d_i, $i = 1, \ldots, k$ **do**

    $int(m, i) \leftarrow \emptyset$

    $currentInterval \leftarrow [NIL, NIL]$

    foreach $j = 1, \ldots, dom_i$ **do**

        $s \leftarrow supp(\mathcal{T}(rep_i^{-1}(j)), m)$

        if $s < \sigma$ **then**

            if $currentInterval = [\alpha, NIL]$ *where* $\alpha \neq NIL$ **then**

                /* close the current interval at position $j - 1$, and set the
current interval to the empty interval */

                $int(m, i) \leftarrow int(m, i) \sqcup \{[\alpha, rep_i^{-1}(j - 1)]\}$

                $currentInterval \leftarrow [NIL, NIL]$

        else

            if $currentInterval = [NIL, NIL]$ **then**

                /* start a new current interval at position j */

                $currentInterval \leftarrow [rep_i^{-1}(j), NIL]$

            if $j = dom_i$ *and* $currentInterval = [\alpha, NIL]$ *where* $\alpha \neq NIL$
then

                $int(m, i) \leftarrow int(m, i) \sqcup \{[\alpha, rep_i^{-1}(j)]\}$

    $\mathcal{L}_1(m) \leftarrow \mathcal{L}_1(m) \sqcup int(m, i)$

$\mathcal{B}_1(m) \leftarrow \{b = \delta_1 \times \ldots \times \delta_k \quad (\exists i)(\delta_i \in int(m, i))$ and $(\forall j \neq i)(\delta_j = ALL_j)$ and $conf(b, m) \geq \gamma\}$

Figure 3. Occurences of measure value 8

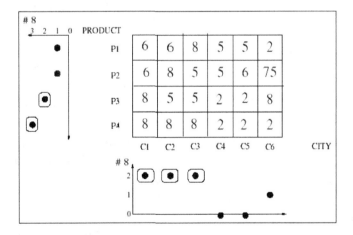

Algorithm 2. Discovery of MS-blocks

Algorithm 2: Discovery of MS-blocks

Data: A k-dimensional data cube C, a measure value m, a support
  threshold σ, and a confidence threshold γ.
Result: The set of blocks $\mathcal{B}$ associated with C
foreach *measure value m from C* **do**

    Compute $\mathcal{L}_1(m)$ and $\mathcal{B}_1(m)$
    for $l = 2$ *to* k **do**

       $\mathcal{B}_l(m) \leftarrow \emptyset$
       Generate from $\mathcal{L}_{l-1}$ all candidates $\delta_{i_1} \times \ldots \times \delta_{i_l}$ such that
       $(\forall p, p' \in [1..l])(i_p \neq i_{p'})$. Let $\mathcal{L}_l(m)$ be this set.
       Pruning: Delete from $\mathcal{L}_l(m)$ all candidates $\delta_{i_1} \times \ldots \times \delta_{i_l}$ such that
       $(\exists p \in \{1, \ldots, l\})(\delta_{i_1} \times \ldots \times \delta_{i_{p-1}} \times \delta_{i_{p+1}} \times \ldots \times \delta_{i_l} \notin \mathcal{L}_{l-1})$
       foreach *remaining candidate* $\delta_{i_1} \times \ldots \times \delta_{i_l}$ **do**

          Let b be the block $\delta_1 \times \ldots \times \delta_k$ where $\delta_p = \delta_{p_j}$ if dimension d_p
          has been treated and $\delta_p = ALL_p$ otherwise
          if $supp(b.m) < \sigma$ **then**
             Remove $\delta_{i_1} \times \ldots \times \delta_{i_l}$ from $\mathcal{L}_l(m)$
          else
             if $conf(b.m) \geq \gamma$ **then** $\mathcal{B}_l(m) \leftarrow \mathcal{B}_l(m) \cup \{b\}$

    $\mathcal{B}(m) \leftarrow \{b \in \bigcup_{l=1}^{l=k} \mathcal{B}_l(m) \mid b$ is an MS-block$\}$
    /* If MG-blocks are to be computed then replace MS with MG is the
    previous statement */
$\mathcal{B} \leftarrow \bigcup_m \mathcal{B}(m)$

It should also be noted from proposition 2 that blocks based on intervals and fuzzy intervals of measure values are larger than blocks based on single values.

Complexity Issues

In this section, we show that our method for computing blocks is polynomial in time with respect to the size of the cube C, but not complete, in the sense that blocks that fulfill the threshold conditions might not be output by our algorithms.

Let m be a measure value. In algorithm 1, the cube is scanned once for each dimension d_i. Thus, this step requires k scans of the cube C. Regarding the complexity of algorithm 2, at each level, the whole cube is scanned at most once, since the intervals produced by algorithm 1 for a given measure value do not overlap. As in algorithm 2, at most k iterations are processed, its execution requires at most k scans of the cube C. As a consequence, the computation of all frequent blocks associated to a given measure value m is in O(k.|C|). As computing the confidence of a block does not require the scanning of the cube (because the size of a block is the product of the sizes of the intervals defining this block), the time complexity of algorithm 2 is in O(k.|C|).

Hence, in the case of single measure values, the computation of all blocks is in O(k.|C|²), because C contains at most |C| distinct measure values. We note that although polynomial, the complexity of our method is not linear.

On the other hand, in the cases of (fuzzy) intervals of measure values, if we denote by N the number of these intervals, then the computation of blocks is in O(k.|C|.N), that is, linear with respect to the size |C| of C. The experiments reported in section 5 show the influence of the three factors (i.e., k, |C| and N) on the computation time.

As mentioned in the introductory section, the general problem of computing blocks of in a cube is known to be NP-hard, and the polynomial method proposed in the chapter computes an approximation of the solution, meaning that our method is not complete. As an example, we recall from example 1 that the block b = [C1;C2] x [P1;P2] is not an output, although its support and confidence are greater than the support and confidence thresholds, respectively. This is due to the fact that the slice T(C2) is not frequent for 6, which implies that the interval [C1;C2] is not computed by algorithm 1.

However, the following example shows that this is not the only reason for noncompleteness. More precisely, even if completeness would mean the computation of all blocks b such that, for a given measure value m:

1. $sup(b, m) \geq \sigma$ and $conf(b, m) \geq \gamma$, and
2. $(\forall i = 1,..., k)(\forall v \in \delta_i)(sup(T(v), m) \geq \sigma)$

then example 2 shows that our method is not complete either.

Example 2: Consider the cube C as shown in Figure 4 in which blocks are to be computed according to support and confidence thresholds equal to 1/15 and 80%, respectively.

Using algorithm 1 for the measure value 8, we obtain the intervals [C1;C6] and [P1;P4] because

all slices contain at least two 8-cells. However, since the confidence for 8 of the block [C1;C6] x [P1;P4] is equal to 12/24, which is less than 80%, this block is not computed by algorithm 2. On the other hand, it is easy to see that the two 8-blocks [C1;C3] x [P3;P4] and [C4;C6] x [P1;P2] satisfy the two items above.

In the next section, we study how to modify algorithm 1 so as to take into account situations as in example 2. Then we study the completeness of this modified method.

REFINING THE COMPUTATION OF BLOCKS

In this section, we take into account the cell neighborhoods in order to enhance the completeness of our method. Intuitively, cells are considered as neighbors if they share one side in the representation. For instance, in Figure 4 the cells $\langle P2, C3, 5\rangle$ and $\langle P2, C4, 8\rangle$ are neighbors.

Cell Neighborhood

Definition 11. Neighbor: Two distinct cells $c = \langle v_1,..., v_k, m\rangle$ and $c' = \langle v'_1,..., v'_k, m'\rangle$ are neighbors if there exists a unique i_0 in $\{1,..., k\}$ such that:

* $|rep_{i0}(v_{i0}) - rep_{i0}(v'_{i0})| = 1$ and
*   for every $i = 1,..., k$ such that $i \neq i_0$, $v_i = v_i'$.

Figure 4. The cube for example 2

PRODUCT						
P1	5	5	5	8	8	8
P2	5	5	5	8	8	8
P3	8	8	8	6	6	6
P4	8	8	8	6	6	6
	C1	C2	C3	C4	C5	C6	CITY

We note that in a k-dimensional cube, a cell has at most 2.k neighbors. Moreover, considering a slice T(v) where v is a member value of the domain dom_i, we denote by v- and v+ the member values of dom_i such that $rep_i(v-) = rep_i(v) - 1$ and $rep_i(v+) = rep_i(v) + 1$, respectively.

Clearly, every cell c in T(v) has exactly one neighbor in each of the slices T(v-) and T(v+).

As will be seen next, the refined computation of blocks requires to count, for every cell c, the number of neighbors of c that contain the same value. Clearly, this counting depends on whether we consider single measure values or intervals or fuzzy intervals. The following definition states how neighbors of a cell are counted in each of these cases.

In order to state this definition, we recall from Kaufmann (1973) that assessing the fact that the contents of two cells c and c' both belong to a given fuzzy interval φ, denoted by (c, φ) ⊗ (c', φ), can be done according to the following t-norms:

- Probalistic t-norm: $\mu((c, \varphi) \otimes (c', \varphi)) = \mu(c, \varphi) . \mu(c', \varphi)$
- Zadeh's t-norm: $\mu((c, \varphi) \otimes (c', \varphi)) = \min(\mu(c, \varphi), \mu(c', \varphi))$
- Lukasiewicz's t-norm: $\mu((c, \varphi) \otimes (c', \varphi)) = \max(\mu(c, \varphi) + \mu(c', \varphi) - 1, 0)$

Definition 12. Neighborhood counting: Let v be a member value.

1. If single measure values are considered, then for every such measure value m, we denote by n(v-, m), respectively n(v+, m), the number of m-cells in T(v) whose neighbor in T(v-), respectively in T(v+), is also an m-cell. Then neighbors(v-, m) and neighbors(v+, m) are defined as follows:

$$neighbors(v-, m) = \frac{n(v-, m)}{count(T(v), m)}$$

and

$$neighbors(v+, m) = \frac{n(v+, m)}{count(T(v), m)}$$

2. If intervals of measure values are considered, then for every such interval [m1;m2], given a member value v, we denote by i_n(v-, [m1;m2]), respectively i_n(v+, [m1;m2]), the number of cells in T(v) whose content is in [m1;m2] and whose neighbor in T(v-), respectively in T(v+), is a cell whose content is in [m1;m2].

Then, i_neighbors(v-, [m1;m2]) and i_neighbors (v+, [m1;m2]) are defined as follows:

$$i\_neighbors(v-, [m1;m2]) = \frac{i\_n(v-, [m1;m2])}{i\_count(T(v), [m1;m2])}$$

and

$$i\_neighbors(v+, [m1;m2]) = \frac{i\_n(v+, [m1;m2])}{i\_count(T(v), [m1;m2])}$$

3. If fuzzy intervals are considered, then given one of the above t-norms, a member value v and a fuzzy interval φ, we denote by f_neighbors(v-, φ) and f_neighbors(v+, φ) the following:

$$f\_neighbors(v-, \varphi) = \frac{\sum_{c \in T(v)}^{f} \mu(c\varphi) \otimes \mu(c-\varphi)}{fCount(T(v), \varphi)}$$

and

$$f\_neighbors(v+, \varphi) = \frac{\sum_{c \in T(v)}^{f} \mu(c\varphi) \otimes \mu(c+\varphi)}{fCount(T(v), \varphi)}$$

where c- and c+ are the neighbors of c in T(v-) and T(v+), respectively.

Intuitively, neighbors(v-, m) and neighbors(v+, m) are respectively the ratios of m-cells in a given slice having m-cells as neighbors in the previous slice, respectively in the next slice. The same remark also holds in the cases of intervals and fuzzy intervals.

Modified Computation of Blocks

Based on the notation previously introduced, our method works roughly as follows: We assume that, in addition to the support and confidence thresholds, we are given a new threshold called the neighbor threshold, denoted by v. When scanning dimension i for a given measure value m, let v be the member in dom_i of which the slice is being considered. If an interval of the form [V;NIL] where $V \neq NIL$ is under construction and if the support of T(v) is greater than the support threshold, then:

- If neighbors(v-, m) < v, then the interval [V;v-] is output and the computation of the new interval [v;NIL] is considered.
- If neighbors(v+, m) < v, then the interval [V;v] is output and the computation of the new interval [v+;NIL] is considered.
- Otherwise, the next slice, that is, the slice defined by v+, is considered for the interval [V;NIL].

Algorithm 3.

Algorithm 3: Modified Computation of $\mathcal{L}_1(m)$

Data: A k-dimensional data cube C, a measure value m, a support threshold σ, a neighbor threshold ν

Result: The set of intervals $\mathcal{L}_1(m)$, the set of corresponding blocks $\mathcal{B}_1(m)$

$\mathcal{L}_1(m) \leftarrow \emptyset$

foreach *dimension d_i, $i = 1, \ldots, k$* **do**

  $int(m, i) \leftarrow \emptyset$

  $currentInterval \leftarrow [NIL, NIL]$

  foreach $j = 1, \ldots, |dom_i|$ **do**

    $s \leftarrow supp(T(rep_i^{-1}(j)), m)$

    if $j < |dom_i|$ **then**

      $n^+ \leftarrow neighbors(rep_i^{-1}(j+1), m)$

    if $j > 1$ **then**

      $n^- \leftarrow neighbors(rep_i^{-1}(j-1), m)$

    if $s < \sigma$ **then**

      if $currentInterval = [\alpha, NIL]$ *where $\alpha \neq NIL$* **then**

        $int(m, i) \leftarrow int(m, i) \cup \{[\alpha, rep_i^{-1}(j-1)]\}$

        $currentInterval \leftarrow [NIL, NIL]$

    else

      /* $s = supp(T(rep_i^{-1}(j)), m) \geq \sigma$ */

      if $currentInterval = [NIL, NIL]$ **then**

        /* start a new current interval at position j */

        $currentInterval \leftarrow [rep_i^{-1}(j), NIL]$

      if $currentInterval \neq [NIL, NIL]$ **then**

        /* $currentInterval = [\alpha, NIL]$ */

        if $j > 1$ *and* $j \neq \alpha$ **then**

          if $n^- < \nu$ **then**

            $int(m, i) \leftarrow int(m, i) \cup \{[\alpha, rep_i^{-1}(j-1)]\}$

            $currentInterval \leftarrow [rep_i^{-1}(j), NIL]$

        if $j < |dom_i|$ **then**

          if $n^+ < \nu$ **then**

            $int(m, i) \leftarrow int(m, i) \cup \{[\alpha, rep_i^{-1}(j)]\}$

            $currentInterval \leftarrow [j+1, NIL]$

        else

          /* $j = |dom_i|$ */

          $int(m, i) \leftarrow int(m, i) \cup \{[\alpha, rep_i^{-1}(j)]\}$

  $\mathcal{L}_1(m) \leftarrow \mathcal{L}_1(m) \cup int(m, i)$

$\mathcal{B}_1(m) \leftarrow \{b = \delta_1 \times \ldots \times \delta_k \mid (\exists i)(\delta_i \in int(m, i))$ and $(\forall j \neq i)(\delta_j = ALL_j)$ and $conf(b, m) \geq \gamma\}$

The corresponding algorithm is given below and is referred to as algorithm 3. In the remainder of the chapter, we call algorithm 2.1 the algorithm obtained from algorithm 2 by replacing algorithm 1 with algorithm 3 for the computation of L_1. It should also be clear that in the case of intervals (respectively fuzzy intervals) of measure values, in algorithm 3, sup and neighbors should respectively be replaced by i_sup and i_neighbors (respectively by f_sup and f_neighbors).

Example 3: We illustrate algorithm 3 using the cube of Figure 4 and we consider the same thresholds as in example 2, that is: $\sigma = 1/15$ and $\gamma = 80\%$. Moreover, let the neighbor threshold ν be 60%.

In this case, for dimension CITY and measure value 8, algorithm 3 starts with [NIL;NIL] as the value for currentInterval and processes the first slice T(C1). As its support is greater than 1/12, and as j = 1, only n+ is computed, and is found equal to 1. Therefore the value of currentInterval is set to [1;NIL] and the next slice, that is, T(C2) is processed. In this case, n+ and n- are computed and both are found equal to 1. Thus, the slice T(C3) is processed.

At this stage, we find n- = 1 and n+ = 0. Since $0 \le \nu$, the interval [C1;C3] is output, the value of currentInterval is set to [C4;NIL] and the slice T(C4) is processed. Now, we find n- = 0 and n+ = 1. As in this case, j = α in algorithm 3, no computation is done and the slice T(C5) is processed,

which does not lead to any change. Finally the processing of the slice T(C6) results in the interval [C4;C6], since $|\text{dom}_{\text{CITY}}| = 6$.

It can be seen that, for dimension PRODUCT and measure value 8, the computation is similar and outputs the two intervals [P1;P2] and [P3;P4]. Therefore, for measure value 8, we obtain L1(8) = {[C1;C3], [C4;C6], [P1;P2], [P3;P4]}.

Regarding the computation of the blocks, it is easy to see that, in this example, algorithm 2.1 computes the two blocks [C1;C3] x [P3;P4] and [C4;C6] x [P1;P2], since their confidence is 1.

Completeness Properties

In this section, we study the completeness of our approach in the case of single measure values. In particular, we show that if we consider a cube that can be partitioned into nonoverlapping blocks containing the same measure value, then algorithm 2.1 computes these blocks.

First, we show that, for limit thresholds, our approach is complete for any cube C, in the sense that Algorithm 2.1 outputs blocks that represent exactly the content of C. In what follows, we call limit thresholds:

- A support threshold such that $0 \le \sigma < 1/|C|$,
- A confidence threshold such that $\gamma = 1$,
- A neighbor threshold such that $\nu = 1$.

Figure 5. The cube for example 4

PRODUCT							
P1	5	5	5	5	6	6	
P2	5	8	5	5	6	6	
P3	5	8	8	5	6	6	
P4	8	8	8	8	6	6	
	C1	C2	C3	C4	C5	C6	CITY

Before giving the corresponding theorem, we note that considering limit thresholds implies the following:

- A block b is frequent for m if and only if b contains at least one m-cell.
- A block b such that conf(b, m) > γ contains only m-cells.
- If in algorithm 3, $L_1(m)$ is computed according to ν = 1, then for every m-cell c in a block b returned by algorithm 2.1, all neighbors of c that belong to b are also m-cells.

Now, the completeness of our approach can be stated as follows, in the case of limit thresholds.

Theorem 1

Let C be a k-dimensional cube. Then for limit thresholds, algorithm 2.1 outputs a set of blocks B such that for every cell $c = \langle v_1,..., v_k, m \rangle$ in C, there exists one and only one block b in B associated with m that contains c.

- **Proof**: Let us first consider a cell $c = \langle v_1,..., v_k, m \rangle$ in C. Since we assume that $0 \leq \sigma \leq 1/|C|$, every slice $T(v_i)$ is frequent for m. Therefore, according to algorithm 3, each v_i is in an interval δ_i of $L_1(m)$. Let us consider the block $b = \delta_1 \times ... \times \delta_k$ that, clearly, contains c.
  Since we assume limit thresholds, all neighbors of c in b are m-cells, and thus, so are all cells of b. As a consequence, conf(b, m) = 1 and thus b is output by algorithm 2.1, which shows that there exists at least one block b in B associated with m that contains c.

Assuming that two such blocks b and b' can exist implies that b and b' overlap and that they both contain only m-cells. However, this situation cannot happen because for any given measure value m, algorithm 3 computes nonoverlapping intervals. So, the proof is complete.

We note that, although Theorem 1 shows an important theoretical feature of our approach, its impact in practice is of little relevance. Indeed, as shown in the following example, in the worst case, algorithm 2.1 outputs blocks that are reduced to one single cell. However, the following example also shows that, with realistic threshold values, our approach can compute relevant blocks, even if in C, the measure values are not displayed in the form of blocks.

Example 4: Let us consider the 2-dimensional cube C of Figure 5 and limit thresholds, for instance σ = 0 and γ = ν = 1. In this case, for measure values 5 and 8, algorithm 2.1 computes blocks that are reduced to one single cell, whereas for the measure value 6, algorithm 2.1 computes the block $[C5;C6] \times ALL_{PRODUCT}$.

To see this, let us consider the computation of L1(8) for dimension CITY. First, for σ = 0, every slice $T(Ci)$, i = 1,...,6, is frequent for 8. Moreover, for all slices, neighbors(Ci-, 8) or neighbors(Ci+, 8) are less than 1. Therefore, algorithm 3 computes the intervals [Ci;Ci], for i = 1,..., 6. For dimension PRODUCT, a similar computation is produced and we obtain:

$$L_1(8) = \{[Ci;Ci] \mid i = 1,..., 6\} \cup \{[Pj;Pj] \mid j = 1,..., 4\}$$

Then, when combining these intervals, algorithm 2.1 outputs each 8-cell of C as a block.

It can be seen that a similar computation is done for the measure value 5, whereas, for measure value 6 the block $[C5;C6] \times ALL_{PRODUCT}$ is returned by algorithm 2.1.

Now, we would like to emphasize that if we consider nonlimit thresholds, our approach computes relevant blocks, even in the case of this example. Indeed, let us consider as in example 2, σ = 1/15, γ = 80% and ν = 60%. Then, algorithm 3 returns the following:

$$L_1(5) = \{[C1;C1], [C3;C4], [P1;P3]\},$$

$L_i(6) = \{[C1;C1], [P1;P4]\}$,
$L_i(8) = \{[C2;C3], [P3;P4]\}$.

Applying algorithm 2.1, we obtain the following blocks:

• For measure value 5: [C1;C1] x [P1;P3] and [C3;C4] x [P1;P3].
• For measure value 6: [C5;C6] x [P1;P4].
• For measure value 8: [C2;C3] x [P3;P4].

We note that, in this case, two blocks overlap and that only two cells (namely $\langle C2, P1, 5\rangle$ and $\langle C4, P4, 8\rangle$) do not belong to any of these blocks.

Now, the following proposition shows that, when in C, measure values are displayed in the form of blocks, then algorithm 2.1 actually computes these blocks. To this end, we use the following terminology: a block b with all cells containing the same measure value m is called an m-block. Moreover, we introduce the notion of block partition as follows.

Definition 12. Block partition: Let C be a k-dimensional cube and $B = \{b_1,..., b_n\}$ a set of blocks such that, for every i = 1,..., n, all cells of b_i contain the same measure value mi. B is called a block partition of C if:

• For all distinct i and i' in {1,..., n}, $b_i \cap b_{i'} = \varnothing$

• $b_1 \cup ... \cup b_n$ is equal to the set of all cells of C.

The block partition $B = \{b_1,..., b_n\}$ of C is said to be maximal if for any measure value m, there does not exist an m-block in C that contains an m-block b_i in B.

It is easy to see that, for the cube C of Figure 3.3, the set B = {[C1;C3] x [P3; P4], [C4;C6] x [P1; P2], [C1;C3] x [P1;P2], [C4;C6] x [P3;P4]} is a maximal block partition of C in which [C1;C3] x [P3;P4] and [C4;C6] x [P1;P2] are two 8-blocks, [C1;C3] x [P1;P2] is a 5-block, and [C4;C6] x [P3;P4] is a 6-block.

Moreover, it can also be seen that, considering limit thresholds (e.g., $\sigma = 0$, $\gamma = \nu = 1$), Algorithm 2.1 computes exactly these blocks.

The following proposition generalizes this remark, and thus shows that our method is complete when the cube can be maximally partitioned into m-blocks.

Proposition 3: Let C be a k-dimensional cube and let $B = \{b_1,..., b_n\}$ be a maximal block partition of C. Assume that, for every measure value m, it is the case that for all m-blocks $b_i = \delta_{i,1} \times ... \times \delta_{i,k}$ and $b_j = \delta_{j,1} \times ... \times \delta_{j,k}$ in B, $\delta_{i,p} \cap \delta_{j,p} = \varnothing$ for every p = 1,..., k. Then, for limit thresholds, algorithm 2.1 returns B.

Figure 6. The cube for example 5

PRODUCT

	C1	C2	C3	C4	C5	C6
P1	5	5	5	8	5	5
P2	5	5	5	8	5	5
P3	8	8	8	8	8	8
P4	5	5	5	5	5	8

CITY

• **Proof**: We first note that theorem 1 shows that algorithm 2.1 computes sub-blocks of blocks in B. So, we have to show that for every m-block $b_i = \delta_{i,1} \times ... \times \delta_{i,k}$ in B, algorithm 3 returns exactly each interval $\delta_{i,p}$ for every $p = 1, ..., k$.

Given one of these intervals for dimension p, say $\delta_{i,p} = [\alpha, \beta]$, let us assume that algorithm 3 returns an interval $\delta'_{i,p} = [\alpha', \beta']$ such that $\delta'_{i,p} \subset \delta_{i,p}$.

Hence, one of the following two inequalities hold: $rep_p(\alpha) < rep_p(\alpha')$ or $rep_p(\beta') < rep_p(\beta)$. Assuming that $rep_p(\alpha) < rep_p(\alpha')$, let us consider the slice $T(\alpha')$. According to our hypothesis on the intervals, b_i is the only m-block in B that intersects $T(\alpha')$. As a consequence, $T(\alpha')$ contains at least one m-cell, and thus is frequent for m.

Moreover, since b_i is a block and since $rep_p(\alpha) < rep_p(\alpha')$, for every m-cell $c = \langle v_1, ..., v_{p-1}, \alpha', v_{p+1}, v_k, m \rangle$ in $T(\alpha')$, the cell $c- = \langle v_1, ..., v_{p-1}, v, v_{p+1}, v_k, m' \rangle$ where $v = rep^{-1}_p(rep_p(\alpha) - 1)$ is such that $m = m'$ (i.e., c- is an m-cell). Therefore, in algorithm 3, the value of n- for the slice $T(\alpha')$ is 1, in which case no new interval is considered. Thus, we have $\alpha = \alpha'$. As it can be shown in the same way that $\beta = \beta'$, the proof is complete.

The following example shows that, if in the maximal partition B of C two m-blocks $b = \delta_1 \times ... \times \delta_k$ and $b' = \delta'_1 \times ... \times \delta'_k$ are such that $\delta_i \cap \delta'_i \neq \varnothing$ for some i, then algorithm 2.1 does not compute B.

Example 5: Consider the cube C as shown in Figure 6 in which blocks are to be computed according to the limit thresholds. In this case, a maximal partition B of C is:

B = {[C1;C3] x [P1;P2], [C4;C4] x [P1;P2], [C5;C6] x [P1;P2], [C1;C6] x [P3;P3], [C1;C6] x [P4;P4]}.

It is clear that B does not satisfy the hypothesis of proposition 3, due, for instance, to the two 5-blocks [C1;C3] x [P1;P2] and [C1;C6] x [P4;P4].

On the other hand, running algorithm 2.1 on the cube C of Figure 6 does not produce B, since the 5-block [C1;C3] x [P4; P4] is split into [C4;C4] x [P4;P4] and [C5;C6] x [P4;P4] by the algorithm.

Figure 7. Number of discovered blocks w.r.t. the numbers of dimensions

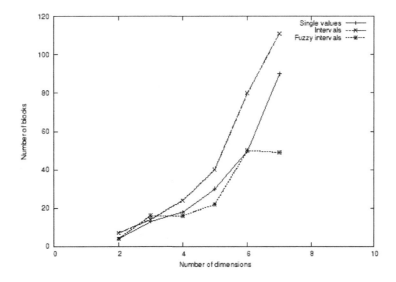

Figure 8. Number of discovered blocks w.r.t. the numbers of members

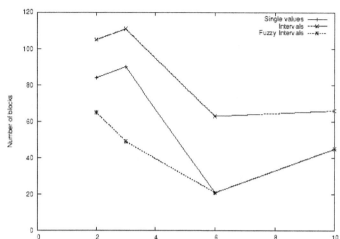

Figure 9. Runtime w.r.t. the size of the cube

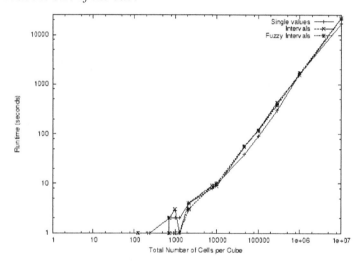

Figure 10. Runtime w.r.t. the size of the cube

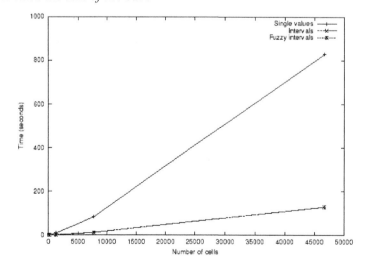

In fact, Theorem 1 shows that in this case, algorithm 2.1 outputs a nonmaximal partition of C that refines B in the following sense: for every block b computed by algorithm2.1, there exists a block b' in B such that $b \subset b'$.

It should be noticed that, in the case of intervals, theorem 1 and proposition 3 still hold since pairwise disjoint intervals can be thought of as single values.

However, in the case of fuzzy intervals, we conjecture that our completeness results do not hold, because in this case, a member value v may belong to more than one interval. On the other hand, based on proposition 2, it is conjectured that blocks computed by our method still cover the whole cube C, *i.e.*, it can be shown that:

1. For theorem 1, each cell belongs to at least one block in B, and
2. For proposition 3, algorithm 2.1 outputs super blocks of blocks in B.

EXPERIMENTS

In this section, we report on experiments in terms of runtime, number of blocks, and rate of overlapping blocks. Experiments have been performed on synthetic multidimensional data randomly generated. Depending on the experiments, the cubes contain up to 10^7 cells, the number of dimensions ranges from 2 to 9; the number of members per dimension ranges from 2 to 10, and the number of cell values ranges from 5 to 1000.

The first experiments report on the impact of taking into account single values, or intervals, or fuzzy intervals.

Figure 7 shows the number of blocks output by the three methods (single values, intervals, and fuzzy intervals) according to the number of dimensions, and Figure 8 shows the number of blocks output by the three methods (single values, intervals, and fuzzy intervals) according to the number of members per dimension.

It should be noted that we obtain more blocks based on intervals than blocks based on single values. This is due to the fact that taking intervals

Figure 11. Rate of overlapping block w.r.t. the number of dimensions

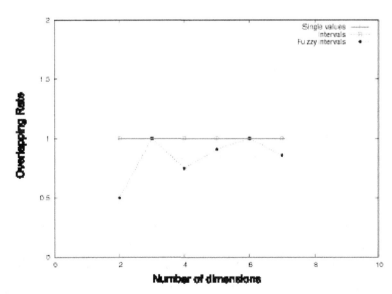

Figure 12. Runtime w.r.t. the number of measure values with and without neighbors (5 dimensions, 9 members per dimension)

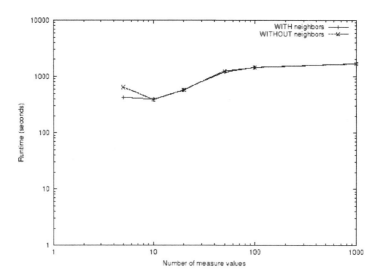

Figure 13. Number of blocks w.r.t. the number of measure values with and without neighbors (5 dimensions, 8 members per dimension; v = 50%)

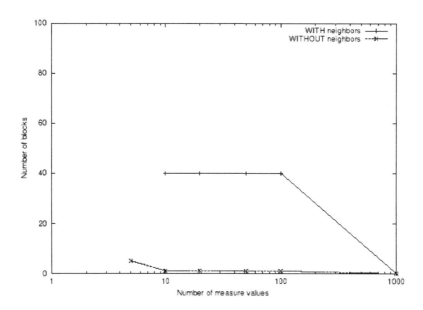

into account increases the chance for a value to match a block value. However, the number of blocks based on fuzzy intervals is lower than the number of blocks based on the other two methods. This is due to the fact that fuzzy blocks can merge several blocks (which would have overlapped, as shown below).

Figure 9 and Figure 10 show the runtime of the three methods (single values, intervals, fuzzy intervals) according to the size of the cube (number of cells). It can be seen that taking intervals and fuzzy intervals into account leads to slightly higher runtimes, if compared with the case of single measure values. However, all runtimes are still comparable and behave the same way.

Figure 11 shows the rate of overlapping blocks depending on the method (single values, intervals of fuzzy intervals) according to the number of dimensions of the cube. This figure suggests that, in the case of this dataset, using crisp methods leads to the fact that many blocks overlap (100% in the case of this experiment), while taking fuzziness into account reduces the rate of overlapping. This fact could be put in relation with the imprecision/uncertainty trade, that is, the more certain, the less precise and conversely.

We also conducted experiments in order to assess the impact of taking neighbors into account. Figure 12 shows the behavior of the runtime according to the number of cell values. It can be seen that taking neighbors into account has no significant effect on the runtime.

Figure 13 shows the behavior of the number of blocks according to the number of measure values. It can be seen that taking neighbors into account leads to the discovery of more blocks.

We have also applied our method on the Titanic database (Blake, Newman, Hettich, & Merz, 1998). In this case, the database is organized according to four dimensions:

1. Dimension called PASSENGER CLASS and defined on $dom_{PASSENGER\ CLASS}$ = {1st, 2nd, 3rd, crew}.
2. Dimension called AGE and defined on dom_{AGE} = {adult, child}
3. Dimension called SEX and defined on dom_{SEX} = {male, female}
4. Dimension called SURVIVED and defined on $dom_{SURVIVED}$ = {yes, no}

Moreover, we have considered a representation of the cube defined from the usual order as implicitly stated in the Titanic file (Blake et al., 1998), that is:

* $rep_1(1st) < rep_1(2nd) < rep_1(3rd) < rep_1(crew)$
* $rep_2(adult) < rep_2(child)$
* $rep_3(male) < rep_3(female)$
* $rep_4(yes) < rep_4(no)$

The cube consists of 32 cells the content of which being the number of passengers concerned by the combination of one value per dimension. These numbers ranging from 0 to 670, we have partitioned the interval [0;670] into the following four intervals: [0;0],]0;20],]20;192],]192;670].

Considering the actual content of the cube, the first bin corresponds to no passenger, the second bin corresponds to numbers of passengers ranging from 4 to 20 (since there are no values between 0 and 4), the third bin corresponds to numbers of passengers ranging from 35 to 192 (since there are no values between 20 and 35), and the last bin corresponds to numbers of passengers ranging from 387 to 670 (since there are no values between 192 and 387).

We first note that, with a minimum confidence threshold of 50% and a minimum support threshold of 2/32, taking single measure values into account has lead to the discovery of no block. On the other hand, with the same thresholds, when considering the intervals defined above, the following four blocks have been discovered:

1. $b1 = ALL_{PASSENGERCLASS}$ x [child;child] x ALL_{SEX} x [no;no], a]192;670]-block meaning that the number of those passengers who were male children and who did not survive is among the highest.
2. $b2$ = [1st;3rd] x [adult;adult] x ALL_{SEX} x $ALL_{SURVIVED}$, a]20;192]-block meaning that the number of those adult passengers who were not crew members, whatever their sex and whatever their fate (survived or not) was between 35 and 192.

3. b3 = [1st;2nd] x [child;child] x ALL$_{SEX}$ x ALL$_{SURVIVED}$, a]0;20]-block meaning that the number of those children passengers belonging to class 1st or 2nd, whatever their sex and their fate (survived or not), was very low but not null.

4. b4 = [crew;crew] x [child;child] x ALL$_{SEX}$ x ALL$_{SURVIVED}$, a [0;0]-block meaning that there were no children hired as crew members.

RELATED WORK

The work on the building of blocks of similar values in a given data cube as presented in this chapter can be related to the work on data clustering of high dimensional data, which is an important area in data mining. For a large multidimensional database where the data space is usually not uniformly occupied, data clustering identifies the sparse and dense areas and thus discovers the overall distribution patterns (or summary) of the dataset. Some examples of work on clustering of high dimensional data include CLARANS (Ng & Han, 2002), BIRCH (Zhang, Ramakrishnan, & Livny, 1996), CLIQUE (Gunopulos, Agrawal, Gehrke, & Raghavan, 1998), and CURE (Guha, Rastagi, & Shim, 1998). Several subspace clustering methods are introduced to detect clusters residing in different subspaces (i.e., subsets of the original dimensions). In this case, no new dimension is generated. Each resultant cluster is associated with a specific subspace. Some examples of these methods are CLIQUE (Gunopulos et al., 1998) and ORCLUS (Aggrawal & Yu, 2000).

CLustering In QUEst (CLIQUE) adopts a density-based approach to clustering in which a cluster is defined as a region that has higher density of points than its surrounding area. To approximate the density of data points, the data space is partitioned into a finite set of cells. Note that a block in our work is almost similar to the concept unit in Gunopulos et al. (1998) which

is obtained by partitioning every dimension into intervals of equal length. Thus a unit in the subspace is the intersection of an interval from each of the k dimensions of a k-dimensional cube. However, the construction of the blocks in Gunopulos et al. (1998) is not determined by the same measure value, but rather by arbitrary chosen partitions of the member values. Constructing subspaces using various methods can be viewed as related research but the aim is normally directed to tackling the issue of high dimensionality for clustering problems.

Research work on (fuzzy) image segmentation may appear as related works (Philipp-Foliguet, Bernardes, Vieira, & Sanfourche, 2002). Although the goals are the same, it is not possible to apply such methods due to problems of scalability and because also of the multidimensional nature of data. For example, clustering-based color image segmentation (Turi, 2001) is normally limited to a 2-dimensional environment with the possibility of an extension to 3 dimensions.

Segmentation methods (e.g., clustering) have been proposed in the multidimensional context (Ester, Kriegel, Sander, Wimmer, & Xu, 1998; Gunopulos 1998). In Gyenesei (2000), the author studies the generation of fuzzy partitions over numerical dimensions. However, these propositions are not related to our measure-based approach, and thus these propositions are different from our work where the measure value is the central criterion. On the other hand, the feature selection methods are used to select a subset of dimensions for supervised classification problem (Motoda & Huan, 1998). The idea is to produce an optimal pool of good dimension subsets for searching clusters. Therefore, in this approach, clusters are built up according to criteria related to dimensions whereas in our approach, blocks are built up according to similarity criteria on the measure values.

In Lakshmanan, Pei, and Han (2002) the authors aim at compressing data cubes. However there is no consideration on cube representations and homogeneous blocks generation. The work presented in Barbara and Sullivan (1997) proposes a method to divide cubes into regions and to represent those regions. However, the authors aim at representing the whole cube. They use statistical methods to construct an approximation of the cube, while we aim at discovering relevant areas, which may not cover the whole cube. In Wang, Lu, Feng, and Yu (2002), the authors propose the concept of condensed data cube. However, the authors aim at considering the cube without loss of information, while we aim at displaying relevant information to the user, which may be a partial representation of data.

CONCLUSION

In this chapter, we have presented an efficient method for summarizing and visualizing multidimensional data. In our approach, blocks of homogeneous data are built to summarize the content of a given data cube, based on user specified thresholds. We have used a levelwise approach for the computation of the blocks and we have shown that our approach is tractable, in particular when the set of measure values is partitioned into (fuzzy) intervals. Although efficiency results in a noncomplete method, completeness issues have been considered, and the experimental results obtained on synthetic datasets show that relevant blocks can be obtained efficiently.

In our future work, we plan to run further tests on real data to better assess the effectiveness and the accuracy of our approach. Moreover, we are also investigating the following research issues:

- How to combine the work in Choong et al. (2003) and the work presented in this chapter, in order to find a representation of the data cube for which large blocks can be computed?
- How standard OLAP operators such as roll-up or drill-down impact the blocks?

More precisely, having built the blocks for a given level of details, can we optimize the construction of the blocks on the same data cube on which a roll-up or drill-down operation has been applied?
- The visualization of the blocks computed by our approach is also an issue we want to investigate further, based on our preliminary work reported in Choong et al. (2007).

NOTE

This work is supported by the French Ministry of Foreign Affairs and French Council of Scientific Research (CNRS) under the STIC-Asia project *EXPEDO* framework.

REFERENCES

Aggrawal, C. C., & Yu, P. S. (2000). Finding generalized clusters in high dimensional spaces. In *Procceedings of the ACM International Conference on Management Of Data (SIGMOD '00)*.

Agrawal R., Imielinski, T., & Swami, A. (1993). Mining association rules between sets of items in large databases. In *Proceeding of ACM International Conference on Management Of Data (SIGMOD '93)*, SIGMOD Record. 22(2): (pp. 207-216).

Barbara, D., & Sullivan, M. (1997). Quasi-cubes: Exploiting approximation in multidimensional data sets. *SIGMOD Record, 26*(2), 12-17.

Blake, C. L., Newman, D. J., Hettich, S., & Merz, C. J. (1998). UCI repository of machine learning databases. Retrieved March 18, 2007, from http://www.ics.uci.edu/~mlearn/MLRepository.html

Choong, Y. W., Laurent, D., & Laurent, A. (2004). Summarizing multidimensional databases using fuzzy rules. *In Proceedings of the International Conference Information Processing and Manage-*

ment of Uncertainty in Knowledge-Based Systems (IPMU '04) Universdita degli studi di Perugia.

Choong, Y. W., Laurent, D., & Laurent, A. (2007). Pixelizing data cubes: A block-based approach. *In IEEE EMBS Visual Information Expert Workshop (VIEW '06).* Lecture Notes in Computer Science.

Choong, Y. W., Laurent, D., & Marcel, P. (2003). Computing appropriate representation for multidimensional data. *Data and Knowledge Engineering International Journal, 45,* 181-203.

Codd, E. F., Codd, S. B., & Salley, C. T. (1993). *Providing OLAP to user-analysts: An IT mandate* (Tech. Rep.). Arbor Software Corporation. Retrieved March 18, 2007, from http://dev.hyperion.com/resource_library/white_papers/providing_olap_to_user_analysts.pdf

Dubois, D., Hülermeier, E., & Prade, H. (2003). A note on quality measures for fuzzy association rules. In *Proceedings of International Fuzzy Systems Association World Congress on Fuzzy Sets and Systems.*

Ester, M., Kriegel, H.-P., Sander, J., Wimmer, M., & Xu, X. (1998). Incremental clustering for mining in a data warehousing environment. In *Proceedings of the International Conference on Very Large Data Bases (VLDB).*

Guha, S., Rastagi, R., & Shim, K. (1998). CURE: An efficient clustering algorithm for large databases. In *Proceedings of the ACM International Conference on Management Of Data (SIGMOD '98).*

Gunopulos, D., Agrawal, R., Gehrke, J., & Raghavan, P. (1998). Automatic subspace clustering of high dimensional data for data mining applications. In *Proceedings of the ACM International Conference on Management Of Data (SIGMOD '98).*

Gyenesei, A. (2000). *A fuzzy approach for mining quantitative association rules* (Tech. Rep. 336). Turku Center for Computer Science (TUCS).

Inmon, W. H. (1992). *Building the data warehouse.* John Wiley & Sons.

Kaufmann, A. (1973). *Introduction to the theory of fuzzy subsets.* Academic Press.

Lakshmanan, L., Pei, J., & Han, J. (2002). Quotient cube: How to summarize the semantics of a data cube. In *Proceedings of the International Conference on Very Large Data Bases VLDB.*

Motoda, H., & Huan, Liu. (1998). *Feature selection for knowledge discovery and data mining.* Kluwer Academic Publishers.

Ng, R. T., & Han, J. (2002). CLARANS: A method for clustering objects for spatial data mining. *IEEE Transactions on Knowledge and Data Engineering, 14*(5), 1003-1016.

Philipp-Foliguet, S., Bernardes, Vieira, M., & Sanfourche, M. (2002). Fuzzy segmentation of color images and indexing of fuzzy regions. In *Proceedings of the 1st European Conference on Color in Graphics, Image and Vision (CGIV '02).*

Turi, R. H. (2001). *Clustering-based colour image segmentation.* Unpublished doctoral thesis. Monash University, Australia.

Wang, W., Lu, H., Feng, J., & Yu, J. X. (2002). Condensed cube: An effective approach to reducing data cube size. In *Proceedings of the International Conference on Data Engeneering (ICDE).*

Zhang, T., Ramakrishnan, R., & Livny, M. (1996). Birch: An efficient data clustering method for very large databases. In *Proceedings of the ACM International Conference on Management Of Data (SIGMOD '96).*

Chapter VII
Social Network Mining from the Web

Yutaka Matsuo
Japanese Institute of Advanced Industrial Science and Technology, Japan

Junichiro Mori
DFKI GmbH, Germany

Mitsuru Ishizuka
University of Tokyo, Japan

ABSTRACT

This chapter describes social network mining from the Web. Since the end of the 1990s, several attempts have been made to mine social network information from e-mail messages, message boards, Web linkage structure, and Web content. In this chapter, we specifically examine the social network extraction from the Web using a search engine. The Web is a huge source of information about relations among persons. Therefore, we can build a social network by merging the information distributed on the Web. The growth of information on the Web, in addition to the development of a search engine, opens new possibilities to process the vast amounts of relevant information and mine important structures and knowledge.

INTRODUCTION

Social networks play important roles in our daily lives. People conduct communications and share information through social relations with others such as friends, family, colleagues, collaborators, and business partners. Social networks profoundly influence our lives without our knowledge of the implications. Potential applications of social networks in information systems are presented in Staab, Domingos, Mika, Golbeck, Ding, and Finin (2005). Examples include viral marketing through social networks (see also Leskovec, Adamic, & Huberman, 2005) and e-mail filtering based on social networks.

A social network is a social structure comprising nodes, which generally represent individuals or organizations. The structure reflects the ways in which they are connected through various social familiarities ranging from casual acquaintances to close familial bonds. Social network analysis (SNA) is a technique in sociology, by which a node is called an *actor* and an edge is called a *tie*. From the 1930's, social network analysis has been applied to various kinds of relational data, which relate one agent to another; such data cannot be reduced to the properties of individual agents themselves (Scott, 2000). In contrast to the long history of SNA in sociology, research on *complex networks* has received much attention since 1998, led by researchers from statistical physics and computer science fields: D. Watts, A. Barabasi, and A. Newman.

Social networks have become familiar recently because of the increasing use and development of social networking services (SNSs). As a kind of online application, SNSs are useful to register personal information including a user's friends and acquaintances; the systems promote information exchange such as sending messages and reading Weblogs. Friendster[1] and Orkut[2] are among the earliest and most successful SNSs. Increasingly, SNSs target focused communities such as music, medical, and business communities. In Japan, one large SNS has more than 7 million users, followed by more than 70 SNSs that have specific characteristics for niche communities. Information sharing on SNSs is a promising application of SNSs (Goecks & Mynatt, 2004; Mori, Ishizuka, Sugiyama, & Matsuo, 2005) because large amounts of information such as private photos, diaries, and research notes are neither completely open nor closed: they can be shared loosely among a user's friends, colleagues, and acquaintances. Several commercial services such as Imeem[3] and Yahoo! 360°[4] provide file sharing with elaborate access control.

In the context of the Semantic Web studies, social networks are crucial to realize a web of trust, which enables the estimation of information credibility and trustworthiness (Golbeck & Hendler, 2004). Because anyone can say anything on the Web, the web of trust helps humans and machines to discern which contents are credible, and to determine which information is reliably useful. Ontology construction is also related to a social network. For example, if numerous people share two concepts, the two concepts might be related (Mika, 2005). In addition, when mapping one ontology to another, persons who are between the two communities, or those who participate in both, play an important role. Social networks enable us to detect such persons with high *betweenness*.

Several means exist to demarcate social networks. One approach is to compel users to describe relations to others. In studies of the social sciences, network questionnaire surveys are often performed to obtain social networks, for example, asking "Please indicate which persons you would regard as your friend." Current SNSs realize such procedures online. However, the obtained relations are sometimes inconsistent: users do not name some of their friends merely because they are not in the SNS or perhaps the user has merely forgotten them. Some name hundreds of friends, but others name only a few. Therefore, deliberate control of sampling and inquiry are necessary to obtain high-quality social networks on SNSs.

In contrast, automatic detection of relations is possible from various sources of information such as e-mail archives, schedule data, and Web citation information (Adamic, Buyukkokten, & Adar, 2003; Miki, Nomura, & Ishida, 2005; Tyler, Wilkinson, & Huberman, 2003). Especially in some studies, social networks are extracted by measuring the co-occurrence of names on the Web. Pioneering work was done in that area by H. Kautz: the system is called Referral Web (Kautz, Selman, & Shah, 1997). Several researchers have used that technique to extract social networks, as described in the next section.

This chapter presents an overview of social

network mining from the Web. The growth of information on the Web plus the development of a search engine opens new possibilities to handle the vast relevant information and mine important structures and knowledge. Some basic algorithms are described along with advanced algorithms. Such algorithms are summarized and described in brief pseudocodes. Surprisingly, a few components that use search engines comprise various algorithms. New aspects of social networks are investigated: classes of relations, scalability, and a person-word matrix.

This chapter is organized as follows. The following section describes the background and motivations. Then, we address basic algorithms to obtain social networks from the Web. Advanced algorithms are described next, including their evaluations. We discuss several important issues, and briefly overview some examples of social network applications. After describing future trends, we conclude this chapter.

BACKGROUND

In the mid-1990's, Kautz and Selman developed a social network extraction system from the Web, called *Referral Web* (Kautz, Selman, & Shah, 1997). The system particularly records co-occurrence of names on Web pages using a search engine. It estimates the strength of relevance of two persons, X and Y by putting a query "X and Y" to a search engine: If X and Y share a strong relation, we can find much evidence that might include their respective homepages, lists of co-authors among technical papers, citations of papers, and organizational charts. The system automatically obtains a path from a person to a person (e.g., from *Henry Kautz* to *Marvin Minsky*). Later, with development of the WWW and Semantic Web technology, more information on our daily activities has become available online. Automatic extraction of social relations has much greater potential and demand now compared to

when Referral Web was first developed.

Recently, P. Mika developed a system for extraction, aggregation and visualization of online social networks for a Semantic Web community, called Flink (Mika, 2005)[5]. Social networks are obtained using analyses of Web pages, e-mail messages, and publications and self-created profiles (FOAF files). The Web mining component of Flink, similarly to that in Kautz's work, employs a co-occurrence analysis. Given a set of names as input, the component uses a search engine to obtain hit counts for individual names as well as the co-occurrence of those two names. The system targets the Semantic Web community. Therefore, the term "Semantic Web OR Ontology" is added to the query for disambiguation.

Similarly, Y. Matsuo describes a social network mining system from the Web (Matsuo, Tomobe, Hasida, & Ishizuka, 2003; Matsuo, 2004; Matsuo, 2006). Their methods are similar to those used in Flink and Referral Web, but they further developed the processes to recognize different types of relations; they also addressed the scalability. Their system, called *Polyphonet*, was operated at the 17th, 18th, 19th, and 20th Annual Conferences of the Japan Society of Artificial Intelligence (JSAI2003, JSAI2004, JSAI2005, and JSAI2006) and at The International Conference on Ubiquitous Computing (UbiComp 2005) to promote communication and collaboration among conference participants.

A. McCallum and his group (Bekkerman & McCallum, 2005; Culotta, Bekkerman, & McCallum, 2004) present an end-to-end system that extracts a user's social network. That system identifies unique people in e-mail messages, finds their homepages, and fills the fields of a contact address book as well as the other person's name. Links are placed in the social network between the owner of the Web page and persons discovered on that page. A newer version of the system targets co-occurrence information on the entire Web, integrated with name disambiguation probability models.

Other studies have used co-occurrence information: Harada, Sato, and Kazama (2004) develop a system to extract names and person-to-person relations from the Web. Faloutsos, McCurley, and Tomkins (2004) obtain a social network of 15 million persons from among 500 million Web pages using their co-occurrence within a window of 10 words. Knees, Pampalk, and Widmer (2004) classify artists into genres using co-occurrence of names and keywords of music in the top 50 pages retrieved by a search engine. Some social networks on the Web have been investigated in detail: L. Adamic (2003) has classified the social network at Stanford and MIT students, and has collected relations among students from Web link structure and text information. Co-occurrence of terms in homepages can be a good indication to reveal communities. Analysis of FOAF networks is a new research topic. To date, a several studies have analyzed FOAF networks (Finin, Ding, & Zou, 2005; Mika, 2005). Aleman-Meza, Nagarajan, Ramakrishnan, Sheth, Arpinar, Ding, Kolari (2006) proposed the integration of two social networks: "knows" from FOAF documents and "co-author" from the DBLP bibliography. They integrate the two networks by weighting each relationship to determine the degree of conflict of interest among scientific researchers.

In the context of the Semantic Web, a study by Cimiano and his group is a very relevant work to this chapter. That system, pattern-based annotation through knowledge on the Web (PANKOW), assigns a named entity into several linguistic patterns that convey Semantic meanings (Cimiano, Handschuh & Staab, 2004; Cimiano & Staab, 2004; Cimiano, Ladwig, & Staab, 2005). Ontological relations among instances and concepts are identified by sending queries to a Google API based on a pattern library. Patterns that are matched most often on the Web indicate the meaning of the named entity, which subsequently enables automatic or semi-automatic annotation. The underlying concept of PANKOW, *self-annotating Web*, is that it uses globally available Web data and structures to annotate local resources Semantically to bootstrap the semantic Web.

Most of those studies use co-occurrence information provided by a search engine as a useful way to detect the proof of relations. Use of search engines to measure the relevance of two words is introduced in a book, *Google Hacks* (Calishain & Dornfest, 2003), and is well known to the public. Co-occurrence information obtained through a search engine provides widely various new methods that had been only applicable to a limited corpus so far. The present study seeks the potential of Web co-occurrence and describes novel approaches that can be accomplished with surprising ease using a search engine.

We add some comments on the stream of research on Web graphs. Sometimes, the link structure of Web pages is seen as a social network: a dense subgraph is considered as a community (Kumar, Raghavan, Rajagopalan, & Tomkins, 2002). Numerous studies have examined these aspects of ranking Web pages (on a certain topic), such as PageRank and HITS, and of identifying a set of Web pages that are densely connected. However, particular Web pages or sites do not necessarily correspond to an author or a group of authors. In our research, we attempt to obtain a social network in which a node is a person and an edge is a relation, that is, in Kautz's terms, a hidden Web. Recently, Weblogs have come to provide an intersection of the two perspectives. Each Weblog corresponds roughly to one author; it creates a social network both from a link-structure perspective and a person-based network perspective.

SOCIAL NETWORK MINING FROM THE WEB

This section introduces the basic algorithm that uses a Web search engine to obtain a social network. Most related works use one algorithm described in this section. We use the Japan Society for Artificial Intelligence (JSAI) community as an example, and show some results on extracting the community.

Nodes and Edges

A social network is extracted through two steps. First we set nodes and then we add edges. Some studies, including Kautz's and McCallum's studies, have employed network expansion, subsequently creating new nodes and finding new edges iteratively. Nodes in a social network are given in Polyphonet and Flink. In other words, a list of persons is given beforehand. Authors and co-authors who have presented works at past JSAI conferences are presupposed as nodes.

Next, edges between nodes are added using a search engine. For example, assume we are to measure the strength of relations between two names: Yutaka Matsuo and Peter Mika. We put a query:

Yutaka Matsuo AND *Peter Mika*

to a search engine. Consequently, we obtain 44 hits.[6] We obtain only 10 hits if we put another query *Yutaka Matsuo* AND *Lada Adamic*. *Peter Mika* itself generates 214 hits and *Lada Adamic* generates 324 hits. Therefore, the difference of hits by two names shows the bias of co-occurrence of the two names: *Yutaka Matsuo* is likely to appear in Web pages with *Peter Mika* than *Lada Adamic*. We can infer that Yutaka Matsuo has a stronger relationship with Peter Mika. Actually, the targets of this example, Yutaka Matsuo and Peter Mika participated together in several conferences.

That approach estimates the strength of their relation by co-occurrence of their two names. We add an edge between the two corresponding nodes if the strength of relations is greater than a certain threshold. Several indices can measure the co-occurrence (Manning & Sch{\"{u}}tze, 2002): matching coefficient, $n_{X \wedge Y}$; mutual information, $\log(nn_{X \wedge Y} / n_X n_Y)$; Dice coefficient,

$(2n_{X \wedge Y})(n_x + n_y)$; Jaccard coefficient, $(n_{X \wedge Y} / \min(n_x, n_y)$; overlap coefficient, $(n_{X \wedge Y} / \min(n_x, n_y)$; and cosine, $(n_{X \wedge Y} / \sqrt{n_{X \vee Y}})$; where n_X and n_Y denote the respective hit counts of name X and Y, and $n_{X \wedge Y}$ and $n_{X \wedge Y}$ denote the respective hit counts of "X AND Y" and "X OR Y."

Depending on the co-occurrence measure that is used, the resultant social network varies. Generally, if we use a matching coefficient, a person whose name appears on numerous Web pages will collect many edges. The network is likely to be decomposed into clusters if we use mutual information. The Jaccard coefficient is an appropriate measure for social networks: Referral web and Flink use this coefficient. In POLYPHONET, the overlap coefficient (Matsuo, 2004) is used because it fits our intuition well: For example, a student whose name co-occurs almost constantly with that of his supervisor strongly suggests an edge from him to that supervisor. A professor thereby collects edges from the students. The overlap coefficients are verified to perform well by investigating the co-authorship probability (Matsuo, Tomobe, Hasida, & Ishizuka, 2005).

Pseudocode that measures the co-occurrence of two persons is shown in Figure 1. In this paper, we define two functions in pseudocodes:

- *GoogleHit*: Returns the number of hits retrieved by a given query
- *GoogleTop*: Returns k documents that are retrieved by a given query

Those two functions play crucial roles in this chapter. *CoocFunction* is a co-occurrence index. In the case of the overlap coefficient, it is defined as the following.

$$f(n_X, n_Y, n_{X \wedge Y}) = \begin{cases} \dfrac{n_{X \wedge Y}}{\min(n_X, n_Y)} & \text{if } n_Y > k \text{ and } n_Y > k \\ 0 & \text{otherwise} \end{cases}$$

We set $k=30$ for the JSAI case. Alternatively, we can use some techniques for smoothing.

As shown in Figure 2, an alternative means exists to measure co-occurrence using a search engine: using top retrieved documents. *NumEntity* returns the number of mentions in a given document set. *NumCooc* returns the number of co-occurrence of mentions in a given document set. Some related works employ this algorithm, in which we can use more tailored NLP methods. However, when the retrieved documents are much more numerous than *k*, we can process only a small fraction of the documents.

A social network is obtained using the algorithm shown in Figure 3. For each node pair for which co-occurrence is greater than the threshold, an edge is invented. Eventually, a network $G=(V,E)$ is obtained in which V is a set of nodes and E is a set of edges. Instead of using *GoogleCooc*, we can employ *GoogleCoocTop* in the case that documents are not so large and more detailed processing is necessary. If we want to expand the network one node at a time, we can insert a module shown in Figure 4 into the algorithm and iterate the module execution. The module, *ExtractEntities*, returns extracted person names from documents.

Although various studies have applied co-occurrence using a search engine to extract a social network, most correspond to an algorithm described previously: most are surprisingly simple.

Disambiguate a Person Name

More than one person might have the same name. Such similarities of important information cause problems when extracting a social network. To date, several studies have produced attempts at personal name disambiguation on the Web (Bekkerman et al., 2005; Guha & Garg, 2004; Lloyd, Bhagwan, Gruhl, & Tomkins, 2005; Malin, 2005). In addition, the natural language community has specifically addressed name disambiguation as a class of word sense disambiguation (Wacholder, Ravin, & Choi, 1997; Mann & Yarowsky, 2003).

Bekkerman and McCallum use probabilistic models for the Web appearance disambiguation problem (Bekkerman, 2005). The set of Web pages is split into clusters. Then one cluster can be considered as containing only relevant pages: all other clusters are deemed irrelevant. Li, Morie, and Roth (2005) propose an algorithm for the problem of cross-document identification and tracing of names of different types. They build a generative model of how names are sprinkled into documents.

These works identify a person from appearance in the text when a set of documents is given. However, to use a search engine for social network mining, a good keyphrase to identify a person is useful because it can be added to a query. For example, we can use an affiliation (a name of organization one belongs to) together with a

Figure 1. Measure co-occurrence using GoogleHit

Algorithm 3.1: GoogleCooc*(X, Y)*
comment: Given person names *X* and *Y*, return the co-occurrence.
$n_X \leftarrow$ *GoogleHit("X")*
$n_Y \leftarrow$ *GoogleHit("Y")*
$n_{X \wedge Y} \leftarrow$ *GoogleHit("X Y")*
$r_{X,Y} \leftarrow$ *CoocFunction(n_X, n_Y, $n_{X \wedge Y}$)*
return $(r_{X,Y})$

Figure 2. Measure co-occurrence using GoogleTop

Algorithm 3.2: GOOGLECOOCTOP*(X, Y, k)*
comment: Given person names X and Y, return the co-occurrence.
$D_X \leftarrow GoogleTop("X", k)$
$D_Y \leftarrow GoogleTop("Y", k)$
$n_X \leftarrow NumEntity(D_X \cup D_Y, X)$
$n_Y \leftarrow NumEntity(D_X \cup D_Y, Y)$
$n_{X \wedge Y} \leftarrow NumCooc(D_X \cup D_Y, X, Y)$
$r_{X,Y} \leftarrow CoocFunction(n_X, n_Y, n_{X \wedge Y})$
return $(r_{X,Y})$

Figure 3. Extract social network using GoogleCooc

Algorithm 3.3: GETSOCIALNET*(L)*
comment: Given person list L, return a social network G.
for each $X \in L$
  do set a node in G
for each $X \in L$ and $Y \in L$
  do $r_{X,Y} \leftarrow GoogleCooc(X, Y)$
for each $X \in L$ and $Y \in L$ where $r_{X,Y} > threshold$
  do set an edge in G
return (G)

Figure 4. Expand personal names

Algorithm 3.4: EXPANDPERSON*(X, k)*
comment: Extract person names from the retrieved pages.
$D \leftarrow GoogleTop("X", k)$
$E \leftarrow ExtractEntities(D)$
return (E)

Figure 5. Measure co-occurrence with disambiguation

Algorithm 3.5: GOOGLECOOCCONTEXT*(X, Y, W_x, W_y)*
comment: Given X, Y and word(s) W_x, W_y, return co-occurrence.
$n_X \leftarrow GoogleHit("X W_x")$
$n_Y \leftarrow GoogleHit("Y W_y")$
$n_{X \wedge Y} \leftarrow GoogleHit("X Y W_x W_y")$
$r_{X,Y} \leftarrow CoocFunction(n_X, n_Y, n_{X \wedge Y})$

return $(r_{X,Y})$

Figure 6. Classify relation

```
Algorithm 4.1: ClassifyRelation(X, Y, k)
comment: Given personal names X and Y, return the class of
relation.
D_{X∧Y} ← GoogleTop("X Y", k)
for each d ∈ D_{X∧Y}
  do c_d ← Classifier(c, X, Y)
class ← determine on c_d (d∈D_{X∧Y})
return (class)
```

name. We make a query "X AND (A OR B OR …)" instead of "X" where A and B are affiliations of X (including past affiliations and short name for the affiliation). Flink uses a phrase *semantic Web OR ontology* for that purpose.

POLYPHONET uses a name-disambiguation module (Bollegara, Matsuo, & Ishizuka, 2006): for a person whose name is not common, such as *Yutaka Matsuo*, we need add no words; for a person whose name is common, we should add a couple of words that best distinguish that person from others. In an extreme case, for a person whose name is very common such as *John Smith*, many words must be added. The module clusters Web pages that are retrieved by each name into several groups using text similarity. It then outputs characteristic keyphrases that are suitable for adding to a query. A pseudocode, *GoogleCooc-Context*, is used to query a search engine with disambiguating keyphrases, as shown in Figure 5. The code is slightly modified from *GoogleCooc*. We regard keyphrases to be added as implying the context of a person.

ADVANCED MINING METHODS

This section introduces some advanced algorithms for social network extraction.

Class of Relation

Various interpersonal relations exist: friends, colleagues, families, teammates, and so on. RELATIONSHIP (Davis) defines more than 30 kinds of human relationships that often form a subproperty of the *knows* property in FOAF. For example, we can write "I am a collaborator of John (and I know him)" in our FOAF file. Various social networks are obtainable if we can identify such relationships. A person might possibly be central in the social network of a research community but not in the local community. Actually, such overlaps of communities often exist and have been investigated in social network analyses (Wasserman & Faust, 1994). This problem also invites interesting studies recently into the context of complex networks (Palla, Derenyi, Farkas, & Vicsek, 2005).

In POLYPHONET, the relations in a researcher community are targeted. Among them, four kinds of relations are picked up because of the ease at identifying them and their importance in reality:

- **Co-author:** co-authors of a technical paper
- **Lab:** Members of the same laboratory or research institute
- **Proj:** Members of the same project or committee

- **Conf:** Participants in the same conference or workshop

Each edge might have multiple labels. For example, *X* and *Y* have both "Co-author" and "Lab." relations.

We first fetch the top five pages retrieved by the {*X AND Y*} query, that is, using *GoogleTop("X Y", 5)*. Then we extract features from the content of each page, as shown in Table 1. Attributes NumCo, FreqX, and FreqY relate to the appearance of name *X* and *Y*. Attributes GroTitle and GroFFive characterize the contents of pages using word groups defined in Table 2. We produced word groups by selecting high tf-idf terms using a manually categorized data set.

Figure 6 shows the pseudocode to classify relations. The *classifier* indicates any one classifier used in machine learning such as Naive Bayes, maximum entropy or support vector machine. In the JSAI case, C4.5 (Quinlan, 1993) is used as a classifier. Using more than 400 pages to which manually labels are assigned, classification rules are obtained. Some of those obtained rules are shown in Table 3. For example, the rule for co-author is simple: if two names co-occur in the same line, they are classified as co-authors. However, the lab relationship is more complicated.

Table 4 shows error rates of five-fold cross validation. Although the error rate for lab is high, others have about a 10% error rate or less. Precision and recall are measured using manual labeling of an additional 200 Web pages. The co-author class yields high precision and recall even though its rule is simple. In contrast, the lab class

Table 1. Attributes and possible values

Attribute		Values
NumCo	Number of co-occurrences of *X* and *Y*	zero, one, or more_than_one
SampleLine	Whether names co-occur at least once in the same line	yes or no
FreqX	Frequency of occurrence of *X*	zero, one, or more_than_one
FreqY	Frequency of occurrence of *Y*	zero, one, or more_than_one
GroTitle	Whether any of a word group A–F appears in the title	yes or not (for each group)
GroFFive	Whether any of a word group (A–F) appears in the first five lines	yes or not (for each group)

Table 2. Word groups (translated from Japanese)

Group	Words
A	Publication, paper, presentation, activity, theme, award, authors, and so forth.
B	Member, lab, group, laboratory, institute, team, and so forth.
C	Project, committee
D	Workshop, conference, seminar, meeting, sponsor, symposium, and so forth.
E	Association, program, national, journal, session, and so forth.
F	Professor, major, graduate student, lecturer, and so forth.

Table 3. Obtained rules

Class	Rule
Co-author	SameLine=yes
Lab	(NumCo = more_than_one & GroTitle(D)=no & GroFFive(A) = yes & GroFFive(E) = yes) & or (FreqX = more_than_two & FreqY = more_than_two & GroFFive(A) = yes & GroFFive(D)=no) or ...
Proj	(SameLine=no & GroTitle(A)=no & GroFFive(F)=yes) or ..
Conf	(GroTitle(A)=no & GroFFive(B)=no & GroFFive(D)= yes) & or (GroFFive(A)=no & GroFFive(D)=no & GroFFive(E) = yes) or ..

Table 4. Error rates of edge labels, precision and recall

Class	Error rate	Precision	Recall
Co-author	4.1%	91.8% (90/98)	97.8% (90/92)
Lab	25.7%	70.9% (73/103)	86.9% (73/84)
Proj	5.8%	74.4% (67/90)	91.8% (67/73)
Conf	11.2%	89.7% (87/97)	67.4% (87/129)

gives low recall, presumably because laboratory pages have greater variety.

Obtaining the class of relationship is reduced to a text categorization problem. A large amount of research pertains to text categorization. We can employ more advanced algorithms. For example, using unlabeled data also improves categorization (Nigram, McCallum, Thrun, & Mitchell, 1999). Relationships depend on the target domain. Therefore, we must define classes to be categorized depending on a domain.

Vastly numerous pages exist on the Web. For that reason, the *ClassifyRelation* module becomes inefficient when *k* is large. Top-ranked Web pages do not necessarily contain information that is related to the purpose. One approach to remedy that situation is to organize a query in a more sophisticated manner. For example, if we seek to determine whether *X* and *Y* have Lab relations, we can organize a query such as "*X Y* (publication OR

paper OR presentation)" through consultation of Tables 2 and 3. This algorithm works well in our other study for extraction of a social network of corporations (Jin, Matsuo, & Ishizuka, 2006). In Question-Answering systems, query formulation is quite a common technique.

Scalability

The number of queries to a search engine becomes a problem when we apply extraction of a social network to a large-scale community: a network with 1,000 nodes requires $_{1000}C_2 \approx 500,000$ queries and grows with $O(n^2)$, where *n* is the number of persons. Considering that the Google API limits the number of queries to 1,000 per day, the number is huge. Such a limitation might be reduced gradually with the development of technology, but the number of queries remains a great obstacle.

One solution might be that social networks are often very sparse. For example, the network density of the JSAI2003 social network is 0.0196, which means that only 2% of possible edges actually exist. The distribution of the overlap coefficient is shown in Figure 7. Most relations are less than 0.2, which is below the edge threshold. How can we reduce the number of queries while simultaneously preserving the extraction performance? One idea is to filter out pairs of persons that seem to have no relation. That pseudocode is described in Figure 8. This algorithm uses both

good points of *GoogleCooc* and *GoogleCoocTop*. The latter can be executed in computationally low order (if *k* is a constant), but the former gives more precise co-occurrence information for the entire Web.

For 503 persons who participated in JSAI2003, $_{503}C_2$=126253 queries are necessary if we use the *GetSocialNet* module. However, *GetSocialNetScalable* requires only 19,182 queries in case *k=20*, empirically, which is about 15%. The degree to which the algorithm filters out information correctly is shown in Figure 9. For example, where

Figure 7. Number of pairs versus the overlap coefficient

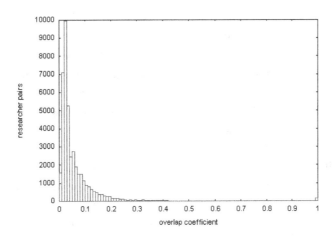

Figure 8. Extract the social network in a scalable manner

```
Algorithm 4.2: GETSOCIALNETSCALABLE(L, k)
comment: Given person list L, return a social network G.
for each X ∈ L
  do set a node in G
for each X ∈ L and Y ∈ L
  do
      D ← GoogleTop("X", k)
      E ← ExtractEntities(D)
      for each Y ∈ L∩E
        do r_{X,Y} ← GoogleCooc(X,Y)
  for each X ∈ L and Y ∈ L where r_{X,Y} > threshold
    do set an edge in G
  return (G)
```

Figure 9. Coverage of GetSocialNetScalable for the JSAI case

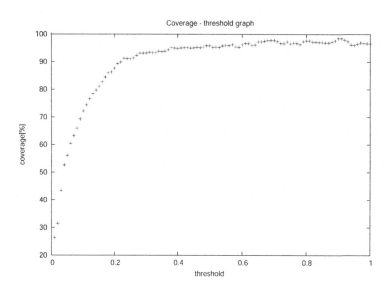

Keyword Extraction

Keywords for a person, in other words personal metadata, are useful for information retrieval and recommendations on a social network. For example, if a system has information on a researcher's study topic, it is easy to find a person of a certain topic on a social network. PANKOW also provides such keyword extraction from information on a person's homepage (Culotta et al., 2004).

Keyword extraction for researchers is implemented in POLYPHONET. A ready method to obtain keywords for a researcher is to search a person's homepage and extract words from the page. However, homepages do not always exist for each person. Moreover, a large amount of information about a person is not recorded in homepages, but is instead recorded elsewhere in conference programs, introductions in seminar Webpages, profiles in journal papers, and so forth. For those reasons, POLYPHONET uses co-occurrence information to search the entire Web for a person's name.

We use co-occurrence of a person's name and a word (or a phrase) on the Web. The algorithm is shown in Figure 10. Collecting documents retrieved by a personal name, we obtain a set of

$k=20$, 90% or more of the relations with an overlap coefficient 0.4 are detected correctly. It is readily apparent that as k increases, the performance improves. As an extreme case, we can set $k=\infty$ and thereby achieve 100%.

The computational complexity of this algorithm is $O(nm)$, where n is the number of persons and m is the average number of persons that remain candidates after filtering. Although m can be a function of n, it is bounded depending on k because a Web page mentions a certain number of person names in a typical case. Therefore, the query number is reduced from $O(n^2)$ to $O(n)$, enabling us to crawl a social network as large as $n=7000$.[7]

Name and Word Co-Occurrence

Personal names co-occur along with many words on the Web. A particular researcher's name will co-occur with many words that are related to that person's major research topic. Below, we specifically address the co-occurrence of a name and words.

Figure 10. Extract keywords for a person

```
Algorithm 4.3: EXTRACTKEYWORDS(X, k₁, k₂)
D ← GoogleTop("X", k₁)
words ← ExtractWords(D)
for each W ∈ words
  do score_W ← GoogleCooc(X, W)
K ← { W| score_W is top k₂}
return (K)
```

Figure 11. Exemplary keywords for Dan Brickley

Dan Brickley	*Dan Connolly*
Libby Miller	*Jan Grant*
FOAF	RDF Interest Group
Semantic Web	xmlns.com=foaf
Dave Beckett	RDF
RDFWeb	*Eric Miller*
ILRT	FOAF Explorer

Table 5. Precision and recall

Method	tf	tf-idf	*ExtractKeywords*
precision	0.13	0.18	0.60
recall	0.20	0.24	0.48

words and phrases as candidates for keywords. Termex (Nakagawa, Maeda & Kojima, 2003) is used for term extraction in Japanese as *Extract-Words*. Then, the co-occurrence of the person's name and a word / phrase is measured. This algorithm is simple but effective. Figure 12 shows an example of keywords for *Dan Brickley*. He works with XML/RDF and metadata at W3C and ILRT; he created the FOAF vocabulary along with *Libby Miller*. Some important words, such as FOAF and Semantic Web, are extracted properly. Table 5 shows the performance of the proposed algorithm based on a questionnaire. Both tf and tf-idf are baseline methods that extract keywords from D_X. In the tf-idf case, by collecting 3981

pages for 567 researchers a corpus is produced. For *ExtractKeywords*, we set $k_1=10$ and $k_2=20$ (as similarly as tf and tf-idf). We gave questionnaires to 10 researchers and defined the correct set of keywords carefully. For details of the algorithm and its evaluation, see Mori et al. (2005). The tf outputs many common words: tf-idf outputs very rare words because of the diversity of Web document vocabularies. The proposed method is far superior to that of the baselines.

Affiliation Network

Co-occurrence information of words and persons forms a matrix. Figure 12 shows a person-word co-occurrence matrix, which represents how likely a person's name is to co-occur with other words on the Web. In social network analysis literature, this matrix is called an *affiliation matrix* whereas a person-person matrix is called an *adjacent matrix* (Wasserman et al., 1994). Figure 13 presents an example of a person-to-word matrix obtained in POLYPHONET. For example, the name of *Mitsuru Ishizuka* co-occurs often with words such as *agent* and *communication*. *Koiti Hasida* co-occurs often with *communication* and *cognition*. Conceptually speaking, by measuring the similarity between two-word co-occurrence vectors (i.e., two rows of the matrix), we can calculate the similarity of the two people's contexts. In the researchers' cases, we can measure how mutually relevant the two researchers' research topics are: if two persons are researchers of very similar topics, the distribution of word co-occurrences will be similar.

Figure 14 describes the pseudocode for calculating the context similarity of two persons. We should prepare a word / phrase list W_L, which is a controlled vocabulary for the purpose, because rare words do not contribute greatly to the similarity calculation. In POLYPHONET, we obtain 188 words that appear frequently (excluding stop words) in titles of papers at JSAI conferences. Actually, the affiliation matrix is stored for a list of persons and a list of words before calculating

similarity to avoid inefficiency. Popular words such as *agent* and *communication* co-occur often with many person names. Therefore, statistical methods are effective: We first apply χ^2 statistics to the affiliation matrix and calculate cosine similarity (Chakrabarti, 2002).

One evaluation is shown in Figure 15. Based on the similarity function, we plot the probability that the two persons will attend the same session at a JSAI conference. We compare several similarity calculations: χ^2 represents using the χ^2 and cosine similarity, the idf represents using idf weighting and cosine similarity, and hits represents the use the hit count as weighting and cosine similarity. This session prediction task is very difficult and its precision and recall are low: among the weighting methods, χ^2 performs best.

A network based on an affiliation matrix is called an *affiliation network* (Wasserman et al., 1994). A relation between a pair of persons with similar interests or citations is sometimes called an *intellectual link*. Even if no direct mutual relation exists, we infer that they share common interests, implying an intellectual relation, or a potential social relationship.

Figure 12. Affiliation matrix and adjacent matrix

	W_1	W_2	W_3 ...	W_m	
X_1	...				
X_2	...				
X_3	...				
...	...	...	...	...	...
X_n	...				

	X_1	X_2 ...	X	X_M
X_1			...	
X_2			...	
X_3			...	
...	...	...	...	...
X_n			...	

Figure 13. Example of a person-to-word co-occurrence matrix

	Agent	Mining	Communication	Audio	Cognition	...
Mitsuru Ishizuka	454	143	414	382	246	...
Koiti Hasida	412	156	1020	458	1150	...
Yutaka Matsuo	129	112	138	89	58	...
Nobuaki Minematsu	227	22	265	648	138	...
Yohei Asada	6	6	6	2	0	...
...	...	...	...	...	...	...

Figure 14. Measure contextual similarity of two persons

Algorithm 4.4: CONTEXTSIM(X, Y, W_L)
comment: Given names X, Y and word list W_L, return the similarity.
for each $W \in W_L$
do
  $a_w \leftarrow GoogleCooc(X, W)$
  $b_w \leftarrow GoogleCooc(Y, W)$
  $s_{X,Y} \leftarrow$ similarity of two vectors $a = \{a_w\}$ and $b = \{b_w\}$
return $(s_{X,Y})$

Figure 15. Precision and recall for session identification

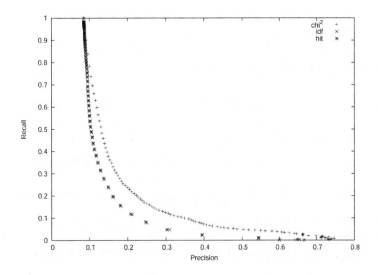

IMPORTANT ISSUES

Entity Identification

In the field of artificial intelligence, various forms of Semantic representation have been speculated upon for decades, including first-order predicate logic, Semantic networks, frames, and so on. Such a representation enables us to describe relations among objects; it is useful for further use of the Web for integration of information and inference. On the other hand, studies of social network analyses in sociology provide us a means to capture the characteristics of a network as an integration of relations. For example, the concept of centrality quantifies the degree to which a person is central to a social network. A measure of centrality, that is, the degree to which a researcher is central to a research community, sometimes correlates with other measures of an individual's characteristics or achievements, e.g., their number of publications. Social networks (and their individual relations) are defined properly in terms of a certain purpose if the correlation is high. Such feedback from an extracted network to individual relations is important when we target extraction of a large-scale social network from the Web.

In accordance with that concept, the following points are important for the further development of an algorithm:

- **Scalability:** Using very simple modules with a search engine to attain scalability.
- **Relate-identify process:** For identifying entities[8] and extracting relations of entities, more advanced algorithms are necessary: Based on the overall network structure and statistics, we improve the means to identify entities.

To attain scalability, we allow two operations using a search engine: *GoogleTop* and *GoogleCooc*. These two are permissible operations even if the Web grows more. *GoogleTop* enables us to investigate a small set of samples of Web pages using text processing, whereas *GoogleCooc* provides statistics that pertain to the entire Web. We note that as the Web grows, *GoogleTop* returns fewer and fewer Web pages relative to all retrieved documents, thereby rendering it less effective. A more effective means to sample documents from the Web must be developed, as described in (Anagnostopoulos, Broder & Carmel, 2005). In contrast, *GoogleCooc* yields a more precise number if the Web grows because the low-frequency problem is improved. Therefore, a good combination of *GoogleCooc* and *GoogleTop* is necessary for Super Social Network Mining. For other kinds of operations by a search engine such as "obtain the number of documents where word X co-occurs with Y within the word distance of 10," whether they are permissible or not remains unclear in terms of scalability because the index size grows very rapidly. A search engine that is specially designed for NLP (Cafarella & Etzioni, 2005) will benefit our research importantly if it actually scales properly.

Integration of Social Networks

Some flaw would hinder any method we might take for obtaining a social network. For example, SNSs data and FOAF data, which are based on self-report surveys, suffer from data bias and sparsity. Users might name some of their work acquaintances, but would not include private friends. Others might name hundreds of friends, but others would name only a few. Automatically obtained networks, for example, Web-mined social networks, would provide a good view of prominent persons, but would not work well for novices, students, and other "normal" people. Social networks observed using wearable devices (Pentland, 2005) are constrained using their device-specific characteristics; they might have detection errors, limited detection scopes, and the bias of usage.

How can we integrate multiple social networks? In social network analysis, a network is called a *multi-plex* graph in which actors are connected in multiple ways simultaneously (Hanneman & Riddle, 2005). Several techniques are available to reduce the multiple network matrices into one: we can use sum, average, maximum, multiplication for each corresponding element of the matrices.

In typical social science studies, a social network is obtained according to survey purposes. Otherwise, a network is only a network that represents nothing. In the context of the Semantic Web, social networks are useful for several purposes:

- Locating experts and authorities (Mika, 2005; Matsuo et al., 2004)
- Calculating trustworthiness of a person (Golbeck & Hendler, 2005; Goldbeck & Persia, 2006; Massa & Avesani, 2005)
- Detecting relevance and relations among persons, for example, COI detection (Aleman-Meza et al., 2006)
- Promoting communication, information exchange and discussion (Matsuo et al., 2006)
- Ontology extraction by identifying communities (Mika, 2005)

To locate experts and authorities, it is useful to use a *collaborator* network and calculate centralities based on the network. Correlation to research performance, for example, publication and citation, is used to measure whether the network is appropriate or not. To calculate trustworthiness and aggregate information, the *knows* relation works well because of its inherent requirement of an explicit declaration.

For promoting communication and finding referrals, *knows* links are useful: a person is likely to introduce friends to others if one explicitly declares knowing some of his friends. *Meets* links are also useful, which is a relation through face-to-face interaction detected by wearable devices and ubiquitous sensors (Matsuo et al., 2006, Pentland, 2005). The *meets* link is a key because a person actually meets others on-site; the person feels at ease talking again to introduce someone.

For (light-weight) ontology extraction, it is important to detect the community precisely under consistent criteria. In that sense, the *collaborator* network is the best in an academic context. Integration of *collaborator* plus *knows* might improve the result because it increases the probability that the two are in the same community.

In summary, integration of multiple social networks depending on purposes is an important issue; some methodology is necessary for further utilization of social networks.

SOCIAL NETWORK ANALYSIS

Once we obtain a social network, we can analyze the network structure in various ways. A major analysis in social network analysis is calculating the centrality of each actor. Sometimes (for example in the case of a network of Web pages) it can be considered as the *authoritativeness* of the node. On the other hand, an egocentric network is used to calculate trust that can be accorded to a person. This section first describes these two kinds of authoritativeness, then various applications using a social network, using information recommendation, information sharing, and navigation.

Authoritativeness

Freeman (1979) proposes a number of ways to measure node *centrality*. Considering an actors' social network, the simplest means to determine centrality is to count the number of others with whom an actor maintains relations. The actor with the most connections, for example, the highest *degree*, is most central. Another measure is *closeness*, which calculates the distance from each person in the network to another person based on the connections among all network members. Central actors are closer to all others than are other actors. A third measure is *betweenness*, which examines the extent to which an actor is situated between others in the network, that is, the extent to which information must pass through them to get to others, and thus the extent to which they will be exposed to information that circulates through the network.

The Google[9] search engine uses the link structure for ranking Web pages, called PageRank (Brin & Page, 1998). A page has a high rank if the sum of the ranks of its backlinks is high. The rank of a page is divided among its forward links evenly to contribute to the ranks of the pages they point to. PageRank is a global ranking of all Web pages; it is known to perform very well.

The PageRank model is useful to measure authoritativeness of each member. Each node v has an authority value $A_n(v)$ on iteration n. The authority value propagates to neighboring nodes in proportion to the relevance to the node:

$$A_{n+1}(v') = c \sum_{v' \in Neighbor(v)} \frac{rel(v,v')}{rel\_sum(v')} A_n(v') + cE(v)$$

and

$$rel\_sum(v) = \sum_{v'' \in Neighbor(v)} rel(v,v''),$$

where *Neighbor(v)* represents a set of nodes, each of which is connected to node v, c is a constant, and E represents a source of authority value. We set E as uniform over all nodes (for mathematical details, see Brin & Page, 1998).

Table 6 shows a result applied to the JSAI community extracted from the Web. Among 1,509 people in the community, these people have a high authority value $A(v)$ after 1,000 iterations. Present or former commissioners of JSAI comprise 9 of 15 people. Others are younger: they are not yet commissioners, but are very active researchers who are mainly working in JSAI.

The top listed people by this algorithm are authoritative and reliable in the JSAI community. However, authoritative people are not always listed highly by our approach. For example, JSAI currently has 20 commissioners (including a chairperson and two vice chairpersons), but we can extract only 5 current commissioners of the top 15. In other words, this approach seems to have high precision, but low recall, which is attributable to the lack of information online. Especially, elder authorities tend to have made many publications before the WWW came into daily use.

Table 7 shows a list of people that was created by calculating the PageRank by setting a source node to one person: *Yutaka Matsuo*. Similarly, we can calculate the importance of other persons to that person. In other words, that list is a proxy of individual trust by the person. This corresponds to the algorithm mentioned in Brin and Page (1998) as a personalized ranking of Web pages.

The PageRank algorithm performs better than other measures including degree, closeness, and the number of retrieved pages. For example, by measuring the number of retrieved pages, a famous person tends to be ranked highly irrespective of their contribution to the community. This measure is insufficient for our purposes because we want to know the authoritativeness in the target community. Alternatively, we can measure the topic-sensitive PageRank (Haveliwala, 2002) of one's homepage as that person's authoritativeness. However, the connection between authority of a person and authority of a homepage is not clear; some pages have high PageRanks because their contents are popular, not because authorities have written them.

Applications

We next describe the algorithm used to calculate authoritativeness of a node. A related but different concept is the trust value of a node: The trust calculation in social networks has been addressed in several studies. The EigenTrust algorithm is used in peer-to-peer systems and calculates trust using a variation on the PageRank algorithm (Kamvar, Schlosser, & Garcia-Molina, 2003)

Table 6. Result of authority propagation

	Name	Activation	Freq.	Comment[10]
1	*Toyoaki Nishida*	5.53	624	Former Commissioner of JSAI, Prof.
2	*Toru Ishida*	4.98	574	Former Commissioner of JSAI, Prof.
3	*Hideyuki Nakashima*	4.52	278	Former Commissioner of JSAI
4	*Koiti Hasida*	4.50	345	Commissioner of JSAI
5	*Mitsuru Ishizuka*	4.24	377	Commissioner of JSAI, Prof.
6	*Hiroshi Okuno*	3.89	242	Commissioner of JSAI, Prof.
7	*Riichiro Mizoguchi*	3.60	404	Commissioner of JSAI, Prof.
8	*Seiji Yamada*	3.35	168	Associate Prof.
9	*Hideaki Takeda*	3.22	435	Associate Prof.
10	*Takahira Yamaguchi*	3.10	236	Prof.
11	*Yukio Ohsawa*	2.98	185	Associate Prof.
12	*Hozumi Tanaka*	2.90	465	Chairperson of JSAI, Prof.
13	*Takenobu Tokunaga*	2.89	302	Associate Prof.
14	*Koichi Furukawa*	2.77	141	Former Commissioner of JSAI, Prof.
15	*Tatsuya Kawahara*	2.74	440	Prof.

Table 7. Result of authority propagation from Yutaka Matsuo

	Name	Activation	Freq	Comment
1	*Yutaka Matsuo*	230.6	136	Himself
2	*Mitsuru Ishizuka*	28.7	377	His former supervisor, co-author
3	*Yukio Ohsawa*	19.5	185	His former project leader, co-author
4	*Toyoaki Nishida*	14.5	624	Professor of lecture at university
5	*Naohiro Matumura*	13.5	82	My former colleague, co-author
6	*Seiji Yamada*	12.7	168	Acquaintance
7	*Takafumi Takama*	12.3	16	Former researcher of my former laboratory
8	*Toru Ishida*	12.1	574	A member of the advisory board of his research center
9	*Takahira Yamaguchi*	11.5	236	Acquaintance
10	*Hidehiko Tanaka*	11.3	842	University professor

for a peer-to-peer system. Richardson, Agrawal, and Domingos (2003) use social networks with trust to calculate the belief a user might have in a statement. Golbeck and Hendler (2005) proposed algorithms for inferring trust relationships among individuals that are not directly connected in the network. These approaches find paths from the source to any node, concatenating trust values along the paths to reveal, eventually, the recommended belief or trust for the path.

Once algorithms for calculating trust have been designed properly, the next step is to use them for applications. With the current large amount of social network data available from the Web, several studies have addressed integrating network analysis and trust into applications. One promising application of trust is a recommendation system. Golbeck and Hendler (2004) developed TrustMail, an e-mail client that uses variations on these algorithms to score email messages in the user's inbox based on the user's participation and ratings in a FOAF network. They developed the Trust Module for FOAF, which extends the FOAF vocabulary by adding a property by which users state how much they trust one another. FilmTrust, which integrates social network and movie reviews, is another trust-based system (Golbeck & Parsia, 2006). System users can rate films and write reviews. In addition, they maintain a set of friends who are rated according to how much the user trusts their opinion of movies. In both systems, trust took on the role of a recommendation system forming the core of algorithms to create predictive rating recommendations for emails and movies.

In addition to recommendation systems, another application in which trust takes on an important role is information sharing. With the current development of tools and sites that enable users to create Web contents, users can easily disseminate various kinds of information. In social networking services (SNSs), a user creates a variety of contents including public and private information. Although these tools and sites enable users to

easily disseminate information on the Web, users sometimes have difficulty sharing information with the right people and frequently have privacy concerns because large amounts of information including private photos, diaries, and research notes in the SNSs are neither completely open nor closed. One approach to tackle the information sharing issue on SNSs is to use a trust network. Availability information in the real world is often closely guarded and shared only with the people in one's trust relationships: Confidential project documents which are limited to share within a division of company might be granted access to data of another colleague who is concerned with the project. By analogy with the examples in the real world, we find that social trust relationships are applicable to the process of disseminating and receiving information on SNSs.

Several studies have addressed integration of social networks and trust into information sharing. Goecks and Mynatt (2004) propose a Saori infrastructure, which uses social networks for information sharing. In their system, access to post and edit Website information is controlled by relationships among users. Mori et al. (2005) propose a real-world oriented information sharing system using social networks, which enables users to control the information dissemination process within social networks. The system enables users to analyze their social networks so that they can decide who will have rights to access their information. For example, if a user wants to diffuse information, he might consider granting access to a person who has both high degree and betweenness on his network. On the other hand, he must be aware of betweenness when the information is private or confidential. The users can also control information access using trust. For example, a user can give information access rights to other users who have certain trust relationships. The user can directly assign trust in a numerical value to a person in his relation. Then, trust can automatically be inferred using several algorithms, as mentioned earlier.

Figure 16. Screenshot of navigation for Yokohama Triennale 2005

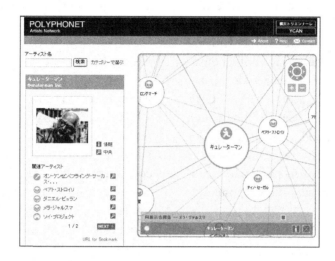

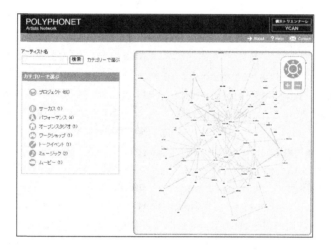

Other applications include navigation using a social network. Polyphonet is used for academic conferences to navigate researchers: If one would like to know someone, that person can see the information of the other person, even the location information at the conference site is available. Flink, developed by Mika, also navigates researchers of semantic Web. It is a very useful site if we wish to know a researcher, and associated collaborators.

Jin et al. (2006) uses the social network of contemporary arts as a navigation site for the International Triennale of Contemporary Art (Yokohama Triennale 2005). At exhibitions, it is usual that participants enjoy and evaluate each work separately. However, our presupposition was that if participants knew the background and relations of the artists, they might enjoy the event more. For that purpose, the system provided relations of artists and the evidential web pages for users. The system interface is shown in Figure 16. It was implemented using Flash display software to realize interactive navigation. The system provides a retrieval function. The information about the artist is shown on the left side if a user clicks a node. In addition, the edges from the nodes are highlighted in the right-side network. The user can proceed to view the neighboring artists' information sequentially, and can also jump to the web pages that show evidence of the relation.

The recent interesting application of extracted social network online is detecting conflict of interests (COI) of researchers (Aleman-Meza et al., 2006). Using the network extracted from FOAF data and DBLP (Computer Science Bibliography), potential COI are suggested. Although the rules are constructed heuristically, the results show the usefulness of the social networks in actual use for assigning reviewers of papers and proposals.

FUTURE TRENDS

Social Network Extraction for General Purpose

Social network mining presents some concrete applications for semantic Web and information retrieval. It can also contribute as a more general data-mining tool.

A possible direction is expansion of the applicability to other named entities such as firms, organizations, books, and so on. Actually, some studies have undertaken such expansion on firms and artists (of contemporary art) (Jin et al., 2006). Because numerous entities are interests of Web users, mining the structure and showing an overview of it is a promising application: It aids users' decision-making and information gathering. Depending on the target entities, appropriate methods will vary: for researchers, the Web count is useful to detect the strength of ties among them, but for corporate purposes, the Web count does not produce a good index. Some corporate relationships receive much more attention than others thereby returning huge hit counts. Therefore more advanced language processing is necessary to identify the individual different relations.

Toward general-purpose social network mining, we must consider what a "good" social network is for a given purpose. A "good" social network depends on its purpose. It should represent a target domain most appropriately. We can first generalize social network extraction as:

$$f(\mathbf{S}_r(X, Y), \Theta) \rightarrow \{0, 1\},$$

where $\mathbf{S}_r(X, Y)$ is an m-dimensional vector space $(S^{(1)}_r(X, Y), S^{(2)}_r(X, Y), \ldots, S^{(m)}_r(X, Y))$ to represent various measures for X and Y in relation r. For example, $S^{(i)}_r(X, Y)$ can be either a matching coefficient, a Jaccard coefficient, or an overlap coefficient. It can be a score function based on sentences including mentions of both X and Y. The parameter Θ is an n-dimensional vector space $(\theta(1), \theta(2), \ldots, \theta(n))$. For example, Θ can be as a combination of thresholds for each co-occurrence measure. The function f determines whether an edge should be invented or not based on multiple measures and parameters.

A social network should represent particular relations of entities depending on purposes. Therefore, function f should not always be the same. We must have a method to infer an appropriate function f. For that reason, the algorithm inevitably consists of an off-line module and an online module: Function f is learned from the training examples and provides good classification to other examples. This view, that is, learning extraction of social network from examples, is a currently neglected research topic. It would be a very important issue to integrate relational learning approach, (e.g., Getoor, Friedman, Koller, & Taskar, 2002).

The resultant network is useful for semantic Web studies in several ways. For example (inspired by (Aleman-Meza et al., 2006)), we can use a social network of artists for detecting COI among artists when they make evaluations and comments on others' work. We might find a cluster of firms and characterize a firm by its cluster. Business experts often make such inferences based on firm relations and firm groups. Consequently, the firm network might enhance inferential abilities on the business domain. As a related work, Gandon, Corby, Giboin, Gronnier, and Guigard (2005) present a Semantic Web server that maintains annotations about the industrial organization of Telecom Valley to partnerships and collaboration.

Mining Ontology and Structural Knowledge

An increasing number of studies are done that use search engines. In natural language processing research, many systems have begun using search engines. For example, Keller, Lapata, and Ourioupina (2002) use the Web to obtain frequencies for unseen bigrams in a given corpus. They count for adjective-noun, noun-noun, and verb-object bigrams by querying a search engine, and demonstrate that Web frequencies (Web counts) correlate with frequencies from a carefully edited corpus such as the British National Corpus (BNC). Aside from counting bigrams, various tasks are attainable using Web-based models: spelling correction, adjective ordering, compound noun bracketing, countability detection, and so on (Lapata & Keller, 2004). For some tasks, simple unsupervised models perform better when *n*-gram frequencies are obtained from the Web rather than a standard large corpus: the web yields better counts than BNC.

Some studies have used a search engine to extract relational knowledge from among entities, thereby harnessing the ontology of a target domain. For example, the relation between a book and an author can be extracted through putting a query to a search engine using the names of the book and the (possible) author, analyzing the text, and determining whether the relation is recognizable. In addition, the pattern which describes an entity and its class is identifiable through a search engine. The popularly known pattern is called Hearst pattern, which include "*A* such as *B*" and "*B* is a (kind of) *A*": We can infer that *A* is a class of *B* if many mentions exist in these patterns. Although this approach is heuristic-based, an important study could be made toward obtaining patterns using supervised / unsupervised learning. Various patterns that describe a specific kind of relation and how to obtain such patterns are important issues.

Recognizing relations among entities is a necessary ingredient for advanced Web systems, including question answering, trend detection, and Web search. In the future, there will increasingly be studies that use search engines to obtain structural knowledge from the web. A search engine can be considered as a database interface for a machine with the huge amount of global information on social and linguistic activities.

CONCLUSION

This chapter describes a social network mining approach using the Web. Several studies have addressed similar approaches. We organize those methods into small pseudocodes. POLYPHONET, which was implemented using several algorithms described in this chapter, was put into service at JSAI conferences over three years and at the UbiComp conference. We also discuss important issues including entity recognition, social network analysis, and applications. Lastly, future trends toward general-purpose social network extraction and structural knowledge extraction are described.

Merging the vast amount of information on the Web and producing higher-level information might foster many knowledge-based systems of the future. Acquiring knowledge through Googling (Cimiano, 2004) is an early work for this concept. Increasing numerous studies of the last few years have been conducted using search engines for these. More studies in the future will use search engines as database interfaces for machines and humans to the world's information.

REFERENCES

Adamic, L., Buyukkokten, O., & Adar, E. (2003). Social network caught in the web. *First Monday, 8*(6).

Aleman-Meza, B., Nagarajan, M., Ramakrishnan, C., Sheth, A., Arpinar, I., Ding, L., Kolari, P., Joshi, A., & Finin, T. (2006). Semantic analytics on social networks: Experiences in addressing the problem of conflict of interest detection. In *Proceedings of the WWW2006.*

Anagnostopoulos, A., Broder, A. Z., & Carmel, D. (2005). Sampling search-engine results. In *Proceedings of WWW 2005.*

Bekkerman, R., & McCallum, A. (2005). Disambiguating web appearances of people in a social network. In *Proceedings of WWW 2005.*

Bollegara, D., Matsuo, Y., & Ishizuka, M. (2006). Extracting key phrases to disambiguate personal names on the Web. In *Proceedings of ECAI 2006.*

Brin, S., & Page, L. (1998). The anatomy of a large-scale hypertextual web search engine. In *Proceeings of 7th WWW Conf.*

Cafarella, M., & Etzioni, O. (2005). A search engine for natural language applications. In *Proc. WWW2005.*

Calishain, T., & Dornfest, R. (2003). *Google hacks: 100 industrial-strength tips & tools.* O'Reilly.

Chakrabarti, S. (2002). *Mining the web: Discovering knowledge from hypertext data.* Morgan Kaufmann.

Cimiano, P., Handschuh, S., & Staab, S. (2004). Towards the self-annotating web. In *Proceedings of WWW2004.*

Cimiano, P., Ladwig, G., & Staab, S. (2005). Gimme' the context: Context-driven automatic Semantic annotation with C-PANKOW. In *Proceedings of WWW 2005.*

Cimiano, P., & Staab, S. (2004). Learning by googling. *SIGKDD Explorations, 6*(2), 24–33.

Culotta, A., Bekkerman, R., & McCallum, A. (2004). Extracting social networks and contact information from email and the web. In *CEAS-1.*

Davis, I., & Jr., E. V. Relationship: A vocabulary for describing relationships between people. http://vocab.org/relationship/

Faloutsos, C., McCurley, K. S., & Tomkins, A. (2004). Fast discovery of connection subgraphs. In *Proceedings of the ACM SIGKDD 2004.*

Finin, T., Ding, L., & Zou, L. (2005). Social networking on the Semantic Web. *The Learning Organization, 12*(5), 418-435.

Freeman, L. C. (1979). Centrality in social networks: Conceptual clarification. *Social Networks, 1,* 215–239.

Gandon, F., Corby, O., Giboin, A., Gronnier, N., & Guigard, C. (2005). Graph-based inferences in a Semantic web server for the cartography of competencies in a telecom valley. In *Proceedings of ISWC05.*

Getoor, L., Friedman, N., Koller, D., & Taskar, B. (2003). Learning probabilistic models of link structure. *Journal of Machine Learning Research, 3,* 679–707.

Goecks, J., & Mynatt, E. D. (2004). Leveraging social networks for information sharing. In *Proceedings of ACM CSCW 2004.*

Golbeck, J., & Hendler, J. (2004a). Accuracy of metrics for inferring trust and reputation in Semantic web-based social networks. In *Proceedings of EKAW 2004.*

Golbeck, J., & Hendler, J. (2004b). Inferring reputation on the Semantic web. In *Proceedings of WWW2004.*

Golbeck, J., & Hendler, J. (2005). Inferring trust relationships in web-based social networks. *ACM Transactions on Internet Technology, 7*(1).

Golbeck, J., & Parsia, B. (2006). Trust network-based filtering of aggregated claims. *International Journal of Metadata, Semantics and Ontologies.*

Guha, R., & Garg, A. (2004). Disambiguating entities in Web search. TAP project, http://tap.stanford.edu/PeopleSearch.pdf

Hanneman, R., & Riddle, M. (2005). *Introduction to social network methods.* University of California, Riverside.

Harada, M., Sato, S., & Kazama, K. (2004). Finding authoritative people from the Web. In *Proceedings of the Joint Conference on Digital Libraries (JCDL2004).*

Haveliwala, T. (2002). Topic-sensitive PageRank. In *Proceedings of WWW2002.*

Jin, Y., Matsuo, Y., & Ishizuka, M. (2006). Extracting a social network among entities by web mining. In *Proceedings of the ISWC '06 Workshop on Web Content Mining with Human Language Techniques.*

Kamvar, S., Schlosser, M., & Garcia-Molina, H. (2003). The eigentrust algorithm for reputation management in P2P networks. In *Proceedings of WWW2003.*

Kautz, H., Selman, B., & Shah, M. (1997). The hidden web. *AI magazine, 18*(2), 27–35.

Keller, F., Lapata, M., & Ourioupina, O. (2002). Using the web to overcome data sparseness. In *Proceedings of the EMNLP 2002.*

Knees, P., Pampalk, E., & Widmer, G. (2004). Artist classification with web-based data. In *Proceedings of the 5th International Conference on Music Information Retrieval (ISMIR).*

Kumar, R., Raghavan, P., Rajagopalan, S., & Tomkins, A. (2002). The web and social networks. *IEEE Computer, 35*(11), 32–36.

Lapata, M., & Keller, F. (2004). The web as a baseline: Evaluating the performance of unsupervised web-based models for a range of nlp tasks. In *Proceedings of the HLT-NAACL 2004.*

Leskovec, J., Adamic, L. A., & Huberman, B. A. (2005). The dynamics of viral marketing. http://www.hpl.hp.com/research/idl/papers/viral/viral.pdf

Li, X., Morie, P., & Roth, D. (2005). Semantic integration in text: From ambiguous names to identifiable entities. *AI Magazine Spring*, pp. 45–68.

Lloyd, L., Bhagwan, V., Gruhl, D., & Tomkins, A. (2005). *Disambiguation of references to individuals* (Tech. Rep. No. RJ10364(A0410-011)). IBM Research.

Malin, B. (2005). Unsupervised name disambiguation via social network similarity. *Workshop Notes on Link Analysis, Counterterrorism, and Security.*

Mann, G. S., & Yarowsky, D. (2003). Unsupervised personal name disambiguation. In *Proceedings of the CoNLL.*

Manning, C., & Schutze, H. (2002). *Foundations of statistical natural language processing.* London: The MIT Press.

Massa, P., & Avesani, P. (2005). Controversial users demand local trust metrics: An experimental study on epinions.com community. In *Proceedings of the AAAI-05.*

Matsuo, Y., Hamasaki, M., Takeda, H., Mori, J., Bollegala, D., Nakamura, Y., Nishimura, T., Hasida, K., & Ishizuka, M. (2006a). Spinning multiple social networks for Semantic web. In *Proceedigs of the AAAI-06.*

Matsuo, Y., Mori, J., Hamasaki, M., Takeda, H., Nishimura, T., Hasida, K., & Ishizuka, M. (2006b). POLYPHONET: An advanced social network extraction system. In *Proceedings of the WWW 2006*.

Matsuo, Y., Tomobe, H., Hasida, K., & Ishizuka, M. (2003). Mining social network of conference participants from the web. In *Proceedings of the Web Intelligence 2003*.

Matsuo, Y., Tomobe, H., Hasida, K., & Ishizuka, M. (2004a). Finding social network for trust calculation. In *Proc. ECAI2004*, pages 510–514.

Matsuo, Y., Tomobe, H., Hasida, K., & Ishizuka, M. (2004b). Finding social network for trust calculation. In *Proceedings of the 16th European Conference on Artificial Intelligence (ECAI2004)*.

Matsuo, Y., Tomobe, H., Hasida, K., & Ishizuka, M. (2005). Social network extraction from the web information. *Journal of the Japanese Society for Artificial Intelligence, 20*(1E), 46–56.

Mika, P. (2005a). Flink: Semantic web technology for the extraction and analysis of social networks. *Journal of Web Semantics, 3*(2).

Mika, P. (2005b). Ontologies are us: A unified model of social networks and Semantics. In *Proceedings of the ISWC2005*.

Miki, T., Nomura, S., & Ishida, T. (2005). Semantic web link analysis to discover social relationship in academic communities. In *Proceedings of the SAINT 2005*.

Milgram, S. (1967). The small-world problem. *Psychology Today, 2*, 60–67.

Mori, J., Ishizuka, M., Sugiyama, T., & Matsuo, Y. (2005a). Real-world oriented information sharing using social networks. In *Proceedings of the ACM GROUP '05*.

Mori, J., Matsuo, Y. & Ishizuka, M. (2005b). Finding user Semantics on the web using word co-occurrence information. In *Proceedings of*

the International Workshop on Personalization on the Semantic Web (PersWeb '05).

Nakagawa, H., Maeda, A., & Kojima, H. Automatic term recognition system termextract. *http://gensen.dl.itc.utokyo.ac.jp/gensenweb_eng. html* .

Nigram, K., McCallum, A., Thrun, S., & Mitchell, T. (2000). Text classification from labeled and unlabeled documents using EM. *Machine Learning, 39*, 103–134.

Palla, G., Derenyi, I., Farkas, I., & Vicsek, T. (2005). Uncovering the overlapping community structure of complex networks in nature and society. *Nature, 435*, 814.

Pentland, A. S. (2005). Socially aware computation and communication. *IEEE Computer.*

Quinlan, J. R. (1993). *C4.5: Programs for machine learning.* CA: Morgan Kaufmann.

Richardson, M., Agrawal, R., & Domingos, P. (2003). Trust management for the Semantic Web. In *Proceedings of the ISWC2003.*

Scott, J. (2000). S*ocial network analysis: A handbook (2nd ed.).* SAGE publications.

Staab, S., Domingos, P., Mika, P., Golbeck, J., Ding, L., Finin, T., Joshi, A., Nowak, A., & Vallacher, R. (2005). Social networks applied. *IEEE Intelligent Systems*, 80–93.

Tyler, J., Wilkinson, D., & Huberman, B. (2003). *Email as spectroscopy: Automated discovery of community structure within organizations.* Kluwer, B.V.

Wacholder, N., Ravin, Y., & Choi, M. (1997). Disambiguation of proper names in text. In *Proceedings of the 5th Applied Natural Language Processing Conference.*

Wasserman, S., & Faust, K. (1994). Social network analysis. *Methods and applications.* Cambridge: Cambridge University Press.

Watts, D., & Strogatz, S. (1998). Collective dynamics of small-world networks. *Nature, 393*, 440–442.

ENDNOTES

1   http://www.friendster.com/
2   http://www.orkut.com/
3   http://www.imeem.com/
4   http://360.yahoo.com/
5   http://flink.Semanticweb.org/. The system won the first prize at the Semantic Web Challenge in ISWC2004.
6   As of October, 2005 by Google search engine. The hit count is that obtained after omission of similar pages by Google.
7   Using the disaster mitigation research community in Japan.
8   We use an *entity* as a broader term of a *person*.
9   http://www.google.com/
10   As of 2004.

Chapter VII
Discovering Spatio-Textual Association Rules in Document Images

Donato Malerba
Università degli Studi di Bari, Italy

Margherita Berardi
Università degli Studi di Bari, Italy

Michelangelo Ceci
Università degli Studi di Bari, Italy

ABSTRACT

This chapter introduces a data mining method for the discovery of association rules from images of scanned paper documents. It argues that a document image is a multi-modal unit of analysis whose semantics is deduced from a combination of both the textual content and the layout structure and the logical structure. Therefore, it proposes a method where both the spatial information derived from a complex document image analysis process (layout analysis), and the information extracted from the logical structure of the document (document image classification and understanding) and the textual information extracted by means of an OCR, are simultaneously considered to generate interesting patterns. The proposed method is based on an inductive logic programming approach, which is argued to be the most appropriate to analyze data available in more than one modality. It contributes to show a possible evolution of the unimodal knowledge discovery scheme, according to which different types of data describing the units of analysis are dealt with through the application of some preprocessing technique that transform them into a single double entry tabular data.

INTRODUCTION

Business processes have always been based on the flow of documents around an organization. The concept of flow is almost synonymous with the concept of paper flow in typical office environments, where the main problem is the amazing number of printed documents that are generated and filed. In fact, much time and effort is wasted in ineffective searches through multiple information sources. Organizations need to extend the scope of Business Intelligence especially to their internal collections of textual data in order to make decisions on the basis of knowledge captured by these collections. Therefore new document management systems with abilities to catalog and automatically organize these documents are necessary. Personal document processing systems that can provide functional capabilities like classifying, storing, retrieving, and reproducing documents, as well as extracting, browsing, retrieving and synthesizing information from a variety of documents are in continual demand (Fan, Sheng, & Ng, 1999). However, they generally operate on electronic documents (e.g., text, word, rtf, pdf, html, and xml files) and not on the more common paper documents, which are made anyway computationally processable through digital scanning.

The pressing need for systems to be used as intelligent interfaces between paper and electronic media has led to the development of a large number of techniques for document image analysis and recognition. The conversion of document images into a symbolic form appropriate for subsequent modification, storage, retrieval, reuse, and transmission is a complex process articulated into several stages. Initially, the document image is preprocessed, for instance, to remove noise. Then it is decomposed into several constituent items, which represent coherent components of the document layout (e.g., text lines or half-tone images). Finally, logically relevant layout components (e.g., title and abstract) are recognized.

Domain-specific knowledge appears essential for document image analysis and understanding: in the literature, there are no examples of attempts to develop document analysis systems that can interpret arbitrary documents (Nagy, 2000). In many applications presented in the literature, a great effort is made to hand-code the necessary knowledge according to some formalism, such as block grammars (Nagy, Seth. & Stoddard, 1992), geometric trees (Dengel, Bleisinger, Hoch, Fein, & Hönes, 1992), and frames (Wenzel & Maus, 2001). However, hand-coding domain knowledge is time-consuming and limits the application of document analysis systems to predefined classes of documents.

To alleviate the burden in developing and customizing document analysis systems, data mining methods can be profitably applied to extract the required domain-specific knowledge. *Document image mining* denotes the synergy of data mining and document analysis system technology to aid in the analysis and understanding of large collections of document images. It is an interdisciplinary endeavor that draws upon expertise in image processing, data mining, machine learning, and artificial intelligence. The fundamental challenge in document image mining is to determine how low-level, pixel representation contained in a raw image of a scanned document can be efficiently and effectively processed to identify high-level spatial objects and relationships. Since the beginning of the 1990's, when the first attempts in applying machine learning techniques to document images were reported in the literature (Esposito, Malerba, & Semeraro, 1990), there has been a growing research focus on document image mining (Aiello, Monz, Todoran, & Worring, 2002; Akindele & Belaïd, 1995; Berardi, Ceci, & Malerba, 2003; Cesarini, Francescani, Gori, Marinai, Sheng, & Soda, 1997; Dengel, 1993; Dengel & Dubiel, 1995; Esposito, Malerba & Semeraro, 1994; Kise, Yajima, Babaguchi, Fukunaga, 1993; Walischewski, 1997) .

More recently, we have also assisted to a growing interest in *text mining*, a technology for analyzing large collections of unstructured documents for the purposes of extracting interesting and nontrivial patterns or knowledge. Knowledge discovered from textual documents can be in various forms including classification rules, which partition document collections into a given set of classes (Sebastiani, 2002), clusters of similar documents or objects composing documents (Steinbach, Karypis, & Kumar, 2000), patterns describing trends, such as emerging topics in a corpus of time-stamped documents (Lent, Agrawal & Srikant, 1997; Mei & Zhai, 2005; Morinaga & Yamanishi, 2004;), concept links, that connect related documents by identifying their commonly shared concepts and allow browsing a documents collection (Ben-Dov, Wu, Cairns, & Feldman, 2004; Sheth, Aleman-Meza, Arpinar, Halaschek, Ramakrishnan, & Bertram, 2004), and semantic graphs that can be used as document summaries (Leskovec, Grobelnik, & Millic-Frayling, 2004).

Document image mining and text mining have always been considered two complementary technologies: the former is applicable to documents available on paper media, while the second is appropriate for documents that are generated according to some textual format. Document image mining aims to identify high-level spatial objects and relationships, while text mining is more concerned with patterns involving words, sentences, and concepts. The possible interactions between spatial information extracted from document images and textual information related to the content of some layout components, have never been considered in the data mining literature.

This chapter introduces a new, integrated approach to mining patterns from document images acquired by scanning the original paper documents. In this approach, both the layout and the textual information available in a document are taken into account. They are extracted by means of a complex process that aims at converting unstructured document images into semi-structured XML documents where textual, graphical, layout and semantic pieces of information coexist. The particular type of patterns extracted in the proposed approach is *spatio-textual association rules* that express regularities among content-enriched logical structures of a set of document images belonging to the same class.

In document image processing, this kind of patterns can be used in a number of ways. First, discovered association rules can be used as constraints defining domain templates of documents both for classification tasks, such as in associative classification approaches (Liu, Hsu & Ma, 1998), and to support layout correction tasks. Second, the rules could be also used in a generative way. For instance, if a part of the document is hidden or missing, strong association rules can be used to predict the location of missing layout/logical components (Hiraki, Gennari, Yamamoto, & Anzai, 1991). Moreover, a desirable property of a system that automatically generates textual documents is to take into account the layout specification during the generation process, since layout and wording generally interact (Reichenberger, Rondhuis, Kleinz, & Bateman, 1995). Association rules can be useful to define the layout specifications of such a system. Finally, this problem is also related to document reformatting (Hardman, Rutledge, & Bulterman, 1998).

The goal of the chapter is also to present a multistep knowledge-intensive process that transforms document images into structured representations allowing images to be mined.

BACKGROUND

In tasks where the goal is to uncover structure in the data and where there is no target concept, the discovery of relatively simple but frequently occurring patterns has shown good promise. Association rules are a basic example of this kind of setting. The problem of mining association rules was originally introduced in the work by Agrawal, Imieliński, and Swami (1993). Association rules can be expressed by an implication:

$$X \rightarrow Y$$

where X and Y are sets of *items*, such that $X \cap Y = \varnothing$. The meaning of such rules is quite intuitive: Given a database D of transactions, where each *transaction* $T \in D$ is a set of items, $X \rightarrow Y$ expresses that whenever a transaction T contains X than T probably contains Y also. The conjunction $X \wedge Y$ is called *pattern*. Two parameters are usually reported for association rules, namely the support, which estimates the probability $p(X \subseteq T \wedge Y \subseteq T)$, and the confidence, which estimates the probability $p(Y \subseteq T \mid X \subseteq T)$. The goal of association rule mining is to find all the rules with *support* and *confidence*, exceeding user specified thresholds, henceforth called *minsup* and *minconf* respectively. A pattern $X \wedge Y$ is *large* (or *frequent*) if its support is greater than or equal to minsup. An association rule $X \rightarrow Y$ is *strong* if it has a large support (i.e., $X \wedge Y$ is large) and high confidence.

Traditionally, association rules are discovered for market basket analysis. However, it is becoming clear that they can be successfully applied to a wide range of domains, such as Web access patterns discovery (Chen, Park, & Yu, 1996), building intrusion detection models (Lee, Stolfo, & Mok, 1998) and mining data streams (Jiang & Gruenwald, 2006). An interesting application is faced in the work by Ordonez and Omiecinski (1999) where a method for mining knowledge from images is proposed. The method is an association rule miner that automatically identifies similarities in images on the basis of their content. The content is expressed in terms of objects automatically recognized in a segmented image. The work shows that even without domain knowledge it is possible to automatically extract some reliable knowledge. Mined association rules refer to the presence/absence of an object in an image, since images are viewed as transactions while objects as items. No spatial relationship between objects in the same image is considered.

Nevertheless, mining patterns from document images raises a lot of different issues regarding document structure, storage, access, and processing.

Firstly, documents are typically unstructured or, at most, semistructured data. In the case of structured data, the associated semantics or meaning is unambiguously and implicitly defined and encapsulated in the structure of data (i.e., relational databases), whereas unstructured information meaning is only loosely implied by its form and requires several interpretation steps in order to extract the intended meaning. Endowing documents with a structure that properly encode their semantics adds a degree of complexity in the application of the mining process. This makes the data preprocessing step really crucial.

Secondly, documents are *message conveyers* whose meaning is deduced from the combination of the written text, the presentation style, the context, the reported pictures, and the logical structure, at least. For instance, when the logical structure and the presentation style are quite well-defined (typically when some parts are pre-printed or documents are generated by following a predefined formatting style), the reader may easily identify the document type and locate information of interest even before reading the descriptive text (e.g., the title of a paper in the case of scientific papers or newspapers, the sender in the case of faxes, the supplier or the amount in the case of invoices, etc.). Moreover, in many contexts, illustrative images fully complement the textual information, such as diagrams in socioeconomic or marketing reports. By considering typeface information, it is also possible to immediately and clearly capture the notion about the historical origin of documents (e.g., medieval, renaissance, baroque, etc.) as well as the cultural origin (e.g., Indic, Kangi, Hangul, or Arabic rather than European scripts). The presence of spurious objects may inherently define classes of documents, such as revenue stamps in the case of legal documents. The idea to consider the multimodal nature of documents falls in the novel research trend of the document understanding field, that encourages the development of hybrid strategies for knowledge capture in order to exploit the different sources of knowledge (e.g., text, images, layout, type style, tabular, and format information) that simultaneously define the semantics of a document (Dengel, 2003).

However, data mining has evolved following a unimodal scheme instantiated according to the type of the underlying data (text, images, etc). Applications of data mining involving hybrid knowledge representation models are still to be explored. Indeed, several works have been proposed to mine association rules from the textual dimension (Ahonen-Myka, 2005; Amir, Aumann, Feldman, & Fresko, 2005; Cherfi, Napoli, & Toussaint, 2005; Raghavan & Tsaparas, 2002; Srinivasan, 2004) with the goal to find rules that express regularities concerning the presence of particular words or particular sentences in text corpora. Conversely, mining the combination of structure and content dimensions of documents has not been investigated yet in the literature, even though some emerging real-world applications are demanding for mining processes able to exploit several forms of information, such as images and captions in addition to full text (Yeh, Hirschman, & Morgan, 2003). Some interesting examples of association rule mining applied to more complex cases of data are proposed in (Li, Wu & Pottenger, 2005), where textual documents come from different distributed sources, and in (Lee, Lin & Chen, 2001) which presents an application on temporal document collections.

Thirdly, documents are a kind of data that do not match the classical attribute-value format. In the tabular model, data are represented as fixed-length vectors of variable values describing properties, where each variable can have only a single, primitive value. Conversely, the entities (e.g., the objects composing a document image) that are observed and about which information is collected may have different properties, which can be properly modeled by as many data tables (relational data model) as the number of object types (Knobbe, Blockeel, Siebes, & Van der Wallen, 1999). Moreover, relationships (e.g., topological or distance relationships that are implicitly defined by the location of objects spatially distributed in a document image or words distributed in text) among observed objects forming the same semantic unit can be also explicitly modeled in a relational database by means of tables describing the relationship. Hence, the classical attribute-value representation seems too restrictive and advanced approaches to both represent and reason in presence of multiple relations among data are necessary.

Lastly, the data mining method should take into account external information, also called expert or domain knowledge, that can add semantics to the whole process and then obtain high-level decision support and user confidence.

All these peculiarities make documents a kind of complex data that require methodological evolutions of data mining technologies as well as the involvement of several document processing techniques. In our context, the extraction of spatio-textual association rules requires the consideration of all these sources of complexity coming from the inherent nature of processed documents.

Since the early work by Agrawal, Imieliński, and Swami (1993), several efficient algorithms to mine association rules have been developed. Studies cover a broad spectrum of topics including: (1) fast algorithms based on the level-wise Apriori framework (Agrawal & Srikant, 1994; Park, Chen, & Yu, 1997); (2) FP-growth algorithms (Han, Pei, & Yin, 2000); (3) incremental updating (Lee et al., 2001); (4) mining of generalized and multilevel rules (Han & Fu, 1995; Srikant & Agrawal, 1995); (5) mining of quantitative rules (Srikant & Agrawal, 1996); (6) mining of multidimensional rules (Yang, Fayyad, & Bradley, 2001); (7) multiple minimum supports issues (Liu, Hsu & Ma, 1999; Wang, He & Han, 2000). However, the blueprint for all the algorithms proposed in the literature is the levelwise method by Mannila and Toivonen (1997), which is based on a breadth-first search in the lattice spanned by a generality order between patterns. Despite all the interesting extensions proposed in the literature, most of these algorithms work on data represented as fixed-length vectors, that is, according to the *single-table assumption*. More specifically, it is assumed that the data to be mined are represented in a single table (or relation) of a relational database, such that each row (or tuple) represents an independent unit of the sample population and the columns correspond to properties of units. This means that all these methods of association rule discovery requires that the database has to be "flattened" somehow in a single table before applying the data mining method. Moreover, discovered patterns are not relational. Relational frequent patters are conversely generated by WARMR (Dehaspe & Toivonen, 1999) which adapts the levelwise method to a search space of conjunctive first-order formulas representing patterns. However, no example of relational association rule discovery that is able to include domain-specific knowledge in the reasoning step is reported in the literature. Indeed, the use of background knowledge generally affects the processing of data to be mined but not the form of patterns. Conversely, mining from documents is the kind of application that may benefit from mechanisms for reasoning in presence of knowledge on the domain and discovery goal too.

MAIN THRUST OF THE CHAPTER: ISSUES

In this chapter we investigate the discovery of *spatio-textual association rules* that takes into account both the layout and the textual dimension of document images acquired by scanning paper documents. However, the extraction of both

layout and textual information from document images is a complex process that is articulated into several stages. Initial processing steps include binarization, skew detection, noise filtering, and segmentation. Then, a document image is decomposed into several constituent items that represent coherent components of the documents (e.g., text lines, half-tone images, line drawings or graphics) without any knowledge of the specific format. This layout analysis step precedes the interpretation or understanding of document images whose aim is that of recognizing semantically relevant layout components (e.g., title, abstract of a scientific paper or leading article, picture of a newspaper) as well as extracting abstract relationships between layout components (e.g., reading order).

The domain-specific knowledge required to perform effective interpretation and understanding of document images is typically restricted to relevant and invariant layout characteristics of the documents. The idea is that humans are generally able to classify documents (invoices, letters, order forms, papers, indexes, etc.) from a perceptive point of view, by recognizing the layout structure of the documents. However, this layout-based characterization of classes of documents is not applicable to all domains. Indeed in many cases it is necessary to use also information on the textual content of the document. These considerations motivate the importance of mining spatio-textual association rules as a means to capture domain-specific knowledge which provides us with both a layout-based and a content-based characterization of a class of documents. In the following, we present solutions implemented in a knowledge-intensive document processing system to extract these content-enriched logical structures from document images.

As to knowledge representation issues, relational formalisms allow us to represent a document image as the composition of layout objects described on the basis of attributes about their geometry, textual content, color, as well as topological relations describing their spatial distribution in a document page. To navigate the relational structure of document data and to express complex background knowledge, we resort to inductive logic programming (ILP) as learning framework to investigate association rule induction. ILP aims to induce general rules starting from specific observations and background knowledge. It is a research area at the intersection of inductive machine learning and logic programming. Logic programming uses as representation language a subset of first-order logic, also called relational logic, which is really appropriate to represent multirelational data. Indeed, the ILP paradigm is the natural candidate for data mining tasks with relational representations and abundant expert knowledge (Flach & Lavrac, 2003).

In this data representation model of documents, their inherent spatial nature raises two further issues. First, the location and the extension of layout components implicitly define spatial relations, such as topological, distance and direction relations. Therefore, complex data transformation processes are required to make spatial relations explicit. Second, layout components can be described at multiple levels of granularity in order to preserve spatial relations.

Multi-level approaches to *spatial association rule mining* allow us to discover association rules involving spatial objects at different granularity levels. A peculiarity of spatial association rule mining is that associations are discovered between *reference objects* (ro) and some *task-relevant objects* (tro). The former are the main subject of the description, while the latter are spatial objects that are relevant for the task at hand and are spatially related to the former. Multi-level association rules can be discovered when taxonomic knowledge (i.e., is-a hierarchies) is expressed on task-relevant objects. Merely representing taxonomic relations is not sufficient since specific mechanisms for taxonomic reasoning are necessary in the mining step. For instance, although is-a hierarchies can be represented in WARMR, the system is not able to perform multi-level analysis. Conversely, we

propose a relational algorithm for multi-level association rule extraction that is explicitly designed for this task and that fully exploits hierarchical knowledge expressed on items of interest.

OUR APPROACH

In our proposal, the system used for processing documents is WISDOM++ (Altamura, Esposito, & Malerba, 2001). WISDOM++ (www.di.uniba. it/~malerba/wisdom++/) is a document analysis system that can transform textual paper documents into XML format. This is performed in several steps. First, the image is segmented into basic layout components (non-overlapping rectangular blocks enclosing content portions). These layout components are classified according to the type of their content (e.g., text, graphics, and horizontal/vertical line). Second, a perceptual organization phase, called layout analysis, is performed to detect structures among blocks. The result is a tree-like structure, named *layout structure*, which represents the document layout at various levels of abstraction and associates the content of a document with a hierarchy of layout components, such as blocks, lines, and paragraphs. Third, the document image classification step aims at identifying the membership class (or type) of a document (e.g., censorship decision, newspaper article, etc.), and it is performed using some first-order rules which can be automatically learned from a set of training examples. Document image understanding (or interpretation) creates a mapping of the layout structure into the *logical structure*, which associates the content with a hierarchy of logical components, such as title/authors of a scientific article, or the name of the censorer in a censorship document, and so on. As previously pointed out, the logical and the layout structures are strongly related. For instance, the title of an article is usually located at the top of the first page of a document and it is written with the largest character set used in the document. Document image understanding also uses first-order rules (Malerba, Esposito, Lisi, & Altamura, 2001). Once the logical and layout structures have been mapped, OCR can be applied only to those textual components of interest for the application domain, and its content can be stored for future retrieval purposes. This way, the system can automatically determine not only the type of document, but is also able to identify interesting parts of a document and to extract the information given in this part plus its meaning. The result of the document analysis is an XML document which makes the document image easily retrievable.

Once the layout/logical structure as well as the textual content of a document have been extracted, association rules are mined by taking into account all sources of complexity described in previous sections and, in particular, by taking into account the inherent spatial nature of the layout structure. For this reason, association rule mining methods developed in the context of spatial data mining are considered and, in particular, we resort to the Spatial Association Rules mining system SPADA (Spatial Pattern Discovery Algorithm) (Appice, Ceci, Lanza, Lisi, & Malerba, 2003) that discovers spatial association rules, that is, association rules involving spatial objects and relations. It is based on an ILP approach which permits the extraction of multi-level spatial association rules, that is, association rules involving spatial objects at different granularity levels. It also exploits the expressive power of first order logic that permits to represent background knowledge on the application domain and to define some form of search bias.

In SPADA, training examples are represented in first order logic representation formalism. Next Section introduces the first-order logic descriptions of documents processed by SPADA.

DOCUMENT DESCRIPTIONS

WISDOM++ has been extended in order to support the generation of document descriptions for SPA-

DA. In a document description, ground facts are used to describe the logical structure of a document image in terms of relational features, attributes and textual features. In particular, we mention *locational* features such as the coordinates of the centroid of a logical component (x_pos_center, y_pos_center), *geometrical* features such as the dimensions of a logical component (width, height), and *topological* features such as relations between two components (on_top, to_right, alignment). We use the *aspatial* feature type_of which specifies the content type of a logical component (e.g., image, text, horizontal line). Other aspatial features, called logical features, are used to define the label associated to the logical components. For example, in the case of scientific papers they are: affiliation, page_number, figure, caption, index_term, running_head, author, title, abstract, formulae, subsection_title, section_title, biography, references, paragraph, table, undefined. In order to represent the textual dimension, we also introduce textual features (e.g. text_in_affiliation, text_in_index_term) describing the presence or the absence of a term in a logical component. In WISDOM++, the use of these features is limited to describe only logical components of interest that are opportunely specified by the user.

In Box 1, we report an example of the document description extracted by WISDOM++ for the document page shown in Figure 1, where tpami1_1_14 represents the page and tpami1_1_14_2,…,tpami1_1_14_15 represent logical components of the page. It is noteworthy that the relation *part_of* is used to express the membership of a component to a page. Numerical features are automatically discretized before mining association rules by means of the RUDE algorithm (Ludl & Widmer, 2000).

Concerning textual predicates, they express the presence of a term in a logical component. Terms have been automatically extracted by means of a text-processing module implemented in WISDOM++. It aims to describe each single textual layout component of interest by means

Box 1.

```
class(h,tpami),
running_head(tpami1_1_14,tpami1_1_14_2).
title(tpami1_1_14,tpami1_1_14_3).
author(tpami1_1_14,tpami1_1_14_4).
abstract(tpami1_1_14,tpami1_1_14_5).
  ...
page_first(tpami1_1_14).
part_of(tpami1_1_14,tpami1_1_14_2).
part_of(tpami1_1_14,tpami1_1_14_3).
part_of(tpami1_1_14,tpami1_1_14_4).
  ...
width(tpami1_1_14_2,[329..390]).
width(tpami1_1_14_3,[488..490]).
width(tpami1_1_14_4,[186..262]).
  ...
height(tpami1_1_14_2,[7..7]).
height(tpami1_1_14_4,[11..54]).
height(tpami1_1_14_3,[11..54]).
  ...
type_of(tpami1_1_14_2, text).
type_of(tpami1_1_14_3, text).
type_of(tpami1_1_14_4, text).
  ...
type_of(tpami1_1_14_8, hor_line).
  ...
x_pos_centre(tpami1_1_14_2,[208..215]).
x_pos_centre(tpami1_1_14_3,[287..288]).
x_pos_centre(tpami1_1_14_4,[288..288]).
  ...
y_pos_centre(tpami1_1_14_2,[26..83]).
y_pos_centre(tpami1_1_14_3,[26..83]).
y_pos_centre(tpami1_1_14_4,[129..216]).
  ...
on_top(tpami1_1_14_2,tpami1_1_14_3).
on_top(tpami1_1_14_3,tpami1_1_14_4).
on_top(tpami1_1_14_3,tpami1_1_14_5).
  ...
```

continued on next page

Box 1. continued

```
to_right(tpami1_1_14_14,tpami1_1_14_12).

to_right(tpami1_1_14_11,tpami1_1_14_12).

to_right(tpami1_1_14_13,tpami1_1_14_12).

...

only_left_col(tpami1_1_14_2,tpami1_1_14_10).

...

text_in_index_term(tpami1_1_14_6,model).

text_in_index_term(tpami1_1_14_6,track).

text_in_abstract(tpami1_1_14_5,base).

text_in_abstract(tpami1_1_14_5,model).

text_in_title(tpami1_1_14_3,algorithm).

...
```

Figure 1. An example of document image processed by WISDOM++ (layout and logical structure)

of the classical *bag-of-words representation*. All textual components are initially tokenized and the set of obtained tokens (words) is filtered in order to remove punctuation marks, numbers and tokens of less than three characters. Only relevant tokens are used in textual predicates. Before selecting relevant features, standard text preprocessing methods are used to:

1. Remove stop words, such as articles, adverbs, prepositions and other frequent words.
2. Determine equivalent stems (stemming), such as "topology" in the words "topology" and "topological," by means of Porter's algorithm for English texts (Porter, 1980).

Feature selection is based on the maximization of the product maxTF•DF2•ICF (Ceci & Malerba, 2007) which scores high terms appearing (possibly frequently) in a logical component *c* and penalizes terms common to other logical components.

More formally: Let *c* be the logical label associated to a logical component. Let *d* be a bag of word representation of a logical component labeled with *c* (after the tokenizing, filtering and stemming steps), *w* a term extracted from *d* and $TF_d(w)$ the relative frequency of *w* in *d*. Then, the following statistics can be computed:

*   The maximum value of $TF_d(w)$ on all logical components *d* labeled with *c*
*   The document frequency, that is, the percentage of logical components labeled with *c* in which the term *w* occurs
*   The category frequency $CF_c(w)$, that is, the number of labels $c' \neq c$, such that *w* occurs in logical components labeled with *c'*.

According to such statistics, the score v_i associated to the *i*-th term w_i belonging to at least one of the logical components labeled with *c* is:

$$v_i = TF_c(w_i) \times DF_c^2(w_i) \times \frac{1}{CF_c(w_i)}$$

According to this function, it is possible to identify a ranked list of "discriminative" terms for each of the possible labels. From this list, we select the best n_{dict} terms in $Dict_c$, where n_{dict} is a user-defined parameter.

The textual dimension of each logical component *d* labeled as *c* is represented in the document description as a set of ground facts that express the presence of a term $w \in Dict_c$ in the specified logical component.

MINING SPATIO-TEXTUAL ASSOCIATION RULES WITH SPADA

Once the document descriptions are generated, SPADA can be used to extract association rules. The problem of mining spatial association rules can be formalized as follows:

*   *Given* a set *S* of *reference objects*, some sets R_k, $1 \leq k \leq m$, of *task-relevant objects*, a background knowledge *BK* including some *spatial hierarchies* H_k on objects in R_k, *M granularity levels* in the descriptions (1 is the highest while *M* is the lowest), a set of *granularity assignments* Ψ_k which associate each object in H_k with a granularity level, a couple of thresholds *minsup[l]* and *minconf[l]* for each granularity level, a language bias *LB* that constrains the search space
*   *Find* strong multi-level spatial association rules, that is, association rules involving spatial objects at different granularity levels.

The reference objects are the main subject of the description, that is, the observation units, while the task relevant objects are spatial objects that are relevant for the task at hand and are spatially related to the former. Hierarchies H_k define *is-a* (i.e., taxonomical) relations on task relevant objects. Both frequency of spatial patterns and strength of rules depend on the granularity level l at which patterns/rules describe data. Therefore, a pattern P (*s%*) at level l is *frequent* if $s \geq minsup[l]$ and all ancestors of P with respect to H_k are frequent at their corresponding levels. A spatial association rule $Q \rightarrow R$ (*s%, c%*) at level l is *strong* if the pattern $Q \cup R$ (*s%*) is frequent and $c \geq minconf[l]$.

SPADA operates in three steps for each granularity level: (1) pattern generation; (2) pattern evaluation; (3) rule generation and evaluation. SPADA takes advantage of statistics computed at granularity level l when computing the supports of patterns at granularity level $l+1$.

The expressive power of first-order logic is exploited to specify both the background knowledge *BK*, such as spatial hierarchies and domain specific knowledge, and the language bias *LB*. Spatial hierarchies allow us to face with one of the main issues of spatial data mining, that is, the representation and management of spatial objects at different levels of granularity, while the domain specific knowledge, encoded in a set of rules, supports qualitative spatial reasoning. On the other hand, the *LB* is relevant to allow

the user to specify the user's bias for interesting solutions, and then to exploit this bias to improve both the efficiency of the mining process and the quality of the discovered rules. In SPADA, the language bias is expressed as a set of constraint specifications for either patterns or association rules. Pattern constrains allow the user to specify a literal or a set of literals that should occur one or more times in discovered patterns. During the *rule generation* phase, patterns that do not satisfy a pattern constraint are filtered out. Similarly, rule constraints are used to specify literals that should occur in the head or body of discovered rules. In addition, a rule constraint permits to specify the maximum number of literals that should occur in the head of a rule.

In our application domain, reference objects are all the logical components for which a logical label is specified. Task relevant objects are all the logical components (including undefined components).

The *BK* is used to specify the hierarchy of logical components (Figure 2) that allows the system to extract spatial association rules at different granularity levels.

Figure 2. Hierarchy of logical components

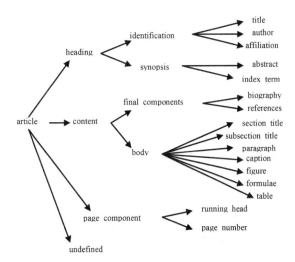

The *BK* also permits to automatically associate information on page order to layout components, since the presence of some logical components may depend on the order page (e.g., *author* is in the first page). This concept is expressed by means of the following Prolog rules seen in Box 2.

Moreover, in the *BK* we can also define the general textual predicate `text _ in _ component`, as seen in Box 3.

It is noteworthy that hierarchies are defined on task relevant objects. This means that, in theory, it is not possible to consider the same reference object at different levels of granularity. To overcome this limitation, we introduced in the BK the fact `specialize(X,X)` which allows us to consider a *ro* as a *tro*. By means of LB constraints we forced the presence of the predicate `specialize` in the head of an extracted association rule.

Concerning the textual dimension, the language bias of SPADA has been extended in order to properly deal with atoms representing tokens. Indeed, SPADA language bias requires that the user specify predicates that can be involved in a pattern. For instance, if we are interested in patterns that contain the predicate `text _`

`in _ abstract(A, paper)` where A is a variable representing a *tro* already introduced in the pattern and "paper" is a constant value representing the presence of the term "paper" in A, we have to specify the following bias rule `lb _ atom(text _ in _ component(old tro, paper))`. This means that it is necessary to specifies a rule for each constant value that could be involved in the predicate.

Although this approach can be profitably used to keep under control the dimension of the search space avoiding the exploration of candidate patterns containing non interesting constants, it turns out to be a severe limitation in our context where there are hundreds of constants representing selected terms (the number depends on the n_{dict} constant and on the number of user-selected logical labels for which the textual dimension is considered). To avoid the manual or semiautomatic specification of different `lb _ atom` biases, we extended the SPADA LB in order to support anonymous variables:

`lb _ atom(text _ in _ component(old tro, _ )).`

Box 2.

at_page_first(X)	:- part_of(Y,X), page_first(Y).
at_page_intermediate(X)	:- part_of(Y,X),page_intermediate(Y).
at_page_last_but_one(X)	:- part_of(Y,X),page_last_but_one(Y).
at_page_last(X)	:- part_of(Y,X), page_last(Y).

Box 3.

```
text_in_component(X,Y) :- text_in_index_term(X,Y).
text_in_component(X,Y) :- text_in_references(X,Y).
text_in_component(X,Y) :- text_in_abstract(X,Y).
text_in_component(X,Y) :- text_in_title(X,Y).
text_in_component(X,Y) :- text_in_running_head(X,Y).
```

This means that we intend to consider in the search phase those patterns involving the predicate text _ in _ component whose second argument is an arbitrary term. The SPADA search strategy has been consequently modified in order to support this additional feature.

APPLICATION TO THE TPAMI CORPORA

We investigate the applicability of the proposed solution to real-world document images. In particular, we have considered 24 multipage documents, which are scientific papers published as either regular or short in the IEEE Transactions on Pattern Analysis and Machine Intelligence in the January and February 1996 issues. Each paper is a multi-page document and has a variable number of pages and layout components for page. A user of WISDOM++ labels some layout components

of this set of documents according to their logical meaning. Those layout components with no clear logical meaning are labelled as *undefined*. All logical labels belong to the lowest level of the hierarchy reported in the previous section. We processed 217 document images in all.

In Table 1, the number of logical components for the whole data set is shown. The number of features to describe the 24 documents presented to SPADA is 38,948, about 179 features for each page document. The total number of logical components is 3,603 (1,014 of which are *undefined*) about 150 descriptors for each document page.

To generate textual predicates we set n_{dict} = 50 and we considered the following logical components: *title, abstract, index_term, references, running_head*, thus the following textual predicates have been included in the document descriptions: *(text_in_title, text_in_abstract, text_in_index_term, text_in_references, text_in_running_head)*. The total number of extracted textual features is 1,681.

Table 1. Logical labels distribution

Label	No Logical components
Affiliation	23
Page_number	191
Figure	357
Caption	202
Index_term	26
Running_head	231
Author	28
Title	26
Abstract	25
Formulae	333
Section_title	65
Biography	21
References	45
Paragraph	968
Table	48
Undefined	1014

An example of association rule discovered by SPADA at the second granularity level (l=2) is the following:

```
is _ a _ block(A) ==> specialize(A,B)
, is _ a(B,heading),
on _ top(B,C),   C\=B,   is _
a(C,heading),
text _ in _ component(C,paper)
support: 38.46 confidence: 38.46
```

This rule considers both relational properties and textual properties. Its spatial pattern involves ten out of 26 (i.e., 38.46%) blocks labelled as *title*. This means that ten logical components which represent a *heading* of some paper are on top of a different logical component C that is a *heading* component and contains the term "paper" (typically adopted in the sentence "In this paper we...").

At a lower granularity level (l=4), a similar rule is found where the logical component B is specialized as *title* and the component C is specialized as *abstract*.

```
is _ a _ block(A) ==> specialize(A,B)
, is _ a(B,title),
on _ top(B,C),     C\=B,     is _
a(C,abstract),
text _ in _ component(C,paper)
support: 38.46 confidence: 38.46
```

The rule has the same confidence and support reported for the rule inferred at the first granularity level.

Another example of association rule is:

```
is _ a _ block(A) ==> specialize(A,B),
is _ a(B,references),
type _ text(B), at _ page _ last(B)
support: 46.66 confidence: 46.66
```

which shows the use of the predicate `at _ page _ last(B)` introduced in the BK. This is an example of pure spatial association rule.

Finally, an example of pure textual association rule discovered by SPADA is

```
is _ a _ block(A) ==> specialize(A,B),
is _ a(B,index _ term),
text _ in _ component(B,index)
support: 92.0 confidence: 92.0
```

which simply states that a logical component index term contains the term 'index'.

The number of mined association rules for each logical component at different granularity levels is reported in Table 2. SPADA has found several spatial associations involving all logical components. Many spatial patterns involving logical components (e.g., *affiliation, title, author, abstract* and *index_term*) in the first page of an article are found. This can be explained by observing that the first page generally has a more regular layout structure and contains several distinct logical components. The situation is different for *references* where most of the rules involve textual predicates because of the high frequency of discriminating terms (e.g., "pp", "vol", "ieee" etc.).

FUTURE TRENDS

Since its definition, knowledge discovery has witnessed the development of numerous efficient methods and studies to extract knowledge in the context of variegated real-world applications, many of which generate various data, organized in different structures and formats, distributed on heterogeneous sources, changing in terms of definition or value at different times. However, intelligent data analysis for this kind of complex data is still at the beginning. Most of data mining methods operate on the classical double entry tabular data, and different types of unstructured or semi-structured data (e.g., images, natural language texts, and HTML documents) are dealt with

Table 2. Number of extracted association rules

No of Rules	Level 1	Level 2	Level 3	Level 4
min_conf	*0.3*	*0.3*	*0.3*	*0.3*
min_supp	*0.3*	*0.3*	*0.3*	*0.3*
Affiliation	18	18	18	18
Page_Number	62	62	61	0
Figure	26	26	26	23
Caption	33	33	33	33
Index_term	45	45	45	51
Running_head	184	184	184	0
Author	30	30	30	30
Title	27	27	32	32
Abstract	103	101	101	101
Formulae	26	26	25	28
Section_Title	23	23	23	23
Biography	23	23	23	23
References	266	265	256	256
Table	30	30	30	18

through the application of some preprocessing techniques that transform them into this tabular format. The knowledge discovery has evolved following a *unimodal scheme* according to which data of a single modality (database transactions, text, images, etc.) are transformed into a single table or database relation.

This unimodal scheme presents two strong limitations for many real world applications.

First, the wealth of secondary data sources creates opportunities to conduct analyses on units described by a combination of data in more than one modality. For instance, a clinical file includes both tabular data (e.g., results of blood tests), and texts (e.g., a diagnosis report) and images (e.g., X-rays and pictures of an ultrasonography), which must be simultaneously considered in order to make correct and appropriate decisions. Moreover, units of analysis can be multimodal in their nature. This is the case of paper documents, which contain text, tables, graphics, images, and maps, as well as Web pages, which may also include time-dependent (or stream) data, such as full-motion videos and sounds. These units should be analyzed by means of multimodal data mining techniques, which can combine information of different nature and associate them with a same semantic unit.

The second main limitation of the unimodal knowledge discovery scheme is the classical tabular representation in which original data are finally converted. For many applications, squeezing data from multiple relations into a single table requires much though and effort and can lead to loss of information. An alternative for these applications is the use of ILP, which can analyze multirelational directly, without the need to convert the data into a single table first. Multirelational data mining is also appropriate to analyze data available in more than one modality, since the normalized representation of these data in a relational database is clearly different and requires multiple tables.

The extension of the unimodal knowledge discovery scheme to data with more than one modality is one of main trends in data mining and involves the development of new algorithms or the deep modification of old ones. Some of the current directions of research concern spatio-temporal data mining (Andrienko, Malerba, May, & Teisseire, 2006), learning in computer vision (Esposito & Malerba, 2001), and multimedia data mining (Simoff, Djeraba, & Zaïane, 2002). Several research issues investigated in these areas still need appropriate answers. For instance, the spatial and temporal relations are often implicitly defined and must be extracted from the data: trading-off pre- computation (eager approach) and extraction on-the-fly (lazy approach) allow us to save much computational resources. Moreover, the resolution or granularity level at which multimodal data are considered can have direct impact on the strength of patterns that can be discovered: interesting patterns are more likely to be discovered at the lowest resolution/granularity level, while large support is more likely to exist at higher levels. A further issue is the generation of patterns expressing human-interpretable properties and relations: this requires that complex transformations be applied to describe the content of maps, images, and videos. For the same reason, a multimodal data mining algorithm should be able to take into account the large amount of domain independent knowledge nowadays available in ontologies and lexical resources.

ILP remained until recently mostly conceptual, due to limited scalability of algorithms, their inability to explicitly handle noise and uncertainty, and a perceived lack of killer applications. Latest research results show that each of these bottlenecks are beginning to disappear (Blockeel & Sebag, 2003; de Raedt & Kersting, 2003; Page & Craven, 2003), so that ILP (or its database-oriented counterpart, *multi-relational data mining* (Domingos, 2003)) is entering a period of rapid expansion and can offer a viable perspective to the evolution of the unimodal knowledge discovery scheme.

This chapter contributes to this evolution by showing a specific case study in which different types of information conveyed in a document (our unit of analysis), can be extracted and simultaneously considered while generating patterns. The proposed algorithm operates on multirelational data and generates (multi)relational patterns at different levels of abstraction, by taking into account background knowledge available on the specific domain.

CONCLUSION

In this chapter we have provided an overview on issues and solutions to the problem of extracting and synthesizing knowledge from document images in form of association rules. The necessity to consider different sources of information when mining document data has inspired the investigation of spatio-textual association rules discovery, since it allows us to fully exploit the intrinsic spatial nature of document images without diminishing the role of content information. This is a challenging task that requires several efforts both on data processing and on the mining strategy. As to data preparation, the definition of a semantic-safe structure of document images involves several processing steps, whose design has been presented in this chapter. Document images are processed to extract semantically interesting layout structures and relevant content portions. Initially, preprocessing and segmentation of a document image are performed. Then, the geometrical arrangement of content portions on a page is analyzed for layout structure extraction. This layout analysis step precedes the interpretation or understanding of document images whose aim is to label relevant layout components by reflecting the logical structure of the document page. Finally, an OCR system is applied only to those logical components of interest for the application domain in order to extract textual content. All these operations are implemented in the WISDOM++ system, which allows us to extract multi-modal data (e.g., textual and spatial) from documents. WISDOM++ generates proper descriptions of document images by representing them as the composition of labeled layout objects containing text and graphic data and that are spatially distributed in the document page. Some issues concerning the spatial nature of document data have been tackled in the mining problem definition. First, implicit relations defined by the spatial distribution of document objects have been extracted and properly represented. Second, different levels of granularity can be defined on spatial objects contained in document images. Hence, the discovery process has been formulated as *multi-level relational association rule* mining from spatio-textual data. We have presented the extension of the spatial association rule miner SPADA to the extraction of spatio-textual association rules. SPADA is based on an ILP approach and permits the extraction of association rules involving spatial objects at different granularity levels. An application of SPADA to scientific papers processed by WISDOM++ has been described. The mining process has been conducted on a set of document images belonging to the same class, namely documents presenting approximately the same layout/logical structure. Hence, discovered patterns capture regularities that implicitly define domain templates of documents and that can be used both for classification tasks and to support layout correction tasks.

REFERENCES

Agrawal, R., Imieliński, T., & Swami, A. (1993). Mining association rules between sets of items in large databases. In P. Buneman and S. Jajodia (Eds.). In *Proceedings of the 1993 ACM SIGMOD International Conference on Management of Data*.

Agrawal, R., & Srikant, R. (1994). Fast algorithms for mining association rules in large databases. In *Proceedings of the 20th International Conference on Very Large Data Bases*.

Ahonen-Myka, H. (2005). Mining all maximal frequent word sequences in a set of sentences. In *Proceedings of the 14th ACM international Conference on information and Knowledge Management*. CIKM '05.

Aiello, M., Monz, C., Todoran, L., & Worring, M. (2002). Document understanding for a broad class of documents. *International Journal of Document Analysis and Recognition IJDAR, 5*(1), 1-16.

Akindele, O. T., & Belaïd, A. (1995). Construction of generic models of document structures using inference of tree grammars. In *Proceedings of the Third International Conference on Document Analysis and Recognition, ICDAR'95*.

Amir, A., Aumann, Y., Feldman, R., & Fresko, M. (2005). Maximal association rules: A tool for mining associations in text. *Journal of Intelligent Information Systems, 25*(3), 333-345.

Andrienko, G., Malerba, D., May, M., & Teisseire, M. (2006). Mining spatio-temporal data. *Journal of Intelligent Information Systems, 27*(3), 187–190.

Appice, A., Ceci, M., Lanza, A., Lisi, F.A., & Malerba, D. (2003). Discovery of spatial association rules in geo-referenced census data: A relational mining approach. *Intelligent Data Analysis, 7*(6), 541-566.

Altamura, O., Esposito, F., & Malerba, D. (2001). Transforming paper documents into XML format with WISDOM++. *International Journal on Document Analysis and Recognition, 4*(1), 2-17.

Ben-Dov, M., Wu, W., Cairns, P., & Feldman, R. (2004). Improving knowledge discovery by combining text-mining and link analysis techniques. In M. W. Berry, U. Dayal, C. Kamath, D. B. Skillicorn (Eds.). In *Proceedings of the Fourth SIAM International Conference on Data Mining*. Lake Buena Vista, Florida, USA.

Berardi, M., Ceci, M., & Malerba, D. (2003). Mining spatial association rules from document layout structures. In *Proceedings of the 3rd Workshop on Document Layout Interpretation and its Application, DLIA'03.*

Blockeel, H., & Sebag, M. (2003). Scalability and efficiency in multi-relational data mining. *SIGKDD Explorations, 5*(1), 17-30.

Ceci, M., & Malerba, D. (2007). Classifying web documents in a hierarchy of categories: A comprehensive study. *Journal of Intelligent Information Systems, 28*(1), 1-41.

Cesarini, F., Francescani, E., Gori, M., Marinai, S., Sheng, J., & Soda, G. (1997). A neural-based architecture for spot-noisy logo recognition. In *Proceedings of the 4th International Conference on Document Analysis and Recognition, ICDAR'97.*

Chen, M. S., Park, J. S., & Yu, P. S. (1996). Data mining for path traversal patterns in a web environment. In *Proceedings of the 16th International Conference on Distributed Computing Systems.*

Cherfi, H., Napoli, A., & Toussaint, Y. (2006). Towards a text mining methodology using association rule extraction. *Soft Computing: A Fusion of Foundations, Methodologies and Applications, 10*(5), 431-441.

de Raedt, L., & Kersting, K. (2003). Probabilistic logic learning. *SIGKDD Explorations, 5*(1), 31-48.

Dehaspe, L., & Toivonen, H. (1999). Discovery of frequent datalog patterns. *Data Mining and Knowledge Discovery, 3*(1), 7–36.

Dengel, A. (1993). Initial learning of document structure. In *Proceedings of the 2nd International Conference on Document Analysis and Recognition, ICDAR'93.*

Dengel, A. (2003). Making documents work: Challenges for document understanding. In *Proceedings of the Seventh International Conference on Document Analysis and Recognition, ICDAR'95.*

Dengel, A., Bleisinger, R., Hoch, R., Fein, F. & Hönes, F. (1992). From paper to office document standard representation. *Computer, 25*(7), 63-67

Dengel, A., & Dubiel, F. (1995). Clustering and classification of document structure-a machine learning approach. In *Proceedings of the Third International Conference on Document Analysis and Recognition, ICDAR'95.*

Domingos, P. (2003). Prospects and challenges for multi-relational data mining. *SIGKDD Explorations, 5*(1), 80-83.

Esposito, F., Malerba, D., & Semeraro, G. (1990). An experimental page layout-recognition system for office document automatic classification: An integrated approach for inductive generalization. In *Proceedings of 10th International Conference on Pattern Recognition, ICPR'90.*

Esposito, F., Malerba, D., & Semeraro, G. (1994). Multistrategy learning for document recognition. *Applied Artificial Intelligence: An International Journal, 8*(1), 33-84.

Esposito, F., & Malerba, D. (2001). Guest editorial: Machine learning in computer vision. *Applied Artificial Intelligence, 15*(8), 1-13.

Fan, X., Sheng, F., & Ng, P. A. (1999). DOCPROS: A knowledge-based personal document management system. In *Procedings of the 10th International Workshop on Database Expert Systems Applications.*

Flach, P. A., & Lavrac, N. (2003). Rule induction. *Intelligent Data Analysis: An Introduction* (pp. 229-267). Springer-Verlag.

Han, J., & Fu, Y. (1995). Discovery of multiple-level association rules from large databases. In U. Dayal, P. M. Gray & S. Nishio (Eds.). In *Pro-*

ceedings of the 21ᵗʰ International Conference on Very Large Data Bases.

Han, J., Pei, J., & Yin, Y. (2000). Mining frequent patterns without candidate generation. In *Proceedings of the 2000 ACM SIGMOD international Conference on Management of Data SIGMOD '00.*

Hardman, L., Rutledge, L., & Bulterman, D. (1998). Automated generation of hypermedia presentation from pre-existing tagged media objects. In *Proceedings of the Second Workshop on Adaptive Hypertext and Hypermedia.*

Hiraki, K., Gennari, J. H., Yamamoto, Y., & Anzai, Y. (1991). *Learning spatial relations from images.* Machine Learning Workshop, Chicago (pp. 407-411).

Jiang, N., & Gruenwald, L. (2006). Research issues in data stream association rule mining. *ACM SIGMOD Record, 35*(1), 14-19.

Kise, K., Yajima, N., Babaguchi, N., & Fukunaga, K. (1993). Incremental acquisition of knowledge about layout structures from examples of documents. In *Proceedings of the 2ⁿᵈ International Conference on Document Analysis and Recognition, ICDAR'93.*

Knobbe, A. J., Blockeel, H., Siebes, A., & Van der Wallen, D. M. G. (1999). Multi-relational data mining. In *Proceedings of the Benelearn 1999.*

Lee, C.,-H., Lin, C.,-R., & Chen, M.-S. (2001). On mining general temporal association rules in a publication database. In *Proceedings of the 2001 IEEE International Conference on Data Mining.*

Lee, W., Stolfo, S., & Mok, K. (1998). Mining audit data to build intrusion detection models. In Agrawal, Stolorz & Piatetsky Shapiro (Eds.). In *Proceedings of the 4ᵗʰ International Conference on Knowledge Discovery and Data Mining.*

Lent, B., Agrawal, R., & Srikant, R. (1997). Discovering trends in text databases. In *Proceedings of 3ʳᵈ International Conference on Knowledge Discovery and Data Mining.*

Leskovec, J. Grobelnik, M., & Millic-Frayling, N. (2004, August). *Learning sub-structures of document semantic graphs for document summarization.* Paper presented at the Workshop on Link Analysis and Group Detection, Seattle, WA.

Li, S., Wu T., & Pottenger, W. M. (2005). Distributed higher order association rule mining using information extracted from textual data. *SIGKDD Explorations Newsletter, 7*(1), 26-35.

Liu, B., Hsu, W., & Ma, Y. (1998). Integrating classification and association rule mining. In Agrawal, Stolorz & Piatetsky Shapiro (Eds.). In *Proceedings of the 4ᵗʰ International Conference on Knowledge Discovery and Data Mining.*

Liu, B., Hsu, W., & Ma, Y. (1999). Mining association rules with multiple minimum supports. In *Proceedings of the Fifth ACM SIGKDD International Conference on Knowledge Discovery and Data Mining.*

Ludl, M. C., & Widmer, G. (2000). Relative unsupervised discretization for association rule mining. In D.A .Zighed, H.J. Komorowski, J.M. Zytkow (Eds.), *Principles of data mining and knowledge discovery* (pp. 148-158). Springer-Verlag.

Malerba, D., Esposito, F., Lisi, F. A., & Altamura, O. (2001). Automated discovery of dependencies between logical components in document image understanding. In *Proceedings of the Sixth International Conference on Document Analysis and Recognition*, Los Vaqueros, California.

Mannila, H., & Toivonen, H. (1997). Levelwise search and borders of theories in knowledge discovery. *Data Mining and Knowledge Discovery, 1*(3), 241–258.

Mei, Q., & Zhai, C. (2005). Discovering evolutionary theme patterns from text: An exploration of temporal text mining. In *Proceedings of the Eleventh ACM SIGKDD International Conference on Knowledge Discovery in Data Mining, KDD '05*.

Morinaga, S., & Yamanishi, K. (2004). Tracking dynamics of topic trends using a finite mixture model. In *Proceedings of the Tenth ACM SIGKDD International Conference on Knowledge Discovery and Data Mining, KDD '04*.

Nagy, G., Seth, S. C., & Stoddard, S. D. (1992). A prototype document image analysis system for technical journals. *IEEE Computer, 25*(7), 10-22.

Nagy, G. (2000). Twenty years of document image analysis in PAMI. *IEEE Transactions on Pattern Analysis and Machine Intelligence, 22*(1), 38-62.

Ordonez, C., & Omiecinski, E. (1999). Discovering association rules based on image content. In *Proceedings of the IEEE Advances in Digital Libraries Conference, ADL'99*, Washington, DC.

Page, D., & Craven, M. (2003). Biological applications of multi-relational data mining. *SIGKDD Explorations, 5*(1), 69-79.

Park, J.-S., Chen, M.-S., & Yu, P. S. (1997). Using a hash-based method with transaction trimming for mining association rules. *IEEE Transactions on Knowledge and Data Engineering, 9*(5), 813–825.

Porter, M. F. (1980). An algorithm for suffix stripping. *Program, 14*(3), 130-137.

Raghavan, P., & Tsaparas, P. (2002). Mining significant associations in large scale text corpora. In *Proceedings of the 2002 IEEE international Conference on Data Mining, ICDM '02*, Washington, DC.

Reichenberger, K., Rondhuis, K. J., Kleinz, J., & Bateman, J. (1995). Effective presentation of information through page layout: A linguistically-based approach. In *Proceedings of the ACM Workshop on Effective Abstractions in Multimedia*. San Francisco, California.

Sebastiani, F. (2002). Machine learning in automated text categorization. *ACM Computing Survey, 34*(1), 1-47.

Sheth, A., Aleman-Meza, B., Arpinar, I. B., Halaschek, C., Ramakrishnan, C., Bertram, C., Warke, Y., Avant, D., Arpinar, F. S., Anyanwu, K., & Kochut, K. (2004). Semantic association identification and knowledge discovery for national security applications. *Journal of Database Management, 16*(1), 133-53.

Simoff, S. J., Djeraba, C., & Zaïane, O. R. (2002). MDM/KDD 2002: Multimedia data mining between promises and problems. *SIGKDD Explorations, 4*(2), 118-121

Srikant, R., & Agrawal, R. (1995). Mining generalized association rules. In *Proceedings of the 21th International Conference on Very Large Data Bases*.

Srikant, R., & Agrawal, R. (1996). Mining quantitative association rules in large relational tables. In *Proceedings of 1996 ACM-SIGMOD Conference on Management of Data*.

Srinivasan, P. (2004). Text mining: Generating hypotheses from medline. *Journal of the American Society for Information Science, 55*(5), 396-413.

Steinbach, M., Karypis, G., & Kumar, V. (2000). A comparison of document clustering techniques. In *Proceedings of KDD-2000 Workshop on Text Mining*.

Walischewski, H. (1997). Automatic knowledge acquisition for spatial document interpretation. In *Proceedings of the 4th International Conference on Document Analysis and Recognition, ICDAR'97*.

Wang, K., He, Y., & Han, J. (2000). Mining frequent itemsets using support constraints. In *Proceedings of 2000 International Conference On Very Large Data Bases.*

Wenzel, C., & Maus, H. (2001). Leveraging corporate context within knowledge-based document analysis and understanding. *International Journal on Document Analysis and Recognition, 3*(4), 248-260.

Yang, C., Fayyad, U., & Bradley, P. (2001). Efficient discovery of error-tolerant frequent itemsets in high dimensions. In *Proceedings of the Seventh ACM SIGKDD International Conference on Knowledge Discovery and Data Mining.*

Yeh, A., Hirschman, L., & Morgan, A. (2003). Evaluation of text data mining for database curation: Lessons learned from the KDD Challenge Cup. *Bioinformatics, 19*(1), 331-339.

Chapter IX
Mining XML Documents

Laurent Candillier
Université Charles de Gaulle, France

Ludovic Denoyer
Université Pierre et Marie Curie, France

Patrick Gallinari
Université Pierre et Marie Curie, France

Marie Christine Rousset
LSR-IMAG, France

Alexandre Termier
Institute of Statistical Mathematics, Japan

Anne-Marie Vercoustre
INRIA, France

ABSTRACT

XML documents are becoming ubiquitous because of their rich and flexible format that can be used for a variety of applications. Giving the increasing size of XML collections as information sources, mining techniques that traditionally exist for text collections or databases need to be adapted and new methods to be invented to exploit the particular structure of XML documents. Basically XML documents can be seen as trees, which are well known to be complex structures. This chapter describes various ways of using and simplifying this tree structure to model documents and support efficient mining algorithms. We focus on three mining tasks: classification and clustering which are standard for text collections; discovering of frequent tree structure, which is especially important for heterogeneous collection. This chapter presents some recent approaches and algorithms to support these tasks together with experimental evaluation on a variety of large XML collections.

INTRODUCTION

The widespread use of semistructured formats like XML for representing data and documents has urged the need to develop tools to efficiently store, access, and organize XML corpus. With the development of such structured textual and multimedia document, the document nature is changing. Structured documents usually have a much richer representation than flat ones. They have a logical structure. They are often composed of heterogeneous information sources (e.g., text, image, video, metadata, etc.). Another major change with structured documents is the possibility to access document elements or fragments. The development of classifiers for structured content is a new challenge for the machine learning (ML) and information retrieval (IR) communities. A classifier for structured documents should be able to make use of the different content information sources present in an XML document and to classify both full documents and document parts. It should easily adapt to a variety of different sources and document models (i.e., different document type definitions). It should be able to scale with large document collections.

Handling structured documents for different IR tasks has recently attracted an increasing attention. Many questions are still open for designing such systems so that we are only in the early stages of this development. Most of the work in this new area has concentrated on ad hoc retrieval in the context of the recent initiative for the evaluation of XML retrieval (INEX) launched in 2002. Besides this mainstream of research, some work is also developing around other generic IR problems like clustering and classification for structured documents.

The use of XML format raises a new challenge for document mining, first because of its new complex data structure, second by the two dimensions that can be dealt with: the (semi-) structured dimension and the content (especially text) dimension, and third because of the possible heterogeneity of the documents. Depending on the application or the mining objective, it may be relevant to consider the structure information alone or both the structure and the content of the documents.

XML documents are usually modeled as ordered trees, which are regarded as complex structures. Indeed algorithms dealing with tree collections may be very costly when the size of the documents and the collection increases. It is often necessary to *simplify* the document tree model in order to implement efficient algorithms or to adapt scalable existing clustering and classification methods. A common simplification, for example, is to ignore the order of tree siblings, yet some algorithms would take this into account when required by the data.

This chapter describes various tree-based representations of XML documents to support efficiently three mining tasks: frequent pattern extraction, classification, and clustering. Frequent pattern extraction from document structure has been studied mostly by the database community, with the objective of clustering large heterogeneous collections of XML documents to support query optimisation. Classification and clustering using document structure, and possibly content, has been studied both by the IR and ML communities.

We first introduce the XML tree-based model. Then we present some advanced algorithms for frequent pattern extraction in XML collections. In the last section we present three flexible classes of document representation that have been used in classification or clustering algorithms. Although we do not cover all the possible representations for XML documents, we show many different working representations that can be derived from the initial complex tree-like structure in order to support XML mining tasks.

TREE-BASED COMPLEX DATA STRUCTURE

XML documents are regarded as semistructured data since they offer a flexible structure compared to more strictly structured databases. For example, elements in XML documents can be optional or have an unfixed number of occurrences. The document structure can be constrained by the definition of a document type description (DTD), or a document can be just *well formed*. A well-formed XML document must conform to the XML grammar, which mostly means that, unlike HTML documents, all the tags must be well parenthesised and that a document must have a single root.

The XML document object model (XML DOM) defines a standard way for accessing and manipulating XML documents. The DOM presents an XML document as a tree-structure (a node tree), with the elements, attributes, and text defined as nodes.

Figure 1 and Figure 2 present a small XML document describing a movie and its associated tree-structure. This description is very typical of the ones to be used for indexing and retrieving

movies, and very different from the ones that would be necessary for describing the frames of the film itself. Note the attribute *lang* in the second title, and the repetition of the elements *title* and *actor*. This document here conforms to the DTD that is referred to in the document model CINEMA (second line of the document), not shown here.

XML documents can be modeled by unranked, ordered labeled trees where labels correspond to XML tags, which may or may not carry semantic information. More precisely, when considering only the tree structure:

- Each node can have an arbitrary number of children.
- The children of a given node are ordered.
- Each node has a label in the vocabulary of the tags.

A labeled node n in a XML document is represented by a couple $n=(s, t)$, where s is the label of n in the structure of the document, and t represents the content of n.

Let $S = \{s_1,...,s_{|S|}\}$ be the set of structural labels, and $\mathcal{B} = \{t_1,...,t_{|\mathcal{B}|}\}$ be the set of possible contents.

Figure 1. An XML document describing the movie "Pierrot le Fou," by Jean-Luc Godard

```
<?xml version = "1.0" encoding="ISO-8859-1"?>
<!DOCTYPE CINEMA SYSTEM "cinema.dtd">
<movie>
        <header>
                <title>Pierrot le Fou</title>
                <title lang ="en">Pierrot Goes Wild</title>
                <lang>French</lang>
                <year>1965</year>
                <genre>Drama</genre>
        </header>
        <dir>Jean-Luc Godard</dir>
        <photos>Raoul Coutard</photos>

        <tech>
                <color> B&W </color>
                <format>35mm</format>
                <time>110mn</time>
        </tech>
        <actors>
                <actor>Anna Karina</actor>
                <actor>Jean-Paul Belmondo</actor>
                <actor>Graziella Galvani </actor>
        </actor>
        <desc>Pierrot escapes his boring society and travels from Paris to the Mediterranean Sea with Marianne, a girl
        chased by hit-men from Algeria. They lead an unorthodox life, always on the run.
        </desc>
</movie>
```

Figure 2. XML tree corresponding to the document in Figure 1; nodes are represented by white round boxes, attributes by square boxes and leaf nodes by grey round boxes

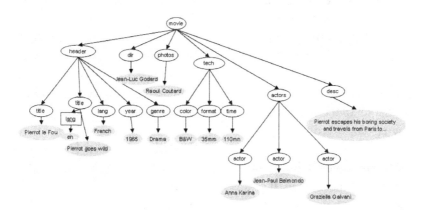

An XML document can then be represented by a **labeled tree**. A labeled tree $T = (N, A, root(T))$ is an acyclic connected graph, where N is the set of nodes,

$A \subseteq N \times N$ is a binary relation over N defining the set of edges, and $root(T)$ is a distinguished node called the **root.**

Let $u \in N$ and $v \in N$ be two nodes of a tree. If there exists an edge $(u, v) \in A$, then v is a **child** of u, and u is the **parent** of v.

For two nodes of a tree u and v, if there exists a set of nodes $\{x_1,...,x_p\}$ such that u is the parent of x_1, x_1 is the parent of x_2,..., and x_p is the parent of v, then $\{x_1,...,x_p\}$ is called a **path** from u to v. If there exists a path from u to v in the tree, then v is a **descendant** of u, and u is an **ancestor** of v.

Finally, for two nodes of a tree u and v, if there exists a node x_1 such that both u and v are children of x_1, then u and v are called **sibling** nodes.

A tree is an **attribute tree** if two sibling nodes cannot have the same label **(Arimura et al., 2005) describe attribute trees in more detail)**. This is mostly not the case in XML documents where lists of elements with the same label are quite common. However it is possible to transform the original trees into attribute trees without losing their most canonical structural properties.

- **Document transformation:** Most tree mining algorithms do not directly operate on XML documents. They need a preprocessing step, which takes as input the XML documents and outputs a labeled tree for each document. This labeled tree reflects the tree structure of the original document, where the node labels are the tags of the XML document. Then the documents will be further transformed depending on the document model used by the intended mining task and the specific algorithm. Pre-processing may involve:
  - Stripping off the textual content of the document when dealing with structure only
  - Stripping off the XML attributes when they are not regarded as relevant for the mining task, or transforming them to fit in the tree structure just like XML elements
  - Replace some tag labels with equivalent labels, for example if a DTD defines different types of paragraphs (p1, p2, p3), it may be advised to rename them by a common label such as *parag*

(this type of transformation requires some semantic knowledge of the DTD or the collection)

○ Stripping off low levels of the tree which would be irrelevant in some mining tasks, for example *italic* or *bold* elements, or the details of a mathematic formula

○ Text processing similar to the one done for flat textual documents, such as removing stop words

In document collections, content information may be composed of text and images that are associated with the leaves of the trees. In this chapter, we consider only textual parts of documents. The textual content is usually contextually dependent of the logical structure, which means that, even when interested in mining the content of documents, taking the structure into account may have a positive impact on the results. We also consider the case where we are interested only on the structure of the documents, without taking into account their content.

DISCOVERING FREQUENT TREE STRUCTURE

The broad use of XML as an exchange format for data exported from databases results in the availability of huge collections of XML documents in which the labels and their nesting represent the underlying tree schema of the data. Those collections of XML documents are possibly structurally heterogeneous because exported from a mass of different and autonomous data sources. Discovering commonalities between their structures is of primary importance for information integration and classification. In this setting, the focus is not the textual content of the documents but the labeled trees corresponding to their structure.

The discovery of frequent tree patterns from a huge collection of labeled trees is costly but has

multiple applications, such as schema extraction from the web (or from frequent user queries like as proposed by (Ji, Wei, Han, & Sheng, 2005), automatic creation of DTDs or XML schemas for sub-collections, uniform querying over heterogeneous data, and clustering together data supporting a given frequent tree pattern. Note that the resulting clusters are not necessarily disjoint, which offers different viewpoints on the data and different entry points for querying them.

Definitions and Examples

The most important operation when searching for frequent tree patterns in a collection of tree data is to determine if a tree pattern is included in a tree of the data. The definition used for this **tree inclusion** operation will determine the nature of the patterns that can be discovered, as well as the complexity of the discovery problem.

A tree inclusion definition is based on a tree homomorphism between the tree pattern and the trees of the data (Kilpeläinen, 1992). Different definitions of tree inclusion can be considered according to the preservation or not of (1) the labels (2) the ancestor relation (3) the order of siblings by the homomorphism.

For the first property concerning label preservation, we will only consider homomorphisms preserving labels as most modern approaches use this kind of homomorphism, and because with XML it is important to preserve the labels as they correspond to the tags of the XML documents.

The second property determines the tolerance to "noise" in the nesting of the nodes. If the parent-child relation is preserved, then the paths from root to leaves in the pattern will mimic exactly paths or sub-paths of the original tree. This definition is suitable for relatively homogeneous data (for example data coming from a single source). However, for truly heterogeneous data it is likely that a semantic relation between A and B will be expressed by different structural relationships between A and B within different XML documents

Figure 3. Academic hierarchical relations in Japan and in France, common pattern between both

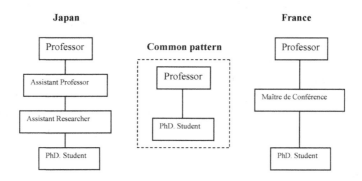

Figure 4. Two tree structure describing car ads, the same contents is expressed with a different sibling order

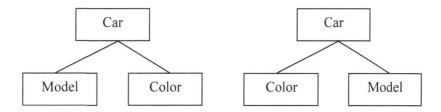

written by different organizations. In such cases, the ancestor preserving definition is the only one capable of finding common patterns. Consider for example the trees of Figure 3 describing the hierarchical relations in a public university in Japan and in France.

Even if both hierarchies are different, in both cases "Professor" is an ancestor of "PhD Student", so the common pattern can be found. As simple as this pattern is, it shows that there are some common points between both trees.

On the other hand, an inclusion definition based on the preservation of parent-child relation would not have found any common pattern because of the differences between the internal nodes of both trees.

The third property about the order of the siblings has also an influence on the kind of data that it is possible to handle. As XML documents are ordered, one could expect the preservation of the order of siblings in the tree inclusion definition to be mandatory. This may be true for homogeneous collections of data, but with heterogeneous data, different organizations may order the nodes of the documents differently. Consider the two example documents of Figure 4 about car descriptions: the important point when discovering patterns is that a "car" has a "model" and a "color", no matter their order.

The complexity of testing the tree inclusion varies with the definition used (Kilpeläinen, 1992).

Frequent Tree Discovery Algorithms

Frequent tree discovery is a very computationally intensive task; hence the design of the discovery algorithm is of a central importance. The algorithm must ensure at the same time the quality of the outputs, a fast execution, and avoid consuming too much memory especially when datasets are big. There is currently no perfect algorithm, but many algorithms have been designed and each of them has its strengths and weaknesses. We review the existing algorithms, classifying them according to two main design principles, namely the edge-centric approach and the tile-centric approach.

Basic Definitions

Let the data be a set of trees $\{T_1,...,T_N\}$.

A tree T **occurs** in the data if there exists a tree T_i in the data such that T is included in T_i.

A tree T is **frequent** in the data according to an absolute frequency threshold ε if T occurs in more than ε trees of the data. The trees of the data $\{T_{i1},...T_{im}\}$ where T occurs are called the **support** of T.

A tree T is a **closed frequent** tree of the data if T is frequent with support $\{T_{i1},...T_{im}\}$ and T is the biggest tree for this support, that is, there exist no other frequent tree T' with support $\{T_{i1},...T_{im}\}$ such as T is included in T'.

Edge-Centric Approaches

Designing a tree-mining algorithm from scratch is quite a challenge, and as is often the case with such problems, it is good to start on solid well known ground. A tree can be seen as a set of edges, so a frequent tree can as well be seen as a frequent set of edges.

Finding a frequent set of edges is easy, and since the seminal paper on the Apriori algorithm (Agrawal & Srikant, 1994), there has been a tremendous amount of research on algorithms for discovering frequent itemsets in transactional data (a transaction is a set of elements and an itemset is a set of elements being a subset of one or more transactions). This was the starting point of the TreeFinder algorithm (Termier, Rousset, & Sebag, 2002), which first finds all the frequent set of edges, and then rebuilds the trees from the edges using an operation borrowed from inductive logic programming (ILP), the Least General Generalization (Plotkin, 1970). Though being able to find interesting patterns by application of well know algorithms, the method falls short of completeness in some cases, reducing its practical usability.

However, many other methods for mining structured data have been derived from the very principle of the Apriori algorithm. Inokuchi, Washio, and Motoda (2000) presented AGM (Apriori Graph Miner), an algorithm for mining general graphs, based on the *generate and test* principle which is the heart of Apriori. Later on, many tree-mining algorithms were designed upon this principle, including specificities for efficient tree mining.

The idea of Apriori to find all the frequent itemsets is to generate candidate itemsets, and to evaluate the frequency of such candidates against the transaction database. If a candidate is frequent, it is flagged as such, and it will also be the base of new, longer candidates. The Apriori algorithm is levelwise: it starts from candidates with only one element, and then processes iteratively candidates with 2,3,...,n elements. The efficiency of the search is ensured by the antimonotony principle, which states that if an itemset I is infrequent, then all the itemsets $I' \supseteq I$ are also infrequent. So when a candidate is evaluated as infrequent, it is not necessary to expand it further, which reduces considerably the search space.

This method can be transposed nicely to trees, by replacing the set elements by tree edges. The first iteration will be to find frequent trees with one edge; the second one will join these trees with one edge to find all frequent trees with two

Figure 5. All the paths to build a single tree by edge adding, and the redundancies induced by creating all these intermediary steps

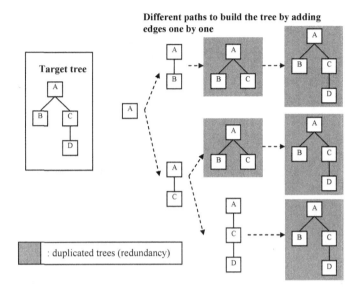

edges, and so on. However, a problem specific to trees arises: a tree can be built by adding edges in many different ways, and so all the different intermediary steps leading to the same tree will be considered by the algorithm, as shown in Figure 5.

This would result in doing a lot of redundant work for each tree. The solution to this problem, found independently by Asai, Abe, Kawasoe, Arimura, Sakamoto, and Arikawa (2002) and Zaki (2002), is to force the edge expansion to be done in a unique way, along the rightmost branch of the tree. This technique is called *rightmost tree expansion* and is the basis of most frequent tree mining algorithms. Both of the previously cited algorithms mine ordered trees. To be able to mine unordered trees, (Asai, Arimura, Uno, and Nakano, 2003) and Nijssen and Kok (2003) independently proposed to use *canonical forms*. A canonical form of a tree pattern is a unique representative for all tree patterns that differ only on the order of the siblings.

However, finding all the frequent tree patterns is a very computation-time expensive task. Chi,

Yang, Xia, and Muntz (2004) proposed the CM-TreeMiner algorithm that improves the previous algorithms by searching only closed frequent trees, with performance improvements over one order of magnitude. Recently, Arimura and Uno (2005) proposed the CLOATT algorithm for mining closed frequent attribute trees, with a proved output-polynomial complexity.

Tile-Centric Approach

The previous approaches discover the frequent tree patterns by reconstructing the tree's edge by edge. However, especially in case of trees with large number of nodes, it can be beneficial to have an approach that expands trees with several edges at a time instead of single edges. Such an approach is represented by the Dryade family of algorithms (Termier, Rousset, & Sebag, 2004; Termier, Rousset, Sebag, Ohara, Washio, & Motoda, 2005), in which the closed frequent trees of a given step are built by *hooking* at the leaves of the (closed) frequent trees of the previous step full subtrees of depth 1 called *tiles*. In this way,

Figure 6. Example data

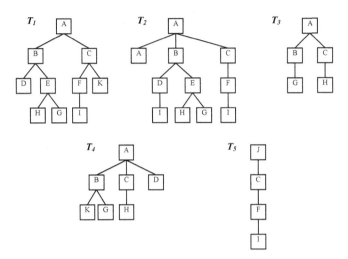

the closed frequent trees are built by increasing levels of depth.

- **Definition:** A *tile* is a closed frequent tree of depth 1.

It can easily be shown that any closed frequent tree can be decomposed into a set of tiles. So the approach used by the Dryade family of algorithms is to first compute all the tiles that are in the data, and then to assemble these tiles together in order to discover the closed frequent trees.

This approach will be illustrated through the DryadeParent algorithm (Termier et al., 2005). This algorithm uses the same tree inclusion definition as CMTreeMiner (the isomorphism preserves the parent-child relation and does not preserve siblings order), but is limited to the discovery of *attribute trees*. The trees of Figure 6 will be used as data for a running example, with a minimal frequency threshold of two trees.

The algorithm can be divided into several steps. The preliminary step is to discover the tiles. Then the iterative part of the algorithm consists in *hooking* together those tiles.

- **Discovering the tiles:** As defined before, the tiles are the closed frequent trees of depth 1. Instead of finding all the tiles, it is simpler to solve the problem of finding all the tiles whose root has label *a*, for any $a \in S$. This problem boils down to finding all the closed frequent sets of children for the nodes of label *a* in the data. Using any closed frequent itemset miner can easily solve this problem. DryadeParent uses the LCM2 algorithm (Uno, Kiyomiet, & Arimura, 2004), which is the fastest algorithm available for this task. By iterating this method on all the labels of *S*, it is then easy to find all the tiles shown in Figure 7.

- **Hooking the tiles:** The previously computed tiles can then be *hooked* together, that is, a tile whose root has label *a* becomes a subtree of another tile having a leaf of label *a* to build more complex trees. A proper strategy is needed to avoid as much as possible constructing attributes trees that would be found unclosed in a later iteration. The DryadeParent's strategy consists in constructing attributes trees, which are isomorphic to the *k* first depth levels of the

Figure 7. The tiles found in trees of figure 6 with minimal frequency threshold set to 2

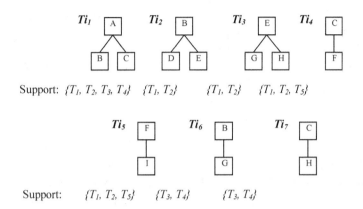

patterns, each iteration adding one depth level to the isomorphism.

For this purpose, the first task of DryadeParent is to discover in the tiles those corresponding to the depth levels 0 and 1 of the patterns, the **root tiles**. Some of these tiles can be found immediately as they cannot be hooked on any other tile: they will be the starting point for the first iteration of DryadeParent. This is the case for Ti_1 in the example. For the rest of the root tiles, they can also be used as building blocks for other patterns: they will be used as root of a pattern only when it will become clear that they are not only a building block, to avoid generating unclosed attribute trees. In the example, this is the case for Ti_4, which can be hooked on Ti_1. Only in iteration 2 will this tile be used as a root tile to construct the pattern

Figure 8. DryadeParent discovery process: The closed frequent attribute trees outputted as result are enclosed in dashed boxes

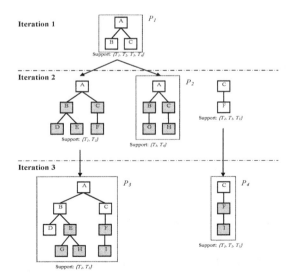

P$_4$ (see Figure 8 for the closed frequent patterns discovered in the data). The computation of the set of tiles that must be hooked to the root tiles for building the next depth level of closed frequent attribute trees is delegated to a closed frequent itemset mining algorithm. They become starting points for the next iteration.

The whole process is shown in Figure 8. On the root tile Ti$_1$ (which is also the closed frequent pattern P$_1$), one can hook the tiles {Ti$_2$, Ti$_4$} or the tiles {Ti$_6$, Ti$_7$}, the latter leading to the pattern P$_2$. Note the different supports of the two constructed attribute trees. From the hooking of {Ti$_2$, Ti$_4$} on Ti$_1$, one can then hook the tile Ti$_3$, leading to the pattern P$_3$. The tile Ti$_4$ is not only a building block of P$_1$, it also has an occurrence which does not appear in P$_3$ (see tree T$_5$): it is used as a root tile, and the only possible hooking on it is Ti$_5$, leading to the pattern P$_4$.

The soundness and completeness of this hooking mechanism have been proved (Termier, 2004). It has also been shown (Termier et al., 2005) that DryadeParent has excellent computation-time performances. It over performs by several orders of magnitude CMTreeMiner when the closed frequent trees to be found have a high average branching factor. Concretely, this means that when handling thousands of XML documents, containing a pattern having 100 nodes, DryadeParent will be able to answer in few seconds, sometimes nearly instantly, allowing real-time use in an interactive

process. On the other hand, CMTreeMiner will need several minutes to handle the same data, making interactive use problematic.

CLASSIFICATION AND CLUSTERING

In this section, we consider various approaches to XML document classification and clustering, two important mining tasks largely explored for data or textual documents. As for XML documents, these tasks can be split into sub-tasks that involve the structure only or both the structure and content of the documents.

Classification and clustering are based on a notion of distance. Since XML documents are represented by trees, a natural idea to adapt traditional methods to XML documents would be to use a tree distance, for example, the edit distance between two ordered labeled trees proposed by Zang and Shasha (1989) that consists in counting the number of editing operations (add, delete, change the label of a node, etc.) needed to transform a tree into another one. Tree edit distances may differ by the set of editing operations they allow. However, algorithms based on tree edit distances (Chawathe, et al., 1996; Costa, et al., 2004; Nierman & Jagadish, 2002) have a time complexity O(MN), M and N being the number of nodes in the two trees to be compared, which

Figure 9. Tree summary

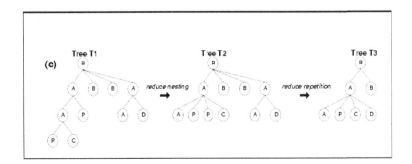

is too high for practical applications. Some approaches therefore replace the original trees by structural summaries (Dalamagas, Cheng, Winkel, & Sellis, 2004) or s-graphs (Lian, Cheung, Mamoulis, & Yiu, 2004) that only retain the intrinsic structure of the tree: for example reducing a list of elements to a single element, or flattening recursive structures. Figure 9 gives an example of tree summary.

Other distances have been proposed. Flesca, Manco, Masciari, Pontieri, and Pugliese (2002) define a Discrete Fourier transform distance using a linear encoding of the document trees based on the depth-first, left-to-right traversal order. Lian et al. (2004) use a distance based on bit string encodings of the edges of the s-graphs.

However, the above approaches are limited to clustering documents based only on their structure. Besides, computing distances directly between trees may consume a lot of time, and the problem of providing interpretable results remains an open issue. That is why some methods based on different ways for representing XML documents were recently designed.

In the next sections we present three different XML document representations, based on structure or both structure and content that have been used in combination with different clustering or classification approaches. First we present an attribute-value representation combined with classification and clustering methods based on decision-trees or probabilistic models; second a representation based on document paths, regarded as words, with a k-means like clustering algorithm; finally a Bayesian network model used as a generative process model for classification.

Representation Using Attribute-Value Structure

Candillier, Tellier, and Torre (2006) investigate the use of a different kind of representation for the manipulation of XML documents. The idea is to transform the trees into sets of attribute-values pairs, so as to be able to apply various existing methods of classification and clustering on such data, and benefit from their strengths. They propose to construct the following attributes from a set of available XML trees:

- The set of tags labeling the nodes of the trees
- The set of parent-child and next-sibling relations (whose domain is the set of pairs of tags labeling the nodes)
- The set of distinct paths (including subpaths), starting from the root (whose domain is the set of finite sequences of tags labeling the nodes)

So they create as many new attributes as distinct features are encountered in the training set. And for each of them, their value for a given document is the number of their occurrences in this document. Finally, they also define as many new attributes as there are absolute distinct node positions in the trees. For every identifier of a node position, the value of the attribute for a document is the arity of the node, which is the count of its child nodes in the document. So the new introduced attributes all take their value into the set of natural numbers.

Such representation could lead to a high number of generated attributes. So the algorithms used to tackle such new datasets should be able to handle many attributes, and to perform feature selection during their learning process. In a classification task, C5 (Quinlan, 1998) is for example well suited. In a clustering task, a subspace clustering algorithm, that is a clustering algorithm able to characterize every distinct cluster on a limited number of attributes (eventually distinct for each cluster), should be used.

Thus, they used SSC (Candillier, Tellier, Torre, & Bousquet, 2005), a subspace-clustering algorithm that has been shown to be effective, and that is able to provide as output an interpretable representation of the clusters found, as a set of rules. They adapted SSC for the clustering and the classification of XML documents, so that the new methods also benefit from the major advantage of producing classifiers that are understandable.

So far, this strategy has been applied to the INEX 2005 collections for mining XML documents, both for the classification task and for the clustering task using the structural description of XML documents alone. The results obtained with such a strategy are very good. In particular, it has been shown to be robust even with noisy data. Besides, the produced classifiers are very understandable. Figure 10 shows for example the decision tree obtained when classifying a collection of movie description into eleven classes. For instance, the membership to class 8 only depends on the presence of tags named *movie, film, table,* and *li*, and the absence of parent-child relation between tags named *p* and *i* in the document.

Tag(T) refers to the number of occurrences of the given tag T in the document, Parent(A-B) to the number of parent-child relations between

tags A and B, Nb(0.0.0) to the arity of the first grand-child node from the root, S* to comparisons between models based on the next-sibling relations, and P* to a comparison based on the paths in the document.

By using such a transformation strategy, part of the information included in the trees is lost, but the data are manipulated more easily and the results are more understandable. However, some differences between trees could be hidden when using such a transformation. Indeed, a swap between two sub-trees of a given tree can lead to a very different tree, although its attribute-value representation proposed here would be very similar to the one of the initial tree. So other types of transformation should be considered when the order of siblings is to be taken in account.

Finally, such a strategy should be generalized in order to perform classification or clustering of XML documents collections using both the structural description and the textual content of the documents. The most direct way to do this would

Figure 10. Example of understandable classifier obtained on an XML data collection by transforming the documents into sets of attribute-values.

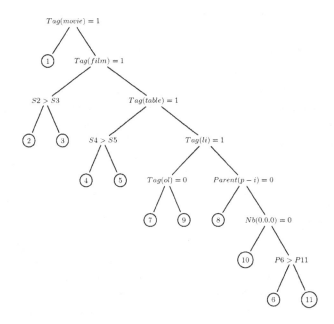

be to consider the textual content of the documents as simple bag-of-words, but more complex transformations could also be considered.

Representing Documents by a Set of Paths

Vercoustre, Fegas, Gul, and Lechevallier (2006) have been motivated by clustering XML documents based on their structure only or both the structure and content. Like in the previous approach, they use a simplified tree representation to avoid the complexity problems of tree clustering. They define a flexible representation of XML documents based on a subset of their paths, generated according to some criteria, such as the length of the paths, whether they start at the root (root paths), or end at a leaf (leaf ending paths). By considering those sub-paths as words, they can use standard methods for vocabulary reduction (based on their frequency), and simple clustering methods such as K-means that scale well.

Basic Definitions

Let $p= \{x_1,...,x_p\}$ be a path of tree T as defined in section 2:

- p is a **root path** if x_1 = root(T); p is a **leaf ending path** if x_p is a leaf of T; p is a **complete path** if it is a root path and a leaf ending path. The **length** of a path is the number of nodes in the path. A path expression is represented by the expression $s= s_1.s_2...s_{p-1}.s_p$ where s_i =label(x_i). Such expressions do not distinguish between two siblings with the same label, which means that, in this approach, two paths are regarded as equivalent of they correspond to the same path expression.

Let $u=(s, t)$ be a node of tree T, where t is the textual content of u. Let w be a word.

u **contains** w if $w \subset t$ or if there exists a path $\{u, ..., v\}$, $v=(s',t')$ such that $w \subset t'$.

If u contains w, and p= $\{x_1,...,u\}$ is a path, we call p' =(p,w) a **text path** and we code it by $s_1.s_2...s_{p-1}.s_p.w$ where s_i =label(x_i).

It means that a text path extends a path p (possibly nonterminal) with a word contains in any of the leaves of its subtrees.

If $W=\{w_i \mid w_i \subset t\}$ then $s_1.s_2...s_{p-1}.s_p.w_i$ for w_i $\in$ W, are all the text paths associated to path p.

Using those definitions, we can now introduce a family of representations for an XML document d using the standard vector model, as:

$$R(d) = \Sigma_i f_i p_i$$

for all path $p_{i=} s_1.s_2...s_{p-1}.s_p$ in d where m $\leq |p_i| \leq$ n, $1 \leq m \leq n$, m and n two numbers given a priori; f_i is the frequency of the path p_i in d.

When interested by both the structure and the content of documents, it is possible to use both text paths and paths, or text paths only. For specific values of m and n, this model is equivalent to some other models that have been proposed before: for m=n=1, it corresponds to the *naïve* model used by Doucet & Ahonen-Myka (2002), where documents are represented by a bag of tags, or a bag of words and tags. Representing documents by their complete paths has been proposed by Yoon, Raghavan, Chakilam, and Kerschberg (2001) in their bitmap model, as well as an extension using complete text paths.

Yi and Sundaresan (2000) propose the structure vector model where a document is represented by all its paths of length between 1 and the height h of the document tree. The frequency of terms associated with a path is relative to the subtree associated with that path. The representation developed by Liu, Wang, Hsu, and Herbert (2004) is based on paths of length smaller than L, although they can also fix the level in the tree where the paths must start. It also includes the definitions of leaf-ending paths as well as root-beginning paths, of length less than L.

The motivation for a flexible choice of paths in the document is that some analysis or clustering tasks may be interested in the top part of the tree, the lower parts of the tree, or possibly parts in the middle. An example would be clustering very heterogeneous collections based on the structure, where the partition can be done by looking at the top-level elements only. At the opposite end of the spectrum, if one wants to cluster documents based mostly on the text, it could be appropriate to add some limited context just above the text (leaf-ending paths). Another motivation in using paths was to fully represent lists of elements, through their path frequency, as lists are an important feature of XML documents that should be taken into account in some clustering tasks.

By considering those paths as words (with their frequency), it is possible to use standard methods for vocabulary reduction, and simple clustering methods such as K-means. However, clustering algorithms based on the vector model rely on the independence of the various dimensions (modalities) for calculating the distance between the vectors.

Although it is not always verified in practice with words in texts, it usually works fine. In the case where words are paths in the document tree, there is an obvious dependency between embedded sub-paths. To deal with the problem of dependency, one can partition the paths by their length and treat each set of paths as a different variable, using a clustering algorithm such as the one proposed by Celeux, Diday, Govaert, Lechevallier, and Ralambondrainy (1989) in which the standard Euclidian distance between clusters is replaced by a distance that takes in account the different variables and the modalities within the variables as follows:

$$d(x, y) = \sqrt{\sum_{k=1}^{p} \sum_{j=1}^{m_k} (x_j^k - y_j^k)^2}$$

where p is the number of variables, and m_k is the number of modalities for the variable k.

The approach has been successfully applied to the INEX collections for the structure only tasks.

As an output, the clustering algorithm provides not only the set of clusters but discriminate representatives for each cluster that characterize each of them. Since the representatives are paths, it could be interesting to reconstruct subtrees from those paths in order to provide a more compact representation of the clusters. This should be feasible, at least for root paths.

When considering document content as well as structure, paths are extended with the individual words of the text contained in the terminal node of each path (not necessarily a leaf node). While it works well for relatively small collections, it does not scale well for very large collections and broad trees where the number of paths, especially leaf-ending paths would grow exponentially. Complementary ways of reducing the vocabulary are needed, possibly from relative frequency of words within their specific paths rather than within the document they belong to.

Stochastic Generative Model

Generative models are well known in the field of Machine Learning. They are used for different applications and particularly for classification and clustering. Generative models allow us to compute the probability of an XML document using a set of parameters describing a stochastic process (that is $P(d/\theta)$ where d is an XML document and θ is a set of parameters). In this part, we describe the family of models proposed by Denoyer and Gallinari (2004). They propose to model the statistical dependencies between the nodes of a semistructured document using the belief network formalism. These models consider that a document d is the realization of a random vector D whose elements are discrete random variables corresponding to each structural node or content node (text nodes) of the document. Each document is transformed into a belief network, all the networks sharing the same set of parameters. The probability of a document is then computed as the joint probability of the corresponding network

Figure 11. A tree representation for a structured document composed of an introduction and two sections. White-background nodes and pink/grey background nodes are respectively structural and content nodes.

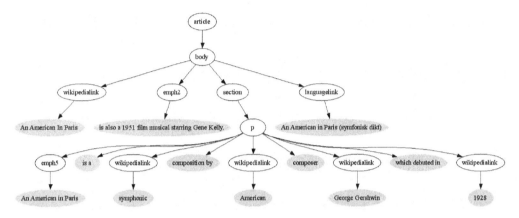

and this probability can be computed under different assumptions of statistical dependencies. Each assumption aims at capturing a particular type of structural information, for example the left-sibling information, or the parent information.

This model is able to deal with a very large amount of data. Moreover, its learning complexity is linear with respect to the size of the documents. This type of model has been used both for the categorization and the clustering of XML documents and the authors have proposed extensions that take into account different information content (text, pictures, etc.) for the multimedia-filtering task (Denoyer, Vittaut, Gallinari, Brunesseaux, & Brunesseaux, 2003). A discriminative algorithm has also been developed for the categorization task. On different XML corpora, this model has better performances than state-of-the art models for categorization of textual documents that do not use the structural information (Denoyer & Gallinari, 2004).

For simplification, we describe the model only for textual documents, using the example of Fig. 11. Extensions for multimedia documents are considered by Denoyer, Wisniewski, and Gallinari (2004).

Modeling Documents with Bayesian Networks

Let us first introduce some notations:

- Let C be a discrete random variable which represents a class from the set of classes C.
- Let Λ be the set of all the possible labels for a structural node.
- Let V be the set of all the possible words. V^* denotes the set of all possible word sequences, including the empty one.
- Let d be a structured document consisting of a set of features where is the label of the i-th structural node of d (), is the textual content of this i-th node () and $|d|$ is the number of structural nodes. d is a realization of a random vector D. In the following, all nodes are supposed to have a unique identifier, indicated here as superscript i.

Bayesian networks offer a suitable framework for modeling the dependencies and relations between the different elements in a structured document. A network model is associated with each document.

Figure 12. The final Bayesian network encoding "is a descendant of" relation

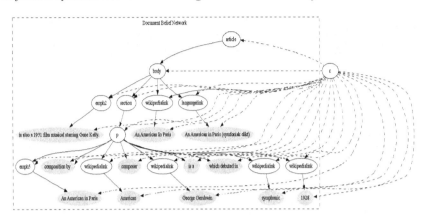

Figure 13. The final Bayesian network making use of a TAN network at each level of the tree

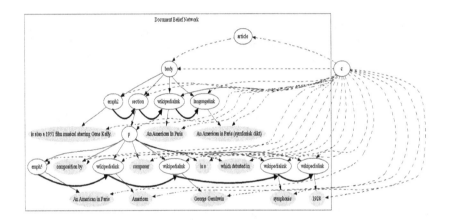

Since the focus here is on the logical document structure, each network is defined according to the corresponding document structure. For the classification task, the network parameters are learned using all the documents from the same class in the training set. Documents from the same class then share their parameters and there is one set of such parameters for each class.

Different networks could be used for modeling a document, depending on which type of relation one would like to take into account. We only consider here the explicit document structure and we will not try to uncover any hidden structure between the document elements. Some of the natural relations which could then be modeled are: "is a descendant of" in the document tree, "is a sibling of", "is a successor of", given a preorder visit of the document tree, and combinations of these different possibilities. Figures 12 and 13 give two examples of document models encapsulating different relations for the document tree in Figure 11. In the simplest one (Figure 12), the network structure is similar to the document tree structure, as it only encodes the "is a descendant of" relation. The second model (Figure 13) makes use of a *tree augmented network* (TAN) at each level of the tree and takes into account an ordering relation between structural siblings and subtrees. As usual there is a trade-off between complexity and efficiency. Tests performed with different models did not show a clear superiority of one model over the others with respect to the classification performances. For simplicity, from now on, we then consider tree-like Bayesian networks. The network structure is built from the document tree, but need not be identical to this tree.

A Tree-Like Model for Structured Document Classification

For this model, we make the following assumptions:

- There are two types of variables corresponding to structure and content nodes.
- Each structure node may have zero or many structure sub-nodes and zero or one content node.
- Each feature of the document depends on the class c we are interested in.
- Each structural variable depends on its parent in the document network.
- Each content variable depends only on its structural variable.

The generative process for the model corresponds to a recursive application of the following process: at each structural node s, one chooses a number of structural sub-nodes, which could be zero, and the length of the textual part if any. Sub-nodes labels and words are then sampled from their respective distribution, which depends on s and the document class. The document depth could be another parameter of the model. Document length and depth distributions are omitted in the model since the corresponding terms fall out for the classification problems considered here.

Using such a network, we can write the joint content and structure probability that document d belongs to class c:

$$P(d,c) = P(c)\left(\prod_{i=1}^{|d|} P(s_d^i \mid pa(s_d^i),c)\right)\left(\prod_{i=1}^{|d|} P(t_d^i \mid s_d^i,c)\right)$$
$$(a) \qquad (b)$$

where (a) and (b) respectively correspond to **structural** and **textual probabilities.** Structural probabilities can be directly estimated from data using some smooth estimator.

Since is defined on the infinite set, we shall make additional hypothesis for estimating the textual probabilities . In the following, we use a Naive Bayes model for text fragments, but this is not a major option and other models could do as well. Let us define as the sequence of words where k and is the number of word occurrences i.e. the length of. Using Naive Bayes for the textual probability, the joint probability for this model is then:

$$P(d,c) = P(c)\left(\prod_{i=1}^{|d|} P(s_d^i \mid pa(s_d^i),c)\right)\left(\prod_{i=1}^{|d|} \prod_{j=1}^{|t^{i,d}|} P(w_j^{i,d} / s_d^i,c)\right)$$

Learning

In order to estimate the joint probability of each document and each class, the model parameters must be learned from a training set of documents. We do not describe here the learning algorithm which is fully explained in (Denoyer & Gallinari, 2004).

Experiments

Many experiments have been made with this model on different corpora (INEX, WebKB, NetProtect,WIPO). Denoyer and Gallinari (2004) for more details on these collections. Table 1 gives the results of different models on three XML corpora:

- The INEX corpus composed of about 12,000 XML documents that describe scientific articles (18 categories)

- The WIPO corpus composed of 10,900 XML documents that describe patents (15 categories)
- The WebKB corpus composed of 8,282 XHTML documents (7 categories).

The different methods are compared using a classic F1 score (micro and macro):

- NB is the Naive Bayes method on flat documents
- RB is the model proposed here
- SVM TF-IDF is the classic SVM method for classification of flat documents using TF-IDF vectors
- Fisher RB is a kernel method that allows us to use our belief network model with a support vector machine.

The results in Table 1 show that the RB model improves the baseline models.

Future Trends for the Stochastic Generative Model

We have presented a generative model for structured documents. It is based on Bayesian networks and allows modeling the structure and the content of documents. It has been tested for the classical task of whole document classification. Experiments show that the model behaves well on a variety of situations. Further investigations are needed for analyzing its behavior on document fragments classification. The model could also be modified for learning implicit relations between document elements besides using the explicit structure. An interesting aspect of the generative model is that it could be used for other tasks relevant to IR. It could serve as a basis for clustering structured documents. The natural solution is to consider a mixture of Bayesian network models where parameters do depend

Table 1. Results of the RB model on different XML textual corpora

	Micro-F1	Macro-F1
NB	0.59	0.605
RB model	0.619	0.622
SVM TF-IDF	0.534	0.564
Fisher RB	0.661	0.668
INEX		
	Micro-F1	Macro-F1
NB	0.801	0.706
RB model	0.827	0.743
SVM TF-IDF	0.737	0.651
Fisher RB	0.823	0.738
WebKB		
	Micro-F1	Macro-F1
NB	0.662	0.565
RB model	0.677	0.604
SVM TF-IDF	0.822	0.71
Fisher RB	0.862	0.715
WIPO		

on the mixture component instead of the class, as it is the case here. Schema-mapping and automatic document structuring are new tasks that are currently being investigated in the database and IR communities. The potential of the model for performing inference on document parts when information is missing in the document will be helpful for this type of application. Preliminary experiments about automatic document structuring are described by Denoyer et al. (2004).

CONCLUSION

XML is becoming a standard in many applications because of its universal and powerful tree structure. On the Internet for example, unstructured documents are being replaced by such structured documents, so that approaches that have been designed to tackle Internet resources need to be revisited in order to take advantage of the new structured nature of the documents.

The tree structure of XML documents can be seen as information by itself. When searching for the origin of a document for example, looking at its tree structure can be sufficient because different sources may use different structures to generate their documents. Clustering XML documents using their structure only can help methods designed to handle homogeneous XML collections work also on heterogeneous collections.

But taking the structure of the documents into account may also have a positive impact on the results even if we are only interested in classifying the documents according to their content. The organization of a document may indeed differ from one context to another. The structure of a document can for example help distinguish an article concerning history to another one about science. Moreover, generic models that combine structure and content may help put the right context or weight on smaller parts of the documents.

On the other hand, many existing approaches designed to handle data represented by trees suffer from high complexities, limiting their use to small volumes of data. Hopefully, as we have shown in this chapter, some transformations of XML tree structures can be used to simplify their representations, still preserving some of their interesting structural properties, and thus providing new ways to efficiently manage high volumes of such data.

As a summary, since XML collections will become more and more important, and since their tree structure can help improve ML and IR tasks on such data, a good compromise has to be found when designing a new method for XML, so that the information contained in the structure is used but does not affect too much its complexity.

Another important challenge concerns the output provided by such methods. In that field, we have highlighted some methods that can exhibit the resulting tree patterns, classifiers or cluster representatives, and therefore can support analysts in mining tasks.

REFERENCES

Agrawa l, R., & Srikant, R. (1994, September). Fast algorithms for mining association rules in large databases. In *Proceedings of the 20th International Conference on Very Large Data Bases, VLDB'94*, Santiago de Chile, Chile.

Arimura, H., & Uno, T. (2005). An output-polynomial time algorithm for mining frequent closed attribute trees. In S. Kramer & B. Bernhard Pfahringer (Eds.). In *Proceedings of the 15th International Conference on Inductive Logic Programming, ILP '05*, Bonn, Germany.

Asai, T., Arimura, H., Uno, T., & Nakano, S. (2003). Discovering frequent substructures in large unordered trees. In *Proceedings of the 6th International Conference on Discovery Science (DS'03)*, Sapporo, Japan, October, LNCS, Springer (Ed.) Volume 2843/2003, (pp. 47-61).

Candillier, L., Tellier, I., & Torre, F. (2006). Transforming XML trees for efficient classification and clustering. In *Proceedings of the 4th International Workshop of the Initiative for the Evaluation of XML Retrieval, INEX '05*, Schloss Dagstuhl, Germany.

Candillier, L., Tellier, I., Torre, F., & Bousquet, O. (2005). SSC: Statistical subspace clustering. In P. Perner & A. Imiya (Eds.). In *Proceedings of the 4th International Conference on Machine Learning and Data Mining in Pattern Recognition, MLDM '05*, Leipzig, Germany.

Chawathe, S., Rajaraman, A., Garcia-Molina, H., & Widom, J. (1996). Change direction in hierarchically structured information. In *Proceedings on the ACM SIGMOD International Conference on Management of Data*, (pp. 493-504), Montreal, Quebec.

Costa, G., Manco, G., Ortale, R., & Tagarelli, A. (2004). A tree-based approach to clustering XML documents by structure. In *Proceedings of the 8th European Conference on Principles and Practice of Knowledge Discovery in Databases, PKDD '04*, Pisa, Italy.

Celeux, G., Diday, E., Govaert, G., Lechevallier, Y., & Ralambondrainy, H. (1989). *Classification Automatique des Données, Environnement statistique et informatique*. Dunod informatique, Bordas, Paris.

Chi, Y., Yang, Y., Xia, Y., & Muntz, R. R. (2004, May). CMTreeMiner: Mining both closed and maximal frequent subtrees. In *Proceedings of the 8th Pacific-Asia Conference on Advances in Knowledge Discovery and Data Mining, PAKDD '04*, Sydney, Australia.

Dalamagas, T., Cheng, T., Winkel, K.-J., & Sellis, T. K. (2004, May). Clustering. In *Proceedings of the 3rd Helenic Conferenceon Methods and Applications of Artificial Intelligence, SETN '04*, Samos, Greece.

Denoyer, L., Vittaut, J.-N., Gallinari, P., Brunesseaux, S., & Brunesseaux, S. (2003). Structured multimedia document classification. In *Proceedings of the ACM Symposium on Document Engineering*, Grenoble, France.

Denoyer, L., & Gallinari, P. (2004). Bayesian network model for semi-structured document classification [Special Issue]. *Information Processing and Management: An International Journal Special Issue: Bayesian networks and information retrieval, 40*(5), 807-827.

Denoyer, L., Wisniewski, G., & Gallinari, P. (2004, July). Document structure matching for heterogeneous corpora. In *Proceedings of the Workshop on XML and Information Retrieval, SIGIR '04*, Sheffield.

Doucet, A., & Ahonen-Myka, H. (2002, December). Naïve clustering of a large XML document collection. In *Proceedings of the 1st ERCIM Workshop of the Initiative for the Evaluation of XML Retrieval, INEX '02*, Schloss Dagsuhl, Germany.

Flesca, S., Manco, G., Masciari, E., Pontieri, L., & Pugliese, A. (2002). Detecting structural similarities between xml documents. In *Proceedings of the 5th International Workshop on the Web and Databases, WebDB '02*, Madison, Wisconsin.

Inokuchi, A., Washio, T., & Motoda, H. (2000). An apriori-based algorithm for mining frequent substructures from graph data. In *Proceedings of the 4th European Conference on Principles of Data Mining and Knowledge Discovery*.

Ji, Z., Wei, W., Han, L., & Sheng, Z. (2005). X-warehouse: Building query pattern-driven data. In *Proceedings of the International World Wide Web Conference (Special interest tracks and posters)*.

Kilpeläinen, P. (1992). *Tree matching problems with applications to structured text databases*.

Unpublished doctoral thesis, University of Helsinki.

Lian, W., Cheung, D. W., Mamoulis, N., & Yiu, S.-M. (2004). An efficient and scalable algorithm for clustering XML documents by structure. *IEEE Transactions and Knowledge Data Engineering, 16*(1), 82-96.

Liu, J., Wang, J. T. L., Hsu, W., & Herbert, K. G. (2004). XML clustering by principal component analysis. In *Proceedings of the 16th IEEE International Conference on Tools with Artificial Intelligence, ICTAI '04.*

Nierman, A., & Jagadish, H. V. (2002). Evaluating structural similarity in XML documents. In *Proceedings of the 5th International Workshop on the Web and Databases, WebDB '02*, Madison, Wisconsin.

Nijssen, S., & Kok, J. N. (2003). Efficient discovery of frequent unordered trees. In *Proceedings of the first International Workshop on Mining Graphs, Trees and Sequences, MGTS '03.*

Plotkin, G. (1970). A note on inductive generalisation. *Machine Intelligence, 5,* 153-163.

Quinlan, R. (1998). *Data mining tools see5 and c5.0.* (Tech. Rep.). RuleQuest Research.

Termier, A., Rousset, M.-C., & Sebag, M. (2002). Treefinder: A first step towards xml data mining. In *Proceedings of the IEEE International Conference on Data Mining, ICDM '02,* Japan.

Termier, A., Rousset, M.-C., & Sebag, M. (2004). DRYADE: A new approach for discovering closed frequent trees in heterogeneous tree databases. In *Proceedings of the 4th IEEE International Conference on Data Mining, ICDM '04,* Brighton, UK.

Termier, A., Rousset, M.-C., Sebag, M., Ohara, K., Washio, T., & Motoda, H. (2005). Efficient mining of high branching factor attribute trees. In *Proceedings of the 5th IEEE International Conference on Data Mining, ICDM '05,* Houston, Texas.

Uno, T., Kiyomiet, M., & Arimura, H. (2004, November). LCM v2.0: Efficient mining algorithms for frequent/closed/maximal itemsets. In *Proceedings of the IEEE ICDM Workshop on Frequent Itemset Mining Implementations, FIMI '04,* Brighton, UK.

Vercoustre, A.-M., Fegas, M., Gul, S., & Lechevallier, Y. (2006). A flexible structured-based representation for XML document mining. In *Proceedings of the 4th International Workshop of the Initiative for the Evaluation of XML Retrieval, INEX '05,* Schloss Dagstuhl, Germany.

Yi, J., & Sundaresan, N. (2000). A classifier for semi-structured documents. In *Proceedings of the 6th ACM SIGKDD International Conference on Knowledge Discovery and Data Mining, KDD '00.*

Yoon, J. P., Raghavan, V., Chakilam, V., & Kerschberg, L. (2001). BitCube: A three-dimensional bitmap indexing for XML documents. *Journal of Intelligent Information Systems, 17*(2-3), 241-254.

Zaki, M. J. (2002). Efficiently mining trees in a forest. In *Proceedings of the 8th ACM SIGKDD International Conference on Knowledge Discovery and Data Mining,* (pp. 71-80), Edmonton, Canada.

Zang, K., & Shasha, D. (1989). Simple fast algorithms for the editing distance between trees and related problems. *SIAM Journal of Computing, 18,* 1245-1262.

Chapter X
Topic and Cluster Evolution Over Noisy Document Streams

Sascha Schulz
Humboldt-University Berlin, Germany

Myra Spiliopoulou
Otto-von-Guericke-University Magdeburg, Germany

Rene Schult
Otto-von-Guericke-University Magdeburg, Germany

ABSTRACT

We study the issue of discovering and tracing thematic topics in a stream of documents. This issue, often studied under the label "topic evolution" is of interest in many applications where thematic trends should be identified and monitored, including environmental modeling for marketing and strategic management applications, information filtering over streams of news and enrichment of classification schemes with emerging new classes. We concentrate on the latter area and depict an example application from the automotive industry—the discovery of emerging topics in repair & maintenance reports. We first discuss relevant literature on (a) the discovery and monitoring of topics over document streams and (b) the monitoring of evolving clusters over arbitrary data streams. Then, we propose our own method for topic evolution over a stream of small noisy documents: We combine hierarchical clustering, performed at different time periods, with cluster comparison over adjacent time periods, taking into account that the feature space itself may change from one period to the next. We elaborate on the behaviour of this method and show how human experts can be assisted in identifying class candidates among the topics thus identified.

INTRODUCTION

"A picture is worth thousand words." However, in many applications, natural language is the main medium of information dissemination, often enriched with acronyms, shorthands or domain-specific jargon. Business analysts, journalists, project managers and project proposers, quality assessors in the manufacturing industry or in pharmaceutics, researchers, reviewers, students, and teachers rely on a stream of texts from multiple document sources to acquire the most up-to-date information and to identify ongoing, respectively declining trends on their subjects of interest. Recently, much research is devoted to the identification of **trends** in texts, with some emphasis on newspaper news, business news and scientific literature.

A particularly demanding application of trend discovery from texts concerns the identification of **emerging topics** that are appropriate as additional classes in an existing document classification scheme. Example areas that exhibit the necessity of refining classification schemes over documents are customer relationship management (CRM) and quality assessment in manufacturing. In CRM, all interaction channels between a customer and the company should be exploited to achieve better customer understanding, proactive portfolio design and increase of customer lifetime value. Of particular interest is the interaction between customers and after-sales support centers that deal with complaints, reclamations, suggestions for product improvements, and requests for product maintenance. The informal documents (also: protocols of phone calls) that capture this interaction can deliver valuable information about the way customers perceive a product and about potential product improvements or extensions. In the manufacturing industry and in pharmaceutics, customer responses, maintenance requests, and reports on shortcomings are also important for quality assessment. Both for CRM and quality assessment, topics that emerge and persist are potential classes

in a taxonomy of customer profiles, of product desiderata, or of product malfunctions.

The information sources containing data about such potential classes are mostly collections of jargon documents: Reports on product maintenance and repairs are written by engineers, while reclamations may combine texts written by customers and texts written by employees of the after-sales service. Since such reports are collected from all service points, they are characterized by differences in language, syntax, sentence formation, presence of typographical and linguistic errors, level of detail and use of abbreviations, and may even differ in their base vocabulary. This makes the discovery of **emerging topics** more challenging than the corresponding analysis of published news or scientific abstracts that have been subjected to a careful reviewing or editorial check before being published for a broad audience.

In this chapter, we study the issue of topic evolution over an accumulating stream of documents. In the next section we discuss advances on **topic evolution**, where a topic is a description of a document group, extracted over an accumulating document stream. Advances in this area have their origin in the field of "topic detection and tracking" (TDT), although the notion of evolving topic is different from the original definition of a topic as a story. In the section *"Monitoring Cluster Evolution,"* we will turn to generic approaches for the discovery and interpretation of changes in clusters. When discussing methods in these two sections, we elaborate on their applicability for the discovery and the evolution of classes over noisy document streams.

Section *"A Topic Evolution Method for a Stream of Noisy Documents"* contains our own approach that builds upon generic methods for cluster evolution. Our method has been motivated by and tested upon a stream of repair and maintenance reports on newly introduced vehicles. This application from the automotive industry is characterized by small noisy **documents** that can deliver insights of immense value for product quality assessment and customer satisfaction. The last section concludes our study with a summary and outlook.

EVOLVING TOPICS IN CLUSTERS

Research methods on **topic evolution** consider a "topic" as a condensed representation of **documents** constituting a group. This group may be a cluster of similar **documents** or may be a whole document collection. For example, Ipeirotis et al. (2005) consider all documents in a text database as one group, which they summarize into a "content summary." Aggarwal and Yu (2006) rather define a "cluster droplet," a summarized representation of the values encountered in the members of a cluster. In other studies, a topic is a "cluster label," comprised of the dominant or otherwise characteristic words of the cluster's members (for instance cf. Mei & Zhai 2005). We use the neutral term *"group description"* as a set of features that are representative of the group's members.

Topic evolution can be observed as a particular thread of "topic detection and tracking" (TDT) as defined in Allan (2002). We briefly describe TDT and its tasks, before concentrating on methods for the detection of changes in document summaries, document cluster labels, and document groups.

Tasks of Topic Detection and Tracking

The subjects of topic detection and topic tracking are defined in Allan (2002), where the five tasks of **TDT** are enlisted. As stated in that book, **TDT** concentrates on the detection and tracking of *stories* (a "topic" is a story) and encompasses the tasks of (1) story segmentation, (2) first story detection, (3) cluster detection, (4) tracking, and (5) story link detection.

There is a conceptual similarity between **TDT** and the identification of **emerging topics** as potential classes over a (noisy) **document** stream. However, these "topics" are not "stories" in the TDT sense: It is not of interest to detect a story and then track it across **documents**, as in tasks (2) and (4), but rather identify **documents** across different time periods, which, when taken together contribute to the same, a priori unknown but statistically important "topic." This separation has been first elaborated in the survey of Kontostathis, Galitsky, Pottenger, Roy, and Phelps (2003), where the new task of topic trend discovery was introduced. However, as we explain in (Schult & Spiliopoulou, 2006a), the methods presented under this task in Kontostathis et al. (2003), such as Pottenger & Yang (2001) and Roy, Gevry, and Pottenger (2002), rely on cross-references among documents. This corresponds to task (5) of the TDT agenda. In a **stream** of independent documents, there are no cross-citations, so these methods do not apply.

Tracing Changes in Summaries

Ipeirotis et al. (2005) trace content summary changes, whereas a "content summary" refers to a database of documents. The motivation is that content summaries are valuable for the selection of the databases that should be queried in the first place. Despite the difference in focus between their work and the issues addressed here, the methodology is transferable: A content summary, as defined by Ipeirotis, Ntoulas, Cho, and Gravano (2005) has similarities to a cluster label. The authors distinguish between a *complete content summary* $C(D)$ that consists of the number of occurrences of each word $w \in D$ and an *approximate content summary* $\hat{C}(D)$ computed by **document** sampling.

To predict when a content summary change occurs, Ipeirotis et al. (2005) apply *survival analysis*, a method originally designed to model/predict the length of survival of patients under different treatments. In particular, they define the "survival time of a summary" as the time until the current database summary is sufficiently different from the old one. To predict this survival time, they consider (a) a measure of difference between summaries at adjacent time points and (b) a probability distribution that is expected to be followed by the content summary change. The measures or "content summary change indicators" they use to this purpose are the Kullback-Leibler divergence, that is, the difference in the word distribution between the old and the current summary, and the simpler "precision" (defined as the number of words in the current summary that were also in the old one) and "recall" (defined as the number of words in the old summary that are also in the current one). The probability with which a content summary change may occur within time t is assumed to follow an exponential distribution $S(t) = e^{-\lambda t}$, in which the value of λ should be predicted for a specific database. In their experiments with text collections from the Internet domains GOV, EDU and COM, Ipeirotis et al. (2005) assessed differences in the *speed of change*: The GOV collection changes more slowly than the others, while COM and other commercial site collections change faster than the rest. Moreover, large databases tend to change faster than small ones.

Ipeirotis et al. (2005) consider content summaries over whole databases of documents. Aggarwal and Yu (2006) rather derive content summaries for clusters over accumulating **streams**. They introduce the notion of "droplet" as a statistical summary of data that is stored and inspected at regular intervals (Aggarwal & Yu, 2006). In particular, a droplet consists of two vectors, one accommodating co-occurring pairs of words and one accommodating the words occurring in the cluster and their weights. The members of a cluster are weighted and contribute to the cluster's weight. This weight is part of the droplet and subject to a decaying function: A cluster's weight decays if no new points are added to it.

Aggarwal and Yu (2006) achieve the identification of new clusters by juxtaposing cluster droplets and new data: A new **document** is assigned to the cluster whose droplet has the highest similarity to it, according to some similarity/distance function. A cluster becomes "inactive," if no documents are added to it for some time. If a document cannot be assigned to a cluster, then it becomes a new cluster itself—replacing the oldest inactive cluster. Hence, new data form new clusters while old clusters decay gradually, if they are not fed with new documents. This approach conforms to the intuition behind topic detection and tracking in the conventional **TDT** sense: A new topic is a document that does not fit to any existing topic; a topic decays and disappears if no new documents are inserted to it any more.

Monitoring Changes in Cluster Labels

In the method of Aggarwal and Yu (2006), the cluster summary is not associated with semantics: A droplet is a condensed cluster representation appropriate for matching and maintenance but not necessarily for human inspection and interpretation. Methods on the **monitoring** of **cluster labels** are rather assuming that a label is a human-understandable representation of a cluster's content. Accordingly, they focus on the evolution of semantics captured in the cluster's label.

In the **topic evolution** mechanism of Moringa and Yamanichi, a topic consists of the words with the largest information gain (Moringa & Yamanichi, 2004). The topics reflect the contents of soft clusters, built with an incremental Expectation-Maximization algorithm. Finite mixture models are learned at each timestamp and dynamic model selection is performed to choose the optimal one. The key idea of this model selection is to first build a large number of components and then select the main ones on the basis of Rissanen's predictive stochastic complexity. The emphasis of that work is on the adaptation of the topics rather than the tracing of topic changes.

Mei and Zhai studied the tracing and interpretation of topic change (2005). Similarly to Moringa and Yamanichi (2004), they consider mixture models to build document clusters and also use the Expectation-Maximization algorithm. A document may belong to multiple clusters and, consequently, topics describing different clusters may overlap. To derive the topics themselves (as combinations of words describing a cluster), they assume a background model. Then, the evolution of topics is traced using Kullback-Leibler divergence, similarly to Ipeirotis et al. (2005). Mei and Zhai (2005) introduce topic transition types and build a **topic evolution** graph, in which transitions are traced using Hidden-Markov-Models. A remarkable aspect of the **topic evolution** graph is that edges/transitions are not restricted to topics derived at consecutive periods: A topic is connected to any topic discovered at an earlier period, if the former turns to be a transition of the latter (according to the KL-divergence).

The clustering of text **streams** is also considered by Shi Zhong (2005), albeit the emphasis is on adapting clusters rather than detecting changes in their labels. Shi Zhong proposes an online variation of k-means, the "online spherical k-means": documents are modeled as TFxIDF vectors normalized into unit length, whereupon the clustering algorithm builds k clusters, maximizing the average cosine similarity within each cluster. A new document is assigned to the cluster with the closest centroid, whereupon the cluster itself is adjusted (Zhong, 2005). **Cluster labels** are not derived nor used by the algorithm itself; they are only used for the evaluation upon prelabeled experimental data. Algorithms that perform document clustering but do not derive topics from the clusters nor consider topic change are not considered further in this chapter.

Among all methods described thus far, the approach of Mei and Zhai (2005) is the closest to our task of topic **monitoring** for the extension of

a class taxonomy: Similarly to Mei and Zhai, we are interested in identifying **emerging topics** that persist over a number of time periods. Moreover, a document may also refer to more than one topic, so that soft clustering seems appropriate at first. However, soft clustering does not agree with our ultimate objective of extending an original classification of topics with new, emerging and long-lived topics, since classes may not overlap.[1] Furthermore, a stream of noisy documents does not lend itself to a time-independent background model, as is assumed in Mei and Zhai (2005).

In our earlier work (Schult & Spiliopoulou, 2006a; Schult & Spiliopoulou, 2006b), we have studied the evolution of topic labels with the objective of tracing emerging and declining topics. One of the focal points was the study of changes in the feature space, whereupon cluster quality degradation has been used as an indicator of a shift in the feature space. We used an evolving document collection for our experiments, the ACM Digital Library section 2.8. We have observed the increasing domination of some topics (most prominently: "data mining") and the gradual disappearance of others. In these experiments, the documents were very small, consisting only of the titles and keywords of the library papers. However, differently from our premises here, the library papers contain very little noise and the vocabulary is limited, thus allowing for a reasonable feature space comprised of the most frequent words. A collection of repair reports or of customer complaints and reclamations has a much wider vocabulary and is expected to contain many typographical errors. In this chapter, we consider therefore all words of the collection as members of the feature space.

To capture the interplay of cluster evolution and **topic evolution**, we have also investigated methods on modeling and detecting **cluster changes** in general, as described in the dedicated section on *"Monitoring Cluster Evolution."*

Remembering and Forgetting in a Stream of Documents

When building and adjusting clusters across an accumulating stream of **documents**, already known documents may have a negative influence on the detection of **emerging topics** and the tracking of changes in existing topics: In the first case, a group of documents that corresponds to an obsolete topic may attract documents that are only marginally relevant to it and that would otherwise form a new topic. In the second case, incoming documents may indicate an evolution inside a topic, for example, the increasing dominance of some terms; if already known documents dominate, this evolution will not become apparent.

The motivation behind forgetting known documents is that they should not be weighted equally to new ones. Methods to this end come from **TDT** but also from incremental clustering and from adaptive classification, ranging from conventional sliding window approaches as in (Mei & Zhai, 2005; Schult & Spiliopoulou, 2006a, 2006b) to reweighting schemes for data records, as in Aggarwal and Yu (2006), Moringa and Yamanichi (2004), Nasraoui, Cardona-Uribe, and Rojas-Coronel (2003), and Zhong (2005).

Shi Zhong (2005) proposes an exponential decay rate for old records: A new record is assigned a weight of 1. Then, for each time segment, the record's contribution to "its" cluster is recomputed using a decay factor $\gamma \in (0,1)$. Gradual decay is also proposed by Aggarwal and Yu (2006) who associate each data record with a weight generated by a nonmonotonic "fading function" that decays uniformly with time: The decay of records leads to a change of the droplets (the cluster content summaries), so that droplets can die out, shift conceptually or merge with other droplets.

Nasraoui et al. (2003) also use a decaying function for the weighting of old records. However, they consider the case of a record's reappearance. While other studies consider this case as the insertion of a new record and assign to it a weight for new

records, Nasraoui et al. (2003) rather increase the weight of the old record that reappeared.

MONITORING CLUSTER EVOLUTION

The detection of emerging and persistent topics can be observed as a special case of **cluster evolution**. This is a rather new research subject that gained in importance in recent years. The scientific contributions come from the fields of pattern comparison and spatiotemporal clustering. There are also some dedicated studies on the *understanding* of **cluster change** (for instance Aggarwal, 2005).

Frameworks for the Identification of Changes

Between 1999 and 2000, Ganti et al. proposed three modules for the observation and analysis of changes in datasets, FOCUS (Ganti, Gehrke, & Ramakrishnan, 1999a), CACTUS (Ganti, Gehrke, & Ramakrishnan, 1999b) and DEMON (Ganti, Gehrke & Ramakrishnan, 2000). When observed as three components of *one* framework, these modules can be used to detect and monitor evolution in datasets or clusters over them, as well as to derive and monitor summary descriptions over the data.

Ganti et al. (2000) proposed DEMON for data evolution and **monitoring** across the temporal dimension. DEMON detects systematic vs. nonsystematic changes in the data and identifies the data blocks (along the time dimension) which have to be processed by the miner in order to extract new patterns. In the context of **topic evolution**, DEMON delivers a mechanism for the selection of those documents that should be considered for the discovery of new clusters. Hence, DEMON can be observed as a mechanism that specifies the data to be forgotten and those to be remembered at each point of time.

The module FOCUS of Ganti et al. (1999a) compares two datasets and computes an interpretable quantifiable *deviation* between them. This deviation is represented as a "model" consisting of a "structure component" and a "measure component." The structure component identifies "interesting regions" and the measure component summarizes the subset of the data that is mapped to each region. Clustered datasets are a special case: Clusters are nonoverlapping regions, where each region is described through a set of attributes (structure component) and corresponds to a set of raw data (measure component). This elaborate and powerful mechanism can split the clusters under comparison down to identical regions and thus provide an overview of their differences. As described later, our approach for the discovery and the **monitoring** of topics is based on a variation of FOCUS.

The "pattern monitor" (PAM) (Baron, Spiliopoulou, & Günther, 2003) models patterns as temporal, evolving objects. A model of changes is more recently proposed in Baron and Spiliopoulou (2005). The main emphasis of PAM is on the **monitoring** of association rules with a more recent extension for clusters. However, topic monitoring is beyond its scope.

The PANDA framework (Bartolini, Ciaccia, Ntoutsi, Patella, & Theodoridis, 2004) delivers mechanisms for the comparison of simple patterns and aggregation logics for the comparison of complex ones. In this framework, a *simple* pattern is built upon raw data, while a *complex* pattern consists of other patterns, for example, a cluster of association rules. Hence, the comparison of complex patterns and the subsequent computation of the dissimilarity score between them is performed in a bottom-up fashion: A complex pattern is decomposed in component patterns which are compared to each other; then, the dissimilarity scores are combined according to a user-defined aggregation logic. In terms of expressiveness, PANDA subsumes FOCUS, as explained in Bartolini et al. (2004). However,

for the purposes of our approach, the expressive power of FOCUS is sufficient.

Closest to our work is the recently published framework MONIC for the **monitoring** of **cluster evolution** (Spiliopoulou, Ntoutsi, Theodoridis, & Schult, 2006): MONIC encompasses a model for "cluster transitions", such as a cluster being split or absorbed by another or changing in size or homogeneity. Its notion of "overlap" among clusters captured at different time points allows for changes in the feature space, thus becoming appropriate for the task of **topic evolution** over a stream of documents. Indeed, MONIC has been tested on an evolving document collection, the ACM Digital Library section H2.8. MONIC is appropriate for the detection of emerging topics, but it has not been designed for interaction with the human expert: It lacks a visualization method that intuitively captures **topic evolution** and assists the human expert in following traces of topic splits and merges. Especially for collections of noisy documents, such assistance seems indispensable, so it is part of our approach presented later.

Spatiotemporal Clustering for Cluster Evolution

Generic methods for **cluster evolution** have been published under the labels "incremental **clustering**" and, more recently, "spatiotemporal **clustering**." The latter methods usually assume the existence of a stationary trajectory with an associated metric.[2]

Ester, Kriegel, Sander, Wimmer, and Xu (1998) proposed an early work on the detection of **cluster change** and the adjustment of spatial clusters. Ester et al. (1998) used the term "incremental **clustering**" for a method that re-computes the clusters after each update of the dataset, paying emphasis on the minimization of the computation overhead. They proposed IncrementalDBSCAN, an adaptive variant of the static DBSCAN proposed earlier by the same group.

DBSCAN is a single scan **clustering** algorithm that groups neighbouring objects into clusters using a *local* **clustering** condition. The condition is that each object in a cluster must have a minimum number of neighbours, whereby a neighbourhood is an area (in the topological sense) with a predefined radius. DBSCAN stands for "Density-Based **Clustering** of Applications with Noise" and pays particular emphasis in preventing cluster distortion through noise/outliers.

IncrementalDBSCAN focuses on cluster adjustment. Nonetheless, the authors propose a typification of cluster changes (Ester et al., 1998): When a new object is inserted, this may cause the creation of a new cluster (a formerly small neighbourhood becomes adequately large), cluster absorption (an existing cluster absorbs the new object and its neighbours) and cluster merger (the members of different clusters become density-connected). When an object is deleted, a cluster may shrink or even disappear (some of its members become disconnected) or be split (the fragments of the original cluster are disconnected but are adequately large to become clusters themselves).

Since noise is a primary characteristic of the documents we consider, methods that are robust against noise are of particular interest. However, DBSCAN has been designed for application areas where proximity of data records is independent of the temporal dimension, i.e. the distance between two data records cannot change from one time point to the next. This holds for spatial databases, including geographical information systems (GIS). Distance among documents might be defined in a similar way, for example, using Euclidean distance or (more usually) cosine distance. However, the feature space across a document stream is not constant, since some terms become obsolete while others emerge. Hence, IncrementalDBSCAN is not trivially applicable.

Aggarwal (2005) proposed a very elaborate method for **cluster evolution**. In his approach, a cluster is a densification of the topological space and is described by a kernel function. The emphasis of Aggarwal (2005) is on studying the *velocity of change* in an evolving cluster and on identifying (a) the dimensions of the feature space, which are most responsible for change and (b) areas or data points that exhibit the highest velocity of change. In the context of topic evolution, this method can be used to identify areas that evolve at different speeds and associate sets of words (labels) with them. However, the constraint of a static, a priori known feature space applies for this method similarly to IncrementalDBSCAN.

For Neill, Moore, Sabhnani, and Daniel (2005) and for Yang, Parthasarathy, and Mehta, (2005), clusters are geometric objects that move or change shape in a metric space. Neill et al. (2005) study the emergence and stability of clusters, observing spatial regions across the time axis. However, their notion of "cluster" is very particular: A cluster is a region where counts (for some property) are higher than expected. This notion cannot be used for topic evolution, because a document cluster is rather a region of objects that are more similar to each other than to the rest of their neighbourhood (cf. cluster definition against a baseline (Mei & Zhai, 2005)).

Yang et al. (2005) detect change events upon clusters of scientific data. They study "Spatial Object Association Patterns" (SOAPs), which are graphs of different types, for example, cliques or stars. A SOAP is characterized by the number of snapshots in the data, where it occurs and the number of instances in a snapshot that adhere to it. With this information, the algorithm detects formation and dissipation events, as well as cluster continuation. The types of **cluster evolution** are also relevant for **topic evolution**, but the methodology itself does not transfer, because it requires the establishment of links among the objects under observation.

A TOPIC EVOLUTION METHOD FOR A STREAM OF NOISY DOCUMENTS

After discussing the literature advances on evolving topics and on evolving clusters, we now introduce our approach for the discovery of topics that should serve as potential new classes over a stream of **documents**. Our problem specification, which is motivated by the application of workshop narratives in the automotive industry is characterized by very small and noisy documents that contain jargon terms, typographical and linguistic errors next to an abundance of potentially synonymous terms. To deal with a stream of those characteristics, we propose a method that (a) discovers clusters at consecutive periods, (b) compares clusters of consecutive clusterings and links each old cluster to its match in the new clustering, if any and (c) graphically depicts chains of matched clusters over time, identifying cluster splits and merges. To this end, we have designed a variation of the FOCUS+DEMON framework (Ganti et al., 1999a; Ganti et al., 2000), adapted to the demands of stream **monitoring** over an evolving feature space. Our method is semi-automatic in the sense that the final decision on adding a topic to the existing classification scheme is left to the human expert. A graphical user interface has been designed to support this task by presenting evolving clusters and the associations among them.

Application Case: Workshop Narratives in the Automotive Industry

In our application case, we study repair & maintenance reports about vehicles that have been newly introduced to the market. The fast and thorough treatment of repair & maintenance requests for new vehicles is paramount for customer satisfaction – and so is the recording of all requests and remarks made by the customers. The documents created to this purpose, termed as "workshop narratives" hereafter, are short texts, written down by the personnel at the front desk of the vendor-affiliated workshops, where the repairs take place. The engineers use these documents to perform the requested maintenance procedures or detect malfunctions.

Workshop narratives contain information that can help answer questions like: What are the experiences of the customers with the vehicles? Which problems do they encounter? If malfunctions are encountered, how do they manifest themselves? Here are two major application areas that demand answers to such questions:

- **Early field feedback:** When a new vehicle is introduced to the market, many functionalities and many pieces of technology are put to test at once. **Emerging topics** in the narratives can deliver a first picture on how the new vehicle is received by the customers and what additional expectations they have for it.
- **Fast response to shortcomings:** The early identification of and the responses to shortcomings or malfunctions in new vehicles are of paramount importance for the quality management and for the image of the automotive vendor.

Those two application areas contribute to quality assessment and to customer satisfaction in the CRM context, as stressed in the introduction to this chapter. The identification and **monitoring** of **emerging topics** is useful for further applications, such as the long-term follow-up of vehicle types in the market and the identification of component-specific requests for repair or maintenance. In the following, we focus on the first two areas.

Description and Preparation of the Document Stream

Our approach is designed for a stream of small noisy documents. Workshop narratives, reclamations and customer letters are good examples of this type of documents, which are characterized by the following properties:

- The documents are small, sometimes limited to a couple of sentences. In our application, a document contains between one (!) and 150 words.
- The documents are written in jargon, containing application-specific abbreviations and encodings.
- There is no agreed-upon terminology, since the authors are independent of each other (e.g., customers of a company or engineers at different workshops). In our application, we counted one million narratives containing more than 150 synonym terms for the concept "maintenance."
- The feature space, comprised of the words in the documents, is not static, since some words, notably product-specific abbreviations, disappear while others emerge.
- There are misspellings and slang expressions, the sentences are not always syntactically complete (e.g., verbs or subjects are missing). This is because such documents are not intended for public use but for the treatment of a particular case.

In the preprocessing phase, we assume that the data arrive (or rather: are collected) in fixed intervals. Our text preparation for the documents collected within each interval includes text normalization, identification of synonyms with help of an existing synonym-list, stop word elimination and deletion of words that appear less than twice in the period under observation.

A conventional **vectorization** according to the vector-space-model introduced by Salton, Wong, and Yang (1975) produced very sparse vectors. Stemming, lemmatization and singular-value-decomposition (SVD) did not result in an applicable dimensionality reduction, most likely because of the many jargon words, abbreviations and the

many types of misspelling. Therefore, we have modeled each document by a pair of vectors, one vector of words and one vector of "quadgrams," that is, 4-grams of letters, built by extracting overlapping 4-letter sequences. The quadgram vector is more robust against orthographical and grammatical errors than the vector of words. The quadgram representation and the n-gram representations in general are language-independent, do not demand linguistic preprocessing and have a rather small vocabulary size. For example, a vocabulary consisting of 25 letters will result in at most of 25^4 different quadgrams. Hence, quadgram vectors form a less sparse data space than vectors of words.

For both the word-vector and the quadgram-vector, we associated each vector element with its TFxIDF value:

$$w_{TF \times IDF}(d,t) = tf(d,t) \times \log \frac{|D|}{df(t)}$$

where $tf(d, t)$ is the term frequency TF for term t in the document d of the collection D, $|D|$ is the cardinality of D and $df(t)$ is the document frequency of term t in D. We further normalize this value into:

$$w(d,t) = \frac{w_{TF \times IDF}(d,t)}{\sqrt{\sum_{i=1}^{m} w_{TF \times IDF}(d,t_i)^2}}$$

Each document is thus represented by a pair of vectors of normalized TFxIDF values. Then, the similarity of two documents d, d' with respect to their word-vectors X and X' is the complement of their cosinus distance: $sim^w(d,d') := sim^w(X,X') = 1-cos(X,X')$. The similarity of the two documents with respect to their quadgram-vectors is defined similarly as: $sim^q(d,d') := sim^q(Y,Y') = 1-cos(Y,Y')$, where Y, Y' denote the quadgram-vectors of the two documents. In the next subsection, we use these two notions of similarity to define the similarity between clusters.

Topic Discovery

We perform the topic discovery step at each period. We use an agglomerative hierarchical **clustering** method, because such methods do not require that we define the number of clusters a priori. The hierarchical **clustering** algorithm operates bottom-up, starting with individual documents as one-element-clusters/nodes and merging the two most similar nodes iteratively, until only one node remains; this is the root of the "dendrogram" or "cluster tree".

To calculate the similarity of two nodes during clustering, we first compute the *Average Neighbor (Group Average)* similarity between word-vectors, resp. quadgram-vectors. In particular, let C,C' be two clusters. Let X, X' denote the word-vectors in C, resp. C' and let Y, Y' denote the quadgram-vectors in C, resp. C'. Then, the word-based group average similarity of C, C' is defined as:

$$sim_{ga}^{w}(C,C') = \frac{\sum_{X \in C, X' \in C'} sim^{w}(X,X')}{|C| + |C'|}$$

and similarly for the quadgram-based group average similarity:

$$sim_{ga}^{q}(C,C') = \frac{\sum_{Y \in C, Y' \in C'} sim^{q}(Y,Y')}{|C| + |C'|}$$

where $sim^{w}(X,X')$ denotes the similarity between two word-vectors and $sim^{q}(Y,Y')$ the similarity between two quadgram-vectors, defined in both cases as the complement of their cosine distance. We then combine the two types of cluster similarity into the final cluster similarity score:

$$sim(C,C') = \frac{n^{w} \times sim_{ga}^{w}(C,C') + n^{q} \times sim_{ga}^{q}(C,C')}{n^{w} + n^{q}}$$

where n^{w} and n^{q} are optional weighting factors indicating the degree of influence of each vector type.

We use this definition of cluster similarity to build and "prune" the dendrogram. Pruning is performed by traversing the completed dendrogram and selecting each cluster C that satisfies both of the following properties: (a) Its children are more similar to each other than a threshold τ-*MinSimilarity* and (b) its cardinality is no less than a threshold τ-*MinClusterSize*. This means that we select only clusters of high homogeneity that correspond to a nontrivial part of the document collection.

It is apparent that this cluster selection/pruning mechanism does not guarantee that the whole collection is covered: We ignore those subsets of the collection that cannot be described by a cluster of acceptable quality and size. This is in accordance with our objective: We are not interested in a clustering that best describes the whole collection, but rather in discovering emerging topics that may serve as document classes over part of the collection. For such topics, we consider only the labels of clusters that satisfy the two requirements.

Topic Evolution Monitoring

We trace and monitor **topic evolution** by a noisy-stream-robust variation of the framework FOCUS+DEMON (Ganti et al., 1999a; Ganti et al., 2000). The reader may recall that the objective of that framework was to compare data (or derived patterns) and test whether they come from the same population: FOCUS has a structure component that identifies interesting regions and a measure component that defines relations between elements and regions. DEMON delivers summaries over the data or the patterns under comparison.

In principle, we might use the original framework for the comparison of clusterings derived at consecutive time periods, except that we are not interested in identifying deviations but rather in tracing topics. However, FOCUS has not been designed for feature spaces with thousands of dimensions; a scalable variation is needed. Moreover, the summaries delivered by DEMON assume a fixed feature space, while in our problem specification the feature space may change from one period to the next. Hence, we derive an appropriate variant of that framework, as described hereafter.

Following the notation of Ganti et al. (1999a) for FOCUS, we denote the clustering derived at some time period t as model m. As we explained in the last section, m consists of the clusters satisfying a quality constraint (intra-cluster similarity is at least τ-*MinSimilarity*) and a cardinality constraint (cluster size is at least τ-*MinClusterSize*). At each period t, we compare the model/clustering m with the clustering m' derived at the previous period t'. The feature spaces of these two periods are not necessarily identical – a fact that is not addressed in DEMON (Ganti et al., 2000).

On the other hand, since the document stream accummulates, there is a data overlap between t and t', consisting of the data records seen until t and not being "forgotten."[3] Hence, instead of computing the "greatest common refinement" between m and m', as in Ganti et al. (1999a), we observe the clusters in each model/clustering as sets of data records and compare the models on the basis of the dataset overlap. This gives us also more scalability towards high-dimensional feature spaces.

To compare clusters in set theoretical terms, we first define a sliding window Θ upon the time axis: For each time period t, it determines the number of subsequent periods, during which the records inserted at t are still remembered. Then, for any two adjacent periods t' and t $(t'<t)$, we compare their models m' and m on the basis of the records

Algorithm 1. Algorithm for cluster comparison and matching

Step	Action
	Input:
	- Set of models $M=\{m_1,...,m_k\}$, where m_i is the model derived at t_i.
	- Size of sliding window Θ
	- Threshold on the ratio of old documents inside a cluster τ-*old*
	Output: directed graph G of connected clusters, as a set of weighted edges
1	$G = \emptyset$;
2	**foreach** $i=1,...,k$ **do**
3	$m :=$ model derived at t_i ; $m' :=$ model derived at t_{i-1} ;
4	**foreach** cluster C in m **do**
5	$X:=Y:=$ set of docs in C that arrived in $[t_i$-$\Theta,t_{i-1})$; // "old" documents
6	**foreach** cluster C' in m' **do**
7	$f = \|C' \cap X\| / \|Y\|$; $g = \|C' \cap X\| / \|C\|$;
8	**if** $f >=$ τ-*old* **then**
9	$X = X - (C' \cap X)$ $G = G \cup \{t, ((C', C,) g)\}$,
10	**else** break;
11	**endif**
12	**end-foreach**
13	**end-foreach**
14	**end-foreach**

in m' that are still remembered and thus appear in m. We stress that these records are not only those inserted at t' but also older records that are still remembered in both t' and t. This FOCUS-variant for cluster comparison and matching is depicted in **algorithm 1** and described in the following.

The algorithm takes as input the set of models derived at the k periods of observation $t_1, ..., t_k$, the size of the sliding window Θ and a lower boundary τ-*old* on the ratio of old documents that may be common to a cluster in time period t_i and a cluster of the immediate previous period t_{i-1}. In this context, "old" documents are those encountered from period $t_i - \Theta$ until period t_{i-1}. For each time period t_i, these documents constitute set X (cf. line 5 of algorithm 1). The initial size of this set depends on the size of the sliding window; if Θ is set to 1, then only the documents inserted during t_{i-1} belong to X, since $t_i - \Theta = t_i - 1 = t_{i-1}$.

The output of algorithm 1 is a directed graph G, the nodes of which are clusters found at different periods. An edge emanates from a cluster *C-old* at period t_{i-1} and points to a cluster *C-new* at period t_i; its existence indicates that *C-old* has "survived into" *C-new*, in the sense that the two clusters overlap for at least τ-*old* records. This corresponds to the notion of "cluster survival" indicated by set overlap, as described in our cluster monitoring MONIC (Spiliopoulou et al., 2006).

To compute graph G, algorithm 1 processes each cluster C of the model m derived at period t_i in turn (line 4). It compares it with the clusters of model m' derived at the previous period (line 5), by taking records of X and finding clusters in m' that intersect with them. Such an intersecting cluster C' is a candidate as source node for a graph edge pointing to C, if the overlap between C' and X exceeds the threshold τ-*old* (line 9). To this purpose, we define two functions that return normalized overlap values. Function *overlapT(C,C',Θ)* ("overlap towards target") returns the intersection of C and C' subject to the common documents for the periods in the sliding window Θ, normalized to the size of the target cluster C.

$$overlapT(C,C',\Theta) = \frac{|C \cap C'|}{|C|}$$

Similarly, *overlapS(C,C',Θ)* ("overlap towards source") returns the intersection of C and C' subject to the common documents for the periods in the sliding window Θ, normalized to the size of the source cluster C'.

$$overlapS(C,C',\Theta) = \frac{|C \cap C'|}{|C'|}$$

In algorithm 1, line 7, we compute dynamic variants of these functions: In each iteration over model m', the set of shared records X is reduced by removing the records belonging to a cluster selected as satisfactory candidate and thus contributing an edge to the graph (cf. line 9). The dynamic variant of *overlapS()* is function f that computes the overlap between C' and X (rather than C) and normalizes it to the original size of the set of common records $|Y|$ (line 7). The dynamic counterpart of *overlapT()* is function g that normalizes the same overlap over C (line 7). The value returned by f in each iteration is compared to the threshold τ-*old*. If the threshold is satisfied, the edge from C' to C is added to the graph, enhanced with a weight equal to the value of g (line 9). A time period is also associated with each inserted edge; it is the period, in which the target cluster has been built (line 9).

By each successful test, X shrinks so that it gradually becomes empty or so small that the test for f fails (line 8). Then, the iterations over m' for cluster C stop and the next cluster of m is studied, until all clusters of m are considered.

It is apparent that Algorithm 1 is sensitive to the order of processing the clusters in each model (lines 4 and 6). Different orderings are feasible here, for example, on size (largest clusters first) or homogeneity (more homogeneous clusters first). The sliding window Θ also affects the results: Large windows result in big sets of old documents and thus increase the influence of past documents

Table 1. An example of cluster monitoring

period	new docs	all docs	Clusters
t_1	A,B,C,D,E,F,G,H	A,B,C,D,E,F,G,H	$C_1=\{A,B,C,D,E\}$ $C_2=\{F,G,H\}$
t_2	I,J,K,L,M,N,O,P	I,J,K,L,M,N,O,P $+ A,B,C,D,E,F,G,H$	$C_3=\{A,I,J,K\}$ $C_4=\{E,F,G,H\}$ $C_5=\{B,C,D,L,M,N,O,P\}$
t_3	Q,R,S,T,U,V,W	Q,R,S,T,U,V,W $+ I,J,K,L,M,N,O,P$	$C_6=\{K,L,O,P,Q,R,T,V,W\}$ $C_7=\{I,J,M,N,S,U\}$

period	cluster intersections	results (τ-*old* = 0.2)
t_2 vs t_1	$C_1 \cap C_5 = \{B, C, D\}$ $C_2 \cap C_5 \{\}$	$f(C_1,C_5)=1.0,\ g(C_1,C_5)=0.375$ $f(C_2,C_5)=0,\ g(C_2,C_5)=0$
t_3 vs t_2	$C_5 \cap C_6 = \{L, O, P\}$ $C_5 \cap C_7 = \{M, N\}$	$f(C_5,C_6)=0.75,\ g(C_5,C_6)=0.33$ $f(C_5,C_7)=0.5,\ g(C_5,C_7)=0.33$

upon current clusters and their topics. Small windows reduce this effect, and, consequently, also the likelihood of cluster survival.

In Table 1 we show and compare example clusterings over three adjacent time periods, setting the size of the sliding window to $\Theta=2$. At each period t "new docs" refers to the records/documents inserted at that period, while "all docs" refers to all documents taken into account at that period. The latter are new docs, inserted at this period, and those among the documents inserted earlier, which are still within the sliding window. For simplicity of notation, we use consecutive id-numbers for the clusters at adjacent periods, that is, $m_1=\{C_1,C_2\}$, $m_2=\{C_4,C_5,C_6\}$ and $m_3=\{C_6,C_7\}$. In the upper part of the table, we see the contents of each example cluster. In the lower part of the table, we observe the influence of C_1 upon C_5 during the second time period (retrospective monitoring for C_5) and the influence of C_5 upon the clusters of the next period (prospective monitoring for C_5).

Visualization of Linked Clusters

For a set of adjacent time periods $\{t_1,...,t_k\}$ and for any pair of adjacent periods t', t in it $(t'<t)$, our algorithm "links" each cluster of model m in t to those clusters of model m' of t' that have survived to it. This allows us to visualize the graph G built by Algorihm 1. We label each node/cluster in the graph with the most frequent words in the word-vectors it contains. This label is a "topic," encountered at the period where the cluster has been discovered. We further label each link with the words shared between the labels of the clusters it connects; this is the "subtopic" that survived from the old to the new time period. In Figure 1, we show a part of the graphical user interface we have designed to assist the human expert in inspecting the links among the clusters and studying the evolving topics represented by them.

The y-axis of Figure 1 depicts the consecutive periods under observation, starting from the earliest period at the bottom of the figure. In the main area of the visualization, we see the linked clusters. The width of a link reflects the value of g for the two linked clusters: the bigger the influence of old documents upon the current cluster, the wider is the link. When the user moves the mouse over the box representing a cluster, the box is highlighted and further information appears, including the cluster label and the value of the

Figure 1. Sample application: Graphical representation of evolving topics

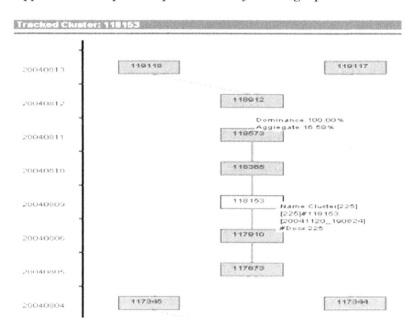

dynamic variant *f* of the function *overlapT()*. In Figure 1, we see a merge of two clusters in the second period of observation, that is, two clusters surviving in a single new one, as well as a cluster split in the last period.

Experimental Evaluation

We have performed a first set of experiments, in which we applied our method to a stream of vehicle workshop narratives, composed of 20 time periods with 15,000 to 80,000 narratives per period. The goal of these experiments was not the identification of new, emerging classes but rather to understand the method's behaviour and the influence of different parameters, like the sliding window size Θ.

We illustrate our results in the figures below. Each figure is partitioned in four charts, where the x-axis always represents the timeline of 20 periods. The chart in the upper left segment (ULS) shows the percentage of topics that survived for 2 to 20 periods: These are topics that appear both in the

source and the target node of at least one link in the graph *G* found by Algorithm 1. We call them "traceable topics;" the clusters containing them are "traceable clusters." The chart in the upper right segment (URS) shows the average cluster size. The chart in the bottom left segment (BLS) shows the average value of *f*, where the average is computed upon the clusters of each period. The chart in the bottom right segment (BRS) depicts the average value of *g*, computed in a similar way. Similarly to the values of *f* and *g*, those averages range in [0,1]; in BLC and BRC, we depict them as percentages.

In Figure 2, we study **cluster evolution** for a cluster size threshold τ-*MinClusterSize=30*, a sliding window size $\Theta=3$ and an overlap threshold τ-*old=0.2*. We vary τ-*MinSimilarity*, the similarity threshold among the children of a cluster in the dendrogram, assigning values within the range [0.2,0.5][4] and thus influencing the number of clusters considered by algorithm 1 at each period. In segment ULS of Figure 2, we observe a fluctuation in the number of traceable clusters;

Figure 2. Experimental results with minimum cluster size set to 30 documents

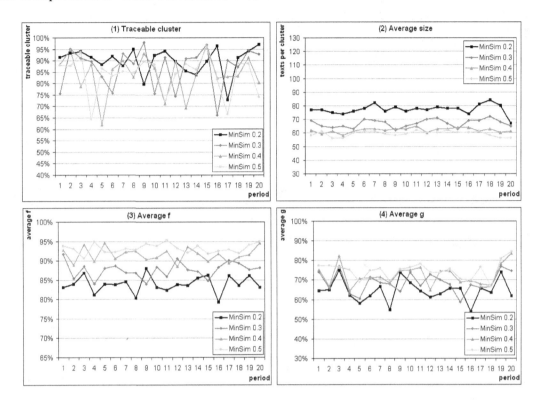

it is most likely due to the different numbers of documents/narratives arriving at each period and thus influencing the size of the clusters and the impact of old documents. In URS we can see that an increase in the similarity threshold results in a slight decrease of cluster size. A possible explanation is that a high threshold value results in fewer matches, for which only small and compact clusters qualify. In BLS and BRS, the curves for *f* and *g* evolve similarly across the time axis and are influenced by threshold changes in much the same way. The two curves have sharp negative peaks at the same periods as for the traceable clusters (ULS), but the asymmetry with respect to the effects of this threshold upon the number of traceable clusters is remarkable.

Figure 3 is the counterpart of Figure 2 for cluster size threshold τ-*MinClusterSize=50*. The curves for the traceable clusters, average *f* and average *g* are similar. The average cluster size

has increased by ca. 20%. This is expected, since this threshold determines the cut-off locations at the dendrogram produced by the hierarchical clustering algorithm.

In Figure 4, we keep the value of the similarity threshold constant, τ-*MinSimilarity=0.3*, set the minimum cluster size to 50 and vary the size of the sliding window Θ from 1 to 7 periods. The number of traceable clusters (ULS) does not seem to be affected by the window size. As Θ increases, the average values of *f* and *g* also increase slightly, since large values of Θ correspond to a higher impact of the old documents. This may also explain why the curves on average cluster size move closer to one another.

Figure 3. Experimental results with minimum cluster size set to 50 documents

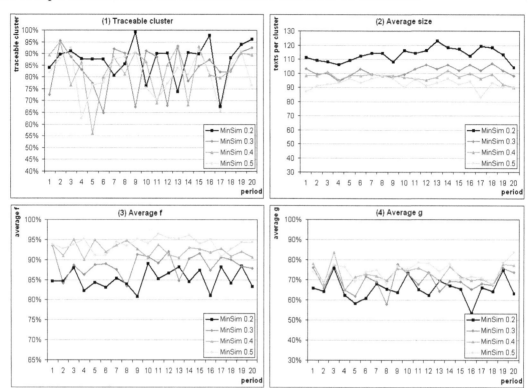

Figure 4. Experimental results for different sizes of the sliding window

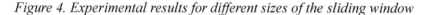
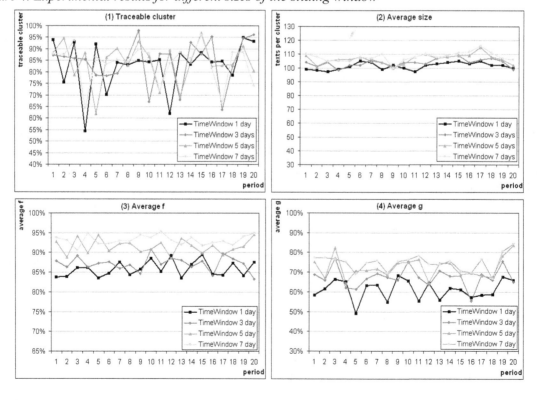

CONCLUSION

We have discussed the issue of **topic evolution** in a document stream, by first elaborating on literature advances and then presenting a new method that puts emphasis on small, noisy documents.

Relevant literature on **topic evolution** in a document stream has been initiated in the domain of "topic detection and tracking" but has concentrated on the discovery of thematic subjects rather than TDT stories and on the evolution of these themes as the underlying clusters evolve. The proposed algorithms are powerful but focus mainly on non-noisy documents; moreover, they do not allow for changes in the feature space. Methods for **cluster evolution** and for the detection of **cluster changes** may also be used for **topic evolution monitoring**. However, as with topic evolution, many methods of this group assume a trajectory over a static feature space. Generic frameworks for **cluster change** detection are more appropriate in this context, although they have not been a priori designed for **monitoring** over a **stream**.

Our **topic evolution** method is motivated by the need to identify potential classes in a stream of small noisy documents. This demand appears in areas like environmental monitoring where business news must be digested or filtered, in quality assessment where repair & maintenance reports must be studied for the discovery of emerging types of malfunction, in customer relationship management where customer reclamations, suggestions or complaints must be processed to understand customer expectations and to increase customer satisfaction. In those application areas, the documents constituting the stream vary in size, terminology[5], presence of slang or jargon terms and in grammatical/syntactic quality. To deal with such data, we have extended a generic framework for **cluster change** detection by a document model that describes a text with two complementary vectors. We have used a set-theoretic notion of overlap between old and new clusters instead of assuming a static trajectory. We have further enriched the framework by a visualization tool that depicts "linked" clusters, that is, old clusters that survive into new ones, and shows the topics and subtopics across each sequence of linked clusters.

Our method attempts to alleviate the problem of noisy documents by using a vector of words and a vector of n-grams and combining them for similarity computation and clustering. The robustness of this two-vector model remains yet to be tested. Also, clustering algorithms specifically designed for noisy datasets should be considered as an alternative. Text preprocessing steps (mainly NLP techniques) may reduce the noise in certain domains and are thus worth considering.

The survived, linked clusters discovered by our approach may give raise to new classes. This may hold for clusters that survive over several periods but also for sequences of linked clusters that are characterized by specific *subtopics*, that is, labels of links that indicate cluster survival but topic change. We are interested in formal and visual aids for the human expert, so that emerging and persistent classes be recognized.

REFERENCES

Aggarwal, C. C. (2005). On change diagnosis in evolving data streams. *IEEE TKDE, 17*(5), 587–600.

Aggarwal, C. C., & Yu, P. S. (2006). A framework for clustering massive text and categorical data streams. In *Proceedings of the 6th SIAM Conference on Data Mining (SDM '06)*.

Allan, J. (2002). *Introduction to topic detection and tracking*. Kluwer Academic Publishers.

Baron, S., & Spiliopoulou, M. (2005). Temporal evolution and local patterns. In Morik et al. (Eds.), *Local patterns detection* (pp. 190–206). Berlin Heidelberg: Springer-Verlag

Baron, S., Spiliopoulou, M., & Günther, O. (2003). Efficient monitoring of patterns in data mining environments. In *Proceedings of 7th East-European Conference on Advances in Databases and Information Systems (ADBIS '03)*.

Bartolini, I., Ciaccia, P., Ntoutsi, I., Patella, M., & Theodoridis, Y. (2004). A unified and flexible framework for comparing simple and complex patterns. In *Proceedings of ECML/PKDD 2004*, Pisa, Italy.

Ester, M., Kriegel, H.-P., Sander, J., Wimmer, M., & Xu, X. (1998). Incremental clustering for mining in a data warehousing environment. In *Proceedings of the 24th International Conference on Very Large Data Bases (VLDB '98)*.

Ganti, V., Gehrke, J., & Ramakrishnan, R. (1999a). A framework for measuring changes in data characteristics. In *Proceedings of the 18th ACM SIGACT-SIGMOD-SIGART Symposium on Principles of Database Systems (PODS '99)*, Philadelphia, Pennsylvania.

Ganti, V., Gehrke, J., & Ramakrishnan, R. (1999b). CACTUS: Clustering categorical data using summaries. In *Proceedings of 5th ACM SIGKDD International Conference on Knowledge Discovery and Data Mining (KDD '99)*.

Ganti, V., Gehrke, J., & Ramakrishnan, R. (2000). DEMON: Mining and monitoring evolving data. In *Proceedings of the 15th IEEE International Conference on Data Engineering (ICDE'2000)*.

Ipeirotis, P., Ntoulas, A., Cho, J., & Gravano, L. (2005). Modeling and managing content changes in text databases. In *Proceedings of the 20th IEEE International Conference on Data Engineering (ICDE '05)*.

Kontostathis, A., Galitsky, L., Pottenger, W., Roy, S., & Phelps, D. (2003). *A survey of emerging trend detection in textual data mining*. Springer Verlag.

Mei, Q., & Zhai, C. (2005). Discovering evolutionary theme patterns from text - An exploration of temporal text mining. In *Proceedings of 11th ACM SIGKDD International Conference on Knowledge Discovery and Data Mining (KDD '05)*, Chicago, Illinois.

Moringa, S. & Yamanichi, K. (2004). Tracking dynamics of topic trends using a finite mixture model. In *Proceedings of 10th ACM SIGKDD International Conference on Knowledge Discovery and Data Mining (KDD '04)*, Seattle, Washington.

Nasraoui, O., Cardona-Uribe, C., & Rojas-Coronel, C. (2003). TECNO-Streams: Tracking evolving clusters in noisy data streams with a scalable immune system learning method. In *Proceedings of the IEEE International Conference on Data Mining (ICDM '03)*. Melbourne, Australia.

Neill, D., Moore, A., Sabhnani, M., & Daniel, K. (2005). Detection of emerging space-time clusters. In *Proceedings of 11th ACM SIGKDD International Conferece on Knowledge Discovery and Data Mining (KDD '05)*, Chicago, Illinois.

Pottenger, W., & Yang, T. (2001). Detecting emerging concepts in textual data mining. In *Proceedings of 1st SIAM International Conference on Data Mining (SDM '01)*.

Roy, S., Gevry, D., & Pottenger, W. (2002). Methodologies for trend detection in textual data mining. In *Proceedings of the TEXTMINE '02 workshop at the 2nd SIAM International Conference on Data Mining*.

Salton, G., Wong, A., & Yang, C. S. (1975). A vector space model for automatic indexing. *Commun. ACM, 18*(11), 613–620.

Schult, R., & Spiliopoulou, M. (2006a). Expanding the taxonomies of bibliographic archives with persistent long-term themes. In *Proceedings of the 21st Annual ACM Symposium on Applied Computing (SAC '06)*, Avignon, France.

Schult, R., & Spiliopoulou, M. (2006b). Discovering emerging topics in unlabelled text collections. In *Proceedings of 10th East-European Conference on Advances in Databases and Information Systems (ADBIS '06)*. Thessaloniki, Greece.

Spiliopoulou, M., Ntoutsi, I., Theodoridis, Y., & Schult, R. (2006). MONIC – Modeling and monitoring cluster transitions. In *Proceedings of 12th ACM SIGKDD International Conference on Knowledge Discovery and Data Mining (KDD '06)*. Philadelphia, Pennsylvania.

Yang, H., Parthasarathy, S., & Mehta, S. (2005). A generalized framework for mining spatio-temporal patterns in scientific data. In *Proceedings of 11th ACM SIGKDD International Conference on Knowledge Discovery and Data Mining (KDD '05)*, Chicago, Illinois.

Zhong, S. (2005). Efficient streaming text clustering. *Neural Networks, 18*(5-6), 790-798.

ENDNOTES

[1] Fuzzy classification is beyond the scope of our study.

[2] The trajectory is determined by the feature space and the distance function. If the feature space changes over time, then the trajectory is not stationary and those methods cannot be used.

[3] Record ageing in a data stream is usually modeled by an ageing function, which ensures that old records are gradually forgotten, or by a sliding window, which determines that records outside the window are forgotten.

[4] The documents in the stream were too noisy for higher similarity threshold values.

[5] This implies that the feature space is volatile.

Chapter XI
Discovery of Latent Patterns with Hierarchical Bayesian Mixed–Membership Models and the Issue of Model Choice

Cyrille J. Joutard
GREMAQ, University Toulouse, France

Edoardo M. Airoldi
Princetone University, USA

Stephen E. Fienberg
Carnegie Mellon University, USA

Tanzy M. Love
Carnegie Mellon University, USA

ABSTRACT

Statistical models involving a latent structure often support clustering, classification, and other data-mining tasks. Parameterizations, specifications, and constraints of alternative models can be very different, however, and may lead to contrasting conclusions. Thus model choice becomes a fundamental issue in applications, both methodological and substantive. Here, we work from a general formulation of hierarchical Bayesian models of mixed-membership that subsumes many popular models successfully applied to problems in the computing, social and biological sciences. We present both parametric and nonparametric specifications for discovering latent patterns. Context for the discussion is provided by novel analyses of the following two data sets: (1) 5 years of scientific publications from the Proceedings of the National Academy of Sciences; (2) an extract on the functional disability of Americans age 65+ from the National Long Term Care Survey. For both, we elucidate strategies for model choice and our analyses bring new insights compared with earlier published analyses.

INTRODUCTION

Statistical models involving a latent structure often support clustering, classification, and other data-mining tasks. Because of their ability to deal with minimal information and noisy labels in a systematic fashion, statistical models of this sort have recently gained popularity, and success stories can be found in a variety of applications; for example, population genetics (Pritchard, Stephens, & Donnelly, 2000; Rosenberg, Pritchard, Weber, Cann, Kidd, & Zhivotovsky, 2002), scientific publications (Blei, Ng, & Jordan, 2003; Erosheva, Fienberg, & Lafferty, 2004; Griffiths & Steyvers, 2004), words and images (Barnard, Duygulu, de Freitas, Forsyth, Blei, & Jordan, 2003), disability analysis (Erosheva, 2002a; Erosheva, 2002b; Erosheva, 2003), fraud detection (Neville, Simsek, Jensen, Komoroske, Palmer, & Goldberg, 2005), biological sequences & networks (Airoldi, Blei, Fienberg, & Xing, 2006b). Specifications of alternative models for the same application can be very different, however, and may lead to contrasting conclusions—we report on two such examples in the introductory section to the case studies. As a consequence, *model choice* becomes a fundamental issue in applications, both methodological and substantive.

Specific models used to support the analyses in the previous list can all be viewed as special cases, or variants, of *hierarchical Bayesian mixed-membership models* (HBMMMs henceforth), a fairly general class of models originally characterized by Erosheva & Fienberg (2005). Furthermore, the class of HBMMMs is closely related to other popular unsupervised data-mining methods such as probabilistic principal component analysis (Tipping & Bishop, 1999), parametric independent component analysis, mixtures of Gaussians, factor analysis (Ghahramani, 2005), hidden Markov models (Rabiner, 1989), and state-space models (Airoldi & Faloutsos, 2004). Few papers recognize that these methods and diverse applications share with HBMMMs a number of

fundamental methodological issues such as that of model choice.

Briefly, HBMMMs allow each object of study, for example, words or individuals, to belong to more than one class, group, or cluster (Erosheva et al., 2004; Erosheva & Fienberg, 2005; Airoldi, Blei, Fienberg, & Xing, 2006a). They are Bayesian models specified in terms of a hierarchy of probabilistic assumptions that involve three sets of quantities:

* Observations, x
* Latent variables, θ
* Parameters for the patterns associated with the groups, or clusters, β

In other words, the quantities (x, θ, β) are organized in a directed acyclic graph. The likelihood of the data (in its general form) can then be written as follows:

$$\ell\left(x \mid \beta\right) = \int_{\theta} \Pi_{k=1}^{\infty} f(x, \theta \mid \beta_k) D_{\alpha}(d\theta), \qquad (1)$$

where the quantity $D_{\alpha}(d\theta)$ is a prior distribution over the latent variables with hyper-parameter α, and the product runs over the (possibly infinite) number of groups, or clusters, and associated patterns. During pattern discovery, that is, posterior inference, we condition on the observed data and maximize the likelihood with respect to the sets of parameters, β_k, that describe the patterns associated with the groups.

The focus in pattern discovery with HBMMMs is not on the variable amount of information about the labels for the objects, but rather it is on the hierarchy of probabilistic assumptions that we believe provide the structure underlying the data and ultimately lead to the likelihood function. Whatever the amount of information about the class labels, full, partial, minimal, or none, we simply treat the information as observations about the attributes and we condition upon it. The missing information about the labels or weights on the classes or groups is recovered during pattern discovery (i.e., posterior inference) as is the information about other nonobservable patterns. In this sense, HBMMMs are essentially *soft-clustering* models in that the *mixed-membership* error model for the labels associates each observation with a vector of memberships that sum to one. The parameters of this error model inform the average abundance of specific class labels without imposing hard constraints, for example, must-belong or must-not belong. Rather, the constraints are soft, probabilistic constraints.

The Issue of Model Choice

As we hinted in the discussion above, in these models classification and clustering tasks correspond to the same mathematical problem of maximizing the likelihood. This, in turn, resolves the mixed membership of observations to categories (which are typically observed only for a negligible portion of the data), and discovers the patterns underlying the data—in other words, we get maximum likelihood estimates for (θ, β). Figure 1 illustrates these concepts. A fundamental issue of HBMMMs is that of *model choice*, that is, the choice of the number of latent categories, groups, or clusters. Positing an explicit model for the category labels requires a choice regarding the number of existing

categories in the population, that is, the "choice" of the model. A parametric model for the labels would assume the existence of a predetermined number, K, of categories, whereas a nonparametric error model would let the number of categories grow with the data.

Figure 1 presents an illustrative example. The raw data (left panel) consist of 3 lists of words; namely {ARC, AND, ART, ANT}, {BIT, BOT, BET, BAT}, and {BAR, BUS, BIN, BAT}. We are interested in finding patterns (word templates) that generate the lists. A hypothetical model that posits 2 latent patterns (central panel) finds A** and B** as good descriptive patterns for the lists of words, and resolves the mixed memberships of lists to patterns, given the lists. A hypothetical model that posits 3 latent patterns (right panel) finds A**, **T, and B** as good descriptive patterns for the lists of words, and resolves the mixed memberships of lists to patterns, given the lists. What is the goal of the analysis? Which model suits it best? In this chapter, we explore and discuss methodology and strategies to answer these questions in the context an application. For now, note that the issue of model choice in this simple example translates into the question of "how many patterns?" there are, underlying the data. Furthermore, note that the issue of model choice depends crucially on the goals of the analysis. Following the intuition developed in the example, in a situation where

Figure 1. A simple example of a mixed membership model applied to word lists

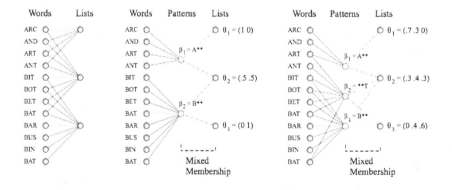

we believe the letter patterns tell us something substantive about the lists of words, we may be interested in estimating the membership of a new list to those patterns. Consider the new list {BAT, CAT, RAT}; in this case the model with 3 patterns would prove more useful in describing the list, when compared to the model with 2 patterns.

In the following sections, we explore the issue of model choice in the context of HBMMMs, both theoretically and computationally, by investigating the nexus between strategies for model choice, estimation strategies, and data integration in the context of data extracted from scientific publications and American elderly.

Overview of the Chapter

In this chapter, we present the following ideas and results: (1) we describe HBMMMs a class of models that respond to the challenges introduced by modern applications, and we characterize HBMMMs in terms of their essential probabilistic elements; (2) we identify the issue of "model choice" as a fundamental task to be solved in each applied data mining analysis that uses HBMMMs; (3) we survey several of the existing strategies for model choice; (4) we develop new model specifications, as well as use old ones, and we employ different strategies of model choice to find "good" models to describe problems involving text analysis and survey data; (5) we study what happens as we deviate from statistically sound strategies in order to cut down the computational burden, in a controlled experimental setting.

Although "common wisdom" suggests that different goals of the analysis (e.g., prediction of the topic of new documents or of the disability profile of a new person age 65 or over, vs. description of the whole collection of documents in terms of topics or of the elderly in terms of disability profiles) would lead us to choose different models, there are few surprises. In fact, from the case studies we learn that:

1. Independently of the goal of the analysis, for example, predictive versus descriptive, similar probabilistic specifications of the models often support similar "optimal" choices of K, that is, the number of latent groups and patterns;

2. Established practices aimed at reducing the computational burden while searching for the best model lead to biased estimates of the "optimal" choices for K, that is, the number of latent groups and patterns.

Arriving at a "good" model is a central goal of empirical analyses. These models are often useful in a predictive sense. Thus our analyses in the present chapter is relevant as input to (1) those managing general scientific journals as they re-examine current indexing schemes or considering the possible alternative of an automated indexing system, and (2) those interested in the implications of disability trends among the US elderly population as the rapid increase in this segment of the population raises issue of medical care and the provision of social security benefits.

TWO MOTIVATING CASE STUDIES

Our study is motivated by two recent analyses about a collection of papers published in the *Proceedings of the National Academy of Sciences* (PNAS) (Erosheva et al. 2004; Griffiths & Steyvers 2004), and by two recent analyses of National Long Term Care Survey data about disabled American elderly (Erosheva, 2002a; Erosheva, 2002b; Erosheva, 2003; Erosheva & Fienberg, 2005; Stallard, 2005).

PNAS Biological Sciences Collection (1997–2001)

Erosheva et al. (2004) and Griffiths and Steyvers (2004) report on their estimates about the number of latent topics, and find evidence that supports a small number of topics (e.g., as few as eight but perhaps a few dozen) *or* as many as 300 latent topics, respectively. There are a number of differences between the two analyses: the collections of papers were only partially overlapping (both in time coverage and in subject matter), the authors structured their dictionary of words differently, one model could be thought of as a special case of the other but the fitting and inference approaches had some distinct and nonoverlapping features. The most remarkable and surprising difference come in the estimates for the numbers of latent topics: Erosheva et al. (2004) focus on values like 8 and 10 but admit that a careful study would likely produce somewhat higher values, while Griffiths & Steyvers (2004) present analyses they claim support on the order of 300 topics! Should we want or believe that there are only a dozen or so topics capturing the breadth of papers in PNAS or is the number of topics so large that almost every paper can have its own topic? A touchstone comes from the journal itself. PNAS, in its information for authors (updated as recently as June 2002), states that it classifies publications in biological sciences according to 19 topics. When submitting manuscripts to PNAS, authors select a major and a minor category from a predefined list of 19 biological science topics (and possibly those from the physical and/or social sciences).

Here, we develop an alternative set of analyses using the version of the PNAS data on biological science papers analyzed in Erosheva et al. (2004). We employ both parametric and nonparametric strategies for model choice, and we make use of both text and references of the papers in the collection, in order to resolve this issue. This case study gives us a basis to discuss and assess the merit of the various strategies.

Disability Survey Data (1982–2004)

In the second example, we work with an excerpt of data from the National Long-Term Care Survey (NLTCS) to illustrate the important points of our analysis. The NLTCS is a longitudinal survey of the U.S. population aged 65 years and older with waves conducted in 1982, 1984 1989, 1984, 1999 and 2004. It is designed to assess chronic disability among the US elderly population especially those who show limitations in performing some activities that are considered normal for everyday living. These activities are divided into *activities of daily living* (ADLs) and *instrumental activities of daily living* (IADLs). The ADLs are basic activities of hygiene and healthcare: eating, getting in/out of bed, moving inside the house, dressing, bathing, and toileting. The IADLs are basic activities necessary to reside in the community: doing heavy housework, doing light housework, doing the laundry, cooking, grocery shopping, moving outside the house, traveling, managing money, taking medicine, and telephoning. The subset of data was extracted by Erosheva (2002a) from the analytic file of the public use data file of the NLTCS. It consists of combined data from the first four survey waves (1982, 1984, 1989, 1994) with 21,574 individuals and 16 variables (6 ADL and 10 IADL). For each activity, individuals are either disabled or healthy on that activity (in the data table, this is coded by 1 if the individual is disabled and 0 if he is healthy). We then deal with a contingency table. Of the $2^{b} = 6,536$ possible combinations of response patterns, only 3,152 are observed in the NLTCS sample.

Here we complement the earlier analyses of Erosheva (2002a) and Erosheva & Fienberg (2005). In particular, these earlier analyses focused primarily on the feasibility of estimation and model selection under the presumption that K was small, that is, equal or less than five. We focus on increasing the number of latent profiles to see if larger choices of K result in better descriptions of the data and to find the value of K which best fits the data.

CHARACTERIZING HBMMMS

There are a number of earlier instances of mixed-membership models that have appeared in the scientific literature, for example, see the review in Erosheva & Fienberg (2005). A general formulation due to Erosheva (2002a), and also described in Erosheva et al. (2004), characterizes the models of mixed-membership in terms of assumptions at four levels. Figure 2 shows a graphical representation of HBMM models and an example of one used in this chapter. In the presentation below, we denote subjects with $n \in [1,N]$ and observable response variables with $j \in [1,J]$.

A1–Population Level. Assume that there are K classes or subpopulations in the population of interest J distinct characteristics. We denote by $f(x_{nj} | \beta_{jk})$ the probability distribution of *j-th* response variable in the *k-th* subpopulation for the *n-th* subject, where β_{jk} is a vector of relevant parameters, $j \in [1,J]$, and $k \in [1,K]$. Within a subpopulation, the observed responses are assumed to be independent across subjects *and* characteristics.

A2–Subject Level. The components of the membership vector $\theta_n = (\theta_{n[1]}, ..., \theta_{n[k]})$ represent the mixed-membership of the *n-th* subject to the various subpopulations. The distribution of the observed response x_{nj} given the individual membership scores θ_n, is then:

$$\Pr(x_{nj} | \theta_n) = \sum_{k=1}^{K} \theta_{n[k]} f(x_{nj} | \beta_{jk}).$$

(2)

Conditional on the mixed-membership scores, the response variables x_{nj} are independent of one another and independent across subjects.

A3–Latent Variable Level. Assume that the vectors θ_n, that is, the mixed-membership scores of the *n-th* subject, are realizations of a latent variable with distribution D_a, parameterized by vector α. The probability of observing x_{nj}, given the parameters, is then:

$$\Pr(x_{nj} | \alpha, \beta) = \int \left(\sum_{k=1}^{K} \theta_{n[k]} f(x_{nj} | \beta_{jk}) \right) D_\alpha (d\theta).$$

(3)

A4–Sampling Scheme Level. Assume that the R independent replications of the J distinct response

Figure 2. Left: A graphical representation of hierarchical Bayesian models of mixed-membership. Right: Models of text and references used in this paper. Specifically, we pair replicates of variables $\{x_1^r, x_2^r\}$ with latent vectors $\{z_1^r, z_2^r\}$ that indicate which latent aspects inform the parameters underlying each individual replicate. The parametric and non-parametric version of the error models for the label discussed in the text refer to the specification of D_a - a Dirichlet distribution versus a Dirichlet process, respectively.

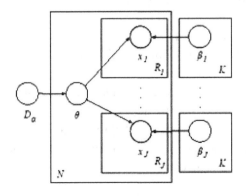

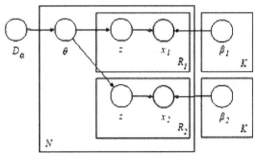

Models of text and references

variables corresponding to the *n-th* subject are independent of one another. The probability of observing $\{x_{n1}^r, \cdots, x_{nJ}^r\}_{r=1}^R$, given the parameters, is then:

$$\Pr(\{x_{n1}^r, \cdots, x_{nJ}^r\}_{r=1}^R \mid \alpha, \beta) =$$

$$\int \left(\prod_{j=1}^J \prod_{r=1}^R \sum_{k=1}^K \theta_{nk} f(x_{nj} \mid \beta_{jk}) \right) D_\alpha (d\theta). \quad (4)$$

The number of observed response variables is not necessarily the same across subjects, that is, $J = J_n$. Likewise, the number of replications is not necessarily the same across subjects and response variables, that is, $R = R_{nj}$.

Example 1: Latent Dirichlet Allocation

Our general framework encompasses popular data mining models, such as the one labeled as the "latent Dirichlet allocation" model (LDA) by Minka and Lafferty (2002) and Blei et al. (2003) for use in the analysis of scientific publications.

For the text component of the PNAS data: subpopulations correspond to latent "topic", indexed by k; subjects correspond to "documents", indexed by n; $J=1$, that is, there is only one response variable that encodes which "word" in the vocabulary is chosen to fill a position in a text of known length, so that j is omitted; positions in the text correspond to replicates, and we have a different number of them for each document, that is we observe n positions filled with words in the *n-th* document. The model assumes that each position in a document is filled with a word that expresses a specific topic, so that each document is the expression of possibly different topics. In order to do so, an explicit indicator variable z_n^r is introduced for each observed position in each document, which indicates the topic that expresses the corresponding word. The function:

$$f(x_n^r \mid \beta_k) = \Pr(x_n^r = 1 \mid z_n^r = k) = \text{Multinomial}\,(\beta_k, 1)$$

where β_k is a random vector the size of the vocabulary, say V, and $\sum_{v=1}^V \beta_{k[v]} = 1$. A mixed-membership vector Θ_n is associated to the *n-th* document, which encodes the topic proportions that inform the choice of words in that document, and it is distributed according to Da (i.e., a Dirichlet distribution). We obtain equation 2 integrating out the topic indicator variable z_n^r at the word level—the latent indicators z_n^r are distributed according to a *multinomial* $(\theta_n, 1)$.

Most of our analyses also incorporate the references and we use the generalization of LDA introduced in Erosheva et al. (2004) for $J=2$, that is, words and references which are taken to be independent.

The issue of model choice we introduced in the introduction translates into the choice about the number of nonobservable word and reference usage patterns (latent topics) that best describe a collection of scientific publications.

Example 2: Grade of Membership Model

The "Grade of Membership," or GoM, model is another specific model that can be cast in terms of mixed-membership. This model was first introduced by Woodbury in the 1970's in the context of medical diagnosis (Woodbury, Clive, and Garson (1978) and was developed further and elaborated upon in a series of papers and in Manton, Woodbury, and Tolley (1994). Erosheva (2002a) reformulated the GoM model as a HBMMM.

In the case of the disability survey data, there are no replications, that is, $R_n = 1$. However we consider several attributes of each elderly American, that is, $J=16$ daily activities. Further, the scalar parameter β_{jk} is the probability of being disabled on the activity j for a complete member of latent profile k, that is:

$$\beta_{jk} = P(x_j = 1 \mid \theta_k = 1)$$

Since we deal with binary data (individuals are either disabled or healthy), the probability distribution $f(x_j \mid \beta_{jk})$ is a Bernoulli distribution with parameter β_{jk}. Therefore, a complete member n of latent profile k is disabled on the activity j, that is, $x_{nj} = 1$, with probability β_{jk}. In other words, introducing a profile indicator variable z_{nj}, we have $P(x_{nj} = 1 \mid z_{nj} = k) = \beta_{jk}$. Each individual n is characterized by a vector of membership scores $\theta_n = (\theta_{n1}, ..., \theta_{nk})$. We assume that the membership scores θ_n follow the distribution D_a (for example a Dirichlet distribution with parameter $a = (a_1, ... a_k, ..., a_K)$. Note that the ratio $\alpha_k / \sum_k \alpha_k$ represents the proportion of the population that belongs to the k-th latent profile).

In this application, the issue of model choice translates into the choice about the number of nonobservable disability propensity profiles (latent profiles) that best describe the population of elderly Americans.

Relationship with Other Data Mining Methods

In order to situate HBMMMs in a familiar landscape, we discuss similarities with other *unsupervised* data mining methods. In fact, in many applications including those we present in this chapter, HBMMMs are used in an unsupervised fashion, with no information about class labels. Recall that in our problem we want to group observations about N subjects $\{x_n^{1:R_n}\}_{n=1}^N$ into, say, K groups. K-means clustering, for example, searches for K centroids $m_{1:K}$ that minimize:

$$MSE = \frac{1}{N} \sum_{k=1}^K \sum_{n=1}^N I(x_n^{1:R_n} \in k) \| x_n^{1:R_n} - m_k \|^2,$$

where the centroids $m_{1:K}$ are centers of respective clusters in the sense of Euclidean norm. Subjects have single group membership in K-means. In the mixture of Gaussians model, a popular HBMMM that extends K-means, the *MSE* scoring criterion is substituted by the likelihood $\sum_{n,k} \ell(n,k)$. Further, we have unknown mixed-membership vectors θ_n, that relax the single membership of K-means. The connection is given by the fact that the mixed-membership vectors θ_n, that is, the class abundances, have a specific form in K-means, that is, for the n-th subject we can write:

$$\theta_{n[k]} = \begin{cases} 1 & if \ k = j_n \\ 0 & otherwise, \end{cases}$$

where $j_n = \arg\min\{\ell(n,k) : k \in [1,K]\}$. In a general specification of HBMMMs we introduce D_a distributed mixed-membership vectors, θ_n, also unknown. Further, in HBMMMs it is possible to have a more complicated likelihood structure, which follows specifications in the section on characterizing HBMMMS.

Methods such as factor analysis (Spearman, 1904; Ghahramani, 2005) and Principal Component Analysis (Hotelling, 1933; Jolliffe, 1986) cannot be subsumed under the general formulation of HBMMMs, however, they too make use of statistical models that include latent patterns, that is, the factors and the components, in order to explain variability in the data. Alternatives exist for classification and clustering that are not *generative*, that is, approaches that are not based on a generating process for the data. Methods that fall under this category are very different in spirit; they study the properties of the cloud of data points with the goal of separating them directly, using some notion of distance. For example, manifold-based methods induce a smooth manifold from the geometry of the cloud of data points, and use the Euclidean distance on such manifold to separate them (Belkin & Niyogi, 2003). Support vector machines project the data points into a high dimensional linear space, and compute distances between them in such a space, implicitly, using a prespecified Kernel (Schölkopf & Smola, 2002). To conclude this brief review, note that HBMMMs also induce a notion of distance on the data space, implicitly, through the likelihood.

STRATEGIES FOR MODEL CHOICE

Although pathological examples can be built, where slightly different model specifications lead to quite different analyses and choices of key parameters, in real situations we expect models with similar probabilistic specifications to suggest roughly similar choices for the number of groups, K.

In our applications to the study of scientific publications and disability survey data we explore the issue of model choice by means of different criteria, of which two popular choices in the data mining community: namely, cross-validation (Hastie, Tibshirani & Friedman, 2001), and a Dirichlet process prior (Antoniak, 1974).

Choice Informed by the Ability to Predict

Cross-validation is a popular method to estimate the generalization error of a prediction rule (Hastie et al., 2001), and its advantages and flaws have been addressed by many in that context, for example, Ng (1997). More recently, cross-validation has been adopted to inform the choice about the number groups and associated patterns in HBM-MMs (Barnard et al., 2003; Wang, Mohanty, & McCallum, 2005)

Guidelines for the proper use of cross-validation in choosing the optimal number of groups K, however, have not been systematically explored. One of the goals of our case studies is that of assessing to what extent cross-validation can be "trusted" to estimate the underlying number of topics or disability profiles.

In particular, given the nonnegligible influence of hyperparameter estimates in the evaluation of the held-out likelihood, that is, the likelihood on the testing set, we discover that it is important

not to bias the analysis with "bad estimates" of such parameters, or with arbitrary choices that are not justifiable using preliminary evidence, that is, either in the form of prior knowledge, or outcome of the analysis of training documents. To this extent, estimates with "good statistical properties," for example, empirical Bayes or maximum likelihood estimates should be preferred to others (Carlin & Louis, 2005).

The Dirichlet Process Prior

Positing a Dirichlet process prior on the number of latent topics is equivalent to assuming that the number of latent topics grows with the log of the number of, say, documents or individuals (Ferguson, 1973; Antoniak, 1974). This is an elegant model selection strategy in that the selection problem becomes part of the model itself, although in practical situations it is not always possible to justify. A nonparametric alternative to this strategy, recently proposed (McAuliffe, Blei, & Jordan, 2006), uses the Dirichlet Process prior is an infinite dimensional prior with a specific parametric form as a way to mix over choices of K. This prior appears reasonable, however, for static analyses of scientific publications that appear in a specific journal. Kuma, Raghavan, Rajagopalan, Sivakumar, Tomkins, and Upfal (2000) specify toy models of evolution, which justify the scale-free nature of the relation between documents and topics using the Dirichlet process prior for exploratory data analysis purposes.

Other Criteria for Model Choice

The statistical and data mining literatures contain many criteria and approaches to deal with the issue of model choice, for example, reversible jump MCMC techniques, Bayes factors and other marginal likelihood methods, cross-validation, and penalized likelihood criteria such as the Bayesian information criterion (BIC) (Schwartz, 1978; Pelleg & Moore 2000), the Akaike information criterion (AIC) (Akaike, 1973), the deviance information criterion (DIC) (Spiegelhalter, Best, Carlin, & Van der Linde, 2002), minimum description length (MDL) (Chakrabarti, Papadimitriou, Modha, & Faloutsos, 2004). See Han & Kamber (2000) for a review of solutions in the data mining community.

AIC has a frequentist motivation and tends to pick models that are too large when the number of parameters is large—it does not pay a high enough penalty. BIC and DIC have Bayesian motivations and thus fit more naturally with the specifications in this chapter. Neither is truly Bayesian for HBMMMs; however DIC involves elements that can be computed directly from MCMC calculations, and the variational approximation to the posterior (described in detail below) allows us to integrate out the nuisance parameters in order to compute an approximation to BIC for different values of K. Therefore, we explore the use of both DIC and BIC in connection with the variational approximation for the NLTCS disability data where we can look at both criteria in action together.

CASE STUDY: PNAS SCIENTIFIC COLLECTION 1997–2001

As mentioned previously, our analyses are motivated by two recent analyses of extracts of papers published in the *Proceedings of the National Academy of Sciences* (PNAS). Erosheva et al. (2004, 2005) and Griffiths & Steyvers (2004) report on wildly different numbers of latent topics, as few as 8 but perhaps a few dozen versus 300. We attempt to provide an explanation for the divergent results here. In the process we explore how to perform the model selection for hierarchical Bayesian models of mixed-membership. After choosing an "optimal" value for the number of topics, K^*, and its associated words and references usage patterns, we also examine the extent to which they correlate with the "actual" topic categories specified by the authors.

Modeling Text and References

In this section we introduce model specifications to analyze the collection of papers published in PNAS, which were submitted by the respective authors to the section on biological sciences. All our models can be subsumed into the general formulation of HBMMMs previously presented. We organize them into finite and infinite mixture models, according to the dimensionality of the prior distribution, D_a, posited at the latent variable level—assumption A3.

We characterize an article, or document, by the words in its abstract and the references in its bibliography. Introducing some notation, we observe a collection of N documents, $D_{1:N}$. The n-th document is represented as $D_n = (x_{1n}^{1:R_{1n}}, x_{2n}^{1:R_{2n}})$ where $1n$ is a word in the abstract and $2n$ is a reference in the bibliography, and where $1n$ is the number of positions in the text of the abstract occupied by a word, and $2n$ is the number of items in the bibliography occupied by a reference. As in the latent Dirichlet allocation example previously introduced, positions (the order of which does not matter), or spots, in the text of the abstracts are modeled as multinomial random variables with 1 coordinates and unitary size parameter. That is, random variables are associated with spots in the text and their values encode which word in the vocabulary (containing 1 distinct words) occupies a specific spot. The number of spots is observed, R_{1n}. We model the references in a similar fashion. Each item in the bibliography is modeled as multinomial random variables with 2 coordinates and unitary size parameter. Values of these variables encode which reference in the set of known citations (2 of them) was used as a specific bibliography item. Again, the number of bibliography items is observed, R_{2n}. That is, words and references are vectors of size V_1, respectively V_2, with a single nonzero, unitary component. We denote by $x_{jn[v]}^r$ the v-th component of x_{jn}^r, for $j=1,2$.

Below, whenever the analysis refers to a single document, the document index n is omitted.

a) Finite Mixture: The Model

In the finite mixture case, we posit the following generative process for each document.

1. Sample the mixed-membership vector $\theta \sim D_a$.
2. For each of the 1 spots in the text of the abstract:
2.1. Sample the topic indicator:

$z_1^r \mid \theta \sim Multinomial(\theta, 1)$
2.2. Sample $x_1^r \mid z_1^r \sim Multinomial(\beta_1 z_1^r, 1)$.
3. For each of the R_2 items in the bibliography:
3.1. Sample topic indicator $z_2^r \mid \theta \sim Multinomial(\theta, 1)$
3.2. Sample $x_2^r \mid z_2^r \sim Multinomial(\beta_2 z_2^r, 1)$.

In this model, α is a Dirichlet $(\alpha_1, \ldots \alpha_K)$ distribution with $\alpha_k = \alpha$ for all k, and (β_1, β_2) are two matrices of size $(V_1 \times K)$ and $(V_2 \times K)$ respectively. The topic indicators, (z_1^r, z_2^r), are latent column vectors of with K coordinates, only one of which assumes a unitary value.

The hyper-parameters of this model are the symmetric Dirichlet parameter α, and the multinomial parameters for words, $(\beta_{1[, k]})$ and references, $(\beta_{2[, k]})$ for each of the latent topics $k=1,\ldots,K$. That is, through pairs of corresponding columns of the two β matrices we define a parametric representation of the K subpopulations (see assumption A1), which we refer to as topics in this application. Technically, they are pairs of latent distributions over the vocabulary and the set of known citations. In other words, element (v, k) of β_1 encodes the probability of occurrence of the v-th word in the vocabulary (containing 1 distinct words) when the k-th topic is active, that is, $\beta_{1[v,k]} = \Pr(x_{1[v]}^r = 1 \mid z_{1[k]}^r)$, with the constraint that $\sum_v \beta_{1[v,k]} = 1$ for each k. Similarly, element (v, k) of β_2 encodes the probability of occurrence of the v-th reference in the set of known citations

(2 of them) when the k-th topic is active. Note that, through the latent topic indicators, we associate each spot in the text, that is, each word instance, with a latent topic. As a consequence, separate instances of the v-th vocabulary word in the same abstract[1] can be generated from different topics.

In this finite mixture model, we assume that the number of latent topics is unknown but fixed at K. Our goal is to find the optimal number of topics, $K*$, which gives the best description of the collection of scientific articles.

b) Infinite Mixture: The Model

In the infinite mixture case we posit a simpler and more traditional type of clustering model, by assuming that each article D_n is generated by one single topic. However, in this case we do not need to fix the unknown number of topics, K, prior to the analysis.

The infinite mixture model is based upon a more compact representation of a document, $D_n = (x_{1n}, x_{2n})$, in terms of a vector of word counts:

$$x_{1n} = \sum_{r=1}^{R_1} x_{1n}^r$$

of size 1, and a vector of reference counts,

$$x_{2n} = \sum_{r=1}^{R_2} x_{2n}^r,$$

of size 2. In fact, given that word instances and bibliography items in the same document cannot be generated by different topics, we do not need the finer representation $(x_{1n}^{1:R_1}, x_{2n}^{1:R_2})$. Further, given that each article can only be generated by a single topic, the mixed membership vectors, $\theta_{1:N}$, become single membership vectors. This means that each θ_n has a single unitary component, while the remaining components equal zero. However, in the infinite mixture model we do not assume a fixed dimensionality, K, for the membership vectors $\theta_{1:N}$. That is, prior to the analysis, the number of subpopulations (see assumption A1) is unknown and possibly infinite.

It is more convenient to write the infinite mixture model as a generative process for the whole collection of documents altogether, $D_{1:N}$, rather than for a single document as in the previous section. In order to promote clarity in this setting, we change the notation slightly. Instead of working with the single membership vectors, $\theta_{1:N}$, it is more convenient to introduce a latent topic indicator vector, c, whose *n-th* component, $c_{[n]}$, encodes the topic assignment of the corresponding document, D_n. That is, $c_{[n]} = k$ if $\theta_{n[k]} = 1$ for $n=1,\ldots,N$. Note that, because of single membership, $\theta_{n[k]} = I(c_{[n]} = k)$ for all k. Further, because of the restriction of one topic per document, if $\theta_{n[k]} = 1$ then $z^r_{1n[k]} = z^r_{2n[k]} = 1$ for all word instances and bibliography items r. This collection of equalities, for a given document D_n, is summarized and simplified by writing $c_{[n]} = k$.

We can now posit the generative process for the whole collection of documents, $D_{1:N}$.

1. $c \sim D_\alpha$.
2. For each of the K distinct values of c:
2.1. $\beta_{1[1:V_1, k]} \sim Dirichlet(\eta_{1[1]},\ldots,\eta_{1[V1]})$.
2.2. $\beta_{2[1:V_2, k]} \sim Dirichlet(\eta_{2[1]},\ldots,\eta_{2[V1]})$.
3. For each of the N documents:
3.1. $x_{1n} \mid \beta_1, c_{[n]} \sim Multinomial(\beta_{1[1:V_1, c_{[n]}]}, R_{1n})$.
3.2. $x_{2n} \mid \beta_2, c_{[n]} \sim Multinomial(\beta_{2[1:V_2, c_{[n]}]}, R_{2n})$.

In this model, D_α is the Dirichlet process prior with parameter α, introduced and discussed in Aldous (1985) and Neal (2000). The distribution D_α models the prior probabilities of topic assignment for the collection of documents. In particular, for the *n-th* document, given the set of assignments for the remaining documents, $c_{[-n]}$, this prior puts on the *k-th* topic (out of K distinct topic assignment observed in $c_{[-n]}$) a mass that is proportional to the number of documents associated with it. It also puts prior mass on a new, *(K+1)-th* topic, which is distinct from the topic assignments $(1,\ldots,K)$ observed in $c_{[-n]}$. That is,

D_α entails prior probabilities for each component of c as follows:

$$\Pr(c_{[n]} = k \mid c_{[-n]}) = \begin{cases} \dfrac{m(-n,k)}{N-1+\alpha} & \text{if } m(-n,k) > 0 \\[2ex] \dfrac{\alpha}{N-1-\alpha} & \text{if } k = K(-n)+1 \\[2ex] 0 & otherwise \end{cases}$$

where $c_{[-n]}$ denotes the latent topic indicator vector without the *n-th* component; $m(-n, k)$ is the number of documents that are associated with the *k-th* topic, other than the *n-th* document, that is, $m(-n,k) = \sum_{i=1}^n I(c_{[i]} = k, i \neq n)$; and $K(-n)$ is the number of observed, distinct topics that are associated with at least one document, other than the *n-th* document.

The hyper-parameters of this model are the scaling parameter of the Dirichlet process prior, α, and the two vectors of Dirichlet parameters, (η_1, η_2), that control the latent topics of words and references, respectively. Note that the topics, that is, latent pairs of distributions, are not hyper-parameters of the model in our specification of the infinite mixture model. Rather, we smooth the topics by positing a pair of Dirichlet priors on them, and the corresponding parameter vectors (η_1, η_2) become the hyper-parameters at the top of the model hierarchy. In our implementation we assume symmetric Dirichlet priors for the topics, such that $\eta_{1[k]} = \eta_1$ scalar, and $\eta_{2[k]} = \eta_2$ scalar, for all components $k=1,\ldots,K$.

In this model, we assume that the number of latent topics, K, is unknown and possibly infinite, through the prior for c, D_α. In order to find the number of topics that best describes the collection of scientific articles, we study the posterior distribution of c.

Inference

In this we develop posterior inference for both the finite and infinite mixture models above. In particular, we use variational methods for the finite mixture model and Monte Carlo Markov chain (MCMC) methods for the infinite mixture model.

a) Finite Mixture: Inference

In the finite mixture case, we assume the number of topics ($K<\infty$) is fixed during inference. Unfortunately, the likelihood of a document according to this model:

$$p(x_1^{1:R_1}, x_2^{1:R_2} | \alpha, \beta_1, \beta_2) \qquad (6)$$
$$= \int \prod_{j=1}^{J} \left(\prod_{r=1}^{R_1} \sum_{k=1}^{K} \prod_{v=1}^{V_1} (\theta_k \beta_{1[v,k]})^{x_{1[v]}^r} \right) \left(\prod_{r=1}^{R_2} \sum_{k=1}^{K} \prod_{v=1}^{V_2} (\theta_k \beta_{2[v,k]})^{x_{2[v]}^r} \right) D_\alpha(d\theta)$$

does not have a closed form solution. We need the likelihood to compute the joint posterior distribution of the mixed-membership scores and the topic and reference latent indicator vectors:

$$p(\theta, z_1^{1:R_1}, z_2^{1:R_2} | x_1^{1:R_1}, x_2^{1:R_2}, \alpha, \beta_1, \beta_2) =$$
$$\frac{p(\theta, z_1^{1:R_1}, z_2^{1:R_2}, x_1^{1:R_1}, x_2^{1:R_2} | \alpha, \beta_1, \beta_2)}{p(x_1^{1:R_1}, x_2^{1:R_2} | \alpha, \beta_1, \beta_2)} \qquad (7)$$

at the denominator of the right hand side of equation 7. The variational method prescribes the use of a mean-field approximation to the posterior distribution in equation 7. Such an approximation leads to a lower bound for the likelihood of a document, which depends upon a set of free parameters ($\gamma, \phi_1^{1:R_1}, \phi_2^{1:R_2}$) for each individual. These free parameters are introduced in the mean-field approximation, and are set to minimize the Kullback-Leibler (KL henceforth) divergence between true and approximate posteriors.

The "variational EM" algorithm we develop for performing posterior inference (see Figure 3) is therefore an approximate EM algorithm. During

Figure 3. The variational EM algorithm to solve the Bayes problem in finite mixture model of text and references, described above (finite mixture case). Note, the M step updates (steps 7 and 8) are performed incrementally in our implementation, within step 6 of the algorithm outlined above, thus speeding up the overall computation.

Variational EM $\left(\{x_{1n}^{1:R_{1n}}, x_{2n}^{1:R_{2n}}\}_{n=1}^{N} \right)$

1. initialize $\alpha_{[k]} := 1/K$ for all k
2. initialize $\beta_{1[kv]} := 1/V_1$ for all v and k
3. initialize $\beta_{2[kv]} := 1/V_2$ for all v and k
4. **do**
5.   for $n = 1$ to N
6. $(\gamma_n, \phi_{1n}^{1:R_{1n}}, \phi_{2n}^{1:R_{2n}}) \longleftarrow$ **Mean-Field Lower-Bound** $(x_{1n}^{1:R_{1n}}, x_{2n}^{1:R_{2n}})$
7. $\beta_{1[vk]} \propto \sum_{n=1}^{N} \sum_{r=1}^{R_{1n}} \phi_{1n[k]}^r x_{1n[v]}^r$ for all v and k
8. $\beta_{2[vk]} \propto \sum_{n=1}^{N} \sum_{r=1}^{R_{2n}} \phi_{2n[k]}^r x_{2n[v]}^r$ for all v and k
9.   normalize the columns of β_1 and β_2 to sum to 1
10.   find pseudo MLE for α using Newton-Raphson—see main text
11. **until** convergence
12. **return** $(\alpha, \beta_1, \beta_2)$

the M step, we maximize the lower bound for the likelihood over the hyperparameters of the model, $(\alpha, \beta_1, \beta_2)$, to obtain to (pseudo) maximum likelihood estimates. During the E step, we tighten the lower bound for the likelihood by minimizing the KL divergence between the true and the approximate posteriors over the free parameters, $\gamma, \phi_1^{1:R_1}, \phi_2^{1:R_2}$, given the most recent estimates for the hyperparameters.

In the M step, we update the hyper-parameters of the model, $(\alpha, \beta_1, \beta_2)$ by maximizing the tight lower bound for the likelihood over such hyperparameters. Given the most recent updates of the free parameters the bound depends on, $\gamma, \phi_1^{1:R_1}, \phi_2^{1:R_2}$. This leads to the following (pseudo) maximum likelihood estimates for the parameters:

$$\beta_{1[vk]} \propto \sum_{n=1}^{N} \sum_{r=1}^{R_1} \phi_{1n[k]}^{r} x_{1n[v]}^{r},$$

$$\beta_{2[vk]} \propto \sum_{n=1}^{N} \sum_{r=1}^{R_2} \phi_{2n[k]}^{r} x_{2n[v]}^{r},$$

where n is the document index, introduced above. The document index is necessary as we make use of the counts about specific words and references observed in all documents in order to estimate the corresponding conditional probabilities of occurrence, that is, the latent topics. Unfortunately a closed form solution for the (pseudo) maximum likelihood estimates of α does not exist. We can produce a method that is linear in time by using Newton-Raphson, with the following gradient and Hessian for the log-likelihood

$$\frac{\partial L}{\partial \alpha_{[k]}} = N\left(\Psi\left(\sum_{k=1}^{K} \alpha_{[k]}\right) - \Psi(\alpha_{[k]}) \right) + \quad (8)$$

$$\sum_{n=1}^{N} \left(\Psi(\gamma_{n[k]}) - \Psi\left(\sum_{k=1}^{K} \gamma_{n[k]}\right) \right),$$

$$\frac{\partial L}{\partial \alpha_{[k_1]} \alpha_{[k_2]}} = N\left(\delta_{k_1=k_2} \cdot \Psi'\left(\alpha_{[k_1]}\right) - \Psi'\left(\sum_{k_2=1}^{K} \alpha_{[k_2]}\right) \right). \quad (9)$$

Figure 4. The mean-field approximation to the likelihood for the finite mixture model of text and references, described above (finite mixture case).

Mean-Field Lower-Bound $\left(x_1^{1:R_1}, x_2^{1:R_2} \right)$

1. initialize $\phi_{1[k]}^{r} := 1/K$ for all r and k
2. initialize $\phi_{2[k]}^{r} := 1/K$ for all r and k
3. initialize $\gamma_{[k]} := \alpha_{[k]} + R_1/K + R_2/K$ for all k
4. do
5.   for $r = 1$ to R_1
6.   for $k = 1$ to K
7. $\phi_{1[k]}^{r} \propto \beta_{1[vk]} \times \exp\left(\Psi(\gamma_{[k]}) - \Psi\left(\sum_{k=1}^{K} \gamma_{[k]}\right) \right)$
8.   normalize ϕ_1^r to sum to 1
9.   for $r = 1$ to R_2
10.   for $k = 1$ to K
11. $\phi_{2[k]}^{r} \propto \beta_{2[vk]} \times \exp\left(\Psi(\gamma_{[k]}) - \Psi\left(\sum_{k=1}^{K} \gamma_{[k]}\right) \right)$
12.   normalize ϕ_2^r to sum to 1
13. $\gamma = \alpha + \sum_{r=1}^{R_1} \phi_1^r + \sum_{r=1}^{R_2} \phi_2^r$
14. until convergence
15. return $(\gamma, \phi_1^{1:R_1}, \phi_2^{1:R_2})$

The variational EM algorithm is summarized in Figure 3.

In the approximate E step, we update the free parameters for the mean-field approximation of the posterior distribution in Equation 7, $\gamma, \phi_1^{1:R_1}, \phi_2^{1:R_2}$, given the most recent estimates of the hyper-parameters of the model, $(\alpha, \beta_1, \beta_2)$, for each individual as follows:

$$\phi_{1[k]}^r \propto \prod_{v=1}^{V_1} \left[\beta_{[vk]} \times \exp\left(\Psi(\gamma_{[k]}) - \Psi\left(\sum_{k=1}^{K} \gamma_{[k]} \right) \right) \right]^{x_{1[v]}^r},$$

(10)

$$\phi_{2[k]}^r \propto \prod_{v=1}^{V_2} \left[\beta_{2[vk]} \times \exp\left(\Psi(\gamma_{[k]}) - \Psi\left(\sum_{k=1}^{K} \gamma_{[k]} \right) \right) \right]^{x_{2[v]}^r},$$

(11)

$$\gamma_{[k]} = \alpha_{[k]} + \sum_{r=1}^{R_1} \phi_{1[k]}^r + \sum_{r=1}^{R_2} \phi_{[k]}^r.$$

(12)

This minimizes the posterior KL divergence between true and approximate posteriors, at the document level, and leads to a new lower bound for the likelihood of the collection of documents. Note that the products over words and references in Equations 10 and 11 serve the purpose of selecting the correct probabilities of occurrence in the respective vocabularies, which correspond to the word and reference observed at a specific position, (r_1, r_2), in the document. That is, the updates of the free parameters $(\phi_{1[k]}^{r_1}, \phi_{2[k]}^{r_2})$ only depend on the probabilities $(\beta_{1[v_1, k]}, \beta_{2[v_2, k]})$, where $v_1 := \{v \in [1, V_1] \, s.t. \, x_{1[v]}^{r_1} = 1\}$ and $v_2 := \{v \in [1, V_2] \, s.t. \, x_{2[v]}^{r_2} = 1\}$. Using this notation, the updates simplify to:

$$\phi_{1[k]}^{r_1} \propto \beta_{1[v_1 k]} \times \exp\left(\Psi(\gamma_{[k]}) - \Psi\left(\sum_{k=1}^{K} \gamma_{[k]} \right) \right)$$

$$\phi_{2[k]}^{r_2} \propto \beta_{2[v_2 k]} \times \exp\left(\Psi(\gamma_{[k]}) - \Psi\left(\sum_{k=1}^{K} \gamma_{[k]} \right) \right)$$

The mean-field approximation to the likelihood we described above is summarized in Figure 4.

In order to develop the mean-field approximation for the posterior distribution in equation 7 we used in the E step above, we posit N independent fully factorized joint distributions over the latent variables, one for each document:

$$q(\theta, z_1^{1:R_1}, z_2^{1:R_2} \mid \gamma, \phi_1^{1:R_1}, \phi_2^{1:R_2}) =$$

$$q(\theta \mid \gamma) \left(\prod_{r_1=1}^{R_1} q(z_1^{(r_1)} \mid \phi_1^{(r_1)}) \prod_{r_2=1}^{R_2} q(z_2^{(r_2)} \mid \phi_2^{(r_2)}) \right),$$

which depends on the set of previously mentioned free parameters, $(\gamma, \phi_1^{1:R_1}, \phi_2^{1:R_2})$. The mean-field approximation consists in finding an approximate posterior distribution:

$$\tilde{p}(\theta, z_1^{1:R_1}, z_2^{1:R_2} \mid \tilde{\gamma}, \tilde{\phi}_1^{1:R_1}, \tilde{\phi}_2^{1:R_2}, \alpha, \beta_1, \beta_2),$$

where the conditioning on the data is now obtained indirectly, trough the free parameters:

$$\tilde{\gamma} = \tilde{\gamma}\left(x_1^{1:R_1}, x_2^{1:R_2} \right),$$

$$\tilde{\phi}_1^{1:R_1} = \tilde{\phi}_1^{1:R_1}\left(x_1^{1:R_1}, x_2^{1:R_2} \right),$$

$$\tilde{\phi}_2^{1:R_2} = \tilde{\phi}_2^{1:R_2}\left(x_1^{1:R_1}, x_2^{1:R_2} \right).$$

The factorized distribution leads to a lower bound for the likelihood; in fact it is possible to find a closed form solution to the integral in Equation 6 by integrating the latent variables out with respect to the factorized distribution. An approximate posterior, $\tilde{p}$, is computed by substituting the lower bound for the likelihood at the denominator of equation 7. The mean-field approximation in then obtained by minimizing the Kullback-Leibler divergence between the true and the approximate posteriors, over the free parameters.

The mean-field approximation has been used in many applications over the years (Bathe, 1996; Parisi, 1988; Rustagi, 1976; Sakurai, 1985). Intuitively, the approximation aims at reducing a complex problem into a simpler one by "decoupling the degrees of freedom in the original problem." Such decoupling is typically obtained

Box 1. Equation 13

$$\Pr(c_{[n]} = k \mid D, c_{[-n]}) \propto \frac{m(-n,k)}{N-1+\alpha}$$

$$\times \binom{R_{1n}}{x_{1n}} \frac{\Gamma(\eta_1 + \sum_v \sum_{i \neq n: c_i = k} x_{1i[v]})}{\prod_v \Gamma(\eta_1 / V_1 + \sum_{i \neq n: c_i = k} x_{1i[v]})} \frac{\prod_v \Gamma(x_{1n[v]} + \eta_1 / V_1 + \sum_{i \neq n: c_i = k} x_{1i[v]})}{\Gamma(\sum_v x_{1n[v]} + \eta_1 + \sum_v \sum_{i \neq n: c_i = k} x_{1i[v]})}$$

$$\times \binom{R_{2n}}{x_{2n}} \frac{\Gamma(\eta_2 + \sum_v \sum_{i \neq n: c_i = k} x_{2i[v]})}{\prod_v \Gamma(\eta_2 / V_2 + \sum_{i \neq n: c_i = k} x_{2i[v]})} \frac{\prod_v \Gamma(x_{2n[v]} + \eta_2 / V_2 + \sum_{i \neq n: c_i = k} x_{2i[v]})}{\Gamma(\sum_v x_{2n[v]} + \eta_2 + \sum_v \sum_{i \neq n: c_i = k} x_{2i[v]})}$$

via an expansion that involves additional, free parameters that are problem dependent, for example, $\{\gamma_n, \phi_{1n}^{1:R_1}, \phi_{2n}^{1:R_2}\}_{n=1}^N$, in our model above. A thorough treatment of such methods, which focus on applications to statistics and machine learning, is given in Jordan, Ghahramani, Jaakkola, and Saul (1999), Wainwright and Jordan (2003), Xing, Jordan, and Russell (2003). We have adapted these methods for other applications in work we hope to report on in the near future.

b) Infinite Mixture: Inference

In the infinite mixture case, we assume the total number of topics, K, to be unknown and possibly infinite. The posterior distribution of c, which is the goal of the posterior inference in this model, cannot be derived in closed form. However, the component-specific full conditional distributions, that is, $\Pr(c_{[n]} \mid c_{[-n]})$ for $n=1,\ldots,N$, are known up to a normalizing constant. Therefore we can explore the desired posterior distribution of the vector c through MCMC sampling methods.

Following algorithm 3 in Neal (2000), we de-

rive the full conditional distribution of the topic assignment vector. The full conditional probability that document D_n belongs in an existing topic k, given all documents, D, and the topic assignment of all other documents, $c_{[-n]}$, is given by equation 13 in Box 1, where $c_{[-n]}$ is the topic assignment vector for all documents other than n. The full conditional probability that document D_n belongs to a topic which no other D_j belongs to is shown in Box 2.

The sparseness of D and symmetry of the Dirichlet prior leads to forms of equations 13 and 14 that are more quickly computed.

The parameters of the model estimated in this way are the vector c of topic assignments and the total number of topics, K. The posterior distributions of c and K can be found using a Gibbs sampler with these full conditional distributions as shown in Figure 5.

In order to assess convergence of the Markov chain, we examine the total number of topics (which varies by Gibbs sample) and consider

Box 2. Equation 14

$$\Pr(c_{[n]} \neq c_{[i]} \forall i \neq n \mid D, c_{[-n]}) \propto \frac{\alpha}{N-1+\alpha}$$

$$\times \binom{R_{1n}}{x_{1n}} \frac{\Gamma(\eta_1)}{\Gamma(\eta_1 / V_1)^{V_1}} \frac{\prod_v \Gamma(x_{1n[v]} + \eta_1 / V_1)}{\Gamma(\sum_v x_{1n[v]} + \eta_1)} \binom{R_{2n}}{x_{2n}} \frac{\Gamma(\eta_2)}{\Gamma(\eta_2 / V_2)^{V_2}} \frac{\prod_v \Gamma(x_{2n[v]} + \eta_2 / V_2)}{\Gamma(\sum_v x_{2n[v]} + \eta_2)}$$

Figure 5. The MCMC algorithm to find posterior distribution of classification in the infinite mixture model of text and references, described above (infinite mixture case).

MCMC $\left(\{x_{1n}, x_{2n}\}_{n=1}^{N} \right)$

1.   initialize K between 1 and N
2.   for $k = 1$ to $(K - 1)$
3.   initialize $c_{[n]} := k$ for $n = (k - 1) \times \lfloor N/K \rfloor + 1$ to $k \times \lfloor N/K \rfloor$
4.   initialize $c_{[n]} := K$ for $n = (K - 1) \times \lfloor N/K \rfloor + 1$ to N
5.   do
6.   for $n = 1$ to N
7.   sample $c_{[n]}$ from a Multinomial with probabilities from Eq. **13** and Eq. **14**
8.   update $K := \max_n(c_{[n]})$
9.   until 50 iterations after convergence (see discussion)
10. return posterior distribution of (c, K)

the Markov chain converged when the number of topics has converged. Convergence was diagnosed when several independent chains sampled close values of K. We started chains with 10, 25, 40, and 11988 topics and they converged after approximately 30 iterations. Thus we are reasonably confident of convergence despite the small number of iterations because of the diversity of chain starting values.

In the estimation of the posterior distribution of c and K, there are two hyperparameters which must be chosen. The prior distribution on c depends on the value of α; values of α greater than one encourage more groups while values of α smaller than one discourage new groups. We interpret α as the number of documents that we *a priori* believe belong in a new topic started by one document. However, once a document has started a new group, other documents will be less likely to join that group based on its small size. Therefore, $\alpha=1$ is used here as the standard value.

The posterior distribution of c also depends, through β, on the η parameters. This is the Dirich-

Figure 6. Left Panel: Log-likelihood (5 fold cv) for K=5,...,50,75,100,200,300 topics. We plot: text only, alpha fitted (solid line); text only, alpha fixed (dashed line). Right Panel: Log-likelihood (5 fold cv) for K=5,...,50,100 topics. We plot: text and references, α fitted (solid line); text and references, α fixed (dotted line).

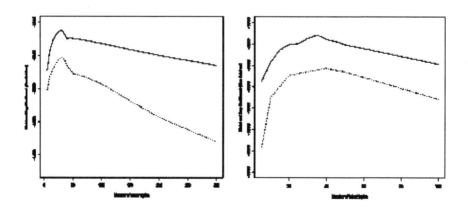

Figure 7. Posterior distribution for the PNAS scientific collection corresponding to the infinite mixture models of text (left panel) and of text and references (right panel)

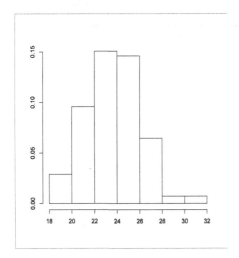 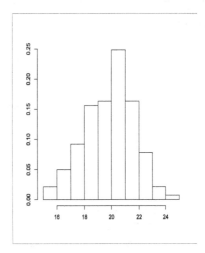

let prior on the probability vector over words or references for each topic. A value of η smaller than *V*, the vocabulary size, implies a prior belief that the word distributions will be highly skewed (a few likely words and many words with almost no probability of use). These values of η cause all documents to appear in one large group, *K*=1. A value of η larger than *V* implies a prior belief that all words are equally likely to be used in a given topic. Here, we take $\eta_1 = 10,000 \times V_1$ and $\eta_2 = 10,000 \times V_2$ as values that encourage a range of values of *K*.

Empirical Results

We fit six models for latent topics in the PNAS dataset: using words alone or with references, finite or infinite mixture models, and (for finite mixture) fitted or fixed Dirichlet parameter α. In Figure 6, we give the log-likelihood obtained for the four finite mixture models (at *K*=5,10,···,5 0,100,200,300).

This suggests we choose a number of topics between 20 and 40 whether words or words and references are used. The infinite model generates a posterior distribution for the number of topics,

K, given the data. Figure 7 shows the posterior distribution ranges from 20 to 28 topics when using only text and 16 to 23 topics when references are also used to identify topics.

By choosing K=20 topics, we can meaningfully interpret all of the word and reference usage patterns. We then fit the data with a 20 topics model for the finite mixture model using words and references and focused on the interpretation of the 20 topics. In Table 1, we list 12 high-probability words from these topics after filtering out the stop words. Table 2 shows the 5 references with the highest probability for 6 of the topics.

Using both tables, we offer the following interpretations of topics:

- Topics 1 and 12 focus on nuclear activity (genetic) and (repair/replication).
- Topic 2 concerns protein regulation and signal transduction.
- Two topics are associated with the study of HIV and immune responses: topic 3 is related to virus treatment and topic 17 concerns HIV progression.
- Two topics relate to the study of the brain

Table 1. Word usage patterns corresponding to the model of text and references, with K=20 topics

Topic 1	Topic 2	Topic 3	Topic 4	Topic 5
Gene	kinase	cells	cortex	species
genes	activation	virus	brain	evolution
sequence	receptor	gene	Visual	population
chromosome	protein	Expression	neurons	populations
analysis	signaling	human	memory	genetic
genome	alpha	viral	activity	selection
sequences	phosphorylation	infection	cortical	data
expression	beta	cell	learning	different
human	activated	infected	functional	evolutionary
dna	tyrosine	vector	retinal	number
number	activity	protein	response	variation
identified	signal	vectors	results	phylogenetic
Topic 6	**Topic 7**	**Topic 8**	**Topic 9**	**Topic 10**
enzyme	plants	protein	protein	cells
reaction	plant	rna	model	cell
Ph	acid	proteins	folding	tumor
activity	gene	yeast	state	apoptosis
site	expression	mrna	energy	cancer
transfer	arabidopsis	activity	time	P53
Mu	activity	trna	structure	growth
state	levels	translation	single	human
rate	cox	vitro	molecules	tumor
active	mutant	splicing	fluorescence	death
oxygen	light	complex	force	induced
electron	biosynthesis	gene	cdata	expression
Topic 11	**Topic 12**	**Topic 13**	**Topic 14**	**Topic 15**
transcription	dna	cells	protein	Ca2+
gene	rna	cell	membrane	channel

continued on next page

Table 1 continued

expression	repair	expression	proteins	channels
promoter	strand	development	atp	receptor
binding	base	expressed	complex	alpha
beta	polymerase	gene	binding	cells
transcriptional	recombination	differentiation	cell	neuron
factor	replication	growth	actin	receptors
protein	single	embryonic	beta	synaptic
dna	site	genes	transport	calcium
genes	stranded	drosophila	cells	release
activation	cdata	Embryos	nuclear	cell
Topic 16	**Topic 17**	**Topic 18**	**Topic 19**	**Topic 20**
peptide	cells	domain	mice	beta
binding	cell	protein	type	levels
peptides	il	binding	wild	increased
protein	hiv	terminal	mutant	insulin
amino	antigen	structure	gene	receptor
site	immune	proteins	deficient	expression
acid	specific	domains	alpha	induced
proteins	gamma	residues	normal	mice
affinity	cd4	amino	mutation	rats
specific	class	beta	mutations	treatment
activity	mice	sequence	mouse	brain
active	response	region	transgenic	effects
Active	response	Region	Transgenic	effects

and neurons: topic 4 (behavioral) and topic 15 (electrical excitability of neuronal membranes).

- Topic 5 is about population genetics and phylogenetics.
- Topic 7 is related to plant biology.
- Two topics deal with human medicine: topic 10 with cancer and topic 20 with diabetes and heart disease.

- Topic 13 relates to developmental biology.
- Topic 14 concerns cell biology.
- Topic 19 focuses on experiments on transgenic or inbred mutant mice.
- Several topics are related to protein studies, for example, topic 9 (protein structure and folding), topic 11 (protein regulation by transcription binding factors), and topic 18 (protein conservation comparisons).

Table 2. Refences usage patterns for 6 of the 20 topics corresponding to the model of text and references, with K=20 topics

Author	Journal	Author	Journal	Author	Journal
Topic 2		**Topic 5**		**Topic 7**	
Thompson,CB	Science, 1995	Sambrook,J	Mol.Cloning Lab. Manu., 1989	Sambrook,J	Mol.CloningLab. Manu., 1989
Xia, ZG	Science, 1995	Altschul,SF	J. Mol. Bio, 1990	Thompson,JD	Nucleic.Acids. Res,1994
Darnel, JE	Science,1994	Elsen,MB	P. Natl. Acad. Sci. USA, 1998	Altschul,SF	J. Mol. Bio, 1990
Zou, H	Cell, 1997	Altschul,SF	Nucleic. Acids.Res, 1997	Saitou,N	Mol. Biol. Evol., 1987
Muzio, M	Cell, 1996	Thompson,JD	Nucleic. Acids.Res, 1994	Altschul,SF	Nucleic. Acids. Res, 1997
Topic 8		**Topic 17**		**Topic 20**	
Sambrook,J	Mol.Cloning Lab. Manu.,1989	Sherrington,R	Nature, 1995	Chomczynski,P	Anal. Biochem., 1987
Kim,NW	Science,1994	Ho,DD	Nature, 1995	Bradford,MM	Anal. Biochem. 1976
Bodnar,AG	Science,1998	Scheuner,D	Nat. Med., 1996	Kuiper,GGJM	P. Natl. Acad. Sci. USA,1996
Bradford,MM	Anal. Biochem. 1976	Thinakaran,G	Neuron,1996	Moncada,S	Pharmacol rev,1991
Fischer,U	Cell, 1995	Wei,X	Nature,1995	Kuiper,GG	Endocrinol-ogy,1998

- Topics 6, 8, and 16 relate to biochemistry.

These labels for the topics are primarily convenience, but they do highlight some of the overlap between the PNAS sections (Plant Biology and Developmental Biology) and the latent topics (7 and 13). However, many plant biologists may do molecular biology in their current work. We can also see by examining the topics that small sections such as Anthropology do not emerge as topics and broad sections such as Medical Science and Biochemistry have distinct subtopics within them. This also suggests special treatment for general sections such as Applied Biology and cutting-edge interdisciplinary papers when evaluating the classification effectiveness of a model.

To summarize the distribution of latent aspects over distributions, we provide graphical representations of the distribution of latent topics for each of thirteen PNAS classifications in Figure 8. The third figure represents the model used for Tables 1 and 2. The two figures on the right represent models where the α parameter of the Dirichlet prior over topics is fixed. These two models are less sparse than the corresponding models with α fit to the data. For twenty latent topics, we fix $\alpha=50/20=2.5>1$ and this means each latent topic is expected to be present in each document and a priori we expect equal membership in each topic. By contrast the fitted values of α are less than one and therefore lead to models that expect articles to have high membership in a small number of

Figure 8. The average membership in the 20 latent topics (columns) for articles in thirteen of the PNAS editorial categories (rows). Darker shading indicates higher membership of articles submitted to a specific PNAS editorial category in the given latent topic and white space indicates average membership of less than 10%. Note that the rows sum to 100% and therefore darker topics show concentration of membership and imply sparser membership in the remaining topics. These 20 latent topics were created using the four finite mixture models with words only (1ˢᵗ, 2ⁿᵈ)or words and references (3ʳᵈ, 4ᵗʰ)and α estimated (1ˢᵗ, 3ʳᵈ)or fixed (2ⁿᵈ, 4ᵗʰ).

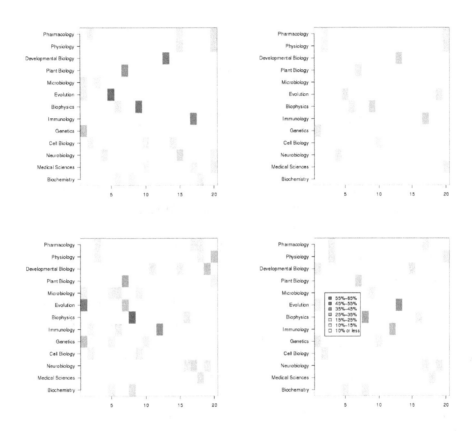

topics. See below the section "Evidence from a Simulation Study: A Practice to Avoid" for further consequences of these assumptions. The articles in each PNAS classification tend to have a few latent topics highly represented when α is fit and low to moderate representation in all topics when α is fixed (as seen by white/light colored rows).

Upon examination of Figure 8, note that topic 1, identified with genetic activity in the nucleus, was highly represented in articles from genetics, evolution, and microbiology. Also note that nearly all of the PNAS classifications are represented by several word and reference usage patterns in all of the models. This highlights the distinction between the PNAS topics and the discovered latent topics. The assigned topics used in PNAS follow the structure of the historical development of biological sciences and the divisions/departmental structures of many medical schools and universi-

Figure 9. Left: 2D symmetric Dirichlet densities underlying mixed-membership vectors θ = (θ₁, θ₂) with parameter (solid black line)and with parameter a = 0.25 < 1 (dashed, red line). Right: held-out log-likelihood for the simulation experiments described in the text. The solid, black line corresponds to the strategy of fitting α = 50/K, whereas the dashed, red line corresponds to the strategy of fitting a via empirical Bayes. K^* is denoted with an asterisk.

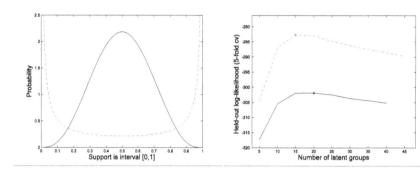

ties. These latent topics, however, are structured around the current interest of biological sciences. Figure 8 also shows that there is a lot of hope for collaboration and interest between separate fields, which are researching the same ideas.

As we saw in Figure 6, the held-out log likelihood plot corresponding to five-fold cross validation suggest a number between 20 and 40 topics for the finite mixture model. Other analyses using finite mixture with words and references supports support values toward the lower end of this range, that is, K=20, more than other choices. This is also true in the posterior distribution of K for the infinite mixture model. We fixed α=50/K following the choice in Griffiths & Steyvers (2004) and estimated α from the data. This produced a similar conclusion. While Griffiths & Steyvers (2004) found posterior evidence for nearly 300 topics, a number on the order of 20 or 30 provides a far better fit to the data, assessed robustly by multiple criteria and specifications. Moreover, we find this simpler more interpretable in a meaningful way that is not possible with 300 topics.

Evidence from a Simulation Study: A Practice to Avoid

To conclude, with the aim of highlighting the dangers of fixing the hyperparameters according to some ad-hoc strategy that is *not* supported by the data, for example, fixing α=50/K in the models of the previous section, we report some anecdotal evidence we gathered from synthetic data. We simulated a set of 3,000 documents according to the finite mixture model of text only previously described, with K^* = 15 and a vocabulary of size 50. We then fitted the correct finite mixture model on a grid for K=5,10,45 that included the true underlying number of groups and associated patterns, using a five-fold cross-validation scheme. In a first batch of experiments we fitted alpha using empirical Bayes (Carlin & Louis, 2005), whereas in a second batch of experiments we set α=50/K, following the analysis in Griffiths & Steyvers (2004). The held-out log-likelihood profiles are reported in the right panel of Figure 9.

In this controlled experiment, the optimal number of nonobservable groups is K^* = 15. This implies a value of a = 50/15 = 3.33 > 1 for the ad-hoc strategy, whereas $\hat{\alpha}$ =0.052<1 according to the empirical Bayes strategy. Intuitively, the fact that $\alpha > 1$ has a disrupting effect on the model fit: each topic is expected to be present in each document, or in other words each document is expected to belong equally to each group/topic, rather than only to only a few of them, as it is the case when $\alpha < 1$. As an immediate consequence, the estimates of the components of mixed-membership vectors, $\{\theta_{nk}\}$, tend to be diffuse, rather than sharply peaked, as we would expect in text mining applications. We can observe this effect, for example, in Figure 8, where the plots in the right column display latent topics that are more "diffuse" than those estimated by fitting the hyperparameter α with maximum likelihood as well. As expected, setting the hyperparameter α to a value greater than one when the simulated data supports values in a dramatically different range, for example, $0.01 < \alpha < 0.1$, ultimately bias the estimation of the number of latent groups. Furthermore, Figure 9 shows that the empirical Bayes strategy correctly recovers $K^* = 15$, whereas the ad-hoc strategy finds $K^* = 20$.

Our experiments in a controlled setting suggest that it is desirable not to fix the hyper-parameters, for example, the nonobservable category abundances α, according to ad-hoc strategies, unless such strategies are supported by previous analyses. Ad-hoc strategies will affect inference about the number of nonobservable groups and associated patterns in noncontrollable ways, and ultimately bias the analysis of data.

CASE STUDY: DISABILITY PROFILES OF AMERICAN ELDERLY

As we mentioned in the section describing our two motivating case studies, the analysis we present here complements the analyses of the data from the *National Long Term Care Survey* (NLTCS) presented in Erosheva (2002a) and Erosheva and Fienberg (2005). In particular, Erosheva (2002a) considers finite mixture models that feature up to

five latent disability profiles and concludes that the model with four profiles is the most appropriate to describe the NLTCS data. In this section, we explore a larger set of finite mixture models that feature up to ten latent disability profiles, and we also present a nonparametric model that does not fix the number of profiles prior to the analysis.[4]

As in the previous case study, the focus on the analysis is on the selection of the number of latent disability profiles, that is, on the selection of the model, which best describes the data.

Modeling Disability

In this section we introduce model specifications to analyze the sample of American elderly included in the NLTC panel survey. For our purposes it will be sufficient to ignore the temporal dimension of the data collection—we refer to Connor (2006) for a longitudinal analysis. All our models can be subsumed into the general formulation of HBMMMs previously presented. We organize them into finite and infinite mixture models, as before, according to the dimensionality of the prior distribution, D_α, posited at the latent variable level—assumption A3.

We characterize an elderly American by a set of responses, x_{jn} for $j = 1, \ldots, J$, which were measured through a questionnaire. In our analysis we selected $J = 16$ binary responses that encode answers to questions about the ability to perform six *activities of daily living* (ADL) and ten *instrumental activities of daily living* (IADL). The *j-th* response, x_{jn}, is recorded as zero if the *n-th* individual does not have problems performing the *j-th* activity (he is considered healthy, to that extent, for the purpose the survey), whereas it is recorded as one if the *n-th* individual has problems performing the *j-th* activity (an individual is considered disabled to that extent for the purpose the survey).

a) Finite Mixture: The Model

To carry out the analysis of the NLTCS data in the finite mixture setting we use the GoM model (previously described in "example 2"), which posits the following generative process for the *n-th* individual.

1. Sample $\theta_n \sim D_\alpha$.
2. For each of the J responses
2.1. Sample $z_{jn} \mid \theta_n \sim Multinomial\ (\theta_n, 1)$.
2.2. Sample $x_{jn} \mid z_{jn} \sim Bernouilli(\beta_{[j,1:K]}z_{jn[1:K]})$.

Here, we take D_α to be a Dirichlet distribution with hyper-parameter $\alpha = (\alpha_1,...,\alpha_K)$. Note that this is not the symmetric distribution we used in the previous case study, in the finite setting. In this model, β is a matrix that encodes the probability of being disabled with respect to each one of the 16 activities for the elderly who display disability characteristics specific to each of the K latent profiles. That is, if we denote as before the latent profile indicator vector with z_{jn}, then $\beta_{[jk]} = P(x_{jn} = 1 \mid z_{jn[k]} = 1)$ is the probability of being disabled with respect to the *j-th* activity for an elderly person who "belongs" completely to the *k-th* latent profile. Note that in this model there are no constraints on the sum of the total probability of having being disabled given any specific profile. For example, $\sum_{j=1}^{J} \beta_{[jk]}$ is not necessarily one as in the model of the PNAS scientific collection section[5]. The hyper-parameters of this model are α and β. In the section on finite mixture inference below, we develop a variational approximation to perform posterior inference on such hyperparameters, and on the latent variables n and jn for all j's and n's.

In our analysis, we also consider a fully Bayesian version of the GoM model, following Erosheva (2002a), which posits the following generative process for all N individuals in the survey.

1. Sample x $\sim D_\alpha$
2. Sample $\alpha_0 \sim Gamma(\tau 1, \tau 2)$

3. Sample $\beta_{[j,k]} \sim Beta(\sigma_1, \sigma_2)$ for all j and k
4. For each of the N individuals
4.1. Sample $\theta_n \sim Dirichlet(\alpha_0\xi_{[1]},...,\alpha_0\xi_{[K]})$.
4.2. For each of the J responses
4.2.1. Sample $z_{jn} \mid \theta_n \sim Multinomial(\theta_n, 1)$
4.2.2. $x_{jn} \mid z_{jn} \sim Bernouilli(\beta_{[j,1:K]}z_{jn[1:K]})$

In this fully Bayesian setting we fix the hyper-parameter for convenience. According to our model specifications D_α is a symmetric Dirichlet distribution with fixed hyper-parameter $\alpha_1 = ... = \alpha_K = 1$. The *k-th* component of ξ, $\xi_{[k]}$, represents the proportion of the elderly in the survey who express traits of the *k-th* latent disability profile. Further, we fix a diffuse Gamma distribution, $\tau_1 = 2$ and $\tau_2 = 0$, to control for the tails of the Dirichlet distribution of the mixed membership vectors, θ_n. The elements of β are sampled from a symmetric Beta distribution with fixed hyper-parameter $\sigma_1 = \sigma_2 = 1$. Note that a symmetric Beta sampling scheme with unitary parameter is equivalent to a Uniform sampling scheme on [0, 1].

In both of the finite mixture models we presented in this section, we assume that the number of latent profiles is unknown but fixed at K. Our goal is to find the number of latent disability profiles, K^*, which gives the best description of the population of the elderly.

b) Infinite Mixture: The Model

In the infinite setting we do not fix the number of subpopulations K underlying the population of surveyed American elderly prior to the analysis. As in the previous case study, the mixed membership vectors $\theta_{1:N}$ reduce to single membership vectors. We denote membership with c, where $c_{[n]} = k$ indicates that $\theta_{n[k]} = 1$. We posit the following generative process.

1. Sample $c \sim D_\alpha$
2. For each of the K distinct values of c
2.1. Sample $\beta_{[j,k]} \sim Beta(\tau_1, \tau_2)$ for all j

3.   For each of the N individuals

3.1.   For each of the J responses

3.1.1. Sample $x_{jn} \mid \beta_{jc_{[n]}} \sim Bernouilli(\beta_{[jc,[n]}])$

Here D_α is the Dirichlet process prior described in the PNAS scientific collection section (infinite mixture model). In our implementation, we specify a symmetric Beta distribution for the disability probabilities, β_{kj}, with $\tau_1 = \tau_2 = \tau$. Further, we fix the hyper-parameter of the Dirichlet process prior D_α at $\alpha=1$, which encodes "indifference" toward additional groups.

In this model, we assume that the number of latent disability profiles, K, is unknown and possibly infinite, through the prior for c, D_α. In order to find the number of profiles that best describes the population of the elderly, we study the posterior distribution of c.

Inference

In this section we develop posterior inference for both specifications of the finite mixture model, and for the infinite mixture model above. In particular, we use variational methods for the "basic" finite mixture model and Monte Carlo Markov chain (MCMC) methods for "fully Bayesian" finite mixture model and for the infinite mixture model.

a) Finite Mixture: Inference

A – The Variational Approximation for the "Basic" Model.

As in the section dealing with the case study on PNAS scientific collection, in the finite mixture case, the coupling between the mixed-membership scores, $\theta_{1:N}$ and the conditional disability prob-

abilities given profile, β, results in an intractable likelihood. Likewise, the algorithm that leads to the mean-field solution to the Bayes problem is a variational EM algorithm. This is an approximate EM algorithm, which involves evaluating a lower bound for the likelihood that depends on additional free parameters.

In the M step we maximize such a lower bound with respect to the hyperparameters of the model, (α, β), given the updates of the free parameters, $(\gamma, \phi_{1:J})$ for each individual. We then obtain the (pseudo) maximum likelihood estimates for the hyperparameters as follows:

$$\beta_{[jk]} \propto \sum_{n=1}^{N} \phi_{jn[k]} x_{jn},$$

where n is the index that runs over the N individuals in the sample. The (pseudo) maximum likelihood estimates for α are derived using the Newton-Raphson algorithm, with gradient and Hessian given in equations 8 and 9.

In the approximate E step we update the free parameters corresponding to each individual, $(\gamma, \phi_{1:J})$, given the update estimates for the parameters of the model, (α, β), as follows:

$$\phi_{j[k]} \propto \beta_{j[k]}^{x_j} (1 - \beta_{j[k]})^{1-x_j} \times \qquad (15)$$
$$\left(\Psi(\gamma_{[k]}) - \Psi(\sum_{\kappa=1}^{K} \gamma_{[k]}) \right),$$

$$\gamma_k = \alpha_k + \sum_{j=1}^{J} \phi_{j[k]}. \qquad (16)$$

As before, the approximation is introduced because the integral used to evaluate the likelihood for an individual:

Box 3. Equation 18

$$p(x,z,\theta,\beta,\alpha_0,\xi) = p(\alpha)p(\beta)\prod_{n=1}^{N}\left(p(\theta_n \mid \alpha_0, \Theta)\prod_{j=1}^{J}\prod_{k=1}^{K}\left(\theta_{n[k]} \beta_{[jk]}^{x_{jn}}(1 - \beta_{[jk]})^{1-x_{jn}} \right)^{z_{jn[k]}} \right)$$

$$p(x_1,\ldots,x_J \mid \alpha, \beta) = \qquad (17)$$

$$\int \left(\prod_{j=1}^{J} \sum_{k=1}^{K} \theta_{[k]} \beta_{[jk]}^{x_j} (1-\beta_{[jk]})^{1-x_j} \right) D_\alpha(d\theta)$$

does not have a closed form solution. As in the model for text and references, we then posit N independent fully factorized joint distributions over the latent variables, one for each individual,

$$q\left(\theta, z_{1:J} \mid \gamma, \phi_{1:J}\right) = q\left(\theta \mid \gamma\right) \prod_{j=1}^{J} q(z_j \mid \phi_j)$$

which depend on a set of free parameters, $(\gamma, \phi_{1:J})$. We then develop a mean-field approximation to the true posterior of the latent variables given data and hyper-parameters, which leads to the approximate EM described above.

b) The MCMC for the "Fully Bayesian" Model

We derived a Metropolis-within-Gibbs MCMC sampler for these model specifications, following Erosheva (2000a). One iteration for this algorithm consists of a Gibbs sampler for drawing z, θ and β and two Metropolis-Hasting steps for drawing α_0 and ξ. The joint distribution for the fully Bayesian version of the GoM model is shown in Box 3 (equation 18), where $p(\beta) = \prod_{j=1}^{J} \prod_{k=1}^{K} p(\beta_{[jk]})$ and $p(\alpha) = p(\alpha_0) p(\xi)$. The exact specifications for $p(\beta_{jk})$, $p(\xi)$ and $p(\alpha_0)$ are given in the paragraph on finite mixture models of this section. From the factorization of the joint distribution in equation

(18), we are able to derive the full conditional distributions of β, z and θ.

The Gibbs sampler algorithm can then be used to obtain the posterior distribution of the model parameters β and θ. To obtain the parameters update for the $(i+1)$-*th* step, we do the following:

- For $n=1,\ldots,N$, for $j=1,\ldots,J$, sample:

$$z_{jn}^{(i+1)} \sim Multinomial\,(q, 1)$$

where $q = (q_1,\ldots,q_K)$ and:

$$q_k = \theta_{n[k]}^{(i)} (\beta_{[jk]}^{(i)})^{x_{jn}} (1-\beta_{[jk]}^{(i)})^{1-x_{jn}}.$$

- For $j=1,\ldots,K$, for $k=1,\ldots,K$, sample:

$$\beta_{[jk]}^{(i+1)} \sim Beta\left(1+\sum_{\{n:z_{jn[k]}^{(i+1)}=1\}} x_{jn}, 1+\sum_{\{n:z_{jn[k]}^{(i+1)}=1\}}(1-x_{jn})\right).$$

- For $n=1,\ldots,N$, sample:

$$\theta_n^{(i+1)} \sim Dirichlet\left(\alpha_{[1]}+\sum_{j=1}^{J} z_{jn[1]}^{(i+1)} \ldots, \alpha_{[K]}+\sum_{j=1}^{J} z_{jn[K]}^{(i+1)}\right).$$

We use Metropolis-Hasting steps to draw from the posterior distribution of α_0 and ξ, given that $\alpha = \alpha_0 \xi$ is random. For α_0, we consider the proposal distribution $p(\alpha_0^* \mid \alpha_0) = Gamma(\gamma, \gamma \alpha_0)$ where γ is an adjustable tuning parameter. The Metropolis-Hasting step for α_0 is:

- Sample $\alpha_0^* \sim p(\alpha_0^* \mid \alpha_0^{(i)})$.
- Compute the proposal ratio:

Box 4.

$$p(c_{[n]} = k \mid c_{[-n]}, x)$$

$$\propto \frac{m(-n,k)\prod_{j=1}^{J} \Gamma\left(\tau + \sum_{\{i:i\neq n, c_i=k\}} x_{ji} + x_{jn}\right) \Gamma\left(\tau + \sum_{\{i:i\neq n, c_i=k\}} (1-x_{ji}) + 1 - x_{jn}\right)}{(N-1+\alpha)(2\tau+m(-n,k))^J (\Gamma(\tau)\Gamma(\tau+1))^J},$$

$$r(\alpha_0) = \frac{q(\alpha_0^* \mid .)p(\alpha_0^{(i)} \mid \alpha_0^*)}{q(\alpha_0^{(i)} \mid .)p(\alpha_0^* \mid \alpha_0^{(i)})}.$$

- Let:

$$\alpha_0^{(i+1)} = \begin{cases} \alpha_0^* & with\ probability\ \min(1, r(\alpha_0)) \\ \alpha_0^{(i)} & with\ probability\ 1 - \min(1, r(\alpha_0)) \end{cases}$$

Here, $q(\alpha_0 \mid .)$ is the full conditional distribution of α_0, conditioning on all of the other variables. From (18), it follows that:

$$(19)$$

$$q(\alpha_0 \mid .) \propto p(\alpha_0) \left(\frac{\Gamma(\alpha_0)}{\Gamma(\xi_{[1]}\alpha_0)...\Gamma(\xi_{[K]}\alpha_0)} \right)^N \prod_{n=1}^{N} \prod_{k=1}^{K} (\theta_{n[k]})^{\xi_{[k]}\alpha_0}.$$

For ξ, we consider the proposal distribution $p(\xi^* \mid \xi) = Dirichlet(\delta K \xi_1, ..., \delta K \xi_K)$ where δ is a tuning parameter, which can be adjusted. The Metropolis-Hasting step for ξ is described below:

- Sample $x^* \sim p(\xi^* \mid \xi^{(i)})$.
- Compute the proposal ratio:

$$r(\xi) = \frac{q(\xi^* \mid .)p(\xi^{(i)} \mid \xi^*)}{q(\xi^{(i)} \mid .)p(\xi^* \mid \xi^{(i)})}$$

- Let:

$$\xi^{(i+1)} = \begin{cases} \xi^* & with\ probability\ \min(1, r(\xi)) \\ \xi^{(i)} & with\ probability\ 1 - \min(1, r(\xi)) \end{cases}$$

Here, $q(\xi \mid .)$ is the full conditional distribution of ξ, conditioning on all of the other variables. From (18), we have:

$$q(\xi \mid .) \propto p(\xi) \left(\frac{\Gamma(\alpha_0)}{\Gamma(\xi_{[1]}\alpha_0)...\Gamma(\xi_{[K]}\alpha_0)} \right)^N \prod_{n=1}^{N} \prod_{k=1}^{K} (\theta_{n[k]})^{\xi_{[k]}\alpha_0}$$

$$(20)$$

b) Infinite Mixture: Inference

In the infinite mixture case, where we assume the total number of disability profiles to be infinite with an unknown number, K of observed profiles in this data, the posterior distribution of c does not have a closed form solution. However, the full conditional distributions of the c_n for $n=1,...,N$ are known up to a normalizing constant. Using the algorithm in Figure 5, we substitute the following full conditional probabilities into step 7. The full conditional probability of the *n-th* elderly person belonging to an existing (without individual n) profile k is shown in Box 4, where $c_{[-n]}$ is the profile assignment vector for all elderly people other than the *n-th*. The full conditional probability that the *n-th* elderly person belongs to a profile, which no other individual belongs to, is the following:

$$p(c_{[n]} \neq c_{[i]} \forall i \neq n \mid c_{[-n]}, x) \propto \frac{\alpha}{2^J (N - 1 + \alpha)}.$$

The parameters of the model estimated in this way are the vector c of profile assignments and the total number of profiles, K. The posterior distributions of c and K can be found using a Gibbs sampler with these full conditional distributions. In order to assess convergence of the Markov chain, we examine the total number of profiles (which varies by Gibbs sample) and consider the Markov chain converged when the number of profiles has converged.

We diagnosed the algorithm to have converged when several independent chains sampled close values of K. We started chains with 10, 25, 40, and 21,574 profiles and they converged after approximately 25 iterations. We can be reasonably confident of convergence despite the small number of iterations because of the diversity of chain starting values.

Again, the posterior distributions of c and K depend on the values of α (the Dirichlet process parameter) and τ (the parameter of the symmetric Beta priors on the β_{jk}. Using $\alpha=1$ is a standard value which assumes prior indifference toward

Table 3. Observed and expected cell counts for frequent response patterns under GoM models with K=2,3,...,10,15. The model with K=9 replicates marginal abundance best

P	Response pattern	observed	K=2	K=3	K=4	K=5	K=6	K=7	K=8	K=9	K=10	K=15
1	0000000000000000	3853	1249	2569	2055	2801	2889	3093	2941	3269	3016	3031
2	0000100000000000	216	212	225	172	177	186	180	180	202	205	187
3	0000001000000000	1107	1176	1135	710	912	993	914	937	1010	944	940
4	0000101000000000	188	205	116	76	113	200	199	181	190	198	201
5	0000001000100000	122	259	64	88	58	199	90	89	116	127	127
6	0000000000010000	351	562	344	245	250	274	274	259	331	303	357
7	0010000000010000	206	69	20	23	116	86	80	137	116	111	149
8	0000001000010000	303	535	200	126	324	255	236	213	273	264	325
9	0010001000010000	182	70	44	71	170	169	162	200	172	187	219
10	0000101000010000	108	99	51	39	162	105	85	117	97	108	116
11	0010101000010000	106	16	32	94	94	123	125	133	142	157	136
12	0000100000001000	195	386	219	101	160	46	25	24	25	31	27
13	0000001000001000	198	369	127	111	108	341	170	169	189	200	163
14	0000001000101000	196	86	41	172	90	104	224	214	174	187	160
15	0000001000011000	123	174	96	86	132	131	120	109	95	108	110
16	0000001000111000	176	44	136	162	97	67	167	149	152	167	157
17	0010001000111000	120	9	144	104	41	57	47	96	75	72	80
18	0000101000111000	101	12	127	90	54	41	68	72	70	74	124
19	0111111111111000	102	57	44	38	22	18	18	85	103	85	61
20	1111111111111010	107	35	88	104	96	84	87	43	37	31	73
21	0111111111111010	104	122	269	239	202	52	50	50	63	53	66
22	1111111111111110	164	55	214	246	272	274	276	224	166	143	115
23	0111111111111111	153	80	291	261	266	250	230	235	189	167	137
24	1111111111111111	660	36	233	270	362	419	418	582	612	474	423

groups of one member. Values of τ less than one represent a prior belief that ADL/IADL disability probabilities will tend to be close to 0 or 1 for each profile. Values of τ greater than one represent a prior belief that many disability probabilities will be close to 0.5. We choose a value of $\tau=50$ to represent a belief that there should be profiles with intermediate probabilities

Empirical Results

We fit three models for disability propensity profiles: the finite mixture with random Dirichlet parameter α, the finite mixture with fixed but unknown α, and the infinite mixture model.

We carry out the analysis of the NLTCS data using both MCMC and variational methods, and fitting the data with K-profiles GoM models, for $K=2,3,\cdots,10,15$. To choose the number of latent profiles that best describes the data, we use a method that focuses on the most frequent response

Table 4. Sum of Pearson residuals for GoM models with K=2, 3,..., 10, 15

No. of latent profiles, K	2	3	4	5	6	7	8	9	10	15
Sum of squares $\times 10^5$	75	20	37	13	11	7.7	9.4	4.4	8.2	8.1
Sum of Pearson residuals	20684	4889	5032	1840	2202	2458	1908	1582	1602	1604

Figure 10. Left panel: DIC for K=2,...,10,15 latent profiles (GoM model). Right panel: BIC for K=2,...,10 latent profiles (GoM model)

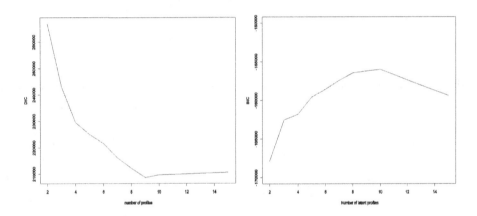

Figure 11. Left panel: Log-likelihood (5 fold cv) for K=2,...,10,15 (GoM model). Right panel: Posterior distribution of K

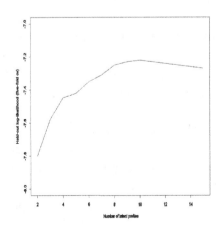 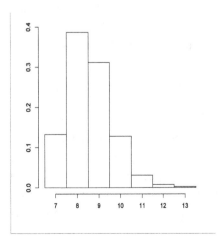

Figure 12. Latent profiles for the GoM model with K=9

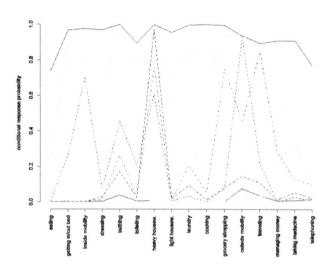

patterns. In the NLTCS data, what we mean by most frequent response patterns are the response patterns with observed counts greater than 100. For example, the "all-zero" response pattern (which concerns individuals with no disabilities on the 16 ADLs/IADLs) has the largest observed count of 3,853. They are actually 24 response patterns with observed counts greater than 100 and they account for 41% of the total number of observations (which is here 21,574). Then, using the estimates of the model parameters obtained via an MCMC algorithm or a variational EM algorithm, we can compute the expected cell counts for the 24 response patterns and compare with the observed cell counts. Eventually, to choose the model that best fits the data, we can compute the sum of absolute values of the "Pearson chi-square" residuals (Bishop, Fienberg, & Holland, 1975), (Observed Count − Expected Count)/Expected Count for each model .

Table 3 provides the expected cell counts for the 24 most frequent response patterns (to be compared with the observed cell counts) using MCMC methods (for K=2,...,10). We observe that the model with K=9 has the best fit for the "all-

zero" response pattern, the "all-one" response pattern and the pattern number P=3 (pattern for individuals on disabled on "doing heavy housework"). The computation of the sum of Pearson residuals shown in Table 4 confirms that K=9 seems to be a good choice. This is also true when one computes the expected cell counts using the variational methods.

To deal with this issue of model choice, we can also compute a version of DIC directly using the output from MCMC simulations. Indeed, if we focus on parameters θ and β, the computation is done using draws from the posterior distribution of $\beta_{[jk]}$ and $\theta_{n[k]}$. Figure 10 (left panel) shows the plot of DIC for models with K=2,3,···,10,15 latent profiles. According to the DIC plot, we choose models with K=9 or K=10 latent profiles. Using variational approximation methods, we also computed an approximate version of BIC based on the variational approximation. Figure 10 (right panel) shows the plot of BIC for models with K=2,3,···,10,15 latent profiles. This criterion suggests a number of profiles around 8 to 10. The cross validation results shown in Figure 10 (left panel) also suggest the choice of 9 or 10 profiles.

The infinite model generates a posterior distribution for the number of profiles, K, given the data. Figure 11 (Right Panel) shows the posterior distribution ranges from 7 to 10 profiles.

According to the array of different criteria we have considered, $K=9$ seems to be an appropriate choice for the NLTCS data. Figure 12 shows the latent profiles obtained for the 9 profiles GoM model using MCMC methods. The conditional response probabilities represented on the Y-axis are the posterior mean estimates of, the probability of being disabled on the activity j for a complete member of latent profile k. The profiles have the following interpretation:

- We can clearly distinguish two profiles for "healthy" individuals; these are the lower curves (the solid, black curve and the solid, grey curve).

- The upper curve (solid, black curve) corresponds to seriously "disabled" individuals since most of the probabilities are greater than 0.8.

- One profile (long-dashed, grey curve) has the second highest values for the IADLs "managing money," "taking medicine" and "telephoning". This focuses on individuals with some cognitive impairment.

- The profile with the second highest probabilities for most of the ADLs/IADLs (solid, grey curve) characterizes "semi-disabled" individuals.

- The profile with very high probabilities for all the activities involving mobility including the IADL "outside mobility" (dashed, grey curve) characterizes mobility-impaired individuals.

- Another profile characterizes individuals who are relatively healthy but cannot do "heavy housework" (long-dashed, black curve). Note that in Table 3, the response pattern $n=3$ has the second largest observed cell count.

- The two remaining profiles (the dot-dashed, black curve and the dashed, black curve) correspond to individuals who are "semi-healthy" since they show limitations in performing some physical activities.

We found similar interpretations with the estimates based on variational methods and MCMC methods despite some differences in the estimated values of the conditional disability propensity probabilities β_{jk}.

Because the NLTCS data is characterized by a large amount of healthy individuals with "all zero" response patterns (there are 3,853 all zero response patterns and they represent a little less than 18% of the sample population), we would like to take into account this excess of healthy individuals. In a forthcoming paper focusing on the results of analyses with the GoM model, we plan carry out an extended analysis using a modified version of the GoM model which adjusts for this excess.

CONCLUDING REMARKS

In this chapter, we have studied the issue of model choice in the context of mixed-membership models. Often the number of latent classes or groups is of direct interest in applications, but it is always an important element in determining the fit and meaning of the model.

We have used "latent Dirichlet allocation" which has some breadth of currency in the data mining literature, and shown extensions to it to analyze a corpus of PNAS biological sciences publications from 1997 to 2001. Among the approaches to select the number of latent topics which we study are k-fold cross-validation and the use of a Dirichlet process prior. Our results focus on six combinations of models and model choice strategies. They lead us to report on and interpret results for $K=20$ topics, a value that appears to be within the range of optimal numbers of topics.

The resulting topics are also easily interpretable and profile the most popular research subjects in biological sciences in terms of the corresponding words and references usage patterns. Much higher choices for *K*, lead to faulty and difficult to interpret conclusions. Incidentally, our 20 topics correlate well with the PNAS editorial categories.

For the analysis of the NLTCS data, we have developed parametric and nonparametric variations the GoM model. We performed posterior inference using variational methods and MCMC. We have used different criteria to assess model fit and choose *K*; in particular a method based on the sum of Pearson residuals for the most frequent response patterns, and information criteria such as DIC and BIC. We have then reached the conclusion that *K*=9 latent profiles is an appropriate choice for the data set. This choice allows us to identify profiles that did not appear in the analysis performed in Erosheva and Fienberg (2005), for example the profile for individuals who are fairly healthy on all the activities but "doing heavy housework." Further, we were able to interpret all nine profiles, whereas with *K*=4 and *K*=5, these profiles could not be ordered by severity. Nonetheless, the fit seems not to improve markedly for models with five to ten latent profiles.

REFERENCES

Airoldi, E. M., Blei, D. M., Fienberg, S. E., & Xing, E. P. (2006a). *Stochastic block models of mixed membership*. Manuscript submitted for publication.

Airoldi, E. M., Blei, D. M., Fienberg, S. E., & Xing, E. P. (2006b). Admixture of latent blocks with application to protein interaction networks. Manuscript submitted for publication.

Airoldi, E. M., & Faloutsos, C. (2004). Recovering latent time-series from their observed sums: Network tomography with particle filters. In *Proceedings of the ACM SIGKDD International Conference on Knowledge Discovery and Data Mining*.

Airoldi, E. M., Fienberg, S. E., Joutard, C., & Love, T. M. (2006). *Discovering latent patterns with hierarchical Bayesian mixed-membership models and the issue of model choice*. (Tech. Rep. CMU-ML-06-101). Pittsburgh, PA: Carnegie Mellon University, School of Computer Science.

Akaike, H. (1973). Information theory and an extension of the maximum likelihood principle. In B. Petrov & F. Csaki (Eds.), *Second international symposium on information theory*, (pp. 267-281).

Aldous, D. J. (1985). Exchangeability and related topics. *Lecture notes in mathematics*, (pp. 1-198). Springer: Berlin.

Antoniak, C. (1974). Mixtures of dirichlet processes with applications to Bayesian nonparametric problems. *The Annals of Statistics, 2*(6), 1152-1174.

Barnard, K., Duygulu, P., de Freitas, N., Forsyth, D., Blei, D. M., & Jordan, M. I. (2003). Matching words and pictures. *Journal of Machine Learning Research, 3*, 1107-1135.

Bathe, K. J. (1996). *Finite element procedures*. Englewood Cliffs, NJ: Prentice Hall.

Belkin, M., & Niyogi, P. (2003). Using manifold structure for partially labeled classification. *Advances in Neural Information Processing*.

Bishop, Y., Fienberg, S. E., & Holland, P. (1975). *Discrete Multivariate Analysis: Theory and Practice*. The MIT press.

Blei, D. M., Ng, A., & Jordan, M. I. (2003). Latent dirichlet allocation. *Journal of Machine Learning Research, 3*, 993-1022.

Carlin, B. P., & Louis, T. A. (2005). *Bayes and empirical Bayes methods for data analysis*. Chapman & Hall.

Chakrabarti, D., Papadimitriou, S., Modha, D., & Faloutsos, C. (2004). Fully automatic cross-associations. In *Proceedings of the ACM SIGKDD International Conference on Knowledge Discovery and Data Mining*.

Connor, J. (2006). *Multivariate mixture models to describe longitudinal patterns of frailty in American seniors*. Unpublished doctoral dissertation, Department of Statistics, Carnegie Mellon University, Pittsburgh, PA.

Erosheva, E. A. (2002). *Grade of membership and latent structure models with application to disability survey data*. Unpublished doctoral dissertation, Carnegie Mellon University, Pittsburgh, PA.

Erosheva, E. A. (2002). Partial membership models with application to disability survey data. In H. Bozdogan (Ed.). In *Proceedings of Conference on the New Frontiers of Statistical Data Mining*.

Erosheva, E. A. (2003). Bayesian estimation of the grade of membership model. *Bayesian statistics* (Vol. 7). Oxford University Press.

Erosheva, E. A., & Fienberg, S. E. (2005). Bayesian mixed membership models for soft clustering and classification. In C. Weihs & W. Gaul, (Eda.), *Classification—The ubiquitous challenge* (pp 11-26). Springer-Verlag.

Erosheva, E. A., Fienberg, S. E., & Lafferty, J. (2004). Mixed-membership models of scientific publications. *Proceedings of the National Academy of Sciences, 97*(22), 11885-11892.

Ferguson, T. (1973). A Bayesian analysis of some nonparametric problems. *The Annals of Statistics, 1*, 209-230.

Ghahramani, Z. (2004). Unsupervised learning. In O. Bousquet, G. Raetsch & U. von Luxburg, (Eds.), *Advanced lectures on machine learning* (Vol. 3176) *Lecture Notes in Computer Science*. Springer-Verlag.

Griffiths, T. L. & Steyvers, M. (2004). Finding scientific topics. *Proceedings of the National Academy of Sciences, 101* (Suppl. 1), 5228-5235.

Han, J., & Kamber, M. (2000). *Data mining: Concepts and techniques*. Morgan Kaufmann.

Hastie, T., Tibshirani, R., & Friedman, J. H. (2001). *The elements of statistical learning: Data mining, inference, and prediction*. Springer-Verlag.

Hotelling, H. (1933). Analysis of a complex of statistical variables into principal components. *Journal of Educational Psychology, 24*, 417-441, 498-520.

Jolliffe, I. T. (1986). *Principal component analysis*. Springer-Verlag.

Jordan, M. I., Ghahramani, Z., Jaakkola, T., & Saul, L. (1999). Introduction to variational methods for graphical models. *Machine Learning, 37*, 183-233.

Kumar R., Raghavan, P., Rajagopalan, S., Sivakumar, D., Tomkins, A., & Upfal, E. (2000). Random graph models for the web graph. In *Proceedings of the Annual Symposium on Foundations of Computer Science*.

Manton, K. G., Woodbury, M. A., & Tolley, H. D. (1994). *Statistical applications using fuzzy sets*. Wiley.

McAuliffe, J., Blei, D. M., & Jordan, M. I. (2006). Nonparametric empirical Bayes for the Dirichlet process mixture model. *Statistics and Computing, 16*(1), 5-14 .

Minka, T., & Lafferty, J. (2002). Expectation-propagation for the generative aspect model. *Uncertainty in Artificial Intelligence*.

Neal, R. (2000). Markov chain sampling methods for Dirichlet process mixture models. *Journal of Computational and Graphical Statistics, 9*(2), 249-265.

Neville, J., Simsek, O., Jensen, D., Komoroske, J., Palmer, K., & Goldberg, H. (2005). Using relational knowledge discovery to prevent securities fraud. In *Proceedings of the ACM SIGKDD International Conference on Knowledge Discovery and Data Mining, Vol. 11.*

Ng, A. (1997). Preventing "overfitting" of cross-validation data. In *Proceedings of the International Conference on Machine Learning, Vol. 14.*

Parisi, G. (1988). *Statistical field theory.* Redwood City, CA: Addison-Wesley.

Pelleg, D., & Moore, A. W. (2000). X-means: Extending K-means with efficient estimation of the number of clusters. In *Proceedings of the International Conference on Machine Learning, Vol. 17.*

Pritchard, J., Stephens, M., & Donnelly, P. (2000). Inference of population structure using multilocus genotype data. *Genetics, 155*, 945-959.

Rabiner, L. R. (1989). A tutorial on hidden Markov models and selected applications in speech recognition. *Proceedings of the IEEE, 77*(2), 257-286.

Rosenberg, N. A., Pritchard, J. K., Weber, J. L., Cann, H. M., Kidd, K. K., Zhivotovsky, L. A., & Feldman, M. W. (2002). Genetic structure of human populations. *Science, 298*, 2381-2385.

Rustagi, J. (1976). *Variational methods in statistics.* New York: Academic Press.

Sakurai, J. (1985). *Modern quantum mechanics.* Redwood City, CA: Addison-Wesley.

Schölkopf, B., & Smola, A. (2002). *Learning with kernels.* Cambridge: MIT Press.

Schwartz, G.. (1978). Estimating the dimension of a model. *The Annals of Statistics, 6*, 461-464.

Spearman, C. (1904). General intelligence objectively determined and measured. *American Journal of Psychology, 15*, 201-293.

Spiegelhalter, D. J., Best, N. G., Carlin, B. P., & Van der Linde, A. (2002). Bayesian measures of model complexity and fit. *Journal of the Royal Statistical Society, Series B, 64*, 583-639.

Stallar, E. (2005). Trajectories of disability and mortality among the U.S. elderly population: Evidence from the 1984-1999 NLTCS. *Living to 100 and Beyond International Symposium.* Society of Actuaries.

Tipping, M. E., & Bishop, C. M. (1999). Probabilistic principal component analysis. *Journal of the Royal Statistical Society, Series B, 61*(3), 611-622.

Wainwright, M. J. & Jordan, M. I. (2003). *Graphical models, exponential families and variational inference.* (Tech. Rep. No. 649). Berkeley, CA: University of California, Department of Statistics.

Wang, X., Mohanty, N., & McCallum, A. K. (2005). Group and topic discovery from relations and text. *Advances in Neural Information Processing Systems* (Vol. 18).

Woodbury, M. A., Clive, J., & Garson, A. (1978). Mathematical typology: Grade of membership techniques for obtaining disease definition. *Computational Biomedical Research, 11*(3), 277-298.

Xing, E. P., Jordan, M. I., & Russell, S. (2003). A generalized mean field algorithm for variational inference in exponential families. *Uncertainty in Artificial Intelligence* (Vol. 19).

ENDNOTES

[1] On the contrary, any given reference that was picked from the set of known citations typically appears as a unique bibliography item. Thus there are no replicates of any given reference in the same bibliography.

2   In this application, we refer to the subpopulations of assumption A.1 as "topics". Despite the suggestive semantics, topics are pairs of latent distributions over the vocabulary and the set of known in citations, from a statistical perspective, as defined by pairs of corresponding columns of the two β matrices.

3   On the contrary, any given reference that was picked from the set of known citations typically appears as a unique bibliography item. Thus there are no replicates of any given reference in the same bibliography.

4   Rather, the nonparametric model implicitly encodes a prior on the number of latent profiles such that $K \approx ln(N)$, where N is the number of elderly in the sample. In the NLTCS data, $N=21,574$ and $ln(N) \approx 10$.

5   Note another subtle difference from the generative process of the section dealing with the PNAS scientific publications (finite mixture case). In this model we loop over 1 replicate of each of the J responses observed for the n-th American senior, whereas in the previous model we loop over R_1 word instances and R_2 bibliography items observed in the n-th document.

Compilation of References

Adamic, L., Buyukkokten, O., & Adar, E. (2003). Social network caught in the web. *First Monday, 8*(6).

Agarwal, R., Aggarwal, C., & Prasad, V. (2000). A tree projection algorithm for generation of frequent itemsets. *Journal of Parallel and Distributed Computing, 61*(3), 350-371.

Aggarwal, C. C. (2005). On change diagnosis in evolving data streams. *IEEE TKDE, 17*(5), 587–600.

Aggarwal, C. C., & Yu, P. S. (2006). A framework for clustering massive text and categorical data streams. In *Proceedings of the 6th SIAM Conference on Data Mining (SDM '06).*

Aggrawal, C. C., & Yu, P. S. (2000). Finding generalized clusters in high dimensional spaces. In *Procceedings of the ACM International Conference on Management Of Data (SIGMOD '00).*

Agrawa l, R., & Srikant, R. (1994, September). Fast algorithms for mining association rules in large databases. In *Proceedings of the 20th International Conference on Very Large Data Bases, VLDB'94*, Santiago de Chile, Chile.

Agrawal R., Imielinski, T., & Swami, A. (1993). Mining association rules between sets of items in large databases. In *Proceeding of ACM International Conference on Management Of Data (SIGMOD'93)*, SIGMOD Record. 22(2): 207-216. ACM Press.

Agrawal, R., & Srikant, R. (1994). Fast algorithms for mining association rules. In *Proceedings of the 20th International Conference on Very Large Data Bases (VLDB) Conference*, 487-499.

Agrawal, R., Gehrke, J., Gunopulos, D., & Raghavan, P. (1998). Automatic subspace clustering of high dimensional data for data mining applications. In *Proceedings of the 1998 ACM SIGMOD International Conference on Management of Data*, 94-105.

Agrawal, R., Imielinski, T., & Swami, A. (1993). Mining association rules between sets of items in large databases. In *Proceedings of SIGMOD Int. Conf. Management of Data* (pp 207–216).

Ahonen-Myka, H. (2005). Mining all maximal frequent word sequences in a set of sentences. In *Proceedings of the 14th ACM international Conference on information and Knowledge Management.* CIKM '05.

Aiello, M., Monz, C., Todoran, L., & Worring, M. (2002). Document understanding for a broad class of documents. *International Journal of Document Analysis and Recognition IJDAR, 5*(1), 1-16.

Airoldi, E. M., & Faloutsos, C. (2004). Recovering latent time-series from their observed sums: Network tomography with particle filters. In *Proceedings of the ACM SIGKDD International Conference on Knowledge Discovery and Data Mining.*

Airoldi, E. M., Blei, D. M., Fienberg, S. E., & Xing, E. P. (2006). *Stochastic block models of mixed membership.* Manuscript submitted for publication.

Airoldi, E. M., Blei, D. M., Fienberg, S. E., & Xing, E. P. (2006). Admixture of latent blocks with application to protein interaction networks. Manuscript submitted for publication.

Airoldi, E. M., Fienberg, S. E., Joutard, C., & Love, T. M. (2006). *Discovering latent patterns with hierarchical Bayesian mixed-membership models and the issue of model choice.* (Tech. Rep. CMU-ML-06-101). Pittsburgh, PA: Carnegie Mellon University, School of Computer Science.

Akaike, H. (1973). Information theory and an extension of the maximum likelihood principle. In B. Petrov & F. Csaki (Eds.), *Second international symposium on information theory,* (pp. 267-281).

Akindele, O. T., & Belaïd, A. (1995). Construction of generic models of document structures using inference of tree grammars. In *Proceedings of the Third International Conference on Document Analysis and Recognition, ICDAR'95.*

Aldous, D. J. (1985). Exchangeability and related topics. *Lecture notes in mathematics,* (pp. 1-198). Springer: Berlin.

Aleman-Meza, B., Nagarajan, M., Ramakrishnan, C., Sheth, A., Arpinar, I., Ding, L., Kolari, P., Joshi, A., & Finin, T. (2006). Semantic analytics on social networks: Experiences in addressing the problem of conflict of interest detection. In *Proceedings of the WWW2006.*

Allan, J. (2002). *Introduction to topic detection and tracking.* Kluwer Academic Publishers.

Altamura, O., Esposito, F., & Malerba, D. (2001). Transforming paper documents into XML format with WISDOM++. *International Journal on Document Analysis and Recognition, 4*(1), 2-17.

Altschul, S. F., Gish, W., Miller, W., Myers, E. W., & Lipman, D. J. (1990). Basic local alignment search tool. *Journal of Molecular Biology, 215,* 403-410.

Altschul, S. F., Madden, T. L., Schaffer, A. A., Zhang, J., Anang, Z., Miller, W., & Lipman, D. J. (1997). Gapped blast and psi-blast: A new generation of protein database search programs. *Nucleic Acids Research, 25,* 3389-3402.

Amir, A., Aumann, Y., Feldman, R., & Fresko, M. (2005). Maximal association rules: A tool for mining associations in text. *Journal of Intelligent Information Systems, 25*(3), 333-345.

Anagnostopoulos, A., Broder, A. Z., & Carmel, D. (2005). Sampling search-engine results. In *Proceedings of WWW 2005.*

Andrienko, G., Malerba, D., May, M., & Teisseire, M. (2006). Mining spatio-temporal data. *Journal of Intelligent Information Systems, 27*(3), 187–190.

Antoniak, C. (1974). Mixtures of dirichlet processes with applications to Bayesian nonparametric problems. *The Annals of Statistics, 2*(6), 1152-1174.

Apostolico, A. (1985). The myriad virtues of subword trees. In A. Apostolico & Z. Galil (Eds.), *Combinatorial algorithms on words* (12, pp. 85-96). Springer-Verlag Publishing.

Apostolico, A., & Crochemore, M. (2000). String pattern matching for a deluge survival kit. In P. M. Pardalos, J. Abello, & M. G. C. Resende (Eds.), *Handbook of massive data sets.* Kluwer Academic Publishers.

Apostolico, A., Bock, M. L., & Lonardi, S. (2003). Monotony of surprise and large-scale quest for unusual words. *Journal of Computational Biology 10*(3/4), 283-311.

Apostolico, A., Comin, M., & Parida, L. (2005). Conservative extraction of over-represented extensible motifs. *ISMB* (Supplement of Bioinformatics), 9-18.

Apostolico, A., Iliopoulos, C., Landau, G., Schieber, B., & Vishkin, U. (1988). Parallel construction of a suffix tree with applications. *Algorithmica, 3,* 347-365.

Appice, A., Ceci, M., Lanza, A., Lisi, F.A., & Malerba, D. (2003). Discovery of spatial association rules in georeferenced census data: A relational mining approach. *Intelligent Data Analysis, 7*(6), 541-566.

Arimura, H., & Uno, T. (2005). An output-polynomial time algorithm for mining frequent closed attribute trees. In S. Kramer & B. Bernhard Pfahringer (Eds.). In *Proceedings of the 15th International Conference on Inductive Logic Programming, ILP '05,* Bonn, Germany.

Armstrong, S. A., Staunton, J. E., Silverman, L. B., Pieters, R., den Boer, M. L., Minden, M. D., Sallan, S. E., Lander, E. S., Golub, T. R., & Korsmeyer, S. J. (2002). MLL translocations specify a distinct gene expression profile that distinguishes a unique leukemia. *Nature Genetics, 30*, 41-47.

Asai, T., Abe, K., Kawasoe, S., Arimura, H., Sakamoto, H., &, Arikawa, S. (2002, April). Efficient substructure discovery from large semi-structured data. In *Proceedings of the 2nd SIAM International Conference on Data Mining, ICDM '02*, Arlington, Virginia.

Barbara, D., & Sullivan, M. (1997). Quasi-cubes: Exploiting approximation in multidimensional data sets. *SIGMOD Record, 26*(2), 12-17.

Barnard, K., Duygulu, P., de Freitas, N., Forsyth, D., Blei, D. M., & Jordan, M. I. (2003). Matching words and pictures. *Journal of Machine Learning Research, 3*, 1107-1135.

Baron, S., & Spiliopoulou, M. (2005). Temporal evolution and local patterns. In Morik et al. (Eds.), *Local patterns detection* (pp. 190–206). Berlin Heidelberg: Springer-Verlag

Baron, S., Spiliopoulou, M., & Günther, O. (2003). Efficient monitoring of patterns in data mining environments. In *Proceedings of 7th East-European Conference on Advances in Databases and Information Systems (ADBIS '03)*.

Barthélemy, J. P. (1978). Remarques sur les propriétés metriques des ensembles ordonnés, *Math. sci. hum.*, 61, 39-60.

Barthélemy, J. P., & Leclerc, B. (1995). The median procedure for partitions. In *Partitioning Data Sets*, (pp. 3-34), Providence, RI.: American Mathematical Society.

Bartolini, I., Ciaccia, P., Ntoutsi, I., Patella, M., & Theodoridis, Y. (2004). A unified and flexible framework for comparing simple and complex patterns. In *Proceedings of ECML/PKDD 2004*, Pisa, Italy.

Bateman, A., Coin, L., Durbin, R., Finn, R. D., Hollich, V., Griffiths-Jones, S., Khanna, A., Marshall, M., Moxon, S., Sonnhammer, E. L. L., Studholme, D. J., Yeats, C., & Eddy, S. R. (2004). The pfam protein families database. *Nucleic Acids Research, 32*, 138-141.

Bathe, K. J. (1996). *Finite element procedures*. Englewood Cliffs, NJ: Prentice Hall.

Bayardo, R. J. (1998). Efficiently mining long patterns from databases. In *Proceedings of the ACM SIGMOD International Conference on Management of Data*, 85-93.

Bayardo, R., Agrawal, R.. & Gunopulous, D. (1999). Constraint-based rule mining in large, dense databases. In *Proceedings of the 15th International Conference on Data Engineering (ICDE)*, 188-197.

Bekkerman, R., & McCallum, A. (2005). Disambiguating web appearances of people in a social network. In *Proceedings of WWW 2005*.

Belkin, M., & Niyogi, P. (2003). Using manifold structure for partially labeled classification. *Advances in Neural Information Processing*.

Ben-Dov, M., Wu, W., Cairns, P., & Feldman, R. (2004). Improving knowledge discovery by combining text-mining and link analysis techniques. In M. W. Berry, U. Dayal, C. Kamath, D. B. Skillicorn (Eds.). In *Proceedings of the Fourth SIAM International Conference on Data Mining*. Lake Buena Vista, Florida, USA.

Benson, D. A., Mizrachi, I. K., Lipman, D. J., Ostell, J., & Wheeler, D. L. (2005). Genbank. *Nucleic Acids Research, 33*.

Benson, G. (1997). Sequence alignment with tandem duplication. *Journal of Computational Biology, 4*(3), 351-67.

Benson, G. (1999). Tandem repeats finder: A program to analyze DNA sequences. *Nucleic Acids Research, 27*(2), 573–580.

Berardi, M., Ceci, M., & Malerba, D. (2003). Mining spatial association rules from document layout structures. In *Proceedings of the 3rd Workshop on Document Layout Interpretation and its Application, DLIA '03*.

Berg, J., & Lassig, M. (2004). Local graph alignment and motif search in biological networks. In *Proceedings of the National Academy of Sciences of the United States of America*, (pp. 14689-14694).

Berman, H. M., Bourne, P. E., & Westbrook, J. (2004). The pdb: A case study in management of community data. *Current Proteomics, 1*, 49-57.

Bhattacharjee, A., Richards, W. G., Staunton, J., Li, C., Monti, S., Vasa, P., Ladd, C., Beheshti, J., Bueno, R., Gillette, M., Loda, M., Weber, G., Mark, E. J., Lander, E. S., Wong, W., Johnson, B. E., Golub, T. R., Sugarbaker, D. J., & Meyerson, M. (2001). Classification of human lung carcinomas by mRNA expression profiling reveals distinct adenocarcinoma subclasses. *PNAS, 98*, 13790-13795.

Bishop, Y., Fienberg, S. E., & Holland, P. (1975). *Discrete multivariate analysis: Theory and practice.* The MIT press.

Blake, C. L., Newman, D. J., Hettich, S., & Merz, C. J. (1998). UCI repository of machine learning databases. Retrieved March 18, 2007, from http://www.ics.uci.edu/~mlearn/MLRepository.html

Blei, D. M., Ng, A., & Jordan, M. I. (2003). Latent dirichlet allocation. *Journal of Machine Learning Research, 3*, 993-1022.

Blockeel, H., & Sebag, M. (2003). Scalability and efficiency in multi-relational data mining. *SIGKDD Explorations, 5*(1): 17-30.

Blum A., & Langley, P. (1997). Selection of relevant features and examples in machine learning. *Artificial Intelligence*, 245-271.

Bollegara, D., Matsuo, Y., & Ishizuka, M. (2006). Extracting key phrases to disambiguate personal names on the Web. In *Proceedings of ECAI 2006*.

Bonchi, F., & Goethals, B. (2004). FP-Bonsai: The art of growing and pruning small fp-trees. In *Proceedings of the Pacific-Asia Conference on Knowledge Discovery and Data Mining (PAKDD '04)* (pp.155–160).

Bonchi, F., & Lucchese, C. (2004). On closed constrained frequent pattern mining. In *Proceedings of the IEEE International Conference on Data Mining (ICDM '04)*.

Bonchi, F., Giannotti, Mazzanti, A., & Pedreschi, D. (2004). Examiner: Optimized level-wise frequent pattern mining with monotone constraints. In *Proceedings of the IEEE ICDM*, Melbourne, Florida.

Brazma, A., Jonassen, I., Eidhammer, I., & Gilbert, D. (1998). Approaches to the automatic discovery of patterns in biosequences. *Journal of Computational Biology, 5*(2), 277-304.

Brazma, A., Jonassen, I., Vilo, J., & Ukkonen, E. (1998). Predicting gene regulatory elements in silico on a genomic scale. *Genome Research, 8*(11), 1998.

Breiman, L., Friedman, J. H., Olshen, R. A., & Stone, C. J. (1998). *Classification and regression trees.* Chapman and Hall, Boca Raton.

Brin, S., & Page, L. (1998). The anatomy of a large-scale hypertextual web search engine. In *Proceeings of 7th WWW Conf.*

Brin, S., Motwani, R., & Silverstein, C. (1997). Beyond market baskets: Generalizing association rules to correlations. In *Proceedings of the 1997 ACM SIGMOD International Conference on Management of Data*, 265–276.

Brown, M. P. S., Grundy, W. N., Lin, D., Cristiani, N., Sugnet, C. W., Furey, T. S, Ares, M., & Haussler, D. (2000). Knowledge-based analysis of microarray gene expression data by using support vector machines. *PNAS, 97*, 262–267.

Brunsdon, C., Fotheringham, A. S., & Charlton, M. (1998). An investigation of methods for visualising highly multivariate datasets. In D. Unwin, & P. Fisher (Eds.), *Case studies of visualization in the social sciences* (pp. 55-80).

Bucila, C., Gehrke, J., Kifer, D., & White, W. (2002). Dualminer: A dual-pruning algorithm for itemsets with constraints. In *Proceedings of the Eight ACM SIGKDD*

International Conf. on Knowledge Discovery and Data Mining (pp. 42–51), Edmonton, Alberta.

Burdick, D., Calimlim, M. J., & Gehrke, J. (2001). *Mafia: A maximal frequent itemset algorithm for transactional databases.* ICDE (pp 443–452).

Burdick, D., Calimlim, M., & Gehrke, J. (2001). MAFIA: A maximal frequent itemset algorithm for transactional databases. In *Proceedings of the 2001 International Conference on Data Engineering (ICDE)*, 443-452.

Butterworth, R., Piatetsky-Shapiro, G., & Simovici, D. A. (2005). On feature extraction through clustering. In *Proceedings of ICDM*, Houston, Texas.

Butterworth, R., Simovici, D. A., Santos, G. S., & Ohno-Machado, L. (2004). A greedy algorithm for supervised discretization. *Journal of Biomedical Informatics*, 285-292.

Cafarella, M., & Etzioni, O. (2005). A search engine for natural language applications. In *Proc. WWW2005*.

Calishain, T., & Dornfest, R. (2003). *Google hacks: 100 industrial-strength tips & tools.* O'Reilly.

Can, F. (1993). Incremental clustering for dynamic information processing. *ACM Transactions for Information Systems, 11*, 143-164.

Can, F., Fox, E. A., Snavely, C. D. & France, R. K. (1995). Incremental clustering for very large document databases: Initial {MARIAN} experience. *Inf. Sci., 84*, 101-114.

Candillier, L., Tellier, I., & Torre, F. (2006). Transforming XML trees for efficient classification and clustering. In *Proceedings of the 4th International Workshop of the Initiative for the Evaluation of XML Retrieval, INEX '05*, Schloss Dagstuhl, Germany.

Candillier, L., Tellier, I., Torre, F., & Bousquet, O. (2005). SSC: Statistical subspace clustering. In P. Perner & A. Imiya (Eds.). In *Proceedings of the 4th International Conference on Machine Learning and Data Mining in Pattern Recognition, MLDM '05*, Leipzig, Germany.

Carlin, B. P., & Louis, T. A. (2005). *Bayes and empirical Bayes methods for data analysis.* Chapman & Hall.

Carpenter, G., & Grossberg, S. (1990). Art3: Hierachical search using chemical transmitters in self-organizing pattern recognition architectures. *Neural Networks, 3*, 129-152.

Carvalho, A. M., Freitas, A. T., Oliveira, A. L., & Sagot, M. F. (2005). A highly scalable algorithm for the extraction of cis-regulatory regions. In *Proceedings of the 3rd Asia-Pacific Bioinformatics Conference*, (pp. 273-282).

Ceci, M., & Malerba, D. (2007). Classifying web documents in a hierarchy of categories: A comprehensive study. *Journal of Intelligent Information Systems, 28*(1), 1-41.

Celeux, G., Diday, E., Govaert, G., Lechevallier, Y., & Ralambondrainy, H. (1989). *Classification Automatique des Données, Environnement statistique et informatique.* Dunod informatique, Bordas, Paris.

Cerquides, J., & López de Mántaras, R. (1997). Proposal and empirical comparison of a parallelizable distance-based discretization method. In *Proceedings of the 3rd International Conference on Knowledge Discovery and Data Mining (KDD '97)*.

Cesarini, F., Francescani, E., Gori, M., Marinai, S., Sheng, J., & Soda, G. (1997). A neural-based architecture for spot-noisy logo recognition. In *Proceedings of the 4th International Conference on Document Analysis and Recognition, ICDAR'97*.

Chakrabarti, D., Papadimitriou, S., Modha, D., & Faloutsos, C. (2004). Fully automatic cross-associations. In *Proceedings of the ACM SIGKDD International Conference on Knowledge Discovery and Data Mining.*

Chakrabarti, S. (2002). *Mining the web: Discovering knowledge from hypertext data.* Morgan Kaufmann.

Charikar, M., Chekuri, C., Feder, T., & Motwani, R (1997). Incremental clustering and dynamic information retrieval. In *STOC*, (pp. 626-635).

Chaudhuri, S. (1998). Data mining and database systems: Where is the intersection? *Bulletin of the Technical Committee on Data Engineering*, p. 21.

Cheeseman, P., & Stutz, J. (1996). Bayesian classification (autoclass): Theory and results. In *Proceedings of* the *ACM KDD International Conference on Knowledge Discovery and Data Mining*, 61-83.

Chen, M. S., Park, J. S., & Yu, P. S. (1996). Data mining for path traversal patterns in a web environment. In *Proceedings of the 16th International Conference on Distributed Computing Systems.*

Cherfi, H., Napoli, A., & Toussaint, Y. (2006). Towards a text mining methodology using association rule extraction. *Soft Computing: A Fusion of Foundations, Methodologies and Applications, 10*(5): 431-441.

Chi, Y., Yang, Y., Xia, Y., & Muntz, R. R. (2004, May). CMTreeMiner: Mining both closed and maximal frequent subtrees. In *Proceedings of the 8th Pacific-Asia Conference on Advances in Knowledge Discovery and Data Mining, PAKDD '04*, Sydney, Australia.

Choong, Y. W., Laurent, D., & Laurent, A. (2004). Summarizing multidimensional databases using fuzzy rules. *In Proceedings of the International Conference Information Processing and Management of Uncertainty in Knowledge-Based Systems (IPMU '04)* Universdita degli studi di Perugia.

Choong, Y. W., Laurent, D., & Laurent, A. (in press). Pixelizing data cubes: A block-based approach. *In IEEE EMBS Visual Information Expert Workshop (VIEW '06).* Lecture Notes in Computer Science.

Choong, Y. W., Laurent, D., & Marcel, P. (2003). Computing appropriate representation for multidimensional data. *Data and Knowledge Engineering International Journal, 45*, 181-203.

Cimiano, P., & Staab, S. (2004). Learning by googling. *SIGKDD Explorations, 6*(2), 24–33.

Cimiano, P., Handschuh, S., & Staab, S. (2004). Towards the self-annotating web. In *Proceedings of WWW2004.*

Cimiano, P., Ladwig, G., & Staab, S. (2005). Gimme' the context: Context-driven automatic Semantic annotation with C-PANKOW. In *Proceedings of WWW 2005.*

Codd, E. F., Codd, S. B., & Salley, C. T. (1993). *Providing OLAP to user-analysts: An IT mandate* (Tech. Rep.).

Arbor Software Corporation. Retrieved March 18, 2007, from http://dev.hyperion.com/resource_library/white_papers/providing_olap_to_user_analysts.pdf

Cohen, E., Datar, M., Fujiwara, S., Gionis, A., Indyk, P., Motwani, R., Ullman, J., & Yang, C. (2000). Finding interesting associations without support pruning. In *Proceedings of the 2000 International Conference on Data Engineering (ICDE)*, 489–499.

Connor, J. (2006). *Multivariate mixture models to describe longitudinal patterns of frailty in American seniors.* Unpublished doctoral dissertation, Department of Statistics, Carnegie Mellon University, Pittsburgh, PA.

Cornujols, A. (1993). Getting order independence in incremental learning. In *Proceeding of the European Conference on Machine Learning*, pages 192-212.

Costa, G., Manco, G., Ortale, R., & Tagarelli, A. (2004). A tree-based approach to clustering XML documents by structure. In *Proceedings of the 8th European Conference on Principles and Practice of Knowledge Discovery in Databases, PKDD '04*, Pisa, Italy.

Cover, T. M., & Hart, P. E. (1967). Nearest neighbor pattern classification. *IEEE Transactions on Information Theory, 1*, 21-27.

Culotta, A., Bekkerman, R., & McCallum, A. (2004). Extracting social networks and contact information from email and the web. In *CEAS-1.*

Dalamagas, T., Cheng, T., Winkel, K.-J., & Sellis, T. K. (2004, May).Clustering. In *Proceedings of the 3rd Helenic Conference on Methods and Applications of Artificial Intelligence, SETN '04*, Samos, Greece.

Daróczy, Z. (1970). Generalized information functions. *Information and Control, 16*, 36-51.

Dasarathy, B. W. (1991) *Nearest neighbor (NN) norms: NN pattern classification techniques.* Los Alamitos, CA: IEEE Computer Society Press.

Davis, I., & Jr., E. V. Relationship: A vocabulary for describing relationships between people. Retrieved from http://vocab.org/relationship/

de Raedt, L., & Kersting, K. (2003). Probabilistic logic learning. *SIGKDD Explorations, 5*(1): 31-48.

Dehaspe, L., & Toivonen, H. (1999). Discovery of frequent datalog patterns. *Data Mining and Knowledge Discovery, 3*(1), 7–36.

Demsar, J., Leban, G., & Zupan, B. (2005). FreeViz - An intelligent visualization approach for class-labeled multidimensional data sets. *IDAMAP-05 Workshop Notes.* Aberdeen, UK.

Demsar, J., Zupan, B., & Leban, G. (2004). Orange: From experimental machine learning to interactive data mining. White Paper, Faculty of Computer and Information Science, University of Ljubljana.

Demsar, J., Zupan, B., Leban, G., & Curk, T. (2004). Orange: From experimental machine learning to interactive data mining. In *Proceedings of the European Conference of Machine Learning.* Pisa, Italy.

Dengel, A. (1993). Initial learning of document structure. In *Proceedings of the 2nd International Conference on Document Analysis and Recognition, ICDAR'93.*

Dengel, A. (2003). Making documents work: Challenges for document understanding. In *Proceedings of the Seventh International Conference on Document Analysis and Recognition, ICDAR'95.*

Dengel, A., & Dubiel, F. (1995). Clustering and classification of document structure-a machine learning approach. In *Proceedings of the Third International Conference on Document Analysis and Recognition, ICDAR'95.*

Dengel, A., Bleisinger, R., Hoch, R., Fein, F. & Hönes, F. (1992). From paper to office document standard representation. *Computer, 25*(7).

Denoyer, L., & Gallinari, P. (2004). Bayesian network model for semi-structured document classification [Special Issue]. *Information Processing and Management: An International Journal Special Issue: Bayesian networks and information retrieval, 40*(5), 807 – 827.

Denoyer, L., Vittaut, J.-N., Gallinari, P., Brunesseaux, S., & Brunesseaux, S. (2003). Structured multimedia document classification. In *Proceedings of the ACM Symposium on Document Engineering*, Grenoble, France.

Denoyer, L., Wisniewski, G., & Gallinari, P. (2004, July). Document structure matching for heterogeneous corpora. In *Proceedings of the Workshop on XML and Information Retrieval, SIGIR '04,* Sheffield.

Diaconis, P., & Friedman, D. (1984). Asymptotics of graphical projection pursuit. *Annals of Statistics, 1,* 793-815.

Domingos, P. (2003). Prospects and challenges for multi-relational data mining. *SIGKDD Explorations, 5*(1), 80-83.

Doucet, A., & Ahonen-Myka, H. (2002, December). Naïve clustering of a large XML document collection. In *Proceedings of the 1st ERCIM Workshop of the Initiative for the Evaluation of XML Retrieval, INEX '02,* Schloss Dagsuhl, Germany.

Dougherty, J., Kohavi, R., & Sahami, M. (1995). Supervised and unsupervised discretization of continuous features. In *Proceedings of the 12th International Conference on Machine Learning,* 194-202.

Dubois, D., Hülermeier, E., & Prade, H. (2003). A note on quality measures for fuzzy association rules. In *Proceedings of International Fuzzy Systems Association World Congress on Fuzzy Sets and Systems.*

Duda, R. O., Hart, P. E., & Stork, D. G. (2000). *Pattern classification.* Wiley-Interscience.

El-Hajj, M., & Zaïane, O. R. (2003). Non recursive generation of frequent k-itemsets from frequent pattern tree representations. In *Proceedings of 5th International Conference on Data Warehousing and Knowledge Discovery (DaWak'2003).*

El-Hajj, M., & Zaïane, O. R. (2005). Mining with constraints by pruning and avoiding ineffectual processing. In *Proceedings of the 18th Australian Joint Conference on Artificial Intelligence,* Sydney, Australia.

El-Hajj, M., & Zaïane, O. R. (2006). Parallel leap: Large-scale maximal pattern mining in a distributed environment. In *Proceedings of the International Conference on Parallel and Distributed Systems (ICPADS'06)*, Minneapolis, Minnesota.

El-Hajj, M., Zaïane, O. R., & Nalos, P. (2005). Bifold constraint-based mining by simultaneous monotone and anti-monotone checking. In *Proceedings of the IEEE 2005 International Conference on Data Mining*, Houston, Texas.

Elloumi, M., & Maddouri, M. (2005). New voting strategies designed for the classification of nucleic sequences. *Knowledge and Information Systems, 1*, 1-15.

Erosheva, E. A. (2002). *Grade of membership and latent structure models with application to disability survey data*. Unpublished doctoral dissertation, Carnegie Mellon University, Pittsburgh, PA.

Erosheva, E. A. (2002). Partial membership models with application to disability survey data. In H. Bozdogan (Ed.). In *Proceedings of Conference on the New Frontiers of Statistical Data Mining*.

Erosheva, E. A. (2003). Bayesian estimation of the grade of membership model. *Bayesian statistics (*Vol. 7). Oxford University Press.

Erosheva, E. A., & Fienberg, S. E. (2005). Bayesian mixed membership models for soft clustering and classification. In C. Weihs & W. Gaul, (Eda.), *Classification---The ubiquitous challenge* (pp 11-26). Springer-Verlag.

Erosheva, E. A., Fienberg, S. E., & Lafferty, J. (2004). Mixed-membership models of scientific publications. *Proceedings of the National Academy of Sciences, 97*(22), 11885-11892.

Eskin, E., & Pevzner, P. A. (2002). Finding composite regulatory patterns in DNA sequences. *Bioinformatics, 18*(Suppl. 1), S354-63.

Esposito, F., & Malerba, D. (2001). Guest editorial: Machine learning in computer vision. *Applied Artificial Intelligence, 15*(8): 1-13.

Esposito, F., Malerba, D., & Semeraro, G. (1990). An experimental page layout-recognition system for office document automatic classification: An integrated approach for inductive generalization. In *Proceedings of*

10th International Conference on Pattern Recognition, ICPR'90.

Esposito, F., Malerba, D., & Semeraro, G. (1994). Multistrategy learning for document recognition. *Applied Artificial Intelligence: An International Journal, 8*(1), 33-84.

Ester, M., Kriegel, H.-P., Sander, J., Wimmer, M., & Xu, X. (1998). Incremental clustering for mining in a data warehousing environment. In *Proceedings of the International Conference on Very Large Data Bases (VLDB)*, (pp. 323-333).

Faloutsos, C., McCurley, K. S., & Tomkins, A. (2004). Fast discovery of connection subgraphs. In *Proceedings of the ACM SIGKDD 2004*.

Fan, X., Sheng, F., & Ng, P. A. (1999). DOCPROS: A knowledge-based personal document management system. In *Procedings of the 10th International Workshop on Database Expert Systems Applications*.

Fassetti, F., Greco, G., & Terracina, G. (2006). Efficient discovery of loosely structured motifs in biological data. In *Proceedings of the 21st Annual ACM Symposium on Applied Computing*, (pp. 151-155).

Fayyad, U. M. (1991). *On the induction of decision trees for multiple concept learning*. Unpublished doctoral thesis, University of Michigan.

Fayyad, U. M., & Irani, K. (1993). Multi-interval discretization of continuous-valued attributes for classification learning. In *Proceedings of the 12th International Joint Conference of Artificial intelligence*, 10222-1027.

Feder, T., & Motwani, R. (1995). Clique partitions, graph compression and speeding-up algorithms [Special Issue]. *Journal of Computer and System Sciences, 51*, 261–272

Ferguson, T. (1973). A Bayesian analysis of some nonparametric problems. *The Annals of Statistics, 1*, 209-230.

FIMI (2003). Itemset mining implementations repository. Retrieved March 6, 2007, from *http://fimi.cs.helsinki.fi/*

Finin, T., Ding, L., & Zou, L. (2005). Social networking on the Semantic Web. *The Learning Organization.*

Fisher, D. (1987). Knowledge acquisition via incremental conceptual clustering. *Machine Learning, 2*, 139-172.

Flach, P. A., & Lavrac, N. (2003). Rule induction. *Intelligent Data Analysis: An Introduction* (pp. 229-267). Springer-Verlag.

Flesca, S., Manco, G., Masciari, E., Pontieri, L., & Pugliese, A. (2002). Detecting structural similarities between xml documents. In *Proceedings of the 5th International Workshop on the Web and Databases, WebDB '02*, Madison, Wisconsin.

Fredkin, E. (1960). Trie memory. *Communications of the ACM, 3*(9), 490-499.

Freeman, L. C. (1979). Centrality in social networks: Conceptual clarification. *Social Networks, 1*, 215–239.

Friedman, J. H., & Tukey, J. W. (1974). A projection pursuit algorithm for exploratory data analysis, *IEEE Transactions on Computers, C-23*, 881-889.

Gandon, F., Corby, O., Giboin, A., Gronnier, N., & Guigard, C. (2005). Graph-based inferences in a Semantic web server for the cartography of competencies in a telecom valley. In *Proceedings of ISWC05.*

Ganti, V., Gehrke, J., & Ramakrishnan, R. (1999). A framework for measuring changes in data characteristics. In *Proceedings of the 18th ACM SIGACT-SIGMOD-SIGART Symposium on Principles of Database Systems (PODS '99)*, Philadelphia, Pennsylvania.

Ganti, V., Gehrke, J., & Ramakrishnan, R. (1999). CACTUS: Clustering categorical data using summaries. In *Proceedings of 5th ACM SIGKDD International Conference on Knowledge Discovery and Data Mining (KDD '99).*

Ganti, V., Gehrke, J., & Ramakrishnan, R. (2000). DEMON: Mining and monitoring evolving data. In *Proceedings of the 15th IEEE International Conference on Data Engineering (ICDE'2000).*

Gavin, A. et al. (2002). Functional organization of the yeast proteome by systematic analysis of protein complexes. *Nature, 415*, 141-147.

Getoor, L., Friedman, N., Koller, D., & Taskar, B. (2003). Learning probabilistic models of link structure. *Journal of Machine Learning Research, 3*, 679–707.

Ghahramani, Z. (2004). Unsupervised learning. In O. Bousquet, G. Raetsch & U. von Luxburg, (Eds.), *Advanced lectures on machine learning* (Vol. 3176) *Lecture Notes in Computer Science.* Springer-Verlag.

Goecks, J., & Mynatt, E. D. (2004). Leveraging social networks for information sharing. In *Proceedings of ACM CSCW 2004.*

Golbeck, J., & Hendler, J. (2004). Accuracy of metrics for inferring trust and reputation in Semantic web-based social networks. In *Proceedings of EKAW 2004.*

Golbeck, J., & Hendler, J. (2004). Inferring reputation on the Semantic web. In *Proceedings of WWW2004.*

Golbeck, J., & Hendler, J. (2005). Inferring trust relationships in web-based social networks. *ACM Transactions on Internet Technology, 7*(1).

Golbeck, J., & Parsia, B. (2006). Trust network-based filtering of aggregated claims. *International Journal of Metadata, Semantics and Ontologies.*

Golub, T. R., Slonim, D. K., Tamayo, P., Huard, C., Gaasenbeek, M., Mesirov, J. P., Coller, H., Loh, M. L., Downing, J. R., Caligiuri, M. A., Bloomfield, C. D., & Lander, E. S. (1999). Molecular classification of cancer: Class discovery and class prediction by gene expression monitoring, *Science, 286*, 531-537.

Grahne, G., Lakshmanan, L. V. S., & Wang, X. (2000). Efficient mining of constrained correlated sets. In *Proceedings of the 2000 International Conference on Data Engineering (ICDE)*, 512-524.

Granovetter, M. (1973). Strength of weak ties. *American Journal of Sociology, 78*, 1360–1380.

Griffiths, T. L. & Steyvers, M. (2004). Finding scientific topics. *Proceedings of the National Academy of Sciences, 101* (Suppl. 1), 5228-5235.

Guha, R., & Garg, A. (2004). Disambiguating entities in Web search. TAP project, http://tap.stanford.edu/PeopleSearch.pdf

Guha, S., Rastagi, R., & Shim, K. (1998). CURE: An efficient clustering algorithm for large databases. In *Proceedings of the ACM International Conference on Management Of Data (SIGMOD '98).*

Gunopulos, D., Agrawal, R., Gehrke, J., & Raghavan, P. (1998). Automatic subspace clustering of high dimensional data for data mining applications. In *Proceedings of the ACM International Conference on Management Of Data (SIGMOD '98).*

Gusfield, D. (Ed.). (1997). *Algorithms on strings, trees and sequences: Computer science and computational biology.* Cambrige University Press.

Gusfield, D., & Stoye, J. (2004). Linear time algorithms for finding and representing all the tandem repeats in a string. *Journal of Computer and System Sciences, 69,* 525-546.

Guyon, E., & Elisseeff, A. (2003). An introduction to variable and feature selection. *Journal of Machine Learning Research,* 1157-1182.

Gyenesei, A. (2000). *A fuzzy approach for mining quantitative association rules* (Tech. Rep. 336). Turku Center for Computer Science (TUCS).

Hall, M.A. (1999). Correlation-based feature selection for machine learning. Unpublished doctoral thesis, University of Waikato, New Zeland.

Han, E., Karypis, G., & Kumar, V. (1998). Hypergraph based clustering in high-dimensional data sets: A summary of results. *Bulletin of the Technical Committee on Data Engineering, 21*(1), 15-22.

Han, J., & Fu, Y. (1995). Discovery of multiple-level association rules from large databases. In U. Dayal, P. M. Gray & S. Nishio (Eds.). In *Proceedings of the 21*[th] *International Conference on Very Large Data Bases.*

Han, J., & Kamber, M. (2000). *Data mining: Concepts and techniques.* Morgan Kaufmann.

Han, J., Pei, J., & Yin, Y. (2000). Mining frequent patterns without candidate generation. In *Proceedings of the 2000 ACM SIGMOD international Conference on Management of Data SIGMOD '00.,* (pp. 1-12).

Hanczar, B., Courtine, M., Benis, A., Hannegar, C., Clement, K., & Zucker, J. D. (2003). Improving classification of microarray data using prototype-based feature selection. *SIGKDD Explorations,* 23-28.

Hanneman, R., & Riddle, M. (2005). *Introduction to social network methods.* University of California, Riverside.

Harada, M., Sato, S., & Kazama, K. (2004). Finding authoritative people from the Web. In *Proceedings of the Joint Conference on Digital Libraries (JCDL2004).*

Hardman, L., Rutledge, L., & Bulterman, D. (1998). Automated generation of hypermedia presentation from pre-existing tagged media objects. In *Proceedings of the Second Workshop on Adaptive Hypertext and Hypermedia.*

Harris, R. L. (1999). *Information graphics: A comprehensive illustrated reference.* New York: Oxford Press.

Hartigan, J. A. (1975). *Clustering algorithms.* New York: John Wiley.

Hastie, T., Tibshirani, R., & Friedman, J. H. (2001). *The elements of statistical learning: Data mining, inference, and prediction.* Springer-Verlag.

Hauth, A. M., & Joseph, D. A. (2002). Beyond tandem repeats: Complex pattern structures and distant regions of similarity. *Bioinformatics, 18*(1), 31-37.

Haveliwala, T. (2002). Topic-sensitive PageRank. In *Proceedings of WWW2002.*

Havrda, J. H., & Charvat, F. (1967). Quantification methods of classification processes: Concepts of structural α-entropy. *Kybernetica, 3,* 30-35.

Hiraki, K., Gennari, J. H., Yamamoto, Y., & Anzai, Y. (1991). *Learning spatial relations from images.* Machine Learning Workshop, Chicago (pp. 407-411).

Hoffman, P., Grinstein, G., & Pinkney, D. (1999). Dimensional anchors: A graphic primitive for multidimensional multivariate information visualizations. In *Proceedings of the 1999 Workshop on new paradigms in information visualization and manipulation.*

Hotelling, H. (1933). Analysis of a complex of statistical variables into principal components. *Journal of Educational Psychology, 24,* 417-441, 498-520.

Hu, H., Yan, X., Huang, Y., Han, J., & Zhou, X., J. (2005). Mining coherent dense subgraphs across massive biological networks for functional discovery. *Bioinformatics, 18*(1), 31-37.

Hulo, N., Sigrist, C. J. A., Le Saux, V., Langendijk-Genevaux, P. S., Bordoli, L., Gattiker, A., De Castro, E., Bucher, P., & Bairoch, A. (2004). Recent improvements to the PROSITE database. *Nucleic Acids Research, 32,* 134-137.

Inmon, W. H. (1992). *Building the data warehouse.* John Wiley & Sons.

Inokuchi, A., Washio, T., & Motoda, H. (2000). An apriori-based algorithm for mining frequent substructures from graph data. In *Proceedings of the 4th European Conference on Principles of Data Mining and Knowledge Discovery.*

Inselberg, A. (1981). *N-dimensional graphics, part I-lines and hyperplanes* (Tech. Rep. No. G320-2711). IBM Los Angeles Scientific Center.

Ipeirotis, P., Ntoulas, A., Cho, J., & Gravano, L. (2005). Modeling and managing content changes in text databases. In *Proceedings of the 20th IEEE International Conference on Data Engineering (ICDE '05).*

Jain, A. K., & Dubes, R. C. (1998). *Algorithms for clustering data.* Prentice Hall.

Jain, A. K., Murty, M. N., & Flynn, P. J. (1999). Data clustering: A review. *ACM Computing Surveys, 31,* 264-323.

Jeffreys, A. J., Wilson, V., & Thein, S. L. (1985). Hypervariable "minisatellite" regions in human DNA. *Nature, 314*(6006), 67-73.

Jeffreys, A. J., Wilson, V., & Thein, S. L. (1985). Individual-specific "fingerprints" of human DNA. *Nature, 316*(6023), 76-9.

Jensen, L. J., & Knudsen, S. (2000). Automatic discovery of regulatory patterns in promoter regions based on whole cell expression data and functional annotation. *Bioinformatics, 16*(4), 326-333.

Ji, Z., Wei, W., Han, L., & Sheng, Z. (2005). X-warehouse: Building query pattern-driven data. In *Proceedings of the International World Wide Web Conference (Special interest tracks and posters).*

Jiang, N., & Gruenwald, L. (2006). Research issues in data stream association rule mining. *SIGMOD Rec., 35*(1), 14-19.

Jin, Y., Matsuo, Y., & Ishizuka, M. (2006). Extracting a social network among entities by web mining. In *Proceedings of the ISWC '06 Workshop on Web Content Mining with Human Language Techniques.*

Jolliffe, I. T. (1986). *Principal component analysis.* Springer-Verlag.

Jonassen, I., Collins, J. F., & Higgins, D. G. (1995). Finding flexible patterns in unaligned protein sequences. *Protein Science, 4,* 1587-1595.

Jordan, M. I., Ghahramani, Z., Jaakkola, T., & Saul, L. (1999). Introduction to variational methods for graphical models. *Machine Learning, 37,* 183-233.

Kamvar, S., Schlosser, M., & Garcia-Molina, H. (2003). The eigentrust algorithm for reputation management in P2P networks. In *Proceedings of WWW2003.*

Kaufman, L., & Rousseeuw, P. J. (1990). *Finding groups in data—An introduction to cluster analysis.* New York: Wiley Interscience.

Kaufmann, A. (1973). *Introduction to the theory of fuzzy subsets.* Academic Press.

Kautz, H., Selman, B., & Shah, M. (1997). The hidden web. *AI magazine, 18*(2), pp. 27–35.

Keim, D. A., & Kriegel, H. (1996). Visualization techniques for mining large databases: A comparison, *Transactions on Knowledge and Data Engineering, 8*, 923-938.

Keller, F., Lapata, M., & Ourioupina, O. (2002). Using the web to overcome data sparseness. In *Proceedings of the EMNLP 2002.*

Khan, J., Wei, J. S., Ringner, M., Saal, L. H., Ladanyi, M., Westerman, F., Berthold, F., Schwab, M., Antonescu, C. R., Peterson, C., & Meltzer, P. S. (2001). Classification and diagnostic prediction of cancers using gene expression profiling and artificial neural networks. *Nature Medicine, 7*, 673-679.

Khan, J., Wei, J. S., Ringner, M., Saal, L. H., Ladanyi, M., Westermann, F., Berthold, F., Schwab, M., Antonescu, C. R., Peterson, C., & Meltzer, P. S. (2001). Classification and diagnostic prediction of cancers using gene expression profiling and artificial neural networks. *Nature Medicine, 7*, 673-679.

Kilpeläinen, P. (1992). *Tree matching problems with applications to structured text databases.* Unpublished doctoral thesis, University of Helsinki.

Kise, K., Yajima, N., Babaguchi, N., & Fukunaga, K. (1993). Incremental acquisition of knowledge about layout structures from examples of documents. In *Proceedings of the 2nd International Conference on Document Analysis and Recognition, ICDAR'93.*

Knees, P., Pampalk, E., & Widmer, G. (2004). Artist classification with web-based data. In *Proceedings of the 5th International Conference on Music Information Retrieval (ISMIR).*

Knobbe, A. J., Blockeel, H., Siebes, A., & Van der Wallen, D. M. G. (1999). Multi-relational data mining. In *Proceedings of the Benelearn 1999.*

Kohavi, R., & John, G. (1997). Wrappers for feature selection. *Artificial Intelligence*, 273-324.

Kolpakov, R. M., Bana, G. & Kucherov, G. (2003). Mreps: Efficient and flexible detection of tandem repeats in DNA. *Nucleic Acids Research, 31*(13), 3672-3678.

Kononenko, I. (1992). Naïve bayes classifiers and continuous attributes. *Informatica, 16*, 1-8.

Kononenko, I. (1993). Inductive and Bayesian learning in medical diagnosis. *Applied Artificial Intelligence, 7*, 317-337.

Kononenko, I. (1994). Estimating attributes: Analysis and extensions of RELIEF. In *Proceedings of the European Conference on Machine Learning (ECML).*

Kontostathis, A., Galitsky, L., Pottenger, W., Roy, S., & Phelps, D. (2003). A survey of emerging trend detection in textual data mining. Springer Verlag.

Koren, Y., & Carmel, L. (2004). Robust linear dimensionality reduction. *IEEE Transactions on Visualization and Computer Graphics, 10*, 459-470.

Koyuturk, M., Kim, Y., Subramaniam, S., Szpankowski, W. & Grama, A. (2006). *Journal of Computational Biology, 13*(7), 1299-1322.

Krauthgamer, R., & Lee, J. (2004). Navigating nets: Simple algorithms for proximity search. In *Proceedings of the 15th Annual Symposium on Discrete Algorithms.*

Kumar R., Raghavan, P., Rajagopalan, S., Sivakumar, D., Tomkins, A., & Upfal, E. (2000). Random graph models for the web graph. In *Proceedings of the Annual Symposium on Foundations of Computer Science.*

Kumar, R., Raghavan, P., Rajagopalan, S., & Tomkins, A. (2002). The web and social networks. *IEEE Computer, 35*(11), 32–36.

Lakshmanan, L., Ng, R., Han, J., & Pang, A. (1999). Optimization of constrained frequent set queries with 2 variable constraints. In *Proceedings of the ACM SIGMOD Conference on Management of Data* (pp 157–168).

Lakshmanan, L., Pei, J., & Han, J. (2002). Quotient cube: How to summarize the semantics of a data cube. In *Proceedings of the International Conference on Very Large Data Bases VLDB.*

Langford, T., Giraud-Carrier, C. G., & Magee, J. (2001). Detection of infectious outbreaks in hospitals through incremental clustering. In *Proceedings of the 8th Conference on AI in Medicine* (AIME).

Lapata, M., & Keller, F. (2004). The web as a baseline: Evaluating the performance of unsupervised web-based models for a range of nlp tasks. In *Proceedings of the HLT-NAACL 2004*.

Leban, G., Zupan, B., Vidmar, G., & Bratko, I. (2006). VizRank: Data visualization guided by machine learning. *Data Mining and Knowledge Discovery, 13*, 119-136.

Lee, C.,-H., Lin, C.,-R., & Chen, M.-S. (2001). On mining general temporal association rules in a publication database. In *Proceedings of the 2001 IEEE International Conference on Data Mining.*

Lee, W., Stolfo, S., & Mok, K. (1998). Mining audit data to build intrusion detection models. In Agrawal, Stolorz & Piatetsky Shapiro (Eds.). In *Proceedings of the 4th International Conference on Knowledge Discovery and Data Mining.*

Lent, B., Agrawal, R., & Srikant, R. (1997). Discovering trends in text databases. In *Proceedings of 3rd International Conference on Knowledge Discovery and Data Mining.*

Lesk, A. (Ed.). (2004). *Introduction to protein science architecture, function, and genomics.* Oxford University Press.

Leskovec, J. Grobelnik, M., & Millic-Frayling, N. (2004, August). *Learning sub-structures of document semantic graphs for document summarization.* Paper presented at the Workshop on Link Analysis and Group Detection, Seattle, WA.

Leskovec, J., Adamic, L. A., & Huberman, B. A. (2005). The dynamics of viral marketing. http://www.hpl.hp.com/research/idl/papers/viral/viral.pdf

Li, S., Wu T., & Pottenger, W. M. (2005). Distributed higher order association rule mining using information extracted from textual data. *SIGKDD Explor. Newsl., 7*(1), 26-35.

Li, X., Morie, P., & Roth, D. (2005). Semantic integration in text: From ambiguous names to identifiable entities. *AI Magazine Spring*, pp. 45–68.

Lian, W., Cheung, D. W., Mamoulis, N., & Yiu, S.-M. (2004). An efficient and scalable algorithm for clustering XML documents by structure. *IEEE Transactions and Knowledge Data Engineering, 16*(1), 82-96.

Liao, C., Wang, X. Y., Wei, H. Q., Li, S. Q., Merghoub, T., Pandolfi, P. P., & Wolgemuth, D. J. (2001). Altered myelopoiesis and the development of acute myeloid leukemia in transgenic mice overexpressing cyclin A1. *PNAS, 98*, 6853-6858.

Lin, J., Vlachos, M., Keogh, E. J., & Gunopulos, D. (2004). Iterative incremental clustering of time series. In *EDBT*, (pp. 106—122).

Liu, B., Hsu, W., & Ma, Y. (1998). Integrating classification and association rule mining. In Agrawal, Stolorz & Piatetsky Shapiro (Eds.). In *Proceedings of the 4th International Conference on Knowledge Discovery and Data Mining.*

Liu, B., Hsu, W., & Ma, Y. (1999). Mining association rules with multiple minimum supports. In *Proceedings of the Fifth ACM SIGKDD International Conference on Knowledge Discovery and Data Mining.*

Liu, B., Hsu, W., & Ma, Y. (1999). Mining association rules with multiple minimum supports. In *Proceedings of the 1999 ACM SIGMOD International Conference on Management of Data*, 175-186.

Liu, H., & Wong, L. (2003). Data mining tools for biological sequences. *Journal of Bioinformatics and Computational Biology, 1*(1), 139-167.

Liu, J., Wang, J. T. L., Hsu, W., & Herbert, K. G. (2004). XML clustering by principal component analysis. In *Proceedings of the 16th IEEE International Conference on Tools with Artificial Intelligence, ICTAI '04.*

Lloyd, L., Bhagwan, V., Gruhl, D., & Tomkins, A. (2005). *Disambiguation of references to individuals* (Tech. Rep. No. RJ10364(A0410-011)). IBM Research.

López de Màntaras, R. (1991). A distance-based attribute selection measure for decision tree induction. *Machine Learning, 6*, 81-92.

Ludl, M. C., & Widmer, G. (2000). Relative unsupervised discretization for association rule mining. In D.A .Zighed, H.J. Komorowski, J.M. Zytkow (Eds.), *Principles of data mining and knowledge discovery* (pp. 148-158). Springer-Verlag.

Maindonald, J., & Brown, J. (2003). *Data analysis and graphics using R*. Cambridge: Cambridge University Press.

Malerba, D., Esposito, F., Lisi, F. A., & Altamura, O. (2001). Automated discovery of dependencies between logical components in document image understanding. In *Proceedings of the Sixth International Conference on Document Analysis and Recognition*, Los Vaqueros, California.

Malin, B. (2005). Unsupervised name disambiguation via social network similarity. *Workshop Notes on Link Analysis, Counterterrorism, and Security*.

Mann, G. S., & Yarowsky, D. (2003). Unsupervised personal name disambiguation. In *Proceedings of the CoNLL*.

Mannila, H., & Toivonen, H. (1997). Levelwise search and borders of theories in knowledge discovery. *Data Mining and Knowledge Discovery, 1*(3), 241–258.

Manning, C., & Sch{\"{u}}tze, H. (2002). *Foundations of statistical natural language processing*. London: The MIT Press.

Manton, K. G., Woodbury, M. A., & Tolley, H. D. (1994). *Statistical applications using fuzzy sets*. Wiley.

Marsan, L., & Sagot, M. F. (2000). Algorithms for extracting structured motifs using a suffix tree with application to promoter and regulatory site consensus identification. *Journal of Computational Biology, 7*, 345-360.

Massa, P., & Avesani, P. (2005). Controversial users demand local trust metrics: An experimental study on epinions.com community. In *Proceedings of the AAAI-05*.

Matsuo, Y., Hamasaki, M., Takeda, H., Mori, J., Bollegala, D., Nakamura, Y., Nishimura, T., Hasida, K., & Ishizuka, M. (2006). Spinning multiple social networks for Semantic web. In *Proceedigs of the AAAI-06*.

Matsuo, Y., Mori, J., Hamasaki, M., Takeda, H., Nishimura, T., Hasida, K., & Ishizuka, M. (2006). POLYPHONET: An advanced social network extraction system. In *Proceedings of the WWW 2006*.

Matsuo, Y., Tomobe, H., Hasida, K., & Ishizuka, M. (2003). Mining social network of conference participants from the web. In *Proceedings of the Web Intelligence 2003*.

Matsuo, Y., Tomobe, H., Hasida, K., & Ishizuka, M. (2004a). Finding social network for trust calculation. In *Proc. ECAI2004*, pages 510–514.

Matsuo, Y., Tomobe, H., Hasida, K., & Ishizuka, M. (2004b). Finding social network for trust calculation. In *Proceedings of the 16th European Conference on Artificial Intelligence (ECAI2004)*.

Matsuo, Y., Tomobe, H., Hasida, K., & Ishizuka, M. (2005). Social network extraction from the web information. *Journal of the Japanese Society for Artificial Intelligence, 20*(1E), 46–56.

McAuliffe, J., Blei, D. M., & Jordan, M. I. (2006). Nonparametric empirical Bayes for the Dirichlet process mixture model. *Statistics and Computing, 16*(1), 5-14 .

McCreight, E. M. (1976). A space-economical suffix tree construction algorithm. *Journal of the ACM, 23*(2), 262-272.

Mei, Q., & Zhai, C. (2005). Discovering evolutionary theme patterns from text - An exploration of temporal text mining. In *Proceedings of 11th ACM SIGKDD International Conference on Knowledge Discovery and Data Mining (KDD '05)*, Chicago, Illinois.

Mika, P. (2005). Flink: Semantic web technology for the extraction and analysis of social networks. *Journal of Web Semantics, 3*(2).

Mika, P. (2005). Ontologies are us: A unified model of social networks and Semantics. In *Proceedings of the ISWC2005*.

Miki, T., Nomura, S., & Ishida, T. (2005). Semantic web link analysis to discover social relationship in academic communities. In *Proceedings of the SAINT 2005*.

Milgram, S. (1967). The small-world problem. *Psychology Today, 2*, 60–67.

Minka, T., & Lafferty, J. (2002). Expectation-propagation for the generative aspect model. *Uncertainty in Artificial Intelligence*.

Mitchell, T. M. (1997). *Machine learning*. New York: McGraw-Hill.

Monjardet, B. (1981). Metrics on partially ordered sets—A survey. *Discrete Mathematics, 35*, 173-184.

Mori, J., Ishizuka, M., Sugiyama, T., & Matsuo, Y. (2005a). Real-world oriented information sharing using social networks. In *Proceedings of the ACM GROUP '05*.

Mori, J., Matsuo, Y. & Ishizuka, M. (2005). Finding user Semantics on the web using word co-occurrence information. In *Proceedings of the International Workshop on Personalization on the Semantic Web (PersWeb '05)*.

Moringa, S., & Yamanichi, K. (2004). Tracking dynamics of topic trends using a finite mixture model. In *Proceedings of 10th ACM SIGKDD International Conference on Knowledge Discovery and Data Mining (KDD '04)*, Seattle, Washington.

Morrison, D. R. (1968). Patricia: Practical algorithm to retrieve information coded in alphanumeric. *Journal of the ACM, 15*(4), 514-534.

Motoda, H., & Huan, Liu. (1998). *Feature selection for knowledge discovery and data mining*. Kluwer Academic Publishers.

Nagy, G. (2000). Twenty years of document image analysis in PAMI. *IEEE Transactions on Pattern Analysis and Machine Intelligence, 22* (1), 38-62.

Nagy, G., Seth, S. C., & Stoddard, S. D. (1992). A prototype document image analysis system for technical journals. *IEEE Computer, 25*(7), 10-22.

Nakagawa, H., Maeda, A., & Kojima, H. Automatic term recognition system termextract. http://gensen.dl.itc.utokyo.ac.jp/gensenweb_eng.html .

Nasraoui, O., Cardona-Uribe, C., & Rojas-Coronel, C. (2003). TECNO-Streams: Tracking evolving clusters in noisy data streams with a scalable immune system learning method. In *Proceedings of the IEEE International Conference on Data Mining (ICDM '03)*. Melbourne, Australia.

Neal, R. (2000). Markov chain sampling methods for Dirichlet process mixture models. *Journal of Computational and Graphical Statistics, 9*(2), 249-265.

Neill, D., Moore, A., Sabhnani, M., & Daniel, K. (2005). Detection of emerging space-time clusters. In *Proceedings of 11th ACM SIGKDD International Conferece on Knowledge Discovery and Data Mining (KDD '05)*, Chicago, Illinois.

Neuwald, A. F., & Green, P. (1994). Detecting patterns in protein sequences. *Journal of Molecular. Biology, 239* (5), 698-712.

Neville, J., Simsek, O., Jensen, D., Komoroske, J., Palmer, K., & Goldberg, H. (2005). Using relational knowledge discovery to prevent securities fraud. In *Proceedings of the ACM SIGKDD International Conference on Knowledge Discovery and Data Mining, Vol. 11*.

Ng, A. (1997). Preventing "overfitting" of cross-validation data. In *Proceedings of the International Conference on Machine Learning, Vol. 14*.

Ng, R. T., & Han, J. (2002). CLARANS: A method for clustering objects for spatial data mining. *IEEE Transactions on Knowledge and Data Engineering, 14*(5), 1003-1016.

Nierman, A., & Jagadish, H. V. (2002). Evaluating structural similarity in XML documents. In *Proceedings of the 5th International Workshop on the Web and Databases, WebDB '02*, Madison, Wisconsin.

Nigram, K., McCallum, A., Thrun, S., & Mitchell, T. (2000). Text classification from labeled and unlabeled documents using EM. *Machine Learning, 39*, 103–134.

Nijssen, S., & Kok, J. N. (2003). Efficient discovery of frequent unordered trees. In *Proceedings of the first International Workshop on Mining Graphs, Trees and Sequences, MGTS '03.*

Nutt, C. L., Mani, D. R., Betensky, R. A., Tamayo, P., Cairncross, J. G., Ladd, C., Pohl, U., Hartmann, C., McLaughlin, M. E., Batchelor, T. T., Black, P. M., von Deimling, A., Pomeroy, S. L., Golub, T. R., & Louis, D. N. (2003). Gene expression-based classification of malignant gliomas correlates better with survival than histological classification. *Cancer Research, 63*, 1602-1607.

Omiecinski, E. (2003). Alternative interest measures for mining associations. *IEEE Transactions on Knowledge and Data Engineering (TKDE),15*(1), 57-69.

Ordonez, C., & Omiecinski, E. (1999). Discovering association rules based on image content. In *Proceedings of the IEEE Advances in Digital Libraries Conference, ADL'99*, Washington, DC.

Page, D., & Craven, M. (2003). Biological applications of multi-relational data mining. *SIGKDD Explorations, 5*(1), 69-79.

Pal, K. P., Mitra, P., & Pal, S. K. (2004). *Pattern recognition algorithms for data mining.* CRC Press.

Palla, G., Derenyi, I., Farkas, I., & Vicsek, T. (2005). Uncovering the overlapping community structure of complex networks in nature and society. *Nature, 435*, 814.

Palopoli, L., Rombo, S., & Terracina, G. (2005). In M.-S. Hacid, N. V. Murray, Z. W. Ras, & S.

Parisi, G. (1988). *Statistical field theory.* Redwood City, CA: Addison-Wesley.

Park, J.-S., Chen, M.-S., & Yu, P. S. (1997). Using a hash-based method with transaction trimming for mining association rules. *IEEE Transactions on Knowledge and Data Engineering, 9*(5), 813–825.

Pasquier, N., Bastide, Y., Taouil, R., & Lakhal, L. Discovering frequent closed itemsets for association rules. In *Proceedings of the International Conference on Database Theory (ICDT)*, (pp 398–416).

Pei, J., Han, J.. & Mao, R. (2000). CLOSET: An efficient algorithm for mining frequent closed itemsets. In *Proceedings of the ACM SIGMOD Workshop on Research Issues in Data Mining and Knowledge Discovery*, 21-30.

Pelleg, D., & Moore, A. W. (2000). X-means: Extending K-means with efficient estimation of the number of clusters. In *Proceedings of the International Conference on Machine Learning, Vol. 17.*

Pentland, A. S. (2005). Socially aware computation and communication. *IEEE Computer.*

Philipp-Foliguet, S., Bernardes, Vieira, M., & Sanfourche, M. (2002). Fuzzy segmentation of color images and indexing of fuzzy regions. In *Proceedings of the 1st European Conference on Color in Graphics, Image and Vision (CGIV '02).*

Pie, J., & Han, J. (2000). Can we push more constraints into frequent pattern mining? In *Proceedings of the ACM SIGKDD Conference* (pp 350–354).

Pie, J., Han, J., & Lakshmanan, L. Mining frequent itemsets with convertible constraints. In *Proceedings of the IEEE ICDE Conference* (pp 433–442).

Plotkin, G. (1970). A note on inductive generalisation. *Machine Intelligence, 5*, 153-163.

Porter, M. F. (1980). An algorithm for suffix stripping. *Program, 14*(3), 130-137.

Pottenger, W., & Yang, T. (2001). Detecting emerging concepts in textual data mining. In *Proceedings of 1st SIAM International Conference on Data Mining (SDM '01).*

Pritchard, J., Stephens, M., & Donnelly, P. (2000). Inference of population structure using multilocus genotype data. *Genetics, 155*, 945-959.

Quinlan, J. R. (1986). Induction of decision trees. *Machine Learning, 1*, 81-106.

Quinlan, J. R. (1993). *C4.5: Programs for machine learning*. CA: Morgan Kaufmann.

Quinlan, R. (1998). *Data mining tools see5 and c5.0*. (Tech. Rep.). RuleQuest Research.

Rabiner, L. R. (1989). A tutorial on hidden Markov models and selected applications in speech recognition. *Proceedings of the IEEE, 77*(2), 257-286.

Raghavan, P., & Tsaparas, P. (2002). Mining significant associations in large scale text corpora. In *Proceedings of the 2002 IEEE international Conference on Data Mining, ICDM '02*, Washington, DC.

Reichenberger, K., Rondhuis, K. J., Kleinz, J., & Bateman, J. (1995). Effective presentation of information through page layout: A linguistically-based approach. In *Proceedings of the ACM Workshop on Effective Abstractions in Multimedia*. San Francisco, California.

Reynolds, H. T. (1977). The analysis of cross-classifications. *The Free Press*.

Richardson, M., Agrawal, R., & Domingos, P. (2003). Trust management for the Semantic Web. In *Proceedings of the ISWC2003*.

Rigoutsos, I., Floratos, A., Parida, L., Gao, Y., & Platt, D. (2000). The emergence of pattern discovery techniques in computational biology. *Journal of Metabolic Engineering, 2*(3), 159-177.

Rijsbergen, C. J. V. (1979). *Information retrieval (2nd ed.)*. Butterworths, London.

Robnik, M. & Kononenko, I. (1995). Discretization of continuous attributes using relieff. In *Proceedings of ERK-95*.

Rosenberg, N. A., Pritchard, J. K., Weber, J. L., Cann, H. M., Kidd, K. K., Zhivotovsky, L. A., & Feldman, M. W. (2002). Genetic structure of human populations. *Science, 298*, 2381-2385.

Roure, J., & Talavera, L. (1998). Robust incremental clustering with bad instance ordering: A new strategy. In *IBERAMIA*, pp. 136-147.

Roy, S., Gevry, D., & Pottenger, W. (2002). Methodologies for trend detection in textual data mining. In *Proceedings of the TEXTMINE '02 workshop at the 2nd SIAM International Conference on Data Mining*.

Rustagi, J. (1976). *Variational methods in statistics*. New York: Academic Press.

Sakurai, J. (1985). *Modern quantum mechanics*. Redwood City, CA: Addison-Wesley.

Salton, G., Wong, A., & Yang, C. S. (1975). A vector space model for automatic indexing. *Commun. ACM, 18*(11), 613–620.

Schölkopf, B., & Smola, A. (2002). *Learning with kernels*. Cambridge: MIT Press.

Schubart, K., Massa, S., Schubart, D., Corcoran, L. M., Rolink, A. G., & Matthias, P. (2001). B cell development and immunoglobulin gene transcription in the absence of Oct-2 and OBF-1. *Nature Immunol, 2*, 69-74.

Schult, R., & Spiliopoulou, M. (2006). Expanding the taxonomies of bibliographic archives with persistent long-term themes. In *Proceedings of the 21st Annual ACM Symposium on Applied Computing (SAC '06)*, Avignon, France.

Schult, R., & Spiliopoulou, M. (2006). Discovering emerging topics in unlabelled text collections. In *Proceedings of 10th East-European Conference on Advances in Databases and Information Systems (ADBIS '06)*. Thessaloniki, Greece.

Schwartz, G.. (1978). Estimating the dimension of a model. *The Annals of Statistics, 6*, 461-464.

Scott, J. (2000). *Social network analysis: A handbook (2nd ed.)*. SAGE publications.

Sebastiani, F. (2002). Machine learning in automated text categorization. *ACM Computing Survey, 34*(1), 1-47.

Sheth, A., Aleman-Meza, B., Arpinar, I. B., Halaschek, C., Ramakrishnan, C., Bertram, C., Warke, Y., Avant, D., Arpinar, F. S., Anyanwu, K., & Kochut, K. (2004). Semantic association identification and knowledge discovery for national security applications. *Journal of Database Management, 16*(1), 133-53.

Shipp, M. A., Ross, K. N., Tamayo, P., Weng, A. P., Kutok, J. L., Aguiar, R. C., Gaasenbeek, M., Angelo, M., Reich, M., Pinkus, G. S., Ray, T. S., Koval, M. A., Last, K. W., Norton, A., Lister, T. A., Mesirov, J., Neuberg, D. S., Lander, E. S., Aster, J. C., & Golub, T. R. (2002). Diffuse large B-cell lymphoma outcome prediction by gene-expression profiling and supervised machine learning. *Nature Medicine, 8*, 68-74.

Simoff, S. J., Djeraba, C., & Zaïane, O. R. (2002). MDM/KDD 2002: Multimedia data mining between promises and problems. *SIGKDD Explorations, 4*(2): 118-121

Simovici, D. A., & Butterworth, R. (2004). A metric approach to supervised discretization. In *Proceedings of the Extraction et Gestion des Connaisances* (EGC 2004) (pp. 197-202), Toulouse, France.

Simovici, D. A., & Jaroszewicz, S. (2000). On information-theoretical aspects of relational databases. In C. Calude & G. Paun (Eds.), *Finite versus infinite*. London: Springer Verlag.

Simovici, D. A., & Jaroszewicz, S. (2002). An axiomatization of partition entropy. *IEEE Transactions on Information Theory, 48*, 2138-2142.

Simovici, D. A., & Jaroszewicz, S. (2003). Generalized conditional entropy and decision trees. In *Proceedings of the Extraction et gestion des connaissances* - EGC 2003 (pp. 363-380), Paris, Lavoisier.

Simovici, D. A., & Jaroszewicz, S. (in press). A new metric splitting criterion for decision trees. In *Proceedings of PAKDD 2006*, Singapore.

Simovici, D. A., & Singla, N. (2005). Semi-supervised incremental clustering of categorical data. In *Proceedings of EGC* (pp. 189-200).

Simovici, D. A., Singla, N., & Kuperberg, M. (2004). Metric incremental clustering of categorical data. In *Proceedings of ICDM* (pp. 523-527).

Singh, D., Febbo, P. G., Ross, K., Jackson, D. G., Manola, J., Ladd, C., Tamayo, P., Renshaw, A. A., D'Amico, A.

V., Richie, J. P., Lander, E. S., Loda, M., Kantoff, P. W., Golub, T. R., & Sellers, W. R. (2002). Gene expression correlates of clinical prostate cancer behavior. *Cancer Cell, 1*, 203-209.

Spearman, C. (1904). General intelligence objectively determined and measured. *American Journal of Psychology, 15*, 201–293.

Spiegelhalter, D. J., Best, N. G., Carlin, B. P., & Van der Linde, A. (2002). Bayesian measures of model complexity and fit. *Journal of the Royal Statistical Society, Series B, 64*, 583-639.

Spiliopoulou, M., Ntoutsi, I., Theodoridis, Y., & Schult, R. (2006). MONIC – Modeling and monitoring cluster transitions. In *Proceedings of 12th ACM SIGKDD International Conference on Knowledge Discovery and Data Mining (KDD '06)*. Philadelphia, Pennsylvania.

Srikant, R., & Agrawal, R. (1995). Mining generalized association rules. In *Proceedings of the 21th International Conference on Very Large Data Bases.*

Srikant, R., & Agrawal, R. (1996). Mining quantitative association rules in large relational tables. In *Proceedings of 1996 ACM-SIGMOD Conference on Management of Data.*

Srinivasan, P. (2004). Text mining: Generating hypotheses from medline. *Journal of the American Society for Information Science, 55*(5), 396-413.

Staab, S., Domingos, P., Mika, P., Golbeck, J., Ding, L., Finin, T., Joshi, A., Nowak, A., & Vallacher, R. (2005). Social networks applied. *IEEE Intelligent Systems*, 80–93.

Stallar, E. (2005). Trajectories of disability and mortality among the U.S. elderly population: Evidence from the 1984-1999 NLTCS. *Living to 100 and Beyond International Symposium*. Society of Actuaries.

Statnikov, A., Aliferis, C. F., Tsamardinos, I., Hardin, D., & Levy, S. (2005). A comprehensive evaluation of multicategory classification methods for microarray gene expression cancer diagnosis. *Bioinformatics, 21*, 631-643.

Steinbach, M., Karypis, G., & Kumar, V. (2000). A comparison of document clustering techniques. In *Proceedings of KDD-2000 Workshop on Text Mining.*

Tan, P., Kumar, V., & Srivastava, J. (2002). Selecting the right interestingness measure for association patterns. In *Proceedings of the 8th ACM SIGKDD International Conference on Knowledge Discovery and Data Mining*, 32-41.

Termier, A., Rousset, M.-C., & Sebag, M. (2002). Treefinder: A first step towards xml data mining. In *Proceedings of the IEEE International Conference on Data Mining, ICDM '02*, Japan.

Termier, A., Rousset, M.-C., & Sebag, M. (2004). DRY-ADE: A new approach for discovering closed frequent trees in heterogeneous tree databases. In *Proceedings of the 4th IEEE International Conference on Data Mining, ICDM '04*, Brighton, UK.

Termier, A., Rousset, M.-C., Sebag, M., Ohara, K., Washio, T., & Motoda, H. (2005). Efficient mining of high branching factor attribute trees. In *Proceedings of the 5th IEEE International Conference on Data Mining, ICDM '05*, Houston, Texas.

Terracina, G. (2005). A fast technique for deriving frequent structured patterns from biological data sets. *New Mathematics and Natural Computation, 1*(2), 305-327.

Ting, R. M., Bailey, J., & Ramamohanarao, K. (2004). Paradualminer: An efficient parallel implementation of the dualminer algorithm. In *Proceedings of the Eight Pacific-Asia Conference, PAKDD* (pp 96–105).

Tipping, M. E., & Bishop, C. M. (1999). Probabilistic principal component analysis. *Journal of the Royal Statistical Society, Series B, 61*(3), 611-622.

Tsumoto (Ed.) *Flexible pattern discovery with (extended) disjunctive logic programming*. (pp. 504-513). Lecture Notes in Computer Science.

Turi, R. H. (2001). *Clustering-based colour image segmentation*. Unpublished doctoral thesis.

Tyler, J., Wilkinson, D., & Huberman, B. (2003). *Email as spectroscopy: Automated discovery of community structure within organizations.* Kluwer, B.V.

Ukkonen, E. (1995). On-line construction of suffix trees. *Algorithmica, 14*(3), 249-260.

Uno, T., Kiyomiet, M., & Arimura, H. (2004, November). LCM v2.0: Efficient mining algorithms for frequent/closed/maximal itemsets. In *Proceedings of the IEEE ICDM Workshop on Frequent Itemset Mining Implementations, FIMI '04*, Brighton, UK.

Vercoustre, A.-M., Fegas, M., Gul, S., & Lechevallier, Y. (2006). A flexible structured-based representation for XML document mining. In *Proceedings of the 4th International Workshop of the Initiative for the Evaluation of XML Retrieval, INEX '05*, Schloss Dagstuhl, Germany.

Vilo, J. (2002). *Pattern discovery from biosequences.* Academic Dissertation, University of Helsinki, Finland. Retrieved March 15, 2007, from http://ethesis.helsinki.fi/julkaisut/mat/tieto/vk/vilo/

Wacholder, N., Ravin, Y., & Choi, M. (1997). Disambiguation of proper names in text. In *Proceedings of the 5th Applied Natural Language Processing Conference.*

Wainwright, M. J. & Jordan, M. I. (2003). *Graphical models, exponential families and variational inference.* (Tech. Rep. No. 649). Berkeley, CA: University of California, Department of Statistics.

Walischewski, H. (1997). Automatic knowledge acquisition for spatial document interpretation. In *Proceedings of the 4th International Conference on Document Analysis and Recognition, ICDAR'97.*

Wang, A., & Gehan, E. A. (2005). Gene selection for microarray data analysis using principal component analysis, *Stat Med, 24*, 2069-2087.

Wang, J., Shapiro, B., & Shasha, D. (Eds.). (1999). *Pattern discovery in biomolecular data: Tools, techniques and applications.* New York: Oxford University Press.

Wang, K., He, Y., & Han, J. (2000). Mining frequent item-sets using support constraints. In *Proceedings of 2000 International Conference On Very Large Data Bases.*

Wang, K., He, Y., Cheung, D., & Chin, Y. (2001). Mining confident rules without support requirement. In *Proceedings of the 2001 ACM Conference on Information and Knowledge Management (CIKM)*, 236-245.

Wang, W., Lu, H., Feng, J., & Yu, J. X. (2002). Condensed cube: An effective approach to reducing data cube size. In *Proceedings of the International Conferece on Data Engeneering (ICDE).*

Wang, X., Mohanty, N., & McCallum, A. K. (2005). Group and topic discovery from relations and text. *Advances in Neural Information Processing Systems* (Vol. 18).

Wasserman, S., & Faust, K. (1994). Social network analysis. *Methods and applications*. Cambridge: Cambridge University Press.

Watts, D., & Strogatz, S. (1998). Collective dynamics of small-world networks. *Nature, 393*, 440–442.

Wenzel, C., & Maus, H. (2001). Leveraging corporate context within knowledge-based document analysis and understanding. *International Journal on Document Analysis and Recognition, 3*(4), 248-260.

Witten, I. H., & Frank, E. (2005). *Data mining: Practical machine learning tools and techniques with Java implementations* (2nd ed.). San Francisco: Morgan Kaufmann.

Witten, I., & Frank, E. (2005). Data mining – Practical machine learning tools and techniques (2nd ed). Amsterdam: Morgan Kaufmann.

Woodbury, M. A., Clive, J., & Garson, A. (1978). Mathematical typology: Grade of membership techniques for obtaining disease definition. *Computational Biomedical Research, 11*(3), 277-298.

Xing, E. P., Jordan, M. I., & Russell, S. (2003). A generalized mean field algorithm for variational inference in exponential families. *Uncertainty in Artificial Intelligence* (Vol. 19).

Xiong, H., He, X., Ding, C., Zhang, Y., Kumar, V., & Holbrook, S. R. (2005). Identification of functional mdodules in protein complexes via hyperclique pattern discovery. In *Proceedings of the Pacific Symposium on Biocomputing (PSB)*, 209-220.

Xiong, H., Steinbach, M., Tan, P-N., & Kumar, V. (2004). HICAP: Hierarchical clustering with pattern preservation. In *Proceedings of 2004 SIAM International Conference on Data Mining (SDM)*. 279–290

Xiong, H., Tan, P., & Kumar, V. (2003). Mining hyperclique patterns with confidence pruning (Tech. Rep. No. 03-006). University of Minnesota, Twin Cities, Department of Computer Science.

Xiong, H., Tan, P., & Kumar, V. (2003). Mining strong affinity association patterns in data sets with skewed support distribution. In *Proceedings of the 3rd IEEE International Conference on Data Mining (ICDM)*, 387-394.

Yang, C., Fayyad, U. M., & Bradley, P. S. (2001). Efficient discovery of error-tolerant frequent itemsets in high dimensions. In *Proceedings of the 1999 ACM SIGKDD International Conference on Knowledge Discovery and Data Mining*, 194-203.

Yang, C., Fayyad, U., & Bradley, P. (2001). Efficient discovery of error-tolerant frequent itemsets in high dimensions. In *Proceedings of the Seventh ACM SIGKDD International Conference on Knowledge Discovery and Data Mining.*

Yang, H., Parthasarathy, S., & Mehta, S. (2005). A generalized framework for mining spatio-temporal patterns in scientific data. In *Proceedings of 11th ACM SIGKDD International Conference on Knowledge Discovery and Data Mining (KDD '05)*, Chicago, Illinois.

Yang, Y., & Webb, G. I. (2001). Proportional k-interval discretization for naive Bayes classifiers. In *Proceedings of the 12th European Conference on Machine Learning*, 564--575.

Yang, Y., & Webb, G. I. (2003). Weighted proportional k-interval discretization for naive Bayes classifiers. In *Proceedings of the PAKDD*

Yeh, A., Hirschman, L., & Morgan, A. (2003). Evaluation of text data mining for database curation: Lessons learned from the KDD Challenge Cup. *Bioinformatics, 19*(1), 331-339.

Yi, J., & Sundaresan, N. (2000). A classifier for semi-structured documents. In *Proceedings of the 6th ACM SIGKDD International Conference on Knowledge Discovery and Data Mining, KDD '00*.

Yoon, J. P., Raghavan, V., Chakilam, V., & Kerschberg, L. (2001). BitCube: A three-dimensional bitmap indexing for XML documents. *Journal of Intelligent Information Systems, 17*(2-3), 241-254.

Zaïane, O. R., & El-Hajj, M. (2005). Pattern lattice traversal by selective jumps. In *Proceedings of the Int'l Conf. on Data Mining and Knowledge Discovery (ACM SIGKDD)* (pp 729–735).

Zaki, M. J., & Aggarwal, C. (2003). XRules: An effective structural classifier for XML data. In *Proceedings of the 9th ACM SIGKDD International Conference on Knowledge Discovery and Data Mining*.

Zaki, M., & Hsiao, C.-J. (2002). CHARM: An efficient algorithm for closed itemset mining. In *Proceedings of the 2nd SIAM International Conference on Data Mining*.

Zang, K., & Shasha, D. (1989). Simple fast algorithms for the editing distance between trees and related problems. *SIAM Journal of Computing, 18*, 1245-1262.

Zhang, T., Ramakrishnan, R., & Livny, M. (1996). Birch: An efficient data clustering method for very large databases. In *Proceedings of the ACM International Conference on Management Of Data (SIGMOD '96)*.

Zhong, S. (2005). Efficient streaming text clustering. *Neural Networks, 18*(5-6), 790-798.

Zongker, D., & Jain, A. (1996). Algorithms for feature selection: An evaluation. In *Proceedings of the International Conference on Pattern Recognition* (pp. 18-22).

About the Contributors

Edoardo M. Airoldi is a postdoctoral fellow at Princeton University, affiliated with the Lewis-Sigler Institute for Integrative Genomics, and the Department of Computer Science. He holds a PhD in computer science from Carnegie Mellon University. His research interests include statistical methodology and theory, Bayesian modeling, approximate inference, convex optimization, probabilistic algorithms, random graph theory, and dynamical systems, with application to the biological and social sciences. He is a member of the Association for Computing Machinery, the American Statistical Association, the Institute of Mathematical Statistics, the Society for Industrial and Applied Mathematics, and the American Association for the Advancement of Science.

Margherita Berardi is an assistant researcher at the Department of Informatics, University of Bari. In March 2002 she received a "laurea" degree with full marks and honors in computer science from the University of Bari. In April 2006 she received her PhD in computer science by defending the thesis "Towards Semantic Indexing of Documents: A Data Mining Perspective." Her main research interests are in data mining, inductive logic programming, information extraction and bioinformatics. She has published about 30 papers in international journals and conference proceedings. She was involved in several national research projects and in the European project COLLATE "Collaboratory for Automation, Indexing and Retrieval of Digitized Historical Archive Material" (IST-1999-20882). She received the best student paper award at SEBD'06 the 15th Italian Symposium on Advanced Database Systems.

Ivan Bratko is professor of computer science at the faculty of computer and information science, Ljubljana University, Slovenia. He heads the AI laboratory at the University. He has conducted research in machine learning, knowledge-based systems, qualitative modelling, intelligent robotics, heuristic programming and computer chess. His main interests in machine learning have been in learning from noisy data, combining learning and qualitative reasoning, and various applications of machine learning including medicine, ecological modelling and control of dynamic systems. Ivan Bratko is the author of widely adopted text, *PROLOG Programming for Artificial Intelligence* (third edition: Pearson Education 2001).

Laurent Candillier received a PhD degree in computer science from Lille 3 University (France) in 2006. His research focuses on machine learning and data mining, and more specifically on personalization technologies (recommender systems, collaborative filtering, profiling, information extraction), knowledge discovery in databases (subspace clustering, cascade evaluation), machine learning methods (supervised, unsupervised, semi-supervised, statistical and reinforcement learning) and XML. He is member of the French Association on Artificial Intelligence (AFIA). http://www.grappa.univ-lille3. fr/~candillier

Michelangelo Ceci is an assistant professor at the Department of Informatics, University of Bari, where he teaches in the courses of "Advanced Computer Programming Methods." In March 2005 he received his PhD in computer science from the University of Bari. During November 2003—March 2004, he visited the Machine Learning Research Group headed by prof. Peter Flach of the Department of Computer Science, University of Bristol, UK. His main research is in knowledge discovery from databases primarily in the development of data mining algorithms for predictive tasks (classification and regression). He has published more than 40 papers in international journals and conference proceedings. He is serving/has served in the program committee of several international conferences and workshops and co-chaired the ECML/PKDD'04 workshop on "Statistical Approaches to Web Mining."

Janez Demsar has a PhD in computer science. Working in the Laboratory of Artificial Intelligence at Faculty of Computer and Information Science, University of Ljubljana, his main interest is the use of machine learning, statistical and visualization methods in data mining. Among other areas, he is particularly involved in adapting these methods for biomedical data and genetics. He is one of the principle authors of *Orange*, a freely available general component-based data mining tool.

Ludovic Denoyer is an associate professor at the university of Paris 6, computer science and machine learning PhD in computer science (2004). Research focused on machine learning with semi-structured document application to categorization and filtering, clustering and structure mapping of xml/web documents. http://www-connex.lip6.fr/~denoyer/

Mohammad El-Hajj is currently working as a researcher/senior developer for the Department of Medicine at the University of Alberta. He received his Masters degree in computing science from the Lebanese American University, Lebanon, and his PhD from the University of Alberta, Canada. His research interest focuses on finding scalable algorithms for discovering frequent patterns in large databases. He is also studding the behavior of clinician at the point of care. El-Hajj published in different journals and conferences such as *ACM SIGKDD, IEEE ICDM, IEEE ICDE, DaWak, DEXA, ICPADS AMIA* and other venues.

Stephen E. Fienberg is a Maurice Falk University professor of statistics and social science at Carnegie Mellon University, with appointments in the Department of Statistics, the Machine Learning Department, and Cylab. His research includes the development of statistical tools for categorical data analysis, data mining, and privacy and confidentiality protection. Fienberg is an elected member of the U. S. National Academy of Sciences, as well as a fellow of the American Academy of Political and Social Science, the American Association for the Advancement of Science, the American Statistical Association, and the Institute of Mathematical Sciences, and the Royal Society of Canada.

Patrick Gallinari is a professor in the computer science and machine learning at the University of Paris 6 lip6. He holds a PhD in computer science (1992). He is director of the lip6 since 2005. His research isfocused on statistical machine learning with application to different fields (speech, pen interfaces, information retrieval, user modeling, diagnosis). He has been in the board of the Neuronet

Network of Excellence (head of the research committee for 4 years) and is currently in the board of the Pascal NoE (machine learning).

Yeow Wei Choong obtained his Master's of Computer Science at the University of Malaya (Malaysia) and he completed his doctorate at the Université de Cergy-Pontoise (France). He is currently the dean of the faculty of information technology and multimedia at HELP University College, Malaysia. His research interests are data warehousing, data mining and search algorithms.

Mitsuru Ishizuka is a professor in the School of Information Science and Technology, Univ. of Tokyo. Previously, he worked at NTT Yokosuka Laboratory and Institute of Industrial Science, University of Tokyo. During 1980-81, he was a visiting associate professor at Purdue University. His research interests are in the areas of artificial intelligence, Web intelligence, next-generation foundations of the Web and multimodal media with lifelike agents. He received his BS, MS and PhD degrees from the Univ. of Tokyo. He is the former president of the Japanese Soc. for Artificial Intelligence (JSAI).

Cyrille J. Joutard received the doctoral degree in applied mathematics/statistics from the University Paul Sabatier (Toulouse, France) in 2004. His PhD research dealt with some problems of large deviations in asymptotic statistics (limit theorems for very small probabilities). After receiving his PhD degree, he worked for two years as a postdoctoral researcher at the Carnegie Mellon University Department of Statistics. His postdoctoral research was on problems of model choice for Bayesian mixed membership models with applications to disability analysis. Cyrille Joutard is currently an assistant professor at University Toulouse I where he continues his research in mathematical and applied statistics.

Vipin Kumar is currently William Norris Professor and head of the Computer Science and Engineering Department at the University of Minnesota. His research interests include high performance computing, data mining, and bioinformatics. He has authored over 200 research articles, and has coedited or coauthored 9 books including widely used textbooks, *Introduction to Parallel Computing* and *Introduction to Data Mining*, both published by Addison Wesley. Kumar has served as chair/co-chair for many conferences/workshops in the area of data mining and parallel computing, including IEEE International Conference on Data Mining (2002) and 15th International Parallel and Distributed Processing Symposium (2001). Kumar serves as the chair of the steering committee of the SIAM International Conference on Data Mining, and is a member of the steering committee of the IEEE International Conference on Data Mining. Kumar is founding co-editor-in-chief of *Journal of Statistical Analysis and Data Mining*, editor-in-chief of *IEEE Intelligent Informatics Bulletin,* and series editor of *Data Mining and Knowledge Discovery Book Series* published by CRC Press/Chapman Hall. Kumar is a Fellow of the ACM, IEEE and AAAS, and a member of SIAM. Kumar received the 2005 IEEE Computer Society's Technical Achievement Award for contributions to the design and analysis of parallel algorithms, graph-partitioning, and data mining.

Anne Laurent completed her PhD at the Computer Science Lab of Paris 6 in the Department of Learning and Knowledge Extraction, under the supervision of Bernadette Bouchon-Meunier. Her PhD research interests covered fuzzy data mining and fuzzy multidimensional databases. During the year 2002-2003, she joined the University Provence/Aix-Marseille I as a postdoctoral researcher and lecturer, working in the Database and Machine Learning group of the Fundamental Computer Science laboratory in Marseille, France. She has been an assistant professor in the University Montpellier 2 at the LIRMM laboratory since September, 2003, as a member of the Data Mining Group. She is interested in fuzzy data mining, multidimensional databases and sequential patterns, investigating and proposing new methods to tackle the problem of remaining scalable when dealing with fuzziness and complex data.

Dominique Laurent received his doctoral degree in 1987 and then his Habilitation degree in 1994 from the University of Orléans. In 1988-1996, he was assistant professor in the University of Orléans, and then, Professor in the University of Tours from September 1996 until September 2003. Since then, he is a professor at the University of Cergy-Pontoise and he leads the database group of the laboratory ETIS (UMR CNRS 8051). His research interests include database theory, deductive databases, data mining, data integration, OLAP techniques and data warehousing.

Gregor Leban received his BS in computer science in 2002 and completed his Ph.D. in 2007 at the Faculty for Computer Science, Ljubljana, Slovenia. Currently he is working as a researcher in the Laboratory for Artificial Intelligence in Ljubljana. His main research includes the development of algorithms that use machine learning methods in order to automatically identify interesting data visualizations with different visualization methods. He is a co-author of *Orange*, an open-source data mining suite available at www.ailab.si/orange.

Tanzy M. Love received her PhD in 2005 from Iowa State University in the Department of Statistics. Her thesis was on methods for microarray data including combining multiple scans and clustering based on posterior expression ratio distributions for maize embryogenesis experiments. Since then, she has been a visiting assistant professor at Carnegie Mellon University in the Statistics Department. Her research interests include Bayesian mixed membership models and other clustering methods for biological applications, methods for quantitative trait loci and bioinformatics, and social network modeling.

Donato Malerba is a professor in the Department of Informatics at the University of Bari, Italy. His research activity mainly concerns machine learning and data mining, in particular numeric-symbolic methods for inductive inference, classification and model trees, relational data mining, spatial data mining, Web mining, and their applications. He has published more than eighty papers in international journals and conference proceedings. He is/has been in the Management Board of the 6FP Coordinate Action KDUbiq (A blueprint for Ubiquitous Knowledge Discovery Systems) and 5FP project KDNet (European Knowledge Discovery Network of Excellence). He is/has been responsible of the Research Unit of University of Bari for both European and national projects.

Yutaka Matsuo is a researcher at National Institute of Advanced Industrial Science and Technology in Japan. He received his BS, MS and PhD degrees in information and communication engineering from the University of Tokyo in 1997, 1999, and 2002. His research interests include information retrieval, Web mining, and online social networks. He is a member of the editorial committee of the Japanese Society for Artificial Intelligence (JSAI).

Junichiro Mori is a PhD student in the School of Information Science and Technology at the University of Tokyo. He received his BS degree in Information Engineering from Tohoku University in 2001 and his MS degree in information science and technology from the University of Tokyo in 2003. With a background in artificial intelligence, he has conducted several researches in user modeling, information extraction and social networks. He is currently a visiting researcher at German Research Center for Artificial Intelligence (DFKI). He is developing an information sharing system using social networks. His research interests include user modeling, Web mining, Semantic Web and social computing.

Minca Mramor was born in Ljubljana in 1978. She studied medicine at the Medical Faculty at the University of Ljubljana in Slovenia. She finished her studies in 2003 and was awarded the Oražen prize for highest grade average in her class. After a year of gaining experience in clinical medicine during which she passed the professional exam for medical doctors she continued her studies in the field of bioinformatics. She is currently working as a young researcher and PhD student at the Faculty of Computer Science and Informatics in Ljubljana. She is also a climber and a member of the Mountain Rescue Team of Slovenia.

Luigi Palopoli has been a professor at University of Calabria since 2001 and currently chairs the School of Computer Engineering. Previously, he held an assistant professorship (1991 - 1998) and an associate professorship in computer engineering (1998 - 2000) at University of Calabria and a full professorship in computer engineering (2000 - 2003) at University of Reggio Calabria "Mediterranea." He coordinates the activity of the research group in bioinformatics at DEIS. His research interests include: bioinformatics methodologies and algorithms, knowledge representation, database theory and applications, data mining and game theory. He is on the editorial board of AI Communications. Luigi Palopoli authored more than 130 research papers appearing in main journals and conference proceedings.

Simona E. Rombo has been a research fellow in CS at University of Calabria since July 2006. She received the Laurea degree in electronic engineering from University of Reggio Calabria in 2002. From February 2003 to March 2006 she was a PhD student in CS at University of Reggio Calabria. During that period, she was a visiting PhD student at the CS dept., Purdue University. From April 2006 to July 2006 she was a research assistant at DEIS, at University of Calabria. Her research interests include: bioinformatics methodologies and algorithms, data mining, combinatorial algorithms, time series analysis and P2P computing.

Marie-Christine Rousset is a professor of computer science at the University of Grenoble1, where she has moved recently from Paris-Sud University. Her areas of research are knowledge representation and information integration. In particular, she works on the following topics: logic-based mediation between distributed data sources, query rewriting using views, automatic classification and clustering of semis-tructured data (e.g., XML documents), peer to peer data sharing, distributed reasoning. She has published over 70 refereed international journal articles and conference papers, and participated in several cooperative industry-university projects. She received a best paper award from AAAI in 1996. She has been nominated ECCAI fellow in 2005. She has served in many program committees of international conferences and workshops and is a frequent reviewer of several journals.

Rene Schult graduated in business informatics at the faculty of informatics at the Otto-von-Guericke-University of Magdeburg in 2001. Since 2003 he is a PhD student at the Faculty of Informatics at the Otto-von-Guericke-University of Magdeburg. His research area is development of text mining and clustering methods at temporal data and topic detection at this streams. Since 2000 he is honorarily involved in the Eudemonia Solutions AG as CTO, a company for software development and consulting in risk management.

Sascha Schulz is a PhD student in the School of Computer Science at Humboldt-University, Berlin, Germany. In 2006 he graduated in computer science from Otto-von-Guericke-University of Magdeburg with major fields business information systems and data analysis. His research areas are the development and enhancement of data and text mining methods with special focus on applied operations. His current work is on abnormality detection under temporal constraints placing emphasis on the joint analysis of textual and categorical data.

Dan Simovici is a professor of computer science at the University of Massachusetts Boston. His current research interests are in data mining and its applications in biology and multimedia; he is also interested in algebraic aspects of multiple-valued logic. His publications include several books (Mathematical Foundations of Computer Science at Springer in 1991, Relational Databases at Academic Press in 1995, Theory of Formal Languages with Applications at World Scientific in 1999) as well as over 120 scientific papers in data mining, databases, lattice theory, coding and other areas. Dr. Simovici participated in the program committees of the major data mining conferences. Dr. Simovici served as the chair of the Technical Committee for Multiple-Valued Logic of IEEE, as a general chair of several multivalued-logic symposia, as Editor-in-Chief of the *Journal for Multiple-Valued Logic and Soft Computing* and as an editor of the *Journal of Parallel, Emergent and Distributed Computing*. He has been a visiting professor at the Tohoku University and at the University of Science and Technology of Lille.

Myra Spiliopoulou is a computer science professor at Otto-von-Guericke-Universität Magdeburg in Germany. She leads the research group KMD on Knowledge Management and Discovery. She has studied mathematics, received her PhD degree in computer science from the University of Athens and the "venia legendi" (habilitation) in business information systems from the Faculty of Economics of the Humboldt University in Berlin. Before joining the tto-von-Guericke-Universität Magdeburg in 2003, she has been a professor of electronic business in the Leipzig Graduate School of Management. Her research is on the development and enhancement of data mining methods for person-Web and person-person-via-Internet interaction, for document analysis and for knowledge management. The main emphasis is on the dynamic aspects of data mining, including the evolution of behavioural patterns, thematic trends and community structures. Her research on Web usage mining and Web log data preparation, text extraction and text annotation, temporal mining and pattern evolution has appeared in several journals, conferences and books. She is regular reviewer in major data mining conferences, including KDD, ECML/PKDD and SIAM Data Mining, of the IEEE TKDE Journal and of many workshops. She was PC co-chair of the ECML/PKDD 2006 international joint conference that took place in Berlin in Sept. 2006. Homepage under http://omen.cs.uni-magdeburg.de/itikmd

Pang-Ning Tan is an assistant professor in the Department of Computer Science and Engineering at the Michigan State University. He received his M.S. degree in Physics and PhD degree in computer science from the University of Minnesota. His research interests include data mining, Web intelligence, medical and scientific data analysis. He has published numerous technical papers in data mining journals, conferences, and workshops. He co-authored the textbook *Introduction to Data Mining*, published by Addison Wesley. He has also served on the program committees for many international conferences. He is a member of ACM and IEEE.

Alexandre Termier was born in 1977 in Châtenay-Malabry, France. Computer Science formation at the University of Paris-South, Orsay. Termier earned a PhD in the I.A.S.I. team of the Computer Science Research Lab of the same university under the supervision of Marie-Christine Rousset and Michèle Sebag, defended in 2004. JSPS fellowship to work under the supervision of Pr. Motoda at Osaka University, Japan. Currently, Termier is a project researcher at the Institute of Statistical Mathematics, Tokyo.

Anne-Marie Vercoustre is a senior researcher at INRIA, France, in the Axis group involved in usage-centred analysis of information systems. She holds a PhD in statistics from the University of Paris-6. Her main research interests are in structured documents (SGML/XML-like), Web technologies, XML search, and the reuse of information from heterogeneous and distributed sources. She spent about five years at CSIRO (2000-2004), Australia, where she was involved in technologies for electronic documents and knowledge She is now focusing on research in XML document mining and XML-based information systems. http://www-rocq.inria.fr/~vercoust

Hui Xiong is currently an assistant professor in the Management Science and Information Systems Department at Rutgers University, NJ, USA. He received the PhD degree in computer science from the University of Minnesota, MN, in 2005. His research interests include data mining, spatial databases, statistical computing, and geographic information systems (GIS). He has published over 30 papers in the refereed journals and conference proceedings, such as *TKDE, VLDB Journal, Data Mining and Knowledge Discovery Journal, ACM SIGKDD, SIAM SDM, IEEE ICDM, ACM CIKM,* and *PSB.* He is the co-editor of the book entitled *Clustering and Information Retrieval* and the co-editor-in-chief of Encyclopedia of Geographical Information Science. He has also served on the organization committees and the program committees of a number of conferences, such as ACM SIGKDD, SIAM SDM, IEEE ICDM, IEEE ICTAI, ACM CIKM and IEEE ICDE. He is a member of the IEEE Computer Society and the ACM.

Osmar R. Zaïane is an associate professor in computing science at the University of Alberta, Canada. Dr. Zaiane joined the University of Alberta in July of 1999. He obtained a Master's degree in electronics at the University of Paris, France, in 1989 and a Master's degree in computer science at Laval University, Canada, in 1992. He obtained his PhD from Simon Fraser University, Canada, in 1999 under the supervision of Dr. Jiawei Han. His PhD thesis work focused on Web mining and multimedia data mining. He has research interests in novel data mining algorithms, Web mining, text mining, image mining, and information retrieval. He has published more than 80 papers in refereed international conferences and journals, and taught on all six continents. Osmar Zaïane was the co-chair of the ACM SIGKDD International Workshop on Multimedia Data Mining in 2000, 2001 and 2002 as well as co-Chair of the ACM SIGKDD WebKDD workshop in 2002, 2003 and 2005. He was guest-editor of the special issue on multimedia data mining of the *Journal of Intelligent Information Systems* (Kluwer), and wrote multiple book chapters on multimedia mining and Web mining. He has been an ACM member since 1986. Osmar Zaïane is the ACM SIGKDD Explorations associate editor and associate editor of the *International Journal of Internet Technology and Secured Transactions* and *Journal of Knowledge and Information Systems.*

Wenjun Zhou is currently a PhD student in the Management Science and Information Systems Department at Rutgers, the State University of New Jersey. She received the BS degree in management information systems from the University of Science and Technology of China in 2004, and the MS degree in biostatistics from the University of Michigan, Ann Arbor, in 2006. Her research interests include data mining, statistical computing and management information systems.

Blaz Zupan is an associate professor at the University of Ljubljana in Slovenia, and a visiting assistant professor at Department of Molecular and Human Biology at Baylor College of Medicine, Houston. His primary research interest is in development and application of artificial intelligence and data mining methods in biomedicine. He is a co-author of *GenePath* (www.genepath.org), a system that uses artificial intelligence approach to epistasis analysis and inference of genetic network from mutant phenotypes, and *Orange* (www.ailab.si/orange), a comprehensive open-source data mining suite featuring easy-to-use visual programming interface. With Riccardo Bellazzi, Zupan chairs a workgroup on intelligent data analysis and data mining at International Federation for Medical Informatics.

Index

A

activities of daily living (ADLs) 244
Akaike information criterion (AIC) 248
a metric incremental clustering algorithm (AMICA)
16

B

Bayesian information criterion (BIC) 248
bioinformatics 86–105
biosequences 85–105
classifier function 90
conservation function 90
data structures 91
suffix trees 91
tries 91
formalization and approaches 92
e-neighbor pattern 100
extraction constraints 93
multi-period tandem repeats (MPTRs) 97
variable length tandem repeats (VLTRs) 97
future trends 101
pattern discovery problems 95
string, suffix, and don't care 90
blocks 128
algorithms 131
complexity issues 134
generation for single measure values 132
processing interval-based blocks 132
refining the computation of 135
support and confidence of 129

C

categorical data 14
incremental clustering 14
dendrogram 18
features 18
feature selection 18
conflict of interests (COI) 170
correlation-based feature (CSF) 21
customer relationship management (CRM) 221

D

data mining 1–31
decision trees 9
J48 technique 12
metric splitting criteria 9
metric methods 1–31
partitions, metrics, entropies 3
geometry 6
metric space 9
data visualization 106–123
classification 117
visualization methods 108
VizRank 108
experimental analysis 112
projection ranking 110
deviance information criterion (DIC) 249

discretization 23
  a metric approach 23

F

frequent
  itemset mining (FIM) 32
    scalability tests 50
  path bases (FPB) 40
  pattern mining 32–56
    constraints 33–35
      anti-monotone 33–35
      bi-directional pushing 35
      monotone 33–35
fuzzy
  partitions 126
  support definition 130

G

geographical information systems (GIS) 227

H

hierarchical Bayesian mixed-membership models (HBM-MMS) 241–275
  characterization 245
  dirichlet process prior 248
  relationship with other data mining methods 247
  strategies for model choice 248
  the issue of model choice 242
  two case studies 243
    disability survey data (1982-2004) 244
    PNAS biological sciences collection (1997-2001) 243
hyperclique patterns 57–84
  all-confidence measure 59
  definition 61
  equivalence between all-confidence measure and H-confidence measure 62
  experimental results 72
  for identifying protein functional modules 80
  h-confidence 61
    as a measure of association 66
    cross-support property 63
    for measuring the relationship among several objects 68
    relationship with correlation 66
    relationship with Jaccard 66
  item clustering approach 72, 78
  miner algorithm 69
    detailed steps 69
    scalability of 77
    the pruning effect 74
      effect of cross-support pruning 76
  quality of 77

I

inductive logic programming (ILP) 182
instrumental activities of daily living (IADLs) 244

L

leap algorithms 38
  closed and maximal patterns 38
  COFI-Leap 38
    with constraints 41
  COFI-trees 40
  HFP-Leap 38
  load distribution strategy 52
  parallel BifoldLeap 44
    sequential performance evaluation 47
      impact of P() and Q() selectivity 50

M

machine learning (ML) 199
mining
  ontology 171
  XML documents 198–219
    classification and clustering 208
    document representation 209
      by a set of paths 211
    edge-centric approaches 204
    feature selection 209
    frequent tree discovery algorithms 204
    frequent tree structure 202
    modeling documents with Bayesian networks 213
    stochastic generative model 212
    tile-centric approach 205
    tree-based complex data structure 200
Monte Carlo Markov chain (MCMC) 252
multidimensional databases 127

N

National Long Term Care Survey (NLTCS) 263

O

on-line analytical processing (OLAP) 125

P

principal component analysis (PCA) 120

S

singular-value-decomposition (SVD) 229
social
  network analysis (SNA) 150, 165
    applications 166
    authoritativeness 165

networking services (SNSs) 150
network mining 149–175
    advanced mining methods 156
    co-occurence
        affiliation network 161
    co-occurrence 160
    from the Web 152
    keyword extraction 160
spatio-textual association rules 181–197
    document descriptions 183
    document management systems 177
    image analysis 177
    mining with SPADA 186
    reference objects (RO) 182
    task-relevant objects (TRO) 182

T

toll-like receptors (TLR) 89
topic and cluster evolution 220–239
    evolving topics in clusters 222
        tasks of topic detection and tracking 222
        tracing changes in summaries 222
    for a stream of noisy documents 228
        application case (automotive industry) 228
    monitoring changes in cluster labels 223
    monitoring cluster evolution 225
        spatiotemporal clustering 226
    remembering and forgetting in a stream of documents
        225
    topic evolution monitoring 230
    visualization of linked clusters 233
translation initiation sites (TIS) 89